AF600544

THE CATHOLIC UNIVERSITY OF AMERICA
CANON LAW STUDIES
Number 89

CONDITIONAL MATRIMONIAL CONSENT

AN HISTORICAL SYNOPSIS AND COMMENTARY

A DISSERTATION

Submitted to the Faculty of Canon Law of the Catholic University of America in Partial Fulfillment of the Requirements for the Degree of

DOCTOR OF CANON LAW

BY

BARTHOLOMEW THOMAS TIMLIN, O.F.M., M.A., J.U.B., J.C.L.,
Priest of the Province of the Most Holy Name of Jesus

THE CATHOLIC UNIVERSITY OF AMERICA
WASHINGTON, D. C.
1934

Nihil Obstat:

Valentinus T. Schaaf, O.F.M., S.T.B., J.C.D.
Censor Deputatus.
Washingtonii, D. C., die X Maii, 1934.

Imprimi potest:

Very Rev. Mathias Faust, O.F.M.,
Minister Provincialis.
die XII Maii, 1934.

Nihil Obstat:

Edward G. Roelker, S.T.D., J.C.D.,
Censor Deputatus.

Imprimatur:

Michael J. Curley, D.D.,
Episcopus Baltimoriensis.
die XIV Maii, 1934.

Printed by
The Paulist Press
New York, N. Y.

TO THE HOLY FAMILY

IN

REVERENCE AND GRATITUDE

"Misericors Deus cum humanae reparationis opus, quod diu saecula exspectabant, perficere decrevisset, ita ejusdem operis rationem ordinemque disposuit, ut prima ipsa ejusdem initia augustam mundo exhiberent speciem Familiae divinitus constitutae, in qua omnes homines absolutissimum domesticae societatis, omnisque virtutis ac sanctitatis intuerentur exemplar. Talis quidem Familia exstitit Nazarethana illa, in qua, antequam gentibus universis pleno lumine emicuisset, Sol justitiae erat absconditus: nimirum Christus Deus, Servator noster, cum Virgine Matre et Joseph, viro sanctissimo, qui erga Jesum paterno fungebatur munere. . . . Ac propterea benigno Providentiae consilio sic illa constitit, ut singuli christiani, qualiscumque conditione vel loco, si ad eam animum advertant, facile possint cujuscumque virtutis exercendae habere causam et invitamentum."

Officium Sanctae Familiae,
Jesu, Mariae, Joseph—Pope Leo XIII.

TABLE OF CONTENTS

PART I

THE CANONICAL EVOLUTION OF THE DOCTRINE

CHAPTER I

PAGE

INTRODUCTION TO THE HISTORICAL STUDY OF CONDITIONAL MATRIMONIAL CONSENT 3

CHAPTER II

CONDITIONS IN HEBREW MARRIAGE 8

ART. I. PRELIMINARY REMARKS 8

ART. II. CONDITIONS IN HEBREW MARRIAGE 10

CHAPTER III

CONDITIONS IN ROMAN LAW 13

ART. I. CONDITIONS IN GENERAL 13

ART. II. IMPROPER CONDITIONS 18

ART. III. THE APPOSITION OF CONDITIONS 21

ART. IV. THE EFFECT OF CONDITIONS 22

CHAPTER IV

SYNOPSIS OF THE CANONICAL HISTORY OF OUR DOCTRINE—OUTLINE OF THE DEVELOPMENT 25

ART. I. THE GERMINATION AND BUDDING OF THE DOCTRINE OF CONDITIONAL MARRIAGE IN THE SCHOOL OF BOLOGNA 25

ART. II. THE OLDEST FORM OF THE DOCTRINE 31

ART. III. THE FIRST INFLUENCE OF PAPAL LEGISLATION, ALEXANDER III AND URBAN III 34

ART. IV. THE COMPLETION OF THE OLDER DOCTRINE IN THE EXPOSITION OF HUGUCCIO 37

PAGE

Art. V. Transition to the New Doctrine 39

Art. VI. The Turning Point in the Doctrine and the Legislation 48

Art. VII. Development and Deepening of the New Doctrine 52

Art. VIII. The Doctrine of the Scholastic Theologians, Antagonism to the New Doctrine 57

Art. IX. The Development of the Doctrine Reaches Its Conclusion. The Liber Sextus. The Teaching of John Andrea and Abbas Siculus 60

Art. X. Retrospect 64

PART II

COMMENTARY ON THE PRESENT LEGISLATION

CHAPTER V

DEFINITIONS OF MARRIAGE 73

CHAPTER VI

THE CONDITION AND ITS VARIOUS SPECIES 79

CHAPTER VII

CAN CONDITIONS BE ADDED VALIDLY TO MATRIMONIAL CONSENT? 89

CHAPTER VIII

RENEWAL OF CONSENT IS NOT NECESSARY FOR VALIDITY 98

CHAPTER IX

PERSEVERANCE OF CONSENT 103

CHAPTER X

LICEITY OF PLACING CONDITIONS 105

PAGE

CHAPTER XI

TIME AND MANNER OF PLACING THE CONDITION 112

CHAPTER XII

THE NATURE AND EFFECTS OF CONDITIONAL CONSENT 131

CHAPTER XIII

NECESSARY, IMPOSSIBLE, AND IMMORAL CONDITIONS IN GENERAL 137

CHAPTER XIV

NECESSARY CONDITIONS 143

CHAPTER XV

IMPOSSIBLE CONDITIONS 146

CHAPTER XVI

DISHONEST OR BASE CONDITIONS WHICH ARE NOT AGAINST THE SUBSTANCE OF MARRIAGE 154

CHAPTER XVII

FUTURE HONEST POSSIBLE CONTINGENT CONDITIONS 161

CHAPTER XVIII

PRESENT AND PAST HONEST POSSIBLE CONDITIONS 183

CHAPTER XIX

VERIFICATION AND FRUSTRATION OF THE CONDITION 188

CHAPTER XX

REVOCATION OF THE CONTRACT OR OF THE CONDITION 195

CHAPTER XXI

INTERCOURSE AS SURROGATE OF FULFILLMENT OF THE CONDITION 198

PAGE

CHAPTER XXII

CONDITIONS THAT INVALIDATE MATRIMONIAL CONSENT 215

ART. I. CONDITIONS AGAINST THE SUBSTANCE OF MARRIAGE IN GENERAL 215

§ 1. Importance of the Subject 215

§ 2. What Kind of an End, Intention or Content of the Will is Necessary in Order That the Act Will Be Essentially Perfect and That Marriage Arises Therefrom? 218

§ 3. De Vitiis Consensus 228

CHAPTER XXIII

CONDITIONS AGAINST THE SUBSTANCE OF MARRIAGE IN PARTICULAR 243

ART. I. CONDITIONS AGAINST THE INDISSOLUBILITY OF MARRIAGE 243

§ 1. The Nature and Importance of the Question 243

§ 2. The Bonum Sacramenti or the Indissolubility of Marriage 244

§ 3. Canon Law on Conditions Contrary to the Indissolubility of Marriage 250

§ 4. Interpretation of This Law 250

1. Is a Simple Intention or Purpose Contrary to Matrimonial Indissolubility Equivalent to an Actual Condition? 251

2. Does a Condition Opposed to the Property of Indissolubility Invalidate Marriage if it is not "deducta in pactum" 255

3. Is Error Juris Whereby Marriage is Considered a Dissoluble Union, Equivalent to a Condition Excluding Indissolubility? 260

4. Summary and Conclusion 275

PAGE

CHAPTER XXIV

CONDITIONS THAT INVALIDATE BECAUSE THEY ARE CONTRARY TO THE BONUM PROLIS 284

ART. I. THE PRIMARY END OF MARRIAGE: ITS MEANING 284

ART. II. CONDITIONS AGAINST THE PRIMARY END OF MARRIAGE 293

1. Bonum Physicum 293

2. Heresy Condition and Immoral Education 310

ART. III. HONEST CONDITIONS AGAINST THE BONUM PHYSICUM PROLIS 311

CHAPTER XXV

CONDITIONS AGAINST THE BONUM FIDEI 331

CHAPTER XXVI

PAST AND PRESENT CONDITIONS AGAINST THE SUBSTANCE OF MARRIAGE 335

CHAPTER XXVII

ENGAGEMENTS AND SO-CALLED CONDITIONS AGAINST THE SUBSTANCE 341

CHAPTER XXVIII

OTHER ADDITIONS TO A CONTRACT 342

ART. I. MODES 342

ART. II. CAUSA AND DEMONSTRATIO 346

CHAPTER XXIX

ACCUSATION OF MARRIAGE ON THE GROUND OF CONDITIONS 350

PAGE

APPENDIX 355

1. CONSENT IN GENERAL AS VIEWED BY MODERN LEGAL CODES 355

2. PRESUMPTIONS IN FAVOR OF INSTRUMENTS IN AMERICAN LAW 358

BIBLIOGRAPHY 361

ALPHABETICAL INDEX 371

BIOGRAPHICAL NOTE 375

CANON LAW STUDIES 377

PART I

THE CANONICAL EVOLUTION OF THE DOCTRINE

CHAPTER I

INTRODUCTION TO THE HISTORICAL STUDY OF CONDITIONAL MATRIMONIAL CONSENT

THE doctrine of Canon Law on the conditional declaration of marriage consent, is quite different in many ways from those in force in Roman Law and in modern codes on the conditional transactions of business affairs. The legislators of the Church knew the Roman civil doctrine on conditions in contracts and other affairs. They freely availed themselves of the Roman Law and adapted and modified it when necessary to the Church's doctrine of marriage contract. That in doing this the canonists and legislators in a degree erroneously interpreted Roman law, is the view of some, while others have said that the applications of the civil law principles of conditional contracts to the Sacrament of Marriage is entirely a mistake.

Mutually declared marital consent between a qualified man and woman makes a marriage, and a Sacrament if the parties are Christians; though this consent together with consummation constituted the essence of the *Sacrament* of Marriage, for those who held the *copula* theory.

Some considered the conditional consent effective immediately; others, later on at the fulfillment of the condition. The older canonical theory taught the first alternative: that no consideration is to be taken of the placing of a condition to the will to marry, the view being that the result which the parties wanted to attain by the condition could be obtained by interpreting the condition as a *modus*. The stipulated marriage contract effects an obligation, but no qualification of consent.

The papal legislations wavered and lent the theory little or no support, till Tancred in his later work, set up the opposing opinion that the fulfillment of conditions placed, was necessary to originate the marriage tie. As long as the condition wavered, he argued, there was no consent at all. This, papal legislation later sanctioned and it holds good today, rightly understood. Thus a true condition protects the sacramentality of the marriage and does due justice to the will of the interested parties. The will of both or one may be so conditioned, that they will to be man and wife, only in such an eventuality, when in the future, a still uncertain, contingent, objective event is realized and verified, provided the character of such event is neither unlawful nor against morals. If they declare this will, then a conditional marriage consent prevails. There is no longer any dispute about the theory and practice of Canon Law that the will to marry can be conditioned, but in times long ago, as well as today, there are questions about the nature and the precise manner of working of this conditional will.

German scholars of the last generation or two, particularly, have studied this question with divers results.

Not a few theories have been advanced, but roughly they have been divided into two groups.[1] It is not our purpose to detail these theories. It is sufficient to say one group holds that the conditional marriage consent operates in the same way as any conditional declaration of will. The question of its effects is answered by the solution of these two questions. From the combination of the effects or general principles of any absolute willing, and the effects or general principles of any conditional willing, one may ascertain the general principles and know the effects of a conditional declaration of marriage will. All operates on general principles. This theory is called the Normal Theory. The second group deny the above and maintain there is a peculiar special law or rule or principle to govern the effects. These effects are in no wise subject to the general rules which hold for absolute willing of marriage, or to the general rules for conditional agreements in general. These are the Singular Theories. With the first opinion, the result will vary according to the opinions which its representatives entertain of the nature and the effect of conditional contracts in general, and of the importance of the declaration of marriage consent.[2]

Some have found it convenient to group these teachings according

[1] Hussarek, *Die Bedingte Eheschliessung,* Wien, 1892, p. 2; *cf. Archiv. für katholisches Kirchenrecht,* Vol. 68, 1892, p. 477.

[2] Hussarek, *op. cit.,* p. 3.

to the conceptions of the *effect* of marriage consent. For instance, the dominant doctrine is: consent makes the marriage; in other words, it is contracted by the mutually declared will of a man and woman to enter marriage at the moment when the will has taken on an exterior form by the expression of the consent. Marriage exists as soon as the consent is declared. This is the basis of the prevailing doctrine. The possibility of the addition of a condition to this marriage consent lies in this, that the substantial requisite for consent is, consent to a union with a *distinct* person, that is appropriate and adequate to the idea of marriage. It is a part of every one's declaration of will to marry in general, and especially to establish conditionally distinct qualifications of the person to be married. Schulte develops this theory, but he, as not a few others, fails to see the rationale of the distinction between the internal and the external forum and what the Church holds concerning these and why.

He who declares his consent to marry, subjects himself through this, to its *canonical* consequences, that is, in the external forum; and it is equally true that he subjects himself to the internal forum (whether being held as to his true internal will, or as to the external declaration which may be contrary to the internal will, is disputed). If, for instance, he places a truly impossible condition and intends it and hangs his consent on its verification there is no marriage in the internal forum or *in re* or in God's sight, though the Church law in the external forum regards it as marriage, till the opposite is proved, which proof in cases of secret conditions or simulations is often impossible to demonstrate. This distinction must always be kept in mind. The Church knows better than her critics that discrepancies can exist between the two *fora*, and it is easily proved that her doctrine and jurisprudence in general, and for the majority of actual cases, rightly and with unerring logic interpret the inner will or the true status of the situation. The canons that outlaw illicit and impossible conditions, and exclude them from lawful review, by considering the consent to have been *pure*, are based on the highest reasoning and the wealth of centuries of the noblest jurisprudence.

It is strange that some scholars are so successful in misunderstanding the point and the plain reasons why the Church *presumes* in the external forum, and enforces this presumption, though admitting proof to the contrary. Such presumptions whether negative, as is the case of impossible conditions, or affirmative as is the case of simulation, is contrary to no doctrine on the essence of marriage consent; neither was the presumption of receding from a condition if, during pendency, cohabitation occurs, contrary to, but in accord with, the best thought concerning the philosophy of the act of willing, or the *voluntarium.*

The conclusions of the recent savants, especially of Germany, about our doctrine of conditional marriage consent are summed up in the introduction to M. Hussarek's important study. One can see that there is hardly any part of the doctrine of the Church about our topic that is not impugned by the contrary tenets found amid so much mystification of the problem.

Following in general, but independently, along the lines of Hussarek's worth-while contribution, not neglecting other authorities like Freisen, and consulting the original sources when possible, the problem and purpose of the historical part of this study will be to offer a synoptic presentation of the history and evolution of the subject as found in the literature of the glosses and the decrees of pontiffs.

An attempt will be made to show the following stages of the evolution. The emergence or budding forth of the doctrine of conditional marital consent in the School of Bologna; the oldest form of the doctrine in the works, *e. g.*, of Joannes Faventinus and Symon de Bisiniano; the first influence of papal legislation (Alexander III and Urban III); the completion of the older doctrine in the exposition of Huguccio; the transition to the new doctrine; the turning point in the doctrine and in the legal code; the development and establishment of the new doctrine; the doctrine of the Scholastics in opposition to the doctrine teaching that a future condition could be added to marriage consent; the completion of the doctrine; the contribution of the *Liber Sextus;* and finally a recapitulation of the entire canonical evolution.

The results of all this will later serve as a basis for the doctrine of the prevailing law. In the commentary of this work each kind of condition will be discussed fully and the interpretation of the various principles applied to the various kinds of conditions. Of especial importance will be the discussion of conditions against the substance of marriage and the *tria bona,* in which discussion will be included the questions pertaining to divorce and to birth control pacts.

The presentation of the canonical evolution will be preceded by some remarks about the Jewish Law; and a general outline of the Roman Law doctrine on conditions, between which latter doctrine and that of Canon Law there is a causal connection.

The writer wishes to take this occasion to give public expression of his gratitude for the privilege of advanced study, to Very Reverend Mathias Faust, O.F.M., Provincial; to Very Reverend Benvenutus Ryan, O.F.M., former Provincial; to Very Reverend Thomas Plassmann, O.F.M., Provincial Prefect of Studies, all three promotors of clerical scholarship and canonical discipline. Sincere thanks are also due to the members of the Faculty of the School of Canon Law, especially to the dean, Dr. Valentine Schaff, O.F.M., and to Dr. Louis Motry, also to Dr. Stanislaus Woywod, for their assistance in the preparation of this monograph, and the use of their libraries, and to all who have aided him by their constant, inspiring encouragement and unfailing support.

CHAPTER II

CONDITIONS IN HEBREW MARRIAGE

Article I

Preliminary Remarks

The Christian Church considered herself bound to the Old Testament Laws on marriage, except when something else was revealed or taught by Christ to the Apostles. Thus the Hebrew Law of marriage as found in the books of Moses and other inspired writings must be received with the exceptions named. Our Lord taught the members of the Church to obey the civil authority in all things that were just and which did not include or imply disobedience to the law of God. Thus the civil laws of Rome on marriage were obeyed by the faithful of the Church. No Christian was at liberty to disobey, as a Christian, any positive requirement of Roman Law on marriage, unless that positive requirement of the civil law was inconsistent with the Christian Law. The permissive parts of the Old Testament Law and the Roman Law were largely modified by the enactments of Christ and the Apostles, *e. g.*, concerning divorce.

After the Apostolic era it was necessary for the Church to declare and insist on the divine law of marriage and impose penance for its violations. From a cumulation of individual cases in particular, the Church formulated, after a time, general rules or canons which were adopted by bishops of an individual diocese, or for a province, and later for the Universal Church.

Many laws of the Church arose not *ex abrupto,* but rather from a general practice or a custom, generally in important localities, *e. g.*, the law of *disparitas cultus,* and the banns of marriage. This is true also of the law among the Hebrews.

The first contract mentioned in Sacred Scripture is that of Abraham buying a burial place for Sara (Gen. xxiii. 3-20). Probably the second example of a contract is the transaction contained in the Book of Ruth (iv. 1-11). In this second transaction the buying of land, and the taking of and marrying of Ruth, was a necessary part of the deal. "You are witnesses this day that I have bought . . . and have taken to wife Ruth . . ." (v. 9, 10). Deuteronomy (xxv. 5-7) speaks of a *law* about marriage "but if he will not take his brother's wife, who by law belongs to him . . ."

In the Old Testament marriage belonged to the sphere of individual law. There was a commercial contract between the man who wished to marry, and the person who was in control of the woman. It concerned also, but to a lesser degree, the whole family, or the local community, but the large public or the State had no interest in the marriage of the Israelites. The legal character of marriage is nowhere specifically described in the Old Testament, but it is presupposed as understood. Exodus for instance (xxi. 9) speaks of the (known) rights of daughters; Ezechiel (xvi. 38-41) of the (known) law about adulteresses. The carefully guarded position of the first born son (Deut. xxi. 15-17) necessarily presuppose fixed regulations about marriage. The married woman is spoken of as "acquired by her husband"; "taken possession of."

However, there is no *ex professo* doctrine of marriage, or conditional marriage consent, elaborated in these venerable books. Yet the writings of the Old Testament abound with conditional transactions. Jehovah makes many kinds of such bargains and agreements with the chosen people and often the Jews take the initiative in these remarkable transactions with God. There can be no doubt that conditional marriage consent was not unknown to these people. The Rabbinical writings, at least in the later centuries, had an embryonic doctrine of conditional marriages, which was, of course, based on their interpretation of Sacred Scripture. The great Jewish scholar Maimonides of Cordova (1135-1204) commented on this doctrine and refuted various interpretations of his predecessors. This doctrine is found in the Jewish jurisprudence of today.[1]

[1] *Jewish Encycl.*, V, "marriage," "contract," "condition"; *Jewish Code of Jurisprudence*, 4th ed., 3 Vol., Part 4, Chap. 38; G. Friedländer, *Laws and Customs of Israel*, 4 Vols.

Article II

Conditions in Hebrew Marriage

The law on conditions is developed in Jewish law books. The conditions of Roman and Common Law: positive, negative, authoritative, dependent, and casual, were known to them, though the classification is different. Express conditions were created by the use of three formulas. Later on other formulas were admitted. Four principal rules had to be observed to create a condition with the word "if" (*im.*). It had to be expressed both in a positive and a negative way, that is the condition had to be doubled. This was probably derived from the Book of Numbers (xxxii. 29, 30). Maimonides gives this example: "If a man say to a woman if thou givest me 200 *zuzim,* thou art betrothed to me by this *denarius* (coin); but if thou does not give them to me thou art not betrothed." After saying this, if he gives her the coin, the condition is a valid one, and she is betrothed on condition. If she gives him the 200 *zuzim* she is betrothed absolutely. If she does not give them she is not betrothed. Some taught and gave decisions to the effect that this doubling was not necessary except in conditions of marriage and divorce. But Maimonides vigorously dissents from this. According to him, if the condition was not properly expressed in double form it was void and the contract was unaffected by it. Thus if the wooer had only expressed the positive part and omitted the negative, "If thou dost not. . ." and had given her the coin, the condition would have been void and she would be betrothed to him absolutely.[2]

The positive must precede the negative form. If changed around, and he gave coin, there would be an unconditional betrothal. The condition must precede the act, or the conclusion of the contract. Again the great Jewish scholar exemplifies it thus: If the man says to the woman "Thou art betrothed me by this coin," then gives the money and adds, "if you will give me 200 *zuzim,* but if not . . ." the condition is void, because the legal act of betrothal was completed before the condition was expressed. "And every condition which is preceded by the act is void," which is the literal meaning of the Misnak. The fourth essential was that the condition must be pos-

[2] *Jewish Encycl.,* Vol. 3. "Marriage," *"Ishut Ishut,"* VI, 5.

sible of fulfillment. Examples of impossible conditions are: to climb to heaven, walk on the sea, swallow a reed 1,000 yards long; with such additions the condition is void and the contract is complete without the condition.

The condition "from now on, if" (*"im"—"me akshaw im"*) is a quasi-condition subsequent. The former condition "if" is a condition precedent. With this second condition the contract is immediately effective but may be ended by the performance of a positive, or the non-performance of a negative condition in the future. With the first kind of a condition, a third party could marry during the pendency. In this latter case if the man says "Thou art betrothed unto me by this coin *from now on, if* I give you 200 *zuzim*" and he eventually gives the 200, she is betrothed from the time of the ceremony of betrothal, even though the condition be not fulfilled till later. Thus a third man could not validly marry her, even before the condition was fulfilled, and even though he would take her absolutely without a condition. This held good also for divorce and business transactions. The third rule of the four necessary for the "if" condition, did not have to be observed when one would use the "from now on, if" condition. Some scholars claimed all four rules were necessary to be observed.

The condition "on condition that" (*"al menat"*) is similar in its legal effects to the second kind of condition. Unlawful conditions are void, *e. g.*, if one marries on condition not to live with his wife, the condition is absolutely void. If the condition was: not to give her food and clothing, it is valid. The reason of the first is that they considered cohabitation of the very essence of marriage, and the second (food and clothing) is not, it reduces itself to a financial consideration. There is another exception. If the condition obliges one to do something contrary to the law, the condition is not *ipso facto* void because the party need not fulfill it. Thus, if the condition is to eat forbidden food, and if one does so, the contract is valid, even though a breach of the dietary law is occasioned thereby. The condition must always be in the power of the party to fulfill. If it is mixed, that is, needs also the power of a third party, the condition is void, because it is presumed the third party will not be a party to a breach of the law. The woman may place the condition.

If the husband went abroad, to sea, or with a caravan, it was customary to give the wife a conditional bill of divorce. The condition was, if the husband did not return within a certain time, the divorce was absolute. This was to save the wife from the levirate marriage, which was valid only on the *first husband's death.* It seems not improbable, that by law (*ipso facto*) the bride became the wife of her brother-in-law. A divorced woman was not subject to this law, for she was his wife as long as he lived, and at his death she was *ipso facto* not his widow but a divorced woman.

If before the expiration of the time mentioned the condition "on condition that" the woman accepts betrothals from another man, she becomes betrothed conditionally until the time limit; if at the end of the time limit, the first man fails to comply with the conditions, the betrothal of the second takes effect and the betrothal of the first becomes void and she is not required to obtain a bill of divorce from the first.

In the case of marriage, if the condition imposed by the man *inures* to his benefit, as when he makes a condition that the woman has no deformities of body, or be not bound by vows, or the like, it is within his power to waive such a condition: but if it *inures* to the benefit of the woman, as when he imposes a condition that the woman shall receive from him 200 *zuzim* or the like, he cannot waive such a condition, and if she does not consent to such a waiver, she does not become betrothed if the condition is not complied with. The above described doctrine of conditions applied to both engagements and marriage consent.

CHAPTER III

CONDITIONS IN ROMAN LAW

Article I

Conditions in General

A contract is an agreement (*conventio*) or the consent of two or more persons to the same thing, entered into with this end, that there will emerge a personal right, or an obligation. It is a convention of wills which directly tends to beget an obligation of law. The manifestation of the mutual consent is called *pactum, pactio*, or even *conventio*.[1] The pact is perfected when that mutual consent manifested externally, is given, no matter what the manner of external manifestation; it may be words, deeds, a nod, and so forth.[2] However, in early Roman Law not every mutual agreement externally manifested begets an obligation. "Nuda pactio obligationem non parit." [3] "Ex pacto actionem non oriri." [4]

In the course of time Roman Law admitted a derogation to the general principle that a nude pact could not originate a legal action or protection. Certain pacts under certain conditions were henceforth given legal recognition. For instance if a condition was added *in continenti* to transactions *bonae fidei*, it was considered to constitute one and the same transaction with the civil convention to which it was joined and hence to beget one and the same civil redress by which the party could demand the fulfillment of that which both the nature of the principal act and of the added pact called for.[5]

Thus besides the common essential elements required for a contract, other elements called accidental may be added to certain agree-

[1] D. 2, 14, de pactis, L. I, par. 2, 3.

[2] Vidal, *Institutiones Juris Civilis Romani*, Prati, 1915, n. 381.

[3] D. 2, 14, de pactis, L. 7, p. 4.

[4] D. 19, 5, L. 15.

[5] D. 2, 14, de pactis, L. 7, par. 4, 5, 6.

ments. These must proceed from the freely expressed will of the parties, must not contradict the essence of the transaction to which they are added, nor change any essential element. It is understood that they cannot be added to every contract or transaction, but only to certain kinds. These accessory declarations of will, at first were only permitted *in negotiis bonae fidei* and *juris praetorii,* and afterwards in all business transactions. This addition may be in the form of a *condicio, modus,* or *causa.* We are here concerned only with the *condicio,* rarely spelled *conditio,* which rather refers to a personal status, and never *condictio* which refers to a judicial matter.

A condition may be defined: "Id quod voluntate partium alligat existentiam juridicae relationis eventui futuro et objective incerto." [6] A *modus* is defined as "onus accessorium adnexum adquisitioni alicujus juris." [7] There is a vast difference between them. The efficacy of the transaction depends on the verification of the condition, while the mode does not affect the efficacy of the transaction at all. When the mode is used the business is done *pure,* but one party has an obligation to perform, *e. g.,* a wife to live in the country of her husband, if that were the *modus* attached to their marriage consent.

Not all systems of law admit conditions because of the difficulty of the concept and its juridical effects. Generally speaking this doctrine appears only when a nation's private law reaches a certain degree of perfection and elaboration; while in very ancient systems it appears not at all or only in an embryonic state. In the Roman law the doctrine is fully developed and perfected especially by the jurists of the classical age. It first appeared only in testamentary documents and secondarily in matters of contracts, and that principally in buying and selling. A *negotium* or transaction without a condition is called in the law *negotium purum;* with a condition, it is designated *negotium condicionatum,* or *sub condicione.*

Marriage in Roman law does not seem to have been, at least in Justinian and ante-Justinian eras, a contract in a legal sense. It was looked upon from the standpoint of the power of the *pater-*

[6] D'Angelo, *Jus Digestorum,* Romae, 1927, 1, n. 720.

[7] D'Angelo, *op. cit.,* n. 767.

familias; just as he alone had the right to buy and sell, to adopt one into his family, in a word, to increase or decrease his patrimony and *potestas,* so he alone had the legal right to consent or not, that a woman become a member of his family by marriage with his son. Of course, the civil law demanded proof of this transaction and of the marriage, and this was evidenced by the various forms used in connection with the marriage, *e. g., confarreatio, coemptio, usus,* which are forms of *manus.* The value of these amount to a *probatio* that the mutual marriage consent was given, but they did not make the marriage.

Marriage is defined in the Institutes of Justinian:[8] "Nuptiae autem sive matrimonium est viri et mulieris conjunctio individuam consuetudinem vitae continens." Modestinus defines it:[9] "Nuptiae sunt conjunctio maris et feminae et consortium omnis vitae, divini et humani juris communicatio." Both these definitions refer rather to the bond by which the husband and wife are bound. Ulpianus [10] says: "Nuptias non concubitus, sed consensus facit." These definitions do not favor the conception of marriage as a contract.[11]

In Roman law the doctrine of conditional contracts, nowhere expressly applies to matrimony in the sense of a conditional marriage consent.[12]

[8] 1, 9, de patr. potest, par. 1.

[9] D. h. t. L. 1.

[10] L. 30, D. 50, 17, de R. I.

[11] "Il matrimonio libero non ha avuto una forma giuridicamente determinata; l'intervento della pubblica autorità non fu. mai ritenuto necessario. Nel diritto classico esso è determinato dalla *maritalis affectio,* che è l'attuale volontà di vivere in comune per formarsi una famiglia ('tecem vivere volt atque aetatem exigere'; Plauto, Mil, 4, 6, 60) assumendo l'uomo la donna a godere della sua posizone sociale e dignità. Ma il matrimonio libero nel concetto romano non è un istituto giuridico per sè stesso: è un istituto etico e sociale, da cui scaturiscono notevoli conseguenze giuridiche e sotto tale aspetto, come sotto l'altro per cui si esige una disposizione permanente degli animi è paragonabile al possesso."—Ferrini, *Manuale di Pandette,* par. 709.

[12] Though this passage is found in the *Code,* VIII, 28, 2, *"de inutilibus stipulationibus":* "Libera matrimonia esse antiquitus placuit. Ideoque pacta, ne liceret divertere, non valere et stipulationes, quibus poenae inrogarentur ei qui divortium fecisset, ratas non haberi constat." "Non è quindi possibile neppure un termine od una condizione sospensiva."—Ferrini, *op. cit.,* n. 712.

In Roman law, matrimonial consent suffered no conditional placing of the same, not only because marriage was no contract in the law, but primarily because of the exalted Roman conception of marriage consent. Their remarkable and noble view of *maritalis affectio* (an essential ingredient of this consent), and what this love denoted and connoted, made it inconceivable to the Romans (before the wealth of empire weakened their character), to hold off by a suspensive condition, or to terminate by a resolutive condition, any marriage consent since the *actual* marital love, by its very nature, excluded the placing of such conditions.[13]

"Sub hoc respectu (*i. e., impossibilitas juridica:* ob naturam voluntatis quam jus requirit ad effectus gigendos, ut in hereditates aditione) etiam *matrimonium* in jure romano respuit omnem condicionem; illud enim requirit *actualem affectionem maritalem;* item in jure italico.[14] "In *jure romano* nullam admittit condicionem" (*i. e.,* in casu matrimonii.[15]

Yet in spite of this fact, the civil law doctrine of conditional transactions has been partly taken over by the first canonists and adopted and modified to the marriage contract. It is therefore necessary to review briefly the Roman law tenets in order to know better the canonical principles and distinctions.

From a logical viewpoint the word "condition" is used in Roman literature as well as our own, in diverse significations. But in a strictly technical sense the word means a future uncertain event upon which the efficacy of an act depends, and, too, the very clause itself which contains this event. D'Angelo defines it: "id quod voluntate partium alligat existentiam juridicae relationis eventui futuro et objective incerto." [16]

From the point of view of efficacy, the jurists divide conditions into suspensive and resolutive. The division into proper and improper is based on the existence of all the requisites for a condition.

[13] Ferrini, Contardo, *Manuale di Pandette,* lib. V, capo II, p. 866. *Cf.* Manenti, *Inapponibilita delle condizione al matrimonio* (1889).

[14] *Cf.* Filomusi-Guelfi, *Enciclop. giurid.,* par. 87; Degni, *Del matrimonio,* I, non vero in jure *canonico* (c. 1092)—D'Angelo, *Jus Digestorum,* I, n. 747 nota 1.

[15] D'Angelo, I, n. 749 note.

[16] *Op. cit.,* I, n. 720.

Proper conditions are either positive or negative, according to their form; or potestative, casual, and mixed according to the causes of the verification of the event.

The nature of the very essence of a conditional law transaction, and more particularly the relation between the condition and the principal transaction to which it is added, is an exceedingly complex and difficult problem.[17] The many opinions are reduced to six by Windscheid, and D'Angelo reduces them to two principal theories to which all the others may be more or less referred. According to some the condition affects immediately the *will itself* so that the will exists or does not exist according to the existence or non-existence of the condition. Another opinion maintains that the condition refers only to the effect. The will always exists, but the effects are produced or not according as the condition is verified or not. Some others teach that the condition should be called a "self-limitation" (*autolimitem*), that there are, as it were, two wills. While finally there are those who say that these accessory clauses to a juridical transaction are in every way purely accidental.

The briefly expressed conclusions of D'Angelo[18] about the above opinions are: as far as the *name* goes, a condition is a self-limitation, and the clause is an accessory addition, but the will is always one and inseparable, the condition being a constitutive and substantial part of this one will: and the condition may be called accidental only by reason of its existence, not by reason of its importance. As far as the *substance* goes, the condition is the *will* (*voluntas*) conditioned, that is, a certain present fact, now existing with a certain quality, and thus the will is now placed and must *now* exist. The existence of the act of the will cannot depend on the event.

Nevertheless the condition is the act of the will *conditioned,* with this peculiarity that it is posited hypothetically, for the judgment on which is based the act of the will is a hypothetical judgment; and this judgment which has every right to be considered as the foundation of the entire condition, is carried out one way or the other. In speech it amounts to and it is expressed, "if (*si,* affirmative)

[17] Windscheid, *Lehrbuch des Pandektenrechts,* 1, par. 86.

[18] D'Angelo, *Jus Digestorum,* I, n. 723 s.

. . . otherwise not" (*nisi,* negative). From this aspect one might say that the will *then* exists or does not exist, according to the outcome, but *now* it does exist as a true and proper conditioned act of the will, which never can be destroyed in the future. Therefore, it follows that speculatively a condition is something accessory and extrinsic since its existence depends on the free will of the party, but practically and in the concrete it is *something substantial* and *intrinsic,* so much so that the validity of the transaction absolutely depends on its verification. It follows, he thinks, that a "negotium juridicum condicionatum" is not a transaction willed simply, to which something else, a condition has been added from which juridical effects arise, but it is one unit, one total whole, "quid unum" not distinct, which has a peculiar conditional or hypothetical nature.

Article II

Improper Conditions

Conditions not endowed with the necessary requisites for a true condition are called improper. These requirements are as follows. That the condition must proceed from the will of the party or parties, not from the very nature of the transaction, which are called *condiciones juris* as opposed to *condiciones facti.* The condition must create a state of *objective* incertitude, therefore, it must concern an event that is uncertain both subjectively and objectively and this event must be possible, contingent, and future, not a present or past event, even though unknown to the parties. This uncertainty refers to the effect of the transaction, to the existence of juridical relations; it does not refer to the will. The *condiciones juris* are improper both because they do not proceed from the will of the parties, and are implicitly and tacitly inherent in the transaction and proceed from the definition of the law, which considers the act as simply placed.[19]

The defect of uncertainty is the reason why necessary conditions are not true ones, for the outcome is certain. They have no impor-

[19] L. 99, D. 35, 1; L. 107, D. 35, 1; L. 21; D. 23. 3.

tance and if placed the transaction is considered as pure and simple.[20]

Past and present conditions are improper, because they exclude the quality of the objective uncertainty of the event. These conditions nevertheless have efficacy, because the fact or event either exists or not, and the validity of the transaction correspondingly depends thereon. Yet the principal characteristic of a true condition, the suspensive effect, is absent.[21] There may, of course, be subjective uncertainty present, when the parties are ignorant of the existence or non-existence of the present or past fact, but this suspension has no juridical effects.[22]

Conditions that are impossible are not true conditions, since they cannot exist, and there is no objective uncertainty about them. A few remarks about the various kinds of impossible conditions and their effects will be helpful. Those that are truly and properly impossible in their very substance are divided into physically, legally or juridically and morally impossible; and by reason of their extension into absolute and relative. The improperly called impossible conditions are such because of a logical contradiction being involved, they are also called perplex, *e. g.*, "Si Titius heres erit, Seius heres esto: si Seius heres erit, Titius heres esto," or *e. g.*, "I marry you, on condition that there be no permanent marital bond between us."

An event that cannot naturally occur is physically impossible, *e. g.*, to drink the ocean. Something which is unlawful (*jure impleri non potest*)[23] is juridically impossible; *e. g.*, for a private citizen to sell a temple, or the city hall. Morally impossible or base conditions are those against morality,[24] *e. g.*, "If you kill your husband." If a *third party* does the immoral thing, this being made the condition, it is not considered as a *condicio turpis*, *e. g.*, "If John robs you." [25] The difference between a base condition and one juridically impossible is that the former is illicit but its execution is possible, but the latter is impossible to execute. An absolutely impossible condition

[20] L. 9, 1; D. 46, 2; Inst., 3, 19, 11.

[21] Inst., 3, 15, 6; LL. 100 and 200; D. 45, 1; 37 and 38 and 39; D. 12, 1.

[22] L. 10, 1; D. 35, 1.

[23] L. 137, 6; D. 45, 1.

[24] L. 15; D. 287; Inst., 3, 19, 24.

[25] D'Angelo, *Jus Digestorum*, I, n. 733.

is present when the fact or event is impossible to *all*, and *always* and *everywhere*. The relatively impossible is had when the event is impossible only to some, or at a definite time or place, or impossible because of certain peculiar but transitory circumstances, *e. g.*, for a non-swimmer to negotiate the English Channel.

One must distinguish in speaking of the *effects* of impossible conditions. The general and logical principle should be that every condition that is permanently and absolutely impossible should bring along with its addition the nullity of the transaction to which it is added, for it is certain that the condition can never be verified. This principle is valid for acts *inter vivos* and may be expressed "omnes condiciones impossibles vitiantur et vitiant." [26] It is rejected in acts "mortis causa." "Condicio vitiatur sed non vitiat," meaning the condition is considered as not added and the main transaction is valid; nor does the general principle hold in cases of relative and transitory impossibility.[27]

There are many disputed points among authorities today about the above principles, both from an historical viewpoint and an intrinsic or logical one. For instance, a complex impossible condition *causa mortis*, vitiates the transaction.[28] Moreover, such a condition, evidently placed as a joke, invalidates in cases "causa mortis," because of the lack of will.[29] The school of Proculus taught that both acts *inter vivos* and *causa mortis*, placed with an impossible condition, were null and void. The Sabinian school to which Gaius belonged, held them void only "inter vivos." The latter opinion prevailed.

If there is a question of physical impossibility which is transient, generally, acts *inter vivos* are null. If it is relatively impossible, generally the condition is considered not added. If juridically impossible at the time of making the condition, the stipulation is also null.[30] If the condition is partly possible, partly impossible, acts

[26] G. III, 98.

[27] L. 57; D. 35, 1.

[28] L. 16; D. 28, 7.

[29] *Cf. analogice*, L. 4, 1; D. 40, 7; Ferrini, *Legati*, L. 333; D'Angelo, *op. cit.*, n. 735.

[30] L. 137, 6; D. 45, 1.

inter vivos are null in general; in acts in view of death, the impossible is considered not added, if the remaining part has the nature of a true condition.[31] If the condition is alternately possible and impossible, it seems [32] that the stipulation is null, though the intention of the party should be ascertained.[33] There are interesting cases of conditions which the Roman law considered as immorally placed. Celibacy or the complete prohibition to marry, if placed as a condition, was held as base and immoral by the *Lex Julia*.[34] The condition to remain a widow was prohibited by the *Lex Julia*, but Justinian later allowed the placing of this condition under certain restrictions.[35] Divorce was (in later ages) permitted if it proceeded from the will of the parties, yet the placing of a condition to divorce was considered illicit.[36] The prohibition of a condition that her husband would never divorce her was referred to above. This condition was void.

Article III

The Apposition of Conditions

The question may arise, whether it was licit in Roman law to add a condition to *all* juridical transactions, and whether it was *always* licit to do so. Historically the first acts to receive this modality were transactions "mortis causa." [37] From the "Twelve Tables" it is known, one could free a slave, on condition of paying a sum of money. Later among acts "inter vivos," stipulations could be conditioned. Then it was extended to other affairs.[38] Juridically and from the nature of the case, there were some legal transactions that admitted no condition; others that admit some conditions, and do not admit other kinds of conditions.

[31] L. 45; D. 28, 5.

[32] From L. 137, 6; D. 45, 1.

[33] *Cf.* for an important case, L. 74; D. 35, 1.

[34] *Cf.* D'Angelo, *op. cit.*, I, n. 742; *cf.* LL. 22, 63; 1, 72; 5, 74; 77.2, 100; D. 35, 1, etc.

[35] D'Angelo, *op. cit.*, I, n. 742; *Novella*, XXII, C. 39, 40.

[36] L. 8, 1; D. 7, 8; L. 5; C. 6, 25; L. 2; C. 8, 39.

[37] Title 7, D. 28; 1 D. 35; 7 D. 40; 25 C. 6; 46 D. 6.

[38] G. 3, 145; L. 6; C. 4, 37.

Those transactions admitting no condition are founded in the 77th law, 17th title of the 50th book of the Digest. This fragment of Papinianus enumerates: "actus legitimi, qui non recipiunt diem vel condicionem, veluti emancipatio, acceptilatio. . . ." Some of the reasons of the prohibition are: especially historical, for it treats of formal acts to which jurists found it most difficult to allow a condition added; there were also intrinsic reasons, *e. g.*, formal, juridical, or social impossibility. Marriage in Roman law forbade all conditions, for this was juridically impossible for several reasons, chiefly because of the nature of the will or consent which the law required in order to beget its effects, for this will must be an *actualis affectio maritalis*. This is true in Italian law also.[39] If a condition were added to these formal transactions, the latter were, as a rule, null and void.

Some acts because of social, juridical, or logical reasons, could only receive certain kinds of conditions. The institution of an heir, *e. g.*, excluded casual and mixed conditions, and admitted only potestative conditions.

Article IV

The Effect of Conditions

The discussion will be confined to the consideration of *suspensive* conditions, and exclude considering the effect of *resolutive* conditions, since these cannot be added to the declaration of marriage consent. A condition from the viewpoint of its effect can be considered from three points of time, namely: the time of pendency, when it is not yet verified, but can be verified (*condicio pendet, condicio in suspenso est*); the time when it is beyond verification (*condicio deficit*); the time when it is verified (*condicio existit*).

That state of uncertainty and expectancy which a condition begets is called pendency, and during this, certain juridical effects may be present, which vary according to the case. The sources of Roman law are not luminously clear nor uniform about a suspensive condition in pendency.[40] It can be said in general that a conditional

[39] *Cf.* Filomusi-Guelfi, *Enciclop. giurid.*, par. 87; Degni, *Del Matrimonio*, 1.
[40] D'Angelo, *Jus Digestorum*, 1, n. 750 s.

transaction does not operate the primary effect to which it tends, for the act is not yet purified or perfected. But it does beget some secondary effects by power of its persevering efficacy which tends to the possible purification.

In obligations this is generally true during pendency: "Interim nihil debetur [41] and "tantum spes est debitum iri";[42] but on the other hand, "etiam pendente condicione creditorem esse";[43] and "ex praesenti vires accipit stipulatio, quamvis petitio ex ea suspensa sit " [44] A creditor cannot seek a debt; but he may demand a safeguard (*cautio*); *e. g.*, a pledge, or bond, or security.[45] The debtor can do nothing to impede the verification.[46] A conditional obligation can be alienated, sold, or novated.[47] The conditioned obligation can beget certain *effectus executivi*, as the separation of goods.[48] If the thing is destroyed, then there is initial impossibility and the obligation perishes with it.

In real transactions (*negotia realia*) which consist in the delivery or the constitution of real rights, this does not yet exist or come to pass till the condition is verified. The owner is owner during this pendency (*interinalis dominus*) and he can vindicate his ownership, own the fruits and so forth, but yet he *cannot* do anything which *per se* does not admit a revocation, as to manumit a slave.

There is a peculiar difference in acts *mortis causa*. While in acts *inter vivos* (obligations and real rights) if the party dies during pendency, the obligations and rights pass to his heir. It is not always thus in transactions in view of death, this effect occurs only when the condition is verified during his life. The reason for this rigid principle: "nullum habetur negotium perfectum ante condicionis eventum" is not exactly known. There are historical reasons given as well as dogmatical, *e. g.*, that these acts presuppose *intuitus personae.*

[41] L. 13, 5; D. 20, 1.
[42] Inst. 3, 15, 4.
[43] L. 42; D. 44, 7.
[44] L. 26; D. 45, 3.
[45] 16 D. 5, 3.
[46] D'Angelo, *Jus Digestorum,* 1, n. 753.
[47] 21 D. 46, 4.
[48] L. 4; D. 42, 6.

A condition is said to fail, when from the nature of the case, or, considering justice and equity, it is entirely impossible that it be verified according to the mind of him who placed it. It is well to note that the failure of a negative condition consists in some positive fact, *e. g.*, when one marries, and the condition is not to marry. Here also the effects vary according to the different cases. The general rule is that the transaction is void.[49]

A condition exists when the fact in the conditional clause, is fully verified according to the intention, reasonably and equitably interpreted, of the person that added it to the transaction. But this statement must be immediately modified and a distinction be made between a condition existing in fact, and one existing in law, the fact not being verified. This latter is true when the fact or condition was not fulfilled either purposely through the fault of him who would gain by its being frustrated, or through the fault of a third party, or by some extrinsic impediment. If the party deceitfully hinders verification for his own interest, in such a way that the condition cannot be verified, then in law it is just the same as if the condition were fulfilled.[50] This principle finally became general and was extended to all cases. If circumstances combine to impede the verification of a potestative condition, even though the party is willing to carry it out, *e. g.*, if the condition is: "if John marries Mary," and meanwhile Mary dies, in this case, some say the condition fails,[51] others say it exists.[52] Ferrini maintains the general rule is that the condition is considered unverified, but those conditions in favor of liberty are exceptions.[53]

When a suspensive condition is verified, either actually or only juridically, the state of pendency or suspension ceases, the transaction becomes perfected, and from some aspects it is considered as if the transaction were originally made purely and simply, but in general its effects are begotten only at the moment of verification (*ex nunc non ex tunc*).

[49] L. 8; D. 18, 6.

[50] L. 1, 161; D. 40, 17; 24 and 66, and 81 and 110; D. 35, 1, etc.

[51] L. 23, 2; D. 9, 2.

[52] L. 54, 2; D. 30.

[53] Ferrini, *Legati*, p. 365 sq.

CHAPTER IV

SYNOPSIS OF THE CANONICAL HISTORY OF OUR DOCTRINE[1]

OUTLINE OF THE DEVELOPMENT

Article I

The Germination and Budding of the Doctrine of Conditional Marriage Contract in the School of Bologna

In discussing the juridical evolution of the doctrine of conditional consent in the marriage contract, authors almost invariably state that the first mention of such conditions occur in the two *paleae* or glosses of an unknown hand, added to the law collection of Gratian.[2] It is truly said that Gratian knew nothing of our doctrine, but it is equally true, but seemingly not realized, that Gratian was the first one to posit the possibility of such a doctrine. He got his cue from St. Augustine. Probably Burchard of Worms (died 1025) in his collection of canons, and Ivo's decretory referred to the same question when they asked: "Is it permitted to sin in order to convert an in-

[1] *Cf.* Hussarek, Max, *Die Bedingte Ehesschliessung,* Wien, 1892, to whom I am indebted for much on the *history* of conditional consent in marriage. Born May 3, 1865, in Pressburg; Austrian statesman; university professor of Church law; from 1911 to 1917 in Ministry of Education. July to October, 1918, Prime Minister. Endeavored in vain to stem the dissolution of the monarchy by transforming it into a Federative State. Last prime minister of the monarchy. Authority on the concordat of 1855. Wrote the history and revocation of this concordat. *Cf. Der Grosse Herder,* Vol. 6, col. 248; *cf. Archiv für Kath. KR.,* CXIII (1933), 309. Freisen, Joseph, *Geschichte des Canonischen Eherechts,* Paderborn, 1893, p. 232. Wernz, F. X., S.J., *Jus Decretalium,* Tomus IV, Titulus X.

[2] *Decretium Gratiani,* c. 7, 8; C. XXVII, q. 2; c. 7: "quod condicio interposita non valeat, ex concilio africano probatur." C. 8: "Quicumque sub condicionis nomine aliquam desponsaverit, et eam postea relinquere voluerit, dicimus quod condicio frangatur, et desponsatio irrefragabiliter teneatur."

fidel?" that is, probably, to marry an infidel, which was forbidden, on condition of his conversion. Burchard gives arguments *pro* and *contra*, but for himself answers, "yes," and the reason is, "of two evils choose the less."

Gratian in the beginning of his *Causa* XXXII puts an interesting case. "Quidam, cum non haberet uxorem . . . Postea de adulterio convictus et punitus quendam rogavit, ut vi uxorem suam opprimeret, ut sic eam dimittere posset, quo facto *quandam infidelem sibi copulavit, ea tamen condicione, ut ad Christianam religionem transiret.*" Immediately thereafter he proposes eight subquestions to clear the ground, in the last of which he says: *"Octavo, si infidelem sub premissa condicione licet alicui fidelium in conjugem ducere?"* He is therefore the first to speak of giving marriage consent with a condition. One must note that the main question is whether one is allowed to marry an infidel, not whether it is allowed to place that condition. He does not answer this question at the proper place. He affirms the first question that it is licit to marry a *meretrix*. The second question also receives his approval, namely, that she is a wife who marries for the sake of incontinency. Though he piles up arguments against this, yet he concludes in the affirmative.

Among the arguments under the second question (c. vi.) he quotes the celebrated case put by Augustine:

> Also the question is wont to be asked, when a male and a female, neither the one the husband nor the other the wife of any other come together, not for begetting children, but by reason of incontinence, for the *mere sexual* intercourse, there being between them this faith, that neither he do it with any other woman, nor she with any other man, whether it is to be called marriage (*nuptiae*).
>
> And perhaps this may, not without reason, be called marriage (*connubium*) if it shall be the resolution (*placuerit*) of both parties until the death of one, and if the begetting of children, although they come not together for that cause, yet they shun not, so as either to be unwilling to have children born to them, or even by some evil work use means that they be not born. But if either both, or one or the other be wanting, I find not how we can call it marriage. For if a man should take unto him anyone for a time, until he find another worthy either of his honors

> or of his means, to marry as his compeer: in his soul itself he is an adulterer, and that not with her whom he is desirous of finding, but with her with whom he so lies, as not to have with her the partnership of a husband. Whence she also herself, knowing and willing this certainly acts unchastely in having intercourse with him, with whom she has not the compact of a wife.[3]

(The language of Gregory IX concerning immoral conditions is in some respects the very words of Augustine.) Under the eighth question, Gratian changes the original question because of the solution of the seven preceding questions. The *"ea tamen condicione ut ad Christinam religionem transiret"* is thus modified: "is it allowed to sin" ("hac condicione peccare, ut infidelem ad fidem adducat?"); this question being put because it was proved that he who has dismissed his wife, cannot marry another, and the above query was suggested. Augustine answered this with an emphatic negation, Burchard and others, Gratian quotes answered that it is allowed (*licet*). The original question "whether it is permitted a Christian to marry an unbaptized on condition of conversion," lost its interest or proved too difficult for Gratian. The query therefore which Question 8 *Causa* XXXII treats, contrary to the program at the beginning of the discussion in Gratian is not "what power of law the marriage consent has between a baptized and a non-baptized with the promise or condition that the latter becomes a Christian," but "is it permitted to sin, (*peccare*), in order to bring one to the faith," a question asked centuries before. Gratian's answer is ***non licet;*** in agreement with Augustine. He is emphatic in his solution of an essentially different question. What he himself thought of the conditional marriage contract, if he really grasped its full significance is not known.

Freisen[4] says Gratian considers the union between baptized and non-baptized illicit, but valid. Gratian did not treat of this *ex professo.* The question he wanted solved is rather, whether unions between unbaptized are marriages at all, and what the law says results

[3] "De Bono Conjugali," *cf.* quaest. in *Heptateuchum,* Liber quintus, 37; *ibid.* 23, 17; Liber secundus, 71 and 20, 1-17; *A Library of the Fathers of the H. C. Church,* Oxford, 1847, Vol. 22, p. 279.

[4] *Geschichte des Canonischen Eherechts,* Paderborn, 1893, p. 640.

from the conversion of one party to the faith. The distinction between *matrimonium legitinum*[5] and *matrimonium ratum* helps Gratian to decide they are married.[6]

Gratian evidently held the view of canon 62 of the Fourth Council of Toledo that the Jews having Christian wives must be converted, else be separated. This puzzled him and he wonders if they were ever married. Of course the Council did not touch on the validity or invalidity of a marriage between Jew and Christian, but on marriages originally contracted between Jews themselves, and then the female is converted: in this case should the marriage be broken if the man remains an infidel? That it can be broken is certain, Augustine says "*. . . hoc inter infideles ratum non, qua non est firmum et inviolabile conjugium eorum.*" The question was not *conjugium inire*, but *permanere* in an already contracted marriage. Freisen[7] is in error on this point. The marriage, in Gratian's opinion, after conversion has become a mere union (*conjunctio*) which is forbidden.

Gratian's decree[8] has the canon of the Council of Agde which was taken from the Council of Laodicea. "*Non oportet cum omnibus hereticis miscere connubia et vel filios vel filias dare sed potius accipere si tamen se profitentur Christianos esse futuros et catholicos.*" It is not certain whether the Council of Laodicea intended herewith a conditional marriage contract, or whether it merely declared that marriage with a heretic is already contracted, when he only promises that in the future he will be converted. Or it may refer to an apostate while doing penance, whom the Council forbade to marry. Gratian probably indicates, without suspecting it, the doctrine of the conditional declaration of marriage consent. Of a condition in a technical sense, of course there is no question here. His original question he did not answer. The substitute was answered in the negative. He proposed it, but found it too difficult because of decrees of Councils and other reasons and leaves the original question in the air. His original query was not immediately taken up and his investigation fell on barren ground.

[5] C. 17, C. XXVII, q. 1.

[6] Hussarek, *Die Bedingte Eheschliessung*, p. 23.

[7] *Loc. cit.*

[8] C. 16, C. XXVIII. q. 1.

The *Summa* of Paucapalea, the disciple of Gratian (c. 1139-1144), mentions the eight questions of Gratian and the original question "quidam, cum non haberet," but takes up the substitute (*Causa* XXXII, qu. 8). Here he has many interesting things to say. He quotes and analyses Augustine and Isidore and the Council of Toledo and his conclusion is: Augustine is right if the man has a wife, or has vows, but others can sin on the condition of conversion of the infidel party. "Ei autem, qui non est his compeditus compedibus dicimus praefata compensatione satis licere." [9]

Whether the two *Paleae* mentioned above are from this pupil of Gratian, is not known. Roland Bandinelli (afterwards Alexander III) composed his *Summa* before 1148 and he did not know of this allegation from the African Council. Whether this gloss refers to conditional matrimonial consent is not certain. It cannot be gathered from the general theme of *Causa* XXXII. Rufinus who wrote his *Summa* and *Glosses* around 1165 and 1171, is the oldest who knows of this allegation from the African Council and with him it is not a *palea*. Huguccio (d. 1210), the prince of the ancient glossators of the *Decretum,* who wrote his *Summa* probably between 1185-1187, confirms it, but not as a *palea*. It might be added here that this passage is not in any African Council nor has it been found anywhere else. Paucapalea wrote his *Summa* certainly before 1150, but after 1139. Roland wrote his before 1148. Rufinus wrote his *Summa* before 1171, probably in 1165.

Roland's [10] *Summa* was composed not later than 1148. He was made a cardinal, and later elected pope, in 1159. He tackles the question of Gratian with energy. His matter is found under matrimonial impediments and in the proper place, *i. e.*, the eighth question of *Causa* XXXII. *Causa* XXVIII "quidam vir infidelis," has for its first question "An conjugium sit inter infideles." The *Causa* is this: "Quidam vir infidelis conjugem habens infidelem ad fidem conversus est." "Uxor odio Christianae fidei eum reliquit, ille aliam accepit fidelem, ea mortua clericus ordinatur, tandem in episcopum eligitur." "Secunda quaestio est, utrum iste vivente prima possit

[9] *Die Summa des Paucapalea,* edited by J. F. von Schulte, Giessen, 1890, p. 129.

[10] *Die Summa Magistri Rolandi,* edited by Fr. Thaner, Innsbruck, 1874.

aliam accipere." To the first question he first gives reasons why it seems there is no marriage among infidels, and then he proves it does exist. The answer to the second is affirmative; yes, if she hated the faith. In *Causa* XXXII he answers the questions of Augustine and Gratian in the affirmative, whether a man can marry a prostitute, and whether there is marriage if the motive of the woman is to avoid incontinency. At the eighth question he puts the original query of Gratian, and remarks that the Master Gratian replied not to this but to another, and then drops it like a hot coal.

In his preface "De Conjugio" to *Causa* XXVII he gives his view of the law of marriage contract in general. Some of his tenets are the following: "Vidimus, quid sit matrimonium; nunc videndum est, quae sunt necessaria ad matrimonium contrahendum. Tria siquidem sunt necessaria; consensus, pactio conjugalis, idoneitas personarum. Consensus juxta illud Nicolai: sufficiat solus consensus eorum . . . Pactio conjugalis est necessaria juxta illud Ambrosii. Non defloratio virginitatis facit matrimonium, sed pactio conjugalis. Idoneitas personarum valde est necessaria, sine qua, consensus et pactio penitus probantur (sunt) inania."

Other views are: if a consummated marriage follows a non-consummated one, then in virtue of ecclesiastical concession, the second marriage is valid and the man keeps the second woman. *Some cannot on account of the vow of celibacy, etc., marry an infidel on condition of promise of conversion.* The *copula* has no legal effect till after one is baptized. The active *matrimonium innitiatum* is present simultaneously with baptism, not before. Max von Hussarek [11] constructs Roland's doctrine on marriage and he gets the first emergence of conditions. He claims that Roland first conceived the idea of conditional marriage contract without any distinction *inter sponsalia de futuro* and *de praesenti.* The doctrine is claimed as the exclusive property of the School of Bologna. It is certain that he is the first to enter deeply into the stimulation and suggestion of Gratian. There is no clue in his work of the Gallican distinction of *sponsalia de futuro* and *de praesenti.* The renowned theologian and contemporary of Gratian, Peter Lombard, whose *Sententiae* are of epochal importance, does not consider conditional marriage contract.

[11] *Op. cit.*, p. 29 s.

Article II

The Oldest Form of the Doctrine

Stephen of Tournay [12] who wrote his *Summa* after 1159 and before 1169, adds his own pertinent opinions to those of Roland. His exposition of the doctrine of marriage is remarkable. Starting with *Causa* XXVII he gives clear cut distinctions and definitions between engagement and marriage, in *Causa* XXVII, qu. 2. "Desponsatio autem de praesenti dicitur, quando vir verbis vel aliis certis signis consensum maritalem mulieri exprimit et e converso mulier viro, cum et ille dicit: accipio te in meam, et illa dicit: concedo me tibi in tuam. Extunc tales sponsi conjuges sunt, et de cetero, si personae idoneae sint, matrimonium non potest, nisi alterutrius morte." Another clarifying statement is: "Nam substantiam quidem sacramenti non solemnitates faciunt, sed consensus de praesenti expressus secundum leges ecclesiasticas; nam matrimonia reguntur hodie jure poli, non jure fori." Stephen is very correct about the Pauline Privilege, but he does not give anything on conditional consent.

John Faventinus used the *Summae* of Stephen and Rufinus to produce his own and completed it about 1171. Therein is found a considerable development in our doctrine. There is a dilemma. The *palea* of the African Council seems to reject all conditions "condito frangatur" yet the canonists finally arrived at the conclusion that marriage on condition of conversion was valid, if one had no wife, or had no vow to the contrary. The Summist solves it thus: "Sed ibidem (palea) de inhonesta condicione agitur, hic vero de honesta." He says in question eight of *Causa* XXXII that it is as clear as day that one cannot sin on condition of conversion of infidel, but the original question was about marriage. He says this is all right. "In principio causae tamen non hoc quaesitum fuit, sed utrum liceat alicui fideli ducere infidelem ea condicione, ut convertatur ad fidem: quod quidem soluto nec voto ligato licet . . . Cognoscere autem non debet eam ante impletam condicionem. . . . Solutis autem sub hac laudabili

[12] *Die Summa des Stephanus Tornacensis*, edited by Fr. von Schulte, Giessen, 1891, pp. 235 s.

condicione, ut Christianam faciat, non cognoscere sed desponsare licet alterius sectae uxorem."[13] Again: "Vel dicemus turpem condicionem non admitti, honestam admitti, ut ista est, et non respui. Vel speciale est in condicione suscipiendae fidei. Magister Ro. etiam cum honesta condicio in contrahendo matrimonio ponitur dicebat distinguendum circa tempus et factum. Si enim dixerit quispiam: 'volo te in meam, si decem dederis tali die,' expirat condicio. Si vero dixerit: 'accipiam te in meam, si tali die decem dederis,' tenet condicio, nisi forte ita de futuro processerint, ut ante diem condicionis matrimonium carnis commixtione perfecerint."[14]

A considerable amount of advancement in the doctrine of conditional marriage contract is decided in these few words. Faventinus is well acquainted with Lombard's distinction between future and present *sponsalia* and uses this distinction. The phrase "sed potius accipere" of the Council of Laodocea, he explains as an engagement (*futurarum nuptiarum promissionem facere*). He knows too that the decree "Quicumque" makes *sponsalia* effective whether the condition is verified or not. He endeavors in a scholastic manner to bring some sense to these contradictions between opinions and original testimonies. He struggles bravely through at great length, trying one solution after the other, of which the net result is that the foundation of the entire doctrine of conditional marriage contract is laid. The last resort was a scholastic distinction to unite two contradictory statements. He makes three attempts. He grapples with the nature of a condition and a *modus*. He thinks the African Council forbids a condition in the Roman Law technical sense.

Condition suspends, does not oblige, mode obliges, does not suspend. "Die Bedingung suspendirt, zwingt aber nicht, der modus swingt, suspendirt aber nicht." Thus does Savigny with remarkable brevity mark the difference.[15] If a *modus,* then the infidel is bound to become a convert, and there would exist an engagement in spite of the impediment of difference of worship.

The second attempt is, dishonorable conditions have to be cancelled, honorable ones not. He does not attempt to show how the

[13] *Cf.* von Hussarek, *op. cit.,* p. 49.

[14] *Loc. cit.,* p. 48.

[15] *System des heutigen Römischen Rechts,* 111, § 231.

decree "Quicumque" can stand this interpretation. The third attempt is none at all, and the only thing he has left is, one condition is admissible, namely of conversion. So he admits conditions positively only at the *desponsatio de futuro,* but it seems (though his words probably can bear a contrary construction) he did not consider those *de praesenti.*

The object of the *Summa* of Simon de Bisiano who wrote between 1174-1179, is the completion of Faventinus. He tells us that already the admissibility of conditional consent *de praesenti* belonged to the disputes of the schools. "Et nota, quod secundum quorundam sententiam distinguitur inter tempus et factum; si enim dixerit quis 'volo te in meam, si X dederis tali die,' expirat condicio, si vero dixerit 'accipiam te in meam, si tali die X dederis' tenet condicio, nisi forte ita de facto processerint, ut antequam extaret condicio matrimonium carnis commixtione perficiatur. Alii sunt, qui dicunt, quod cum matrimonium sub condicione contrahitur, tunc demum matrimonium tenere incipit, cum condicione interposita existit." [16] Simon has no mention of Alexander III's decree "De illis," so evidently this belongs to the latter part of his reign. In speaking of the voluntary alienation of property to the Church, he says it can be given under any condition, but it is understood the condition must not be contrary to canon or civil law, "sicut, si matrimonium fuerit contractum illicita pactione opposita, pactione cessante, matrimonium tenet." Whether all these pacts to marriage were *modes, e. g.,* to follow husband, etc., is unknown.

Sicard of Cremonia wrote the first *manual* of the *Decretum.* He discarded the old exegetical method of explaining each chapter as in Gratian, and made a new systematic division. He wrote his work after 1179 and before 1181, the year Alexander III died. He does not mention the pope's decree "De illis." His doctrine is: Because the consent to the marriage must be free, a condition would frustrate the liberty of consent, therefore every condition, except conversion, is to be dismissed as not placed. ". . . Nam matrimonia libera esse oportet a coactione, temporis adjectione et qualibet condicione. . . . Cum adicitur condicio, pro non adjecta habetur; nam spreta condi-

[16] *Cf.* Hussarek, *op. cit.,* p. 53.

cione matrimonium vires habebit, puta 'consentio, si X dederis, si virgo fueris, si pater meus consenerit,' et quamvis pater dissentiat, nihilominus si nubilis fuerat, illibatum permanet matrimonium. Tamen de hac condicione 'si pater consenerit' quidam aliter sentiunt. Excipitur autem condicio religionis si ad Christianam religionem accesseris. In quo casu non erit matrimonium, nisi condicio sortiatur effectum." "Item quaeritur, si catholicus possit contrahere cum gentili, judaea, vel haeretica. De hoc ambrosius: 'Cave O Christiane ne tradas filiam et cetera.' Ad hoc dicimus, quod potest contrahere cum tali sponsalia sub conditione conversionis sed non sibi commisceri ante conversionem." Why so? *"Favore religionis et spe conversionis."* Why cannot other conditions be added? "Hoc est privilegium matrimonii ergo apposita non apposita intelligitur." [17] One cannot sanction his denial of conditions because they interfere with freedom. The contrary is true, for it is just because of the liberty of the will that our doctrine of conditions exist.

Article III

The First Influence of Papal Legislation, Alexander III and Urban III

Gratian had gathered and systematized a vast store of legal lore. Through the scientific study of his collection the knowledge of the prevailing Church law made considerable progress. The commentators on the *Decretum Gratiani,* the first scientific doctors of canon law expended a tremendous amount of diligence and talent. Their aim was a complete conception, a penetration of the given material, and as a result they stumbled on new visions and entered new regions not yet cultivated or wrongly so. They became the founders of a new law *system;* not of a new church law, as Sohm thinks. There was for the law scholar a new vocation. The two requisites: able men and favorable times were in conjunction, so all was ripe for the formation of the golden era of the 13th century.

Rolandus Bandinelli ("Bononiae resedit in cathedra magistrali in divina pagina") was created a cardinal, and finally in 1159 was

[17] Quoted from Hussarek, *op. cit.,* p. 56.

elected pope and chose the name of Alexander III. He died in 1181. He was followed by Lucius III, 1181-1185. Then Urban III had a two year reign, 1185-1187. The Church had come forth from the combat with the supreme power of the State, mighty, united, and with a powerfully united government, all of which was conducive to the progress of her legislation. So Alexander had full political power, intense scientific training and great prudence. It was reserved for him to establish and reform the common canonical legislation, as his Magister established the common canonical science of law. His legislation concerning the marriage contract law was most important, and he was well aware of the numerous causes dissolving marriage due to Gratian's distinction of *matrimonium innitiatum* and *consummatum.* He limited considerably the number of these causes. The foundations of his reforms are contained in the decree "Licet praeter solitum."[18] Therein he determines exactly what must be the content of the declaration of the will of the nupturients. Herein he uses the doctrine of Peter Lombard and Hugh of St. Victor, that marriage agreements and engagements are both contracts for a specific end. Both are sub-species of one and the same genus. The difference is the modulation of the direction of the will according to time. This will be may be directed to the immediate existence of the marriage tie; then there is present a *consensus de praesenti.* If the parties only declare they are willing in the future to enter marriage, then there is a *consensus de futuro,* which imposes obligations, but does not effect the marriage.

His legislation on our doctrine is, in the decree "De illis" in answer to a query from the Archbishop of Palermo.[19] The case was this. A man took an oath to marry a certain woman if she furnished a sum of money. She did not do so. The pope replied that the man was not guilty of perjury, and he was not bound to take the woman unless they gave *consensus de praesenti* or unless the *copula* intervened. The prelate was in a quandary, the cause of which was the decree "Quicumque" and the decree "Non oportet" together with

[18] C. 3, X, *De sponsa duorum,* IV, 3; *cf.* c. 3 X, *De conversione conjugatorum,* III, 32.

[19] C. 3, X, *de cond. appos.,* IV, 5; *cf.* Jaffe, *Regesta Pontificium Rom.* (1881), n. 9105.

his own knotty case. Urban III ruled as Gregory IX later so interprets it: "Si sponsus de futuro ante copulam ad remota se transfert, sponsa libere cum alio contrahit."[20] And, "Qui juravit aliquam id uxorem accipere, si centum sibi donaverit, centum non datis, recipere non tenetur, nisi postea pure consenerit, vel eam cognoverit." [21]

There had been four attempts to unify and square the two trouble making decrees of the "Quicumque" and the "Non oportet." Of course these attempts worked in the dark, for what these two passages meant was never known at that time, nor today for that matter. The first attempt ignored the decree "Quicumque" and admitted a condition being placed. The other three reckon with the chapter. The second attempt, reduces all to modes, which *per se* are licit. The third attempt uses the Gallican distinction and holds the conditional consent *de futuro* follows the rules of civil law; and the consent *de praesenti sub condicione* follow the usual consequences of marriage contract agreement and no consideration is taken of the condition. The fourth solution distinguishes between honorable and base conditions. The former are permissible, the latter are considered as not having been placed. What are honorable conditions? Some admit only conversion and parental consent; others admit as honorable what the Roman law allows. The case before Alexander III for decision is a *desponsatio de futuro.* Whether his same reasoning applies to a *desponsatio de praesenti,* it is impossible to know. In his opinion the pontiff equalizes (for the *forum externum*) the consent *de praesenti* and the *copula carnalis,* but not *qua copula carnalis,* but only as a presumption or concluding expression of the marriage will. Is the concluding sentence of the decree "De illis" pregnant with hidden meaning? Does it mean more than it says? Already those immediately following Alexander see more in these words than appears on the surface, "nisi consensus de praesenti aut carnalis sit inter eos commixtio subsecuta." What is the ground of the assumption built on the *copula?* A new act of the will presumed or the persevering conditional will to marry?

Urban III accepted the decree of Alexander and gave rules for the conditional contracting of marriage in his answer to two proposed

[20] C. V, X, *de sponsalibus et matrimoniis,* IV, 1.

[21] C. III, X, *de cond. appositis,* IV, 5.

cases. He issued the decree, "Quum in apostolica." [22] The two marriage cases are entirely different, though both marriages are in suspense or a state of doubt. The first case is: during a dispute about the existence of their marriage, the man steps into a new union. After this fact the first marriage is declared null by the judges of the first trial. The decision of the second trial was: During such a trial concerning validity, the consent and the second marriage, given before the decision of nullity, is valid but illicit. The second case was: where a man gave consent on condition of his father's assent. It seems the condition was not fulfilled and the question was, should he be forced to consummate the marriage. The questioner seems to have no doubt of the validity of the marriage, and the point was should the man be forced to consummate or (in view of the still lingering ease in breaking a *matrimonium ratum*), to annul the marriage. The pope said there was no marriage at all. There was no free consent. The part of the decree beginning with "Super eo" [23] (the second case) caused the canonists much trouble, and still does. Urban says therein that his decision is not contrary to that of Alexander III, and it is only sensible to accept his word. "Ac conditionem ispam canonica non improbent instituta, *quae consonet honestati* . . ." He says honest conditions may be placed, and it seems he admits the admissibility of a certain kind of condition *de praesenti*. He may not have intended this decision as law, but Gregory IX confirmed it: "Contrahens matrimonium sub condicione non improbata non compellitur matrimonium consummare ante conditionis eventum," [24] and the authority he quotes is the "Super eo" section of the decree "Quum in apostolica."

Article IV

The Completion of the Older Doctrine in the Exposition of Huguccio

Huguccio of Pisa is easily the prince of the ancient glossators of Gratian's Decree. The future Innocent III was his disciple. His *Summa* was written before 1187 and after 1185. Having the decree

[22] C. 18, X, *de sponsal et matr.*, IV, 1; *cf.* C. 5, X, *de cond. app.*, IV, 5.

[23] C. 5, X, *de cond. app.*, IV, 5.

[24] C. 5, X, *de cond. app.*, IV, 5.

of Urban III before him, his work shows a considerable deepening of our doctrine. His commentary on the decree "Non oportet" runs into many words. The gist is:[25] Conditional *sponsalia de futuro* (condition at betrothal) are allowed, and if the condition is verified, one is bound *to marry*. A *consensus de praesenti sub condicione* is not allowed, it seems, for a new consent is needed for marriage. One should not marry with a conditional consent, but if he does, then "conditio frangi et desponsatio valet"; as the African Council says.

"Sed securius dicitur, quod sive praedicta condicio sive alia honesta apponatur, cum quis contrahit cum aliqua per verba de praesenti, valet et tenet matrimonium sive adimpleatur sive non. Pure enim intelliguntur consentire, ut c. 27 q. 2. c. quicumque. Ex his ergo, quae dicta sunt, patet, quod triplex condicio attenditur in matrimonio contrahendo. Est enim condicio *cum qua* non potest esse matrimonium sive desponsatio de praesenti vel de futuro, ut condicio, quae repugnat contractui matrimonii, scil, quae continet conventionem de liberis non procreandis vel procreatis suffocandis vel cohabitatione temporali et hujusmodi. Est condicio, *sine qua non* potest esse, ut hic, scil. cum contrahuntur sponsalia inter christianam et paganum adjecta condicione, quod debeat illa converti ad fidem; aliter nihil agitur. Est enim condicio indifferens, scil. *sine qua et cum qua* potest esse, ut quaelibet licita et honesta."

He explicitly says: no Christian can *marry* an infidel *sub condicione* or absolutely without a condition because of the impediment, but he can become conditionally engaged. A valid distinction is this: "Et nota, quod si aliqui sic contrahunt, quod non habent voluntatem habendi prolem, non impeditur matrimonium; si vero sic, quod habent voluntatem non habendi, impeditur matrimonium. Similiter impeditur si habet voluntatem vitandi vel necandi prolem."

In the *Summa* of Huguccio, a complete, clear, penetrating doctrine is given. Its most important opinions are: The addition of a condition to a *desponsatio de praesenti* regularly effects nothing. A condition *de praesenti* whether verified or not, has the same effect as the unconditional transaction. Some conditions would invalidate. Even the internal placing by one party of a condition against the

[25] *Cf.* Hussarek, *op. cit.*, pp. 69-87.

substance of marriage, renders the will void. Indecent conditions are considered not added. The *copula carnalis sequens* is accepted as a declaration of marriage consent. He is very explicit about conditions contrary to the substance of marriage. About the *bonum prolis* he distinguishes very cleverly. He enters into a dispute with those who say the intention *contra bonum* must be expressed to invalidate the marriage. "Ego autem dico, quod non est, licet probari non possit."

Article V

Transition to the New Doctrine

Bernard of Pavia,[26] Archbishop of Faenza, finished his *Summa Decretalium* somewhere between the years 1191 and 1198. It is a summarized presentation of canon law as the author taught it at Bologna and practiced it at the Curia of Rome. This double character of his work and the orientation of the author is the key to many obscure points.[27]

The doctrine at that time had distinguished two classes of *sponsalia, de futuro* and *de praesenti,* opening a welcome possibility in two ways: first the conditional marriage in view of conversion was part and parcel of the legal doctrine; and secondly, the decree "Quicumque" which eliminated apparently every condition, was correspondingly interpreted. The canonists, especially Huguccio formulated the doctrine that the declaration of will to contract marriage is not invalidated by adding to it a condition, since in spite of this condition, which is secondary, all the essentials of marriage (*bona tria*) are willed as being present and the condition was to be eliminated. Conditional engagement could be made, with the same effects as other legal transactions. This doctrine found its support in the decree "De illis" of Alexander III, though it seemed to contradict a later law, *viz.,* Urban's decree "Cum in apostolica." Urban's legal

[26] H. Singer, *Neue Beiträge uber die Dekretalensammlugen, . . . Bernhard von Pavia,* Wien, 1913. E. Friedberg, *Die Canones—Sammlungen zwischen Gratian und Bernhard von Pavia,* Leipzig, 1897.

[27] Hussarek, *Die Bedingte Eheschliessung,* p. 87.

maxim seems sound, and the prevailing doctrine unsound. Urban's attempt to interpret away this contradiction failed, as Huguccio proves. Between legislation and canonical doctrine there was a wide cleft which the masters of law could not ignore.

Bernard, a pupil of Huguccio, occupied the older standpoint, but as bishop he could hardly fight against the legislation, so he is careful in his words and his true opinion is veiled. The *condicio* is to him a *promissionis suspensio per conjunctionem condicionalem.* That which is deferred, therefore, is a *promise* of a future act. He defines: "sponsalia sunt futurarum promissio nuptiarum, dicta a spondendo ie. a promittendo." Only the promise of future acts, in this case, the promise to contract marriage, can become conditioned, but not marriage itself. He avoids saying whether this *desponsatio* is of any kind, or exclusively *de futuro.* Yet he achieves this: till his time our doctrine appeared as a matter of little importance, superficially alluded to in reference to the impediment of *disparitatis cultus.* Even Huguccio lets it remain in this connection. His treatment shows a separate doctrine has originated, due to its own independence, and since it does not belong where it was, he assigns the doctrine to its appropriate place. His compilation consolidates the scattered sources of law on conditional betrothal, and the decretals on condition, under a special title, "The Contraction of Marriage," there he discusses too, the *modus, causa,* and *demonstratio.* Thus a foundation is laid for the future development of the doctrine.[28]

His method in detail is something like this: First he gives a series of various kinds of conditions: Possible conditions which are past, present, or future. Impossible ones he divides into potestative, casual, mixed. He is aware that we can speak only in a fashion of past or present conditions. Another division is honorable and dishonorable. Honorable are either necessary, for instance an infidel to embrace the faith; or arbitrary. This terminology of "arbitrary" is new. He has the terms necessary and voluntary, approved by later canonists. Without the necessary conditions, *e. g.*, marriage between a Catholic and a Jew, is void. The arbitrary condition, in case of verification,

[28] Laspeyres, Theod., *Summa Decratalium Bernardi Papiensis,* Titulus V, p. 146.

imports the obligation of the person betrothed. Likewise the dishonorable conditions are twofold: contrary to the essence of marriage and then to the betrothal the general rule of contracts applies, namely the nullity of the act; and those that are base but not contrary to the essentials of marriage, these are considered non added. He proves this last from decree "Quicumque." This is of decisive importance over against Huguccio. Then he discusses the impossible conditions. They have the effect on betrothals as on contracts in general, they involve the nullity of the legal transaction. He knows and quotes Roman Law on the elimination of such conditions in deeds of will. In spite of this he treats betrothal like any other *contract*. It is remarkable that the man who introduced the category of conditions in canon law holds an opinion concerning their effect, so essentially different from that of his successors.

In his first work "Summula de Matrimonio" not even a reference to our doctrine occurs. Bernard is a follower of Huguccio, but his manner of presentation caused the doctrine of Huguccio to leave the track pointed out by the latter and move in an essentially new direction. He strengthened the interest, and gave the doctrine greater importance by positing it correctly. He used extensively Roman Law to support Church Law and thereby stimulated a more thorough study of Roman Law and led to the development of Canon Law, along the lines of the civil law. His purpose was to find adaptable legal maxims and the result was that canonical science gradually abandoned the point of view he still maintained, though hesitatingly defended, and adopted a standpoint opposed to the doctrine of Bernard but in harmony with his words. This change of front, however, materialized very slowly. Evidence that even after the writing and spreading of Bernard's Compilation, the older doctrine (that is, with regard to the *consensus de praesenti* any condition is eliminated), was not immediately dethroned, is contained in the few but clear glosses on the *Compilatio Prima*,[29] which are found in the Codex p. 11, 7 of the Royal Library of Bamberg.[30]

In these glosses a more solid foundation of the doctrine is at-

[29] Wernz, *Jus Matrimoniale*, n. 238.

[30] Hussarek, *op. cit.*, 95, where these glosses are quoted.

tempted. Evidently the realization of the irregularity of the legal maxim was dawning. The older canonists did not go beyond the fact that the maxims or doctrine had been expressed in ecclesiastical law. Now a very different reading of the decree "Quicumque" was broached, which seemed to harmonize with Roman Law on wills, justifying the elimination of dishonorable conditions. No longer was it possible to accept two opposed interpretations of the same passage. Thus the glossators looked to Roman Law for support of the older opinion and it was found in the legal rule, "Utile per inutile non vitiatur." Thus one gloss *sub verbo* "frangatur" reads: "Nota, quod utile non vitiatur per inutile."

Richard Anglicus [31] in his *Distinctiones* probably formulated in the last decade of the XII century, occupies the same position. His work is an epitome of canon law and it conformed to the accepted doctrine, therefore there is no new development therein. It seems, in spite of contradictory opinions on condition, he reaches the inadmissibility of a condition to a *consensus de praesenti*.

Innocent III in his law "Per tuas nobis" [32] given in July, 1203, did not end the ambiguity of the doctrine, though it offered points of support for the later conception of a conditional marriage consent. The case submitted for papal solution was a consent *de praesenti* on condition that the father and uncle of the man assent. Cohabitation took place. The woman claimed that before the third parties dissented, she and her husband had consented *pure* and had the *copula*. This was denied by others. The decision was a foregone conclusion due to the consummation, whether the relationship between the two was a conditional engagement or a conditional marriage, which is unknown; or unconditional for that matter. The decision could have been based on the decrees "De illis" of Alexander III and "Super eo" of Urban III. Yet the way this traditional law conception was expressed, caused a tendency to essentially new maxims. The disputed point, whether with a *sponsalia de praesenti* a condition was allowed, was not touched at all. The situation was that a prior law had on the

[31] Died 1237.

[32] *Cf.* C. 6, X, *de conditionibus app.*, IV, 5, where the case and solution is quoted.

occasion of a scientific dispute, taken pains to state that its formulations, in spite of utterances, in no way contradicts a former law and the current doctrine.[33] Innocent refrains from such a theoretical observation, though his decision seems to contradict one of the theories. Probably his sympathy was no longer in favor of the doctrine as it formerly was. The pope did not base his decision on the testimony of witnesses, which was contradictory and defective, but on the three facts: of the conditional consent, the cohabitation following, and the opposition of the third parties. The first two facts create a right, and the third could become destructive of this right only when its temporal relations were known, and they were unknown; therefore, the dissent was indifferent in the case, for although the time of dissent was known, the date of first cohabitation was not, though the woman declared it was prior to the contradiction of the relatives. This she did not prove. The pope is not influenced by the doctrine of his teacher, Huguccio, but by the principle of *favor matrimonii,* he finds a way out. The plaintiff petitioned for the recognition of the marriage. The decision reads after summing up the *species facti:* " . . . pro matrimonio est *vehementer quidem* praesumendum, quia videtur condicione opposita recessisse." We must remember that the irrefutability of this presumption which excludes all counter evidence was unknown in the age of Innocent III. It was Gregory IX who by law established this point, basing it on Innocent's solution "Per tuas nobis." Gregory's law reads: "Qui sub honesta conditione sponsalia contrahit, et ante conditionis eventum desponsatam cognoscit, a conditione recedit." [34]

Now since the principle was legally (at least implicitly) established that marriage could be contracted under the condition of the consent of other persons besides the parents (the uncle in our case) canonists bestirred themselves. The rationale for the doctrine of the legislator and the opinions held by science was the honorableness of these conditions. Thus a harmonious accord was attained. The fulfillment of duties of pious respect was valued as a sufficient reason for a condition; thus the road was smoothed for the admission of

[33] *Cf.* end of chapter three.

[34] C. 6, X, *de conditionibus, app.,* IV, 5.

numerous other conditions besides the consent of third persons. Although from the above considerations a modification of the current practice was not immediately effected through this law, yet there was an inducement to prepare indirectly at least the field for scientific convictions which till then received scant approval. They gradually entered triumphantly into the doctrine and eventually into the legislation.

The characteristic of the immediately following development was that more and more tenets of Roman law were incorporated into the ecclesiastical law. This detail work pushed into the background the main question, whether also the *consensus de praesenti* could be given under condition. Most of the canonists treat this point *obiter* and by no means clearly. These secondary matters concern the moment of the positing of the condition, the discussion of impossible, perplexed, and resolutive conditions, and whether a condition referring to the past or present operated as a condition, *i. e.,* whether there is any pendency. The canonists, it seems, are dominated by the Roman law; they seldom express their own personal views, or consider whether the civil rules fit the peculiar legal situation that confronts them. Right here is found a testimony showing the power with which civil law entered in and permeated with its tenets, our doctrine on conditions.

Tancred's older works exhibit the achievements of these times. Tancred was "*Decretorum magister Bononinae.*" He died between 1234 and 1236. His *Summa* on marriage was written about 1214. Then he wrote his *Apparatus,* a commentary on the first three *Compilationes.* In the *Summa* and the *Apparatus* to the *Compilatio Prima* he takes no definite attitude to the disputed question about conditional consent *de praesenti* to marry. He only discusses conditional engagements and gives the history of them, and gives the well known answer that *conditiones turpes* are not considered as being placed, and conditions contrary to the essence of marriage invalidate the consent and the betrothal *ipso facto.* A licit condition excludes compulsion before its fulfillment, yet this same conditional consent is a sufficient basis for the instant origination of the marriage tie by the latter occuring cohabitation.

He, as Huguccio, unequivocally teaches that agreements contrary to the nature of marriage also affect the validity of the declaration of the will to marry. Discussing the condition of conversion, he like Bernard, uses *desponsatio* only with the connotation of betrothal.

His *Apparatus* to the first compilation treats our doctrine in more detail but with no great profundity. There seems to be a half-way reserve as to the main point. Impossible and base conditions are eliminated, saying expressly that a marriage or engagement with an impossible condition is valid. But the important question, what is the effect of adding an honest condition to the will to marry, is nowhere answered. At the chapter, "Super eo," the ideal place to define his attitude, he merely says: "here marriage is contracted conditionally like a purchase or other contract," probably referring to the consent of third parties. Yet the *Apparatus* achieved much in the development of the doctrine. So far a thesis for the doctrine was not formulated.[35]

Some teachers taught that agreements contrary to the essence of marriage have their annihilating effects *only* when immediately expressed: "si in primo contractu exprimantur." This principle is now generalized. A declaration of will is considered conditional only when the condition is at once attached. "Condicione mox adjecta; quae ex intervallo admitti non debet." Laurentius the glossator is probably the representative of this doctrine; taken rightly or wrongly from Roman law. Huguccio declared that these will wield their peculiar influence on the declaration of the will to betroth or to marry, even when not uttered, but remain hidden in the breast of the contracting parties. It might be added here that this very point concerning the time of adding a condition is disputed to this day. Canonists vary about it. Even the practice of the Roman Curia has changed its jurisprudence on this point in deciding cases of marriage. The difficulty is the phrase *deducta in pactum condicio.* This will be discussed separately in the doctrinal part of this dissertation.

Bernard, as we saw, characterized the effect of impossible conditions as the frustration of the entire transaction. He treated the

[35] *Cf.* Hussarek, *op. cit.*, p. 124.

desponsatio following the analogy of contracts and not of testamentary regulations. His followers did not receive this with favor. But the gloss differs. It arranges the three varieties of conditions under an amplified concept of impossible conditions as follows: the immoral ones as legally impossible, the naturally impossible, and the perplexed, which last seems to be contrary to the essence of marriage, and thus the will is void. The other two are considered not added, "quia edictum de matrimonio contrahendo prohibitorium est." Thus the impossible and the base conditions are placed on the same level. This is based on an utterance of Papinian " . . . quae facta laedunt pietatem, existimationem, verecundiam nostram, et, ut generaliter dixerim contra bonos mores fiunt, nec facere non posse credendum est."[36] After adopting the above mentioned identification the decision was removed from doubt. The time we are speaking of applied the chapter "Quicumque" only to dishonorable conditions. After positing the maxim, that both are on the same level, all doubt concerning the outcome evaporated. The elimination of both was a foregone conclusion.

The *Apparatus* furthermore contains a passage which illustrates how the glossator conceived the mutual relations of the betrothed couple during the pendency. At the chapter "Praeterea" under the word "sine condicione" we read: ". . . secus si sub condicione fidem darent, quia tunc deficiente condicione *dissolverentur* sponsalia, ut s. eod. De illis." According to this, there exists already, during the pendency, a betrothal, with the normal legal consequences, but with an additional ground for dissolution. In other words, a betrothal under condition is not a suspensively but a resolutively conditioned legal transaction and relationship; not its origin but its preservation is dependent on the verification of the condition. This treatment would thus lay bare the reason for the resistance against the admission of conditions in contracting marriage. It was easy enough to acquiesce in a latter concellation of a betrothal but in the case of marriage it is different, marriage suffers no resolutive condition.

John Teutonicus, in his *Glossa Ordinaria* (1215) to Gratian's Decree clings to the older doctrine. His view is found at chapter "Solet

[36] L. 15 Digest, *De Condicionibus institutionum*, 28, 7.

quaeri." According to him there are two categories of conditions, each with two sub-classes. The honorable ones are either essential or non-essential; the base, either contrary or not contrary to the nature of marriage. A state of pendency occur only with honorable conditions which are essential for marriage, that is, one by which an impediment (*e. g., disparitas cultus*) preventing the marriage is to be removed. Without adding this condition, then, no legal tie between the parties, can be established. He speaks here, of course, of being essential for a *consensus de praesenti,* which is clear from the context and his examples. There is a passage [37] from whose wording we can assume that through the fulfillment of the condition, marriage would set in at once, while before fulfillment nothing else but the legal effects of a betrothal would be in evidence.

In other cases, outside honorable necessary conditions, no pendency occurs, *e. g.*, a condition of giving a dowry, therefore marriage he says is valid with this condition or without it; fulfilled or not, it is considered not added. "Tenet matrimonium cum illa condicione et sine ea," he deduces this from the decree "De illis." The last classes of conditions, those contrary to the *tria bona* of marriage, annihilate everything. The doctrine of the *Glossa Ordinaria* is consistent and harmonious. A conditional marriage cannot exist, it is contradictory. Marriage arises at one stroke "quam cito est perfectum et consummatum quoad sui essentiam nec recipit sectionem nec interstitia temporum." [38] His dilemma was that a conditional consent of marriage was either instantly null and void, or entirely valid. Vacaillation between "effect" and "no effect" as in other law transactions was not in harmony with his view of marriage, and therefore a successive growth by a gradual amelioration was unthinkable, and this is implied in the conditonal consent.[39]

This attitude induced him to consider whether a conditional consent has the essential content which must be predicated of a marriage consent. This consisted in the *tria bona,* "sine his autem bonis matrimonium contrahi non potest, postea vero sine his esse potest." That is

[37] Cap., *Cave Christiane,* 15; C. 28, q. 1.

[38] C. 5, C. 27, qu. 2; *cf.* Hussarek, *op. cit.*, p. 116.

[39] The Scholastic theologians later on, failed to solve this fictitious dilemma.

why he treats our doctrine under the will to marry. Beyond this consent, neither dowry, consent of parents, nor any other thing is legally necessary for a valid marriage, therefore it is plain, why he considers marriage as present and perfect whenever such unessential moments form the conditioning event, nor does it matter whether these are verified or not. When the content of the parties' consent is defective in essence, then there is no marriage. It is not the condition which frustrates as such the consent, it is only valued as a symptom which points to the essential defectiveness of the consent.

The *Apparatus* of Vicentius Hispanus, to the third *Compilation*, was written between 1210 and 1217. With it was commenced the casuistry concerning the admissibility or exclusion of, and the varied legal consequences of the various individual conditions. This casuistry absorbed much of the time and mental activity which was devoted to our doctrine, and frustrated the gaining of clear and satisfactory results. The author of this *Apparatus* had a comprehensive knowledge of Roman Law and applied it to Canon Law.[40] He admits conditions only for betrothals.

Article VI

The Turning Point in the Doctrine and the Legislation

Tancred, next to Bernard Papiensis, is the prince of ancient Decretalists, as Huguccio is the prince of the Decretists. He finished the *Apparatus* to the third compilation about the year 1217. It marks a significant step in the advance of our doctrine. There are some notable passages.

His thesis is that a consent *de praesenti* may be declared with a condition: "Omnem autem condicionem de futuro dico matrimonium suspendere, nec est contra. de. cond. app. 1; nam illud ca. intelligendum est de condicione resolutoria." What is demanded here is the condition must be a suspensive one referring to a future event. The effect of the condition on the consent *de praesenti* to which it is added, is peculiar: "ex quo ibi est condicio, licet verba sint de praesenti,

[40] Hussarek, *op. cit.*, p. 120.

semper tamen suspenditur consensus et sit de futuro." The conditions attached refer not to the instantaneous but exclusively to the future arising of the marriage tie. Because an absolute consent with a third party, destroys the first and effects the marriage with the third party, which is certain, he has to say that during pendency it is a betrothal consent. Yet it matters little what he calls it, since he attributes to it matrimonial efficacy, if the condition is verified.

Other tenets are: if the conditioning fact has been fulfilled or frustrated in the past, immediately upon the declaration of consent, marriage either exists or does not exist; the necessary condition must be fulfilled that all the effects of the present consent may arise, then when that occurs the entire state of affairs is the same as if the marriage were entirely valid from the beginning. Resolutive conditions are treated as non-existent.

With far greater clearness than in Tancred the change in the orientation of the doctrine at the beginning of the XIII century, is manifested in the "Quaestiones" of Damascus, which he wrote before the fourth Lateran Council of 1215.

"Item quaeritur, utrum sponsalia de praesenti possint contrahi sub condicione? Videtur quod non, quia sponsalia de praesenti nichil aliud sunt quam matrimonium et ideo non recipit condicionem. Actus enim legitimus est, et actus legitimi non recipiunt diem nec condicionem. . . . Sed omnes contractus. . . . Ergo existente condicione incipiat consensus de praesenti, quia condicio talem consesum suspendit, qualis est."

"Item responde ad hanc objectionem: lex dicit, quod in quocumque casu probatur matrimonium contrahi in eodem etiam sponsalia D. de spon *Oratio* (1. 16 D. 23, 1). Sed sponsalia contrahuntur sub condicione, ergo et matrimonium, ut de spons. De illus lib. 1. Solutio: Sciendum quod possunt contrahi sub condicione sponsalia de praesenti." All this he sustains by Roman Law.

Comparing the doctrine of the "Quaestiones" with the utterances of the same author in his *Brocarda* or collection of canonical rules, there is no doubt that from the second decade of the XIII century, this new doctrine had met with approval. It was now recognized that a declaration of will aiming at the instantaneous materialization of marriage underwent by the condition a change of essence. According to the new doctrine the conditioned will was only apparently predicated in the present, while its very essence pointed to the future. Marriage did not arise by it. The new doctrine paid more attention to the contents, than to the tenor of the declaration, therefore it was free to admit conditions even in case of a *consensus per verba de praesenti expressus*.

Now two doctrines faced each other in sharpest contrast. Both founded, developed, and elaborated by masters of the law, but neither of them clearly and decisively supported by legislation. This discord pressed for a legislative decision, as an agreement by scientific antagonism was not hoped for. The legislation of Gregory IX arbitrated the dispute.

To appreciate the achievement of the legislation of Gregory IX [41] in our doctrine, it is well to survey the modifications which Raymond of Pennafort applied to the not voluminous decretals he had at hand. The systematic position of the doctrine was given by Bernard, that is, as a variety of *desponsatio*.

Raymond left this position unchanged, and even the traditional title. In this [42] he incorporated first the apocryphal African canon; next to the canon comes the decretal "Cum sit proprium" of Gregory I, with slight modifications;[43] then follows the pertinent part of the decree "De illis," which is significant.[44] Bernard placed the entire decretal in the first title of marriage law. The context there pointed exclusively to *sponsalia de futuro,* to support Bernard's theory against

[41] "His studies and his experience in dealing with cases which had come before him as Auditor and Legate had taught him that Gratian's Decree was antiquated and that there was great need of simplifying and unifying the existing mass of ecclesiastical laws. He therefore commissioned the Dominican Brother Raymond of Pennafort to omit superfluities and to collect into one volume the decretals of his predecessors and his own"—Mann, *The Lives of the Popes in the Middle Ages,* Vol. XIII, p. 206. Even before his election as Pope, Cardinal Hugolinus was a great, intimate and loving friend of St. Francis, St. Dominic, and St. Clare.

[42] C. 1, X, *de cond.*, IV, 5.

[43] C. 2, X, *de cond.*, IV, 5.

[44] C. 3, X, *de cond.*, IV, 5.

our doctrine *de praesenti.* But the basis for this procedure collapsed by the fact that the decretal was now placed in such a connection that this argument could no longer be derived from the same. Its text remained unchanged.[44] The following chapter, "Verum quum," is taken over without change. The next chapter, "Super eo" of Urban III's decree "Cum in apostolica," is modified. Urban considered that doctrine as sanctioned by law which ignored any condition to the declaration of marriage consent. His decision, seemingly contrary to this, he represented as in harmony, yet with timidity, when he declares that notwithstanding something is ordered and decreed (*nihilominus respondemus*). The dilemma was, the vigor of the law striking out the condition on the one hand, and the claims of filial piety on the other and he satisfied the ethical claim of the parents at the expense of the legal consequences, therefore he adds immediately to the bold thesis "ac conditionem ipsam canonica non improbent instituta," the far-reaching restriction "Quae consonet honestati," which here applied only to duties of filial respect.

All these characteristic phrases the redactor of the Gregorian legislation has destroyed. To him a norm was a norm, not a law, for the latter is given in the teeth of conflicting views. The thesis that conditions are admissible in contracting marriage is now announced in dryest terms without restricting them to filial piety. Nor for the materialization of marriage is any devoted observance of duty required, only the verification of the conditioning event. In place of terms connoting ethical duty, here is the juristic-technical standpoint. "Contrahens matrimonium sub conditione non improbata non compellitur matrimonium consummare ante conditionis eventum." [45] The contrast wherein the legislator of the year 1234 found himself with that of the year 1187, induced Gregory to eliminate the above mentioned phraseology.

The next decretal that Raymond inserts is the "Per tuas nobis" of Innocent III. He erased the entire processual part. This law of a presumed pure consent after cohabitation during pendency of a con-

[44] The first part of the decretal is chapter five, of title one of the fourth book of Gregory IX.

[45] C. 5, X, *de conditionibus app.*, IV, 5.

ditional betrothal, did not contradict the view of Gregory and thus no amendment was needed.

But in order to set at rest any doubt of the question: What is the law concerning declaration of conditional consent to marry, the legislator gives a law which directly and indirectly comprises all possible conditions. This is the chapter *"Si Conditiones."* [46] The reason for the addition of this passage is that he wanted to give a terse and concise statement of the entire doctrine. For no one doubted that conditions contrary to the nature of marriage nullify the consent, nor that dishonorable and impossible conditions are to be considered as not added, on account of the "favor matrimonii." Raymond's task was not to establish incontrovertible doctrines, but to enact laws to clear up doubts about former laws. The "dubium" was neither the annihilative effects of conditions against the nature of marriage nor the elimination of impossible and immoral ones, but the admissibility of the other class of honest and possible conditions. Therefore the interpretation of the chapter, "Si Conditiones," means that there are three kinds of conditions, those contrary to the nature of marriage, illicit, and licit ones. The first category does not allow the arising of marriage; the second has no influence on its instantaneous validity; concerning the third class those rules are valid which can be derived from the three preceding laws which affect these matters. With the Gregorian compilation the view which admitted the conditional contracting of marriage achieved a victory.[47]

Article VII

Development and Deepening of the New Doctrine

Roffredus Epiphanii (died 1243) wrote *Libellus Juris Canonici.* This work for the first time in literature testifies to the victory of the new interpretation according to which a consent *de praesenti sub condicione* may be formulated. He devotes a special title of the third book to the doctrine which opens with these significant words: "Licet matrimonia sint favorabilia et fecerimus plures libellos, per quos

[46] C. 7, X, *de conditionibus app.*, IV, 5.

[47] Hussarek, *op. cit.*, p. 136.

compellitur quis ad matrimonium consummandum; verum quia multae sunt causae, propter quas non compellitur quis matrimonium ideo de illis videamus. Et primo de condicione."[48] He is the first to transfer the doctrine from the law of contracting marriage to the law on matrimonial impediments, a confusing transfer. After treating of conditional engagements, with nothing new therein, he puts the question:

"Item quid, si matrimonium fiat per verba de praesenti et dicam sic 'contraho tecum matrimonium, si dabis mihi centum in dotem,' numquid compellar illud matrimonium consummare, si illa non dabit centum in dotem? Respondeo, credo, quod non; nam cum condicio sit honesta et possibilis, non contra bonas mores servanda est ut dicit decre. ulti. extra de cond. app." Then he goes on to answer objections. "Ceterum si a principio contraho sub illa condicione 'si decem dares pro dote,' valet. Quis unquam contrarium diceret?" His testimony is precious for his work was completed before 1243, and even still nearer to the publication of the *Liber Extra* of Gregory IX. Thus he is an immediate contemporary. He sees in the chapter, *"Si Conditiones,"* the law which has answered in the affirmative the question concerning marriage under an honest condition.

Goffredus de Trano, later cardinal and connected with the court of Gregory IX, as was Roffredus, composed his *Summa* or *Gloss* to the Decretals of Gregory IX, between 1241 and 1245. This *Summa* is a true mirror of the status of the doctrine in his time. It remained for a long time the guide which directed the further development of canon law, and after the invention of printing, it was put in type in 1487. The work is a further authoritative argument for the victory of the new doctrine, but it did not develop anything new concerning the doctrine.

The commentary of Sinibaldus Fliscus (Pope Innocent IV, 1243-1254) was an *Apparatus* to the five books of Gregory IX. This removes the last vestige of doubt concerning the admissibility of a conditional consent *de praesenti.* "Si vero dixerit 'accipio te in uxorem, si dederis C.' suspendetur (scil. matrimonium), quousque det

[48] Hussarek, *op. cit.*, p. 137.

C. infra. eod. cap. Super eo."[49] Under the word *"conditiones"* he shrewdly observes that *"pacta"* would be the more exact term. The conditions enumerated in the chapter, *"Si Conditiones,"* are rather agreements of the parties concerning the content of their matrimonial relationship. It should be observed here, however, that there can be a condition without an agreement.

His classification is: honorable, dishonorable, voluntary, and necessary conditions. He rejects some conditions, *e. g.*, "if I shall find you a virgin," but he proves the objection to this condition, not by being entrapped to talk about *error* concerning the virginity, but wants no other authority than the decree "Quicumque." He enriches casuistry by his provocative questions and their solutions. For instance, he examines the question whether the express agreement of both parties to a condition contrary to the nature of marriage is necessary to involve the nullity of the act, or whether it is likewise incurred if one party remains silent, or opposed to such an agreement. The first he answers in the affirmative, basing it on the chapter VII Aliquando C. 32, qu. 2. Marriage is not impaired by the other two eventualities.

Probably the most important feature of the doctrine of Innocent IV is his study of the effect of the conditional consent. He is the first who penetrated into the core of the problem. The passages are contained in the chapter "Super eo." It is not our purpose to relate his courageous analysis of the effects; suffice it to say that during pendency the relation is a fit basis for the origination of marriage by the consummation of the *copula carnalis.* In the last analysis it amounts to analogy to the declaration of the will to marry by persons who are hindered by ecclesiastical impediments.

The *Summa Aurea* of Hostiensis (Cardinal, 1261, died 1271), a great canonist, follows its motto to be helpful to those "qui . . . diversa scripta utilia in unum volumen quod utrumque jus finaliter redacta habere disiderat."

It undertakes to give an exhaustive elucidation of our doctrine, together with other subjects. It, however, contains little that is new

[49] Cap: Quicumque vb. "desponsatio"—C. 1 to 7, X, *De conditionibus appositis,* IV, 3.

on conditional marriage consent. Hostiensis defines condition "quaedam sponsaliorum vel contractus suspensiva promissio cujus effectus comfirmatio pendet ex futuro." This definition excludes resolutive conditions. True conditions (honorable and possible) have the effect to defer the consent to the occurrence of the conditioning event. He energetically rejects the theory of those who hold only those conditions have a suspensive effect whereby the existence of the marriage is left to the arbitrary decision of persons who have authority over the nupturients. Impossible and immoral conditions, barring those contrary to the essence of marriage, are treated as not added. If the condition is one that necessarily occurs, then marriage sets in at once. Thus an intervening marriage before the fulfillment of this necessary condition encounters the impediment of *ligamen*.

He states with considerable emphasis that the pendency which intervenes, due to the condition, is in no way contrary to the essence of marriage. Therefore the rule: "Actus legitimi neque diem recipiunt neque conditionem" does not apply to marriage. These acts invariably presuppose a judicial verdict or a regulation of a testator. A judgment is never pronounced with a condition. Our doctrine, he says, belongs to the law regulating marriage contract, and not to matrimonial impediments. "Hactenus tractavit autor de matrimoniis puris et condicionalibus docens, qualiter contrahatur . . . nunc incipit tractare de matrimonii impedimentis." The doctrine of Innocent IV and Hostiensis, in their combination embody a like culmination point for the evolution of the new doctrine of conditional marriage contract, as the doctrine of Huguccio does for the older doctrine.

Bernardus de Botone (died c. 1263-1266) was the author of the *Glossa Ordinaria* to the Gregorian decretals. According to this work, conditional marriage contract constitutes no matrimonial impediment. The gloss to our doctrine commences with these words: "Quia quandoque sponsalia contrahuntur pure, de quibus visum est supra; quandoque sub condicione, merito de his post praecedentia submittit." The word *sponsalia* is here used generically. His work consists partly in the compilation of older glosses and their adaptation to the changed legal science of his age, and partly in the presentation of his own views. In our doctrine the majority of the glosses are taken from the two *Apparatus* of Tancred. Only the new chapter *"Si Conditiones"* was in need of a commentary.

The principal tenets of his doctrine are: Some conditions are licit, some illicit, example of which he gives. Dishonorable ones are not considered as being placed, marriage is valid without regard to them. Only those conditions that are incompatible with the *tria bona* of marriage, nullify the consent. As is clear, all this is nothing new.

Of greater importance is his discussion of the conditional declaration of consent. He constructs from [60] passages in the Digest a maxim: "Donatio sub condicione facta non tenet, nisi adveniente condicione sive ea impleta . . . et sic venditio."

Applied to marriage, it assumes the following shape: "hoc facit condicio apposita, quae suspendit contractum usque ad tempus condicionis extantis." Thus instead of deferring only the effects of a declaration of will, on account of the condition, Bernard teaches that the declaration of the will, the consent itself is deferred. Before the fulfillment of the condition there *exists no consent.* "Condicionalis consensus nullus est ante condicionem extantem." This attitude is again pointedly expressed thus: "Nota quod matrimonium sub condicione contrahi potest, non tamen tenet, nisi condicio extiterit vel recessum sit a condicione per contrarium factum." An anology may be found in testamentary law. When a last will is drawn up, it is really uncertain whether its arrangements will ever be realized. Due to change of circumstances it may be given up, or be revoked by the testator. It holds out hope, without giving a solid claim. If the declaration of the last will remains and the legatee survives the testator, then the delation sets in.

Since it was an indubitable legal maxim that the consummation of the marriage during pendency will immediately perfect the conditional consent and the conditional relationship, and since a conditional consent becomes legally valid only with the verification of the condition, Bernard tries to find the rationale of the former maxim, especially since at first sight it seems marriage is effected by the *coitus* without any regard to the concomitant consent. He concludes:

[60] L. 44; D. 35, 1.

"Si ergo nullus praecessit consensus, solus coitus matrimonium non facit."

William Durantis, a disciple of Bernard, gives little that is new, but he is a valuable witness to the interpretation of his time. He rejects the distinction made by some canonists between a condition predicated on the assent of a third party and other honorable conditions. "Non ergo videtur referre, sive condicio apponatur in matrimonio sive in consensu. Unde tale matrimonium 'accipio te in meam, si mihi dederis C.' non obligat, nisi illa C. dederit." The consent to marry with a condition is void, during pendency. If the condition is fulfilled marriage arises *ipso facto*. The petition then of the plaintiff is not for contracting marriage but for the execution or enforcing of an already valid marriage. For the rest he adheres to the prevailing doctrine about base and impossible conditions.

Article VIII

The Doctrine of the Scholastic Theologians, Antagonism to the New Doctrine

The Scholastics bear witness to the status of our doctrine in the XIII century. Their presentation of marriage is essentially that contained in the Commentaries to the Sentences of Peter Lombard. Since the topic of conditional marriage consent is foreign to the Lombard, these theologians had no inducement to expatiate on or elucidate the matter. St. Thomas Aquinas assembles his material from the point of view of consent which suffers from the defect of will, at the passage treating of compulsion. He teaches that the marriage effecting power of conditional consent cannot be maintained, due to two considerations; it should be expressed *simpliciter* and marriage should be *certum,* but it is neither, if a condition is placed.

> Ad quintum sic proceditur. 1: Videtur quod nec per consensum conditionatum fiat matrimonium, quia quod sub condicione ponitur, non simpliciter enunciatur. Sed in matrimonio oportet esse verba simpliciter exprimentia consensum. Ergo conditio alicujus consensus non facit matrimonium. 2: Praeterea, matrimonium debet esse certum. Sed ubi

> dicitur aliquid sub condicione, ponitur illud sub dubio. Ergo talis consensus non facit matrimonium.
>
> Sed contra in aliis contractibus fit obligatio sub condicione, et stat stante conditione. Ergo cum matrimonium sit contractus quidam, videtur quod possit fieri per conditionatum consensum.
>
> Concl: Consensus ex conditione de praesenti non contraria matrimonio vel de futuro et necessaria, matrimonium efficit.
>
> Respondeo dicendum, quod conditio apposita aut est de praesenti, aut de futuro. Si de praesenti, et non est contraria matrimonio, sive sit honesta, sive non honesta, stat matrimonium stante conditione, et ea non stante non stat. Sed si sit contraria bonis matrimonii, non efficitur matrimonium; sicut de sponsalibus dictum est, quaest. 43, art. 1. Si autem sit conditio de futuro, aut est necessaria, sicut solem oriri cras, et tunc est matrimonium, quia talia futura sunt praesentia in causis; aut est contingens, ut datio pecuniae, vel acceptatio parentum; et tunc idem est judicium de tali consensu, sicut de consensu qui fit per verba de futuro: unde non facit matrimonium. Et per haec patet solutio ad objecta.[51]

Hussarek [52] remarks that St. Thomas not being a jurist his expression is not precise. While the jurists as a matter of principle took their departure from the temporary nullity of the consent and only in order to explain certain effects had recourse to the existence of a betrothal, he values the relationship exactly as a betrothal. The result is the requirement of a new declaration of consent after the verification of the condition. St. Thomas clearly denies the doctrine about a future contingent condition being admissible to a marriage consent.

St. Bonaventure (John Fidanza, 1221-1274) seems also to deny our doctrine of a consent *de praesenti* given with a condition.[53]

> Si autem consensus fiat per verba de *praesenti;* aut condicio est *praeterita,* aut *praesens,* aut *futura.* Si condicio est *praeterita,* ut: accipio te in meam, si mortuus est pater tuus;

[51] *Commentarium,* Pars Tertia, *Suppl.,* q. 47, art. 5.
[52] *Die Bedingte Eheschliessung,* p. 160.
[53] Lib. IV, *Sent.,* Dist., 28, art. unicus, q. 111.

> vel de *praesenti,* ut: accipio te in meam, si es virgo; stante condicione, stat matrimonium. Si autem condicio est de *futuro;* aut futuri *necessarii,* aut futuri *contingentis.* Si futuri *necessarii,* ut: accipio te in meam, si sol oriatur cras; tunc est matrimonium. Si autem condicio est *contingens,* dico quod non est matrimonium, eo quod *consensus* pendet de futuro, sicut et *condicio;* et ideo judicandum est tunc, sicut de futuro, nec est matrimonium, nisi carnalis copula subsequatur, quia tunc intelligitur a condicione apposita recessisse.

It seems that both the Seraphic Doctor and the Angelic Doctor missed the point, thinking that there were only two alternatives about a conditional matrimonial consent *de praesenti,* namely the marriage either has to immediately arise or there was no marriage at all. The idea of pendency or a virtually continuing marriage consent, was not considered. That this is true of St. Bonaventure seems evident from the following negative arguments:

> Ad. 2: Item, post consensum istum aut est uxor; aut *non.* Si *uxor;* sed possible est, condicionem non stare, et non consenerat nisi sub condicione: Ergo est uxor sine consensu. Sed non est uxor: ergo talis consensus non efficit matrimonium.
>
> Ad. 3: Item matrimonium est vinculum nullo modo solubile; sed omnis obligatio vel pactio sub condicione facta est solubilis, ergo etc.

It seems he fails to distinguish between *matrimonium in fieri* and *in facto esse,* and between suspensive and resolutive conditions.

The opposition was not entirely silenced even in the second half of the XIII century. The protagonists of this opposition are Petrus de Sampsone and his disciple, the Abbas Antiquus. Peter was a "Magister Bononiae" from 1230 to 1260; he wrote a *Summa Decretalium, Distictiones,* and *Lectura* on the Decretals of Innocent IV. The Abbas Antiquus is called the Decretalist of the XIII century to distinguish him from the Abbas Siculus or Panormitanus of the XV century. He composed a *Lectura* or *Apparatus* to Decretals of Gregory IX, and a *Lectura* on the Constitutions of Innocent IV, and *Distinctiones.*

In Peter's *Summa* his view is very clear. He expressly attacks the common doctrine, as he calls it, and attempts to revive and resuscitate the old abandoned opinion of the inadmissibility of a conditional consent *de praesenti,* whose champion was Vincentius.[54] He holds, but not wisely, that a condition of assent of a third party touches the very essence of marriage consent while this cannot be said of other conditions. As usual, like others before him, he is mislead by the use of the term "consensus" in both cases of the parents and the parties:

> . . . licet communiter aliter intelligatur, quod si aliquis contrahat cum aliqua per verba de praesenti sub condicione puta 'si dederis X'; si condicio non impleatur, nihilominus valere consensum de praesenti; his autem dicitur, quod non valet, donec condicio sit impleta. Respondet huic ut patet . . . valet tamen consensus, licet communiter dicant doctores per istud caput, quod sicut hic non valet consensus in casu hujus capituli 'contraho tecum, si pater meus consenerit,' dones condicio sit completa; ita non valet, si contraho tecum 'si dederis mihi X,' nisi condicio fuerit impleta. Sed certe hoc est contra casum illius decretalis De illis . . .

Then he asked why the difference of interpretation of the decree "De illis," and answers with the distinction above mentioned.

His disciple reasons along similar lines, reducing other conditions to modes which do not touch the substance of the contract. These two scholars did not succeed in establishing their opposition to placing any honest future and possible condition to a marriage consent *de praesenti.*

Article IX

The Development of the Doctrine Reaches Its Conclusion. The Liber Sextus. The Teaching of John Andrea and Abbas Siculus

By comparing the two doctrines whose most important champions are Sinnibaldus Fliscus and Hostiensis, which are in veiled contradiction, the law on conditional marriage consent could be theoretically ascertained with clearness. The difference was this. That cham-

[54] *Cf.* Supra, Section 5.

pioned by Innocent IV inclined to the view that the legal status of the two parties was to be valued in analogy to a betrothal, while Hostiensis emphasized more the temporary nullity of the consent. In practice this meant that the first derived from the case during the pendency, the impediment of *publicae honestatis.* The latter did not. This dispute found its solution in the *Liber Sextus* [55] of Boniface VIII, completed in 1298 and sent to the Universities of Bologna and Paris. The pope declared the matrimonial impediment does not exist during the pendency of a condition. He went further and interpreted very plainly in this Decretal conditional marriage consent.

Such consent is temporarily null in exactly the same way as if concluded by a child or an insane person, or under compulsion or error. This nullity is however temporary, not permanent. As soon as the condition is verified, the marriage is valid, because the nullity was predicated on the ground of defect of consent, but this is at once remedied by the verification. During pendency the conditional *sponsalia* are something vacillating and uncertain. As long as this state of uncertainty persists, they are non-existent as far as the law is concerned, therefore from them the impediment could not originate. It is the intervention of the fulfilled condition which makes the formally declared but legally inoperative consent now operative. It is as if the consent were just given now. This teaching is contained in the sole chapter of the first title of the fourth book. Implicitly this decree upholds another maxim which, though generally taught, had no legal sanction. Marriage with a third party during pendency is valid, even if the condition is later verified, even if contracted with a relative of the other party. No attention is paid to any possible arising of *ligamen.* Thus in indirectly sanctioning the conviction of the validity of this other union during pendency, our doctrine achieves a signal victory.

An orientation from Roman Law, says M. Hussarek,[56] could not have established these two propositions without grave inconsistency, being in sharp contrast to the foundation of the theory of conditions in Roman law. By this step he believes the decretal has impressed the

[55] Cap. un., *De Sponsalibus et Matrimoniis,* IV, I in VI.

[56] *Op. cit.,* p. 169.

stamp of uniqueness on the conditional marriage contract, in contradistinction to any other legal transaction. In the *Liber Sixtus* our legal institute has found its crowning conclusion and completion. Thus a definite theory, developed for all individual consequences, was given reception by legal recognition of its two outstanding corralaries. Papal legislation was nevermore induced to create any new forms. The Council of Trent refrained from further regulations, and the particular evolution of canon law never departed from this foundation. The Code[57] substantiates the doctrine.

For a correct appreciation of the importance of this Bonifacian Decretal there is a witness in John Andreae "aetatis Aureae Decretalistarum est felix clausula." His *Glossa in Sextum* (Canon 1304) later received as the *Glossa Ordinaria* to the Bonifacian collection, at the very beginning states that the decision of the scholastic dispute between Sinibaldus and Hostiensis was given in favor of the latter, and the motive of the decision was the pendency. Only while this lasts, can a defect of the consent be found; when the condition is verified, the consent is immediately given, and is identical with one arising from an unconditional declaration of will. Till the verification "in veritate . . . sponsalia dicenda non sint, ex quo consensus defecerat," after the verification of the condition, "non deesset consensus, sed esse perinde, ac si a principio pure contraxisset." Therefore the term applied is consummation ("*consummare*") not contracting ("*contrahere*") the marriage. The situation is essentially different if an improper condition is added. Here the consent in no way differs from an absolute one, and therefore it creates marriage and the *publica honestas* is safeguarded. Boniface placed eighty eight *regulae juris* in his Collection. John commenting on the fiftieth "actus legitimi conditionem non recipiunt neque diem" says: "Matrimonium, licet non recipiat diem . . . , recipit tamen condicionem de condi. appos."

The last witness to the conflicts of the Schools, is Abbas Siculus, the great scholar of the XV century. He was the last master of the old School whose achievements he collected and handed down for the new evolution of canon law after the Council of Trent. The complete doctrine of his age concerning our subject is found in his writ-

[57] *Cf.* Canons 1092, 1081, 1013.

ings. In 1437 he was made Archbishop of Palermo. Later he accepted the cardinalatial dignity from the pseudo-pope Felix and proudly retained it till his death (1455 or 1453). He wrote ***Lectura in Decretales; Lectura in Sextum,*** and ***Lectura in Clementinas.*** "Quidam tamen dixerunt, quod matrimonio non potest apponi condicio, quia consensus debet esse purus et absolutus; sed hoc est falsum." [58]

It is true, he adds, that the law rejects infamous and impossible conditions, and those contrary to the nature of marriage, but: "nota hic regulam, quod omnis condicio a jure non improbata potest apponi in matrimonio."

During the pendency no marriage exists, but only the future hope of marriage. "Condicio suspendit actum in eventum condicionis, unde antea non potest dici donatio, cum sola spes sit in obligatione . . . licet consensus exprimatur per verba de praesenti, tamen ex quo apponitur condicio, non habet effectum de praesenti sed suspenditur in eventum condicionis." If the *copula carnalis* intervenes: "copula hic operatur duo: purificat enim sponsalia et eodem momento ea transfundit in matrimonium." This basis and expectation is destroyed, of course, by marrying a third party: "non dubito, quin secumdum matrimonium teneat . . . ita et matrimonium condicionale tollitur per sequens purum." On the other hand, it is doubtful, whether (outside the case of actually marrying absolutely a third party) one of the parties is still free to recede from his relationship: "Sed; si non intercessit matrimonium, dubito de decisione glossae, quia ex quo obligavit se sub condicione non potuit recedere ab illa obligatione . . . si supervenerit ergo eventus condicionis primum matrimonium remanet purum, nisi forte aliud dicatur in matrimonio, sed ego non bene video rationem diversitatis." With the fulfillment of the condition "consensus remanet purus et tunc vere incipit tenere matrimonium." Here is the difference between a conditional engagement and a conditional marriage. "Tamen est differentia, utrum dicam '*accipiam* te, si C. dederis'; nam in primo casu existente condicione purificantur sponsalia, sed adhuc non est matrimonium; sed in secundo casu erit matrimonium, quia condicio suspendit consensum de praesenti." With the frustration of the condition however, "sponsalia ex toto evanescunt, adeo quod copula sequens nihil operatur."

[58] Cap. . . . Quicumque *cf.* Hussarek, *op. cit.*, p. 171.

Article X

Retrospect

As long as marriage was looked upon principally from its religious and sacramental side, the peculiarity of a marriage contract under the condition of conversion, between a member of the Church and a heretic or infidel, remained unappreciated. Only when canonists were trained in Roman Law, the study of which was only recently revived, there began a profounder penetration into the legal individualities of a long standing discipline. Gratian and Roland appreciated its particular features by placing the phenomena under the type of conditional law transactions well known in Roman Law. This step was significant and decisive for the whole later development. The road decided upon (whether rightly chosen or not) was pursued. Thus the elaboration of our doctrine is a reception, not an independent creation, but a modified reception.[59]

The next step after Roland was determined by the chapter "Quicumque" of a supposed African Council, which in its external appearance at least denied the law institute of a conditional marriage consent. Rufinus had already taken from the civil law a proposition that immoral conditions are irrelevant for the operation of a conditionally uttered declaration of will to marry.

About this time matured the severance of canonistic jurisprudence from theology. This activity and interpretation of the canonists resulted in the recognition of our doctrine, beginning with Faventinus. Then follows the examination of the maxims which regulate these phenomena. While originally, to explain the peculiarities of a particular case of marriage contract, the elaborate category of conditional transactions from Roman law was utilized, the masters henceforth abandoned this inductive method, and posited the axiom that there is such a thing as a conditional marriage contract, and thereupon by way of deduction inferred from this axiom, norms to regulate the legal phenomena which flow from this axiomatic proposition. From this time on the rejection of the doctrine, which rejection is contained in the *palea* attributed to the African council, has changed to its contrary.

[59] Hussarek, *op. cit.*, p. 173.

There was a multitude of controversies in the schools with the intention of amalgamating its axiom with the supposed legally sanctioned negation of the same. John Faventinus and Symon de Bisinano [60] are witnesses of the multicolored manifoldness of disputes and opinions. The axiom that there could be a conditional marriage consent was till now maintained by canonists, but it was legally sanctioned by Alexander III. His decree "De illis" was generally interpreted wrongly by his contemporaries, namely that a conditional consent expressed in the future tense, was valued as a conditional engagement consent, while one expressed in the present tense, was to be considered as unconditional marital consent, with a few exceptional cases. Being unconditional it operates instantly and effects marriage. Huguccio completed this interpretation of the doctrine.

But already before this juncture another view timidly attempted to gain ground. It took its departure from those exceptional cases, (conditions of conversion, and parental consent) where, in spite of the fact that the tense used was the present, the influence of the condition on the effect of the marriage was conceded. Now there followed another battle. One camp laying the principal stress on the word, the other, making most of the essence of the consent. The struggle ended with victory of the spirit over the letter. In the case of the consent of the father to his son's marriage, the second interpretation was sanctioned by Urban III. It is uncertain whether the decision rested on confusing and confounding the idea of representation and condition.

As the School originated our doctrine by trying to combine two contradictory chapters, the decrees "Quicumque" and "Non oportet" of the council of Laodicea, so now there was much scholastic elaboration endeavoring to harmonize the utterances of Alexander III and Urban III. In this attempt nearly all the individual propositions of our doctrine have been developed. In fact their luxuriance crowded the original question concerning the admissibility of a conditional consent *de praesenti* almost out of the picture.

Among all these detailers Bernard of Pavia deserves credit, for he laid the foundation of the doctrine as a peculiar way to contract marriage. But his championship of the side denying a conditional

[60] See Supra, Section 2.

marriage consent *de praesenti* was so vague that the decadence of the opposing doctrine begins at this time.

The canonists from then on could not help notice that the reason of Urban to justify his approval given to a condition of a father's consent, was based on the essence of a conditional declaration of willing. So they likewise applied his decision to other cases. Since the consent which was dependent on the assent of a third party was incapable of creating *ipso facto* the marriage tie, why should not a contingent event, upon whose occurrence the operation of the consent was made dependent, have the same effect? Vincentius [61] had tangled himself on the double meaning of *consensus*, saying the parent's consent was essentially requisite for marriage, while other conditions were accidental and irrelevant. But there was plenty of excuse for this error in his time. Petrus de Sampsone and the Abbas Antiquus had adhered to this error due to ambiguity and other causes. According to Hussarek [62] the very distinct concepts "assent by a third person" and "marriage by representation" were received as equivalent. There was a custom of parents to betroth their children in tender age which was persisted in in spite of the protests of the Church, and in a number of cases a legal and relevant consent was out of the question. So such a representation was more plausible to our ancestors than to us. Of course to-day we admit representation by proxy, in connection with the act of declaring another's will to marry. But the attempt to maintain the old theory of the general inadmissibility of a condition *de praesenti* was defeated.

Since the decree of Innocent III no longer provided the old doctrine with authoritative support, canonists began to apply the theory, which Urban III had sanctioned for a particular kind of condition, namely that such a conditional *consensus de praesenti* is, in spite of its wording, no consent *de praesenti,* and is therefore not endowed with marriage effecting power, and to extend this principle to all licit conditions. This turning point manifested itself at the time of Tancred, and it is clearly found in the *Quaestiones* of Damascus. The *Liber Sextus* at least indirectly sustains this application. At the same time clear norms were established to treat of immoral and impossible

[61] See Supra, end of Section 5.

[62] *Die Bedingte Eheschliessung*, p. 177.

conditions, and those contrary to the nature of marriage. Thus the older legal development lost all practical significance.

In the beginning our doctrine existed for only one case, gradually others were added; but its effects simmered down to almost nothing, a possible and precarious hope of future marriage. Canonists with the Gregorian compilation before them, were not content to hold the results achieved but pressed on to fix the doctrine more accurately and define the essence of a conditional consent during the pendency, with the result that is found in Sinibaldus Fliscus, that it was in the nature of a betrothal. Nevertheless the great majority admitted that with the fulfillment of the condition, the marriage tie arises *eo ipso*. Further explanation was not required. The conditional consent was thus endowed with a mixture of the effects of engagement and of marriage willing. Some would not admit this double effect during pendency. Quite peculiar consequences were attributed to it, arising from the ideas of temporary inefficacy and later full effect. Hostiensis is the champion of this. Its most important corollaries attained legal sanction in the legislation of the *Liber Sextus*.

In conclusion it is well to note how our doctrine was buffeted from pillar to post due to the doctrine concerning the marriage contract in those centuries from Gratian to Boniface VIII. There was a distinction by some between the foundation act of the legal condition of marriage, and the initial point of the *sacramental* character of the same. The foundation act was the declared agreement of the will of the parties to be man and wife. So far this holds good for Gratian and Rolandus, and with them coincided the representatives of the School of Bologna and the *Ecclesia Gallicana*.

The differences of both these doctrines refer only to the doctrine of the *Sacrament*, the combat of the schools being primarily a theological one, and only secondarily a juristic one.[63] The adherents of the one (Gratian and his followers) attributed sacramentality only to the consummated union. Those of the other (Lombard and his followers) vindicated to the non-consummated marriage a sacramental character. Both Schools held fast to the doctrine that sacramental marriage is indissoluble and the non-sacramental is dissoluble. The proof of this assertion is evident from the fact that neither School

[63] Hussarek, *op. cit.*, p. 180.

attributes the sacramental character to the marriage among infidels. Both taught concerning this last kind of union, that it is marriage, and it is dissoluble, making no distinction between consummated and non-consummated unions. It is merely a law condition and soluble.

The consequence of this contradictory doctrine about the *Sacrament* of marriage was that the School of Bologna, in certain cases, admitted a dissolution of the non-consummated unions among Christians. The Gallican school did not. Just for these opinions was the battle fought. Its theme is *not:* Is the consensus, or only the *affectus maritalis* consummated by a *copula carnalis,* the marriage contract act. If it were this the same distinction would have to be made at the marriage of infidels. The original theme was: Is the marriage between Christians, only from the beginning of its *fulfillment* or *consummation,* or already from the *declaration* of the *mutual consent,* sacramental? The question was practical, only in the case of the dissolution of the marriage relationship.[64]

Legislation took an intermediary role and lessened the practical difference of the contradictory points of view, since Alexander III repealed a number of reasons for dissolving a non-consummated marriage, and his successors those still remaining, excepting one. Before this the development was not to limit the reasons of repeal of the non-consummated marriages.

Here is also the point where our doctrine comes in. Gratian could adopt a conditional marriage contract into his system, because the consensus-created marriage was a soluble law condition, without sacramental character. The Lombard however saw in the *consensus* itself not only the confirmation of the legal condition, but also the starting point of the sacramental nature of the same. With this conception, a conditional marriage contract, which contained the possibility of the latter cessation of the thus founded relationship or condition, seemed incompatible. This was no doubt the reason of the denial of the doctrine by St. Thomas, who said marriage should be "certum," and the consent expressed "simpliciter." So they considered a conditional declaration of consent as equal to an unconditional one, irrespective of its tense or tenor. As the tendency of the time

[64] Of course, it was practical for other reasons from the viewpoint of *moral* theology.

was to limit the reasons for dissolving marriage, it was natural to reject a dissolution of a marriage, when the condition was not verified. They did not wish to lose their hard won victory of the complete indissolubility of the consent-marriage, by admitting any new reason for dissolution, so they were forced by their views, to the opinion that the conditional declaration of marriage has exactly the same effect as the absolute declaration. That a consent *de futuro* was soluable if the condition was not verified, did not bear on the question.

A decisive decision of the dispute between the School of Bologna and the *Ecclesia Gallicana* was not reached, rather a compromise was effected. Though, at least at that time the sacramental doctrine of the former seemed to have serious lawful titles in itself, yet the evolution of the topic bent more and more in practice to the *consensus* doctrine of the Lombard. On account of this, the contrary doctrine simmered to a mere theory, and the juristic consideration of a conditional marriage declaration could, from then on, disregard the no longer acute theological dissension, and begin a revival of the traditional doctrine. What paths this has taken has already been shown. With this synopsis (of the historical evolution of the doctrine of conditions added to marital consent) as a background, our study can better proceed to investigate the laws concerning conditions and their interpretations, together with their applications to each species of conditions.

PART II

COMMENTARY ON THE PRESENT LEGISLATION

CHAPTER V

DEFINITIONS OF MARRIAGE

MARRIAGE is defined in divers ways according to the several correct viewpoints or facts this institution presents. It may be considered and therefore defined; as a natural contract; for baptized persons also as a sacrament;[1] objectively from its ends or purpose; from its effects; from its origin; its moral or social aspects; *in fieri* or *in facto esse,* from its causal (human or divine) viewpoint.

Marriage as a contract is defined: "Contractus quo vir et mulier sibi mutuo tradunt et acceptant jus in corpus, perpetuum et exclusivum, in ordine ad actus per se aptos ad generationem." [2]

Peter Lombard, as most Scholastics, defines matrimony in reference to the union between man and woman: "Sunt igitur nuptiae vel matrimonium viri mulierisque conjunctio maritalis inter legitimas personas, individuam vitam retinens." [3] Other definitions are: "The contract of marriage is a mutual and solemn agreement by which a

[1] The definition of the Church that matrimony is a sacrament relates to the rite by which the *nupturientes* become man and wife. It has, however, been debated whether the indissoluble bond thus established, the *vinculum conjugale,* should not also be so termed. Some eminent theologians have maintained that just as in the Holy Eucharist the name of sacrament is rightly applied both to the act of consecration and to the resultant consecrated elements, so also the Sacrament of Matrimony is twofold, including both the act of consent and the union thus effected. Bellarmine, *De Matr.*, Lib. I, a 6; Sanchez, *De Matr.*, II, disp. 5, n. 7; Palmieri, *De Matr.* (Rome, 1880), p. 95. On the other side: Pontius, *De Sacr. Matr.*, lib. I, a. 7, n. 16. This opinion recently gained weight through its adoption by Pope Pius XI in his encyclical letter on Christian Marriage, *Casti Connubii,* 31 December, 1930; Joyce, *Christian Marriage,* p. 147.

[2] *Cf.* Canon 1081; for a cogent exegesis of this canonical definition *cf.* inter alios, De Smet, *De Sponsalibus et Matrimonio* (4 ed., Bruges, 1927), n. 75.

[3] *Sent.* lib. IV, d. 27, c. 2. Roman law definitions are: "Conjunctio maris et feminae et consortium omnis vitae, divini et humani juris communicatio" L.I.D., XXIII, 2. and "viri mulieris conjunctio individuam vitae consuetudinen continens."—Par. I, *Inst.* 1, 9; cf. Freisen, *Geschichte des Canonischen Eherechts,* p. 23 s., who quotes the Decretists and Decretalists expounding these definitions.

man and woman, who are free to marry, become irrevocably united for the procreation and education of children."[4] "Marriage is a *bilateral contract* made freely and mutually by one man and one woman, by which each grants the other the right to marital intercourse exclusively against all others for the span of their natural life."[5] This definition and the others include the efficient cause, the effect, the substance and the bond of matrimony. "Yet although matrimony is by its very nature of divine institution, the human will too enters into it and performs a most noble part. For each individual marriage, inasmuch, as it is a conjugal union of a particular man and woman, arises only from the free consent of each of the spouses; and this free act of the will, by which each party hands over and accepts those rights proper to the state of marriage, is so necessary to constitute true marriage that it cannot be supplied by any human power. This freedom, however, regards only the question whether the contracting parties really wish to enter upon matrimony, or to marry this particular person; but the nature of matrimony is entirely independent of the free will of man, so that if one has once contracted matrimony he is thereby subject to its divinely made laws and its essential properties."[6]

Schmalzgrueber gives the metaphysical definition of marriage which consists in its definition. The Matter and Form constitute the physical essence of marriage.

> Quaeritur 3. quid sit sacramentum matrimonii, seu quae sit essentia illius physica, et metaphysica? Resp. *essentia metaphysica* matrimonii in definitione illius consistit; physica, in materia et forma. Definito matrimonii, ut sacramentum est, a plerisque D.D. saltem quod sensum, haec ponitur: *est conjunctio maritalis, spiritualis gratiae collativa;* vel; *est contractus, marem et foeminam, nullo jure impeditos, ad indivuam vitae societatem, et corporum ad actus conjugales traditionem mutuam obligans, iisque rite dispositis conferens gratiam sanctificantem.*[7]

[4] Lynch, *Christian Marriage,* p. 1.

[5] Nau, *Manual of the Marriage Laws,* p. 1.

[6] Pius XI, Encycl., *Casti Connubii;* translation, *Three Great Encyclicals,* (Paulist Press, N. Y., p. 75); *cf.* Nau, *Manual on the Marriage Laws,* p. 2.

[7] Schmalzgrueber, lib. IV, tit. 1, n. 288.

Sanseverino[8] in explaining this definition: "Matrimonium est conjunctio maritalis viri et feminae individuae vitae consuetudinem retinens" remarks that it contains three principal things: a conjugal contract between a qualified man and woman, or call it mutual conjugal consent, or call it mutual giving and receiving of the marriage right (*jus*). This act takes place in the beginning and passes away (*matrimonium in fieri*). The result of this first thing is this second thing, *i.e.*, the effect: a permanent bond, or *vinculum* (the essence of which is a *jus exclusivum et perpetuum*), or call it, he says, *potestas, jus, dominium,* which each receives over the body of the other. Or it may be called the mutual *debitum,* a mutual obligation, a mutual subjection, by which each is bound. The third thing is the *copula,* to be exercised by both, which act is fitted in itself to procreate children, which canon law calls the primary end of marriage. Sanseverino and a host of other authorities say the first two things or effects of the marriage consent is ordained for this last mentioned end. The contract or the consent, the *traditio* and *acceptatio, dominium, debitum,* all are understood to refer to this act of generation, and by this the marriage contract is distinguished from all other contracts, the marriage bond from all other bonds, the marriage dominion from all other dominions. There are other kinds of contracts, dominions, etc., and not only concerning things but also concerning persons, by principals and subjects, masters and slaves, but there is a vast difference between these bonds and the marriage bond. It is true, Canon 1013 says the primary end of marriage is the procreation and rearing of children, but this need not be interpreted so that the other two ends (*mutuum adjutorium et remedium concupiscentiae*) are subordinate *per se* to the procreational end, subordinate in the sense that without this end they cannot exist. This would be false, the primacy is a primacy of honor and value rather than an essential, absolute one.[9]

The singular unique characteristics of the marriage agreement from other agreements or contracts have been pointed out by many. Cardinal Gerdilius points out this great distinction in his refutation of the work of the apostate archbishop, Antonius De Dominis. Mar-

[8] *De Ordinis et Matrimonii Sacramentis* (Bononiae, 1642), qu. 11; *De Matr.*, p. 209.

[9] Ivo Zeiger, "Nova Matrimonii Definito?", *Periodica,* XX (1931), p. 38.

riage, he says, is instituted by God. It is a contract by its very nature above human laws, and is subject to Divine Law and therefore it cannot be rescinded by human law. Though those who contract marriage do so of their own free will, yet they must assume the contract and its objects and obligations just as they are. Marriage is natural in purpose, divine in origin, sacred in itself. Marriage is governed by two kinds of laws from a canonical viewpoint. The one kind is fundamental and unchangeable, the other accidental, circumstantial and changeable. The natural law, the divinely revealed and Apostolic laws of marriage are interpreted by the Church but never repealed or dispensed from. The circumstantial or disciplinary laws are enacted by the Church and may vary or be repealed, *e. g.*, laws concerning solemnities of the celebration of marriage, and certain qualifications of the parties.

Marriage has singular unique characteristics that distinguish it from all other agreements or contracts. This difference is twofold; intrinsic, from the very nature of marriage itself, as far as the consent and the parties are concerned; and extrinsic, from divine positive law in so far as God in instituting marriage in the beginning of the world placed two conditions which depend on no human power, unity and indissolubility, once upon a time mitigated by Him in the Old Testament, but restored to its pristine sanctity by Jesus Christ.[10]

Hegel saw this great difference too and criticizes Kant's notion of marriage, that it is a purely civil contract. Thus writing against Saurus he says:

> Matrimonium non est contractus, quia I. ad naturam contractus pertinet, ut ex libero arbitrio prodeat; quia II id quod ex contractu prodit, volitum est *ex arbitrio contrahentium,* ergo volitum ex *universali* quodam lege, non est effectus tou communis *idealis* logici; quia III objectum contractus res externa esse debet, quae alterius fieri potest Essentialis matrimonii non possunt dependere ab arbitrio privato, sed in morali hominis natura posita sunt, ita ut

[10] *Cf.* Cardinal Gerdilius, *Trattato del Matrimonio* (ed. Rom.), tom XV, par. I; *cf.* Perrone, *De Matrimonio Christiano,* II, § I, p. 30.

conjuges, non tam vi contractus, quam spirituali quodam unione, religione et pietate obligentur.[11]

Leo XIII in the encyclical, "*Arcanum divinae sapientiae*" in insisting that marriage is never a mere civil contract, but is always and everywhere a matter of religion writes: "Marriage has God for its Author and was from the beginning a kind of foreshadowing of the Incarnation of His Son: and therefore there abides in it something holy and religious; not extraneous but innate: not derived from men but implanted by nature. Innocent III, therefore, and Honorius III, our predecessors, affirmed not falsely or rashly that the *sacramentum* of marriage exists both among the faithful and infidels." [12]

Cardinal Gasparri too points out the essential difference between marriage and other contracts.[13]

Marriage is ordinarily defined from a twofold viewpoint. First as an *act* by which a qualified man and woman are constituted in the marital state. This act is called *matrimonium in fieri.* Secondly marriage is defined as the very *marital state,* (*matrimonium in facto esse*) which has the relation to the aforesaid *act,* as an effect to its cause. Here we are concerned only with the *matrimonium in fieri* which is defined: "*Contractus* quo vir et femina, nullo jure impediti, mutuo tradunt et acceptant '*jus in corpus, perpetuum et exclusivum,* in ordine *ad actus per se aptos ad prolis generationem*' " (Canon 1081).

Marriage as a state is the perpetual and exclusive union (*conjunctio*) or the bond between a husband and a wife, which bond arises from their consent. This bond or union of both is for the purpose of performing the marital acts which by their nature are ordained for the generation of offspring. The primary end of marriage is the procreation and education of offspring, the secondary end is mutual help and the remedy of concupiscense (Canon 1013). The two essentials or properties of marriage are its unity and indissolubility(Canon 1013).

[11] *Principiis philosophiae junioris* (Berolinae 1821), quoted by Perrone *op. cit.*, p. 30. Thus this rationalist, though with a different end, writes so well on this point. *Cf.* Leo XIII, Encyl. *Arcanum divinae; Acta Leonis* XIII, I, p. 125; Gasparri, *De Matrimonio* (1932), n. 17.

[12] *Acta Leonis* XIII, t. I, p. 125; Joyce, *Christian Marriage,* p. 210.

[13] *De Matrimonio* (1932), I, n. 17.

It is deemed useful to insert these definitions of marriage and remarks about its peculiar nature, and at once enter deeper into their implications, because of the very doctrine of conditional consent as applicable to conditions against the substance of marriage.

Cardinal Gasparri[14] starts off his treatise by quoting Ecclesiasticus XV, 14: "Deus ab initio constituit hominem, et reliquit illum in manu consilii sui"; and he immediately concludes that therefore man can consent to marriage absolutely, or under a condition, or with a mode, or cause, or demonstration.

Sacred Scripture says, "What God hath joined together." The human will cannot cause such effects. God made this economy called marriage and fashioned with His own hands this bond. All the parties do is to will or not will to have this relation, this bond, with all its essentials, between them, just as God made it, perpetual and indissoluble. If its effects come from the human consent or the so-called contract these same could break this bond, modify and limit it; but this is impossible.

The essentials of marriage do not depend as even Hegel points out, on the private will of man, but on the very moral makeup of man and he is obligated to it not *vi contractus* but by a certain spiritual union, religion and piety, in other words because God hath joined them.

Vlaming[15] asks, "is marriage a contract" and answers in the affirmative, *optimo jure.* He says it is a contract in a true sense yet it differs from other contracts. In origin it is from God, not from man; as far as the sex and the number of persons who can contract; as far as its object is concerned, for it is the very person of the parties; as far as the very characteristics peculiar to it, it is not merely civil and juridical but much more religious and moral; it is ruled by positive divine law especially as regards its unity and indissolubility, for God hath joined this union together; its effect differs from other contracts, a certain moral union arises between the parties, and it tends to a certain physical union of two in one flesh.

[14] *Tractatus de Matrimonio* (Paris, 1891), Vol. 2, Chap. 5, Art. 4.

[15] *Praelectiones Juris Matrimonii* (Bussum in Hollandia, 3 ed.), Tomus I, n. 9, p. 7.

CHAPTER VI

THE CONDITION AND ITS VARIOUS SPECIES

> Nomine condicionis venit, stricto aut lato sensu, quaelibet circumstantia cui *alligatur* consensus matrimonialis, seu ex qua pendet *valor* consensus accipitur *sensu stricto,* si valorem matrimonii *suspendit:* tum valor consensus ex eventu futuro atque incerto pendet. *Sensu lato* sumitur, si valorem matrimonii *non suspendit;* tum ex facto praeterito aut praesenti pendit valor consensus.[16]

Cardinal Gasparri [17] defines it thus:

> *Conditio,* ut ab ea incipiamus, in re nostra optime definitur: *circumstantia actui* (promissioni) *adjecta ex qua ipse actus pendet,* idest suspenditur, vel revocatur. Exprimi solet per particulas *si, dummodo, modo,* et interdum *ablativo absoluto.*

The eminent canonist immediately remarks quoting D'Annibale that this is not perpetually true, for if *tacit* conditions, that is, those that are inherent in the act [*e. g.*, "I marry you, if you are not my sister"], are *expressed,* they are not *true* conditions and they effect nothing. From the definition of Payen quoted above, the future necessary condition strictly is not included therein, although in the external forum this condition is reduced to a present one.

The word "condition" has various significations,[18] but throughout our study it is used in this meaning: for a circumstance added to a contract of marriage, or to marital consent, or to the act of willing marriage, and on whose existence or fulfillment the one placing it wishes the validity of the contract to depend, that is, the marriage producing effect of the given consent is suspended or made uncertain by the condition being placed.[19] In this sense it is used and in this

[16] Payen, *De Matrimonio,* II, n. 1725.

[17] *De Matrimonio* (1932), n. 79.

[18] Schmalzgrueber, lib. IV, tit. V, n. 1 s.

[19] Reiffenstuel, lib. IV, tit. V. n. 1.

sense it is applied in a twofold way: strictly and in a wide sense. Strictly: for a future possible contingent event. Widely: for past and present facts. In both cases it is commonly signified by the usual particles or phrases.[20] The condition that suspends in the future is the real true condition, for a condition *per se* is supposed to suspend the effect of an act till verification, yet the canonical doctrine of conditions must consider those that do not suspend but only make the validity of the act subjectively uncertain, that is, past and present conditions.

It is of the greatest importance that the definition of a condition be rightly understood, lest it be confounded with somewhat similar things. Thus the normal effects of a juristic act may be modified by a *condition.* But these acts may also be modified or qualified by other means, *e. g.*, by collateral agreements. Of such modifications (unessential as far as the content of the consent is concerned) which the party or parties engraft on the act and which are called the "qualifications" of a juristic act the three following important ones may be enumerated. Approaching the question first negatively, it may be pointed out here that by a *condition* is not meant a *mode,* nor a *causa,* nor a *demonstration.*

A *mode* is an obligation added to the already perfected and completed marital contract, which if not of immoral content obliges the other party in justice, *e.g.*, "I marry you, but you must assume the obligation to live in my city." "Modus est *onus adjectum* contractui matrimoniali *jam perfecto,* et ex justitia ab altera parte ferendum." [21]

A *cause* (*causa*) is the expression of the *very reason* that moves one to marry this person, *e. g.*, "I marry you *because* you are very honest." "Causa quae est expressio ipsius rationis ad nuptias ineundas moventis." [22]

Nor, when speaking of conditions, must one confuse them with a demonstration, which is the description of the person, or the pointing out of some quality existing actually or putatively in the other party to the contract, *e. g.*, "I marry you *who* are the *legitimate* daughter

[20] *Cf.* Canon 39, Cerato, *De Matrimonio,* p. 39; D'Annibale, *Theol. Moralis,* I, 41; Putney, *Conditional Contracts, Popular Law Library, I,* p. 161.

[21] Payen, *De Matrimonio,* n. 1725.

[22] *Loc. cit.*

of my friend, John." "Demonstratio quae est descriptio personae seu significatio alicujus qualitatis in comparte reapse exsistentis aut saltem pro existente habitae." [23]

The *content* of the above three kinds of additions to an already absolute contract may be morally good or morally bad or indifferent, *e. g.*, "I marry you but you must go to Mass often" or "stay away from Mass;" or "you must take a walk in the park every day." The *causa* may be, *e. g.*, "because you will live by crime," or "because you are very honest," or "because you like music." The *demonstratio* may likewise have a good, bad, or indifferent content, *e. g.*, "I marry you *who* are honest;" "who are a thief," or "who are a chess-player." Immoral *modes* are rejected and beget *no obligation* on the other party. The relation between these three accessories to a contract and the effect of error and ignorance about their content—the effect on the marriage consent—will be treated in the chapter dealing with *conditions* against the substance of marriage; *e. g.*, if one contracts through error with a slave and says: "I marry you *who* are a free-born citizen" (*demonstratio*); "I marry you *because* you are a free-born citizen" (*causa*). There, also, will be discussed whether an immoral mode or cause or demonstration that has some reference to the three essential obligations of marriage, invalidates the consent; *e.g.*, if one adds as a mode something against the marital consent or obligations as for instance: "I marry you but you must become sterile." One must carefully distinguish the conditional consent from the consent *cum modo* which obtains when a clause is merely added to the perfected contract (*jam perfecto*) and which does not enter into the contract itself, it is not a constitutive element of the consent or the contract, and in no way suspends or restricts substantially the consent.[24]

Now approaching the definition of a condition from a positive viewpoint the following remarks are necessary for clarity of discussion. The circumstance added to the consent on which the efficacy of the act depends may be *any kind* of a circumstance, dependent or not on the free will of the other party, *e.g.*, if one demands virginity in the other person, this circumstance does not depend on his free

[23] *Loc. cit.*

[24] *Cf.* De Smet, *De Sponsalibus et Matrimonio*, ed. 4, n. 151.

will (the *placing* of it as a *condition* does of course) or on the free will of the other party; or a certain fortuitous event, *e. g.*, the arrival of a ship, the consent of a parent, are likewise independent for their existence or not of the free will of the other party. But if the circumstance concerns some act that the other party is to do or omit, *e. g.*, "I marry you, if you give me so much money"; or "if you promise to raise the children as Catholics," then such a circumstance does depend on the free will of the other party.

It is entirely of subordinate and irrelevant significance whether the circumstance elevated to a condition is factual or legal, positive or negative, *e. g.*, "I marry you, if the ship arrives;" "I marry you if no impediment exists between us;" "if my father consents," "if you do not continue that friendship." Conditions placed negatively are regularly fulfilled on the death of the person thought of as acting. If this person is one of the parties it is absurd and destroys the consent. Without any particular relevancy, is also whether the condition is wholly and solely to be verified by one party to the marriage or needs the external cooperation of others. Conditions may be required independently of the party or not.

This circumstance must bind the consent, that is, the proper function of a condition, whether suspensive or not (past or present) is to make the efficacy, the marriage-producing result of the consent, namely the permanent marital union, depend for its *existence* on the truth or verification or fulfillment of the condition; and it is equally the function of the condition to *prevent* the arising of the *result* or *effect* of the marital consent, if the condition be not verified. The *existence* of the very *obligation* of the contract is made to depend on the truth of the condition, which is voluntarily placed by one or both parties. The condition thus becomes a substantial constitutive element of the marriage contract. The act, if the condition is supensive, is not *ab initio* valid and perfect, it becomes absolute in the very moment of verification of the condition, *e. g.*, as soon as, and not before, the father consents, if this were the condition. If the condition is past or present in its reference, *e. g.*, "I marry you if you were a judge in the past" or "are a judge now," then the act is immediately valid and marriage is present if the condition is or was verified. It is understood that *resolutive* conditions, if added, immediately *destroy the consent* as far as it is *marital, e.g.*, "I marry you, on condition that it is to last only till I find a wealthier girl." [25]

The division of various classes of conditions arise from the various viewpoints from which they are considered. From the viewpoint of the instant in which the condition is verified and marriage exists, conditions are classed into suspensive and non-suspensive. The other divisions are readily understood by their very names; *e. g.*, from the viewpoint of the time to which the condition refers, there are the past, present, and future conditions, *e. g.*, "I marry you, if you were my brother's friend;" "if you are my brother's friend;" "if you will be my brother's friend." Impossible and possible conditions belong to the classes bearing their names, and refer to the impossibility or possibility of the condition being verified, *e. g.*, "I marry you if you swim the ocean, become a girl, fly to heaven;" "I marry you if you learn to swim, if my father consents." The class of possible conditions is subdivided into contingent, namely those which may or may not be verified, but which are not impossible nor necessary, *e. g.*, "I marry you if my father consents;" and necessary, namely those which must be verified, *e. g.*, "I marry you if the sun rises, if fire burns." Then these possible contingent conditions are divided into *potestative* conditions, namely those that depend only on the free will of one or both of the contractors who is to give, or do, or omit something, thus fulfilling the condition, it rests with a person, *e. g.*, "I marry you if you promise to live in my city," "if you learn to swim;" "if you become a Catholic." A *casual* condition is not uniformly interpreted yet it may be said that it depends on some occurrence, some fact happening, *e. g.*, "if we win the war," or it may depend on some third person, *e. g.*, "if my father consents." The casual condition depends on two things: a future event and the will of a third party, *e. g.*, "I marry you if the emperor conquers the Turks."

A *mixed* condition is partly casual, partly arbitrary, *e. g.*, "I marry you if you come back from Europe;" which depends both on good fortune and the will of the one going away.[26]

Reiffenstuel,[27] says a *mixed* condition depends partly on the party

[25] *Cf.* Payen, *De Matrimonio*, n. 1725.

[26] Schmalzgrueber, lib. IV, tit. V, n. 2.

[27] Lib. IV, tit. V, n. 2.

upon whom it is imposed and partly on the will of another; and a *casual* condition does not depend on the will of him upon whom it is placed, but on a third party or on God; *e. g.*, "I marry you if I have a harvest this year;" or "if the president will make you an admiral."

Then from the viewpoint of law, divine or human, if the condition is contrary to these laws it belongs to the class of immoral (*turpis*) conditions; if the condition is consonant with and not against these laws it belongs to the class of honest and moral (*honesta*) conditions; *e. g.*, "I marry you if you promise to be a thief;" "I marry you if you promise to become a Catholic." Then from the point of view whether the condition is essentially in accord with, or contrary to marriage itself, or its substance, or its essential treasures (*tria bona*), there are two corresponding classes of conditions, namely "those not against the substance of marriage" and "those against the substance of marriage," *e. g.*, "I marry you if you will steal;" "if you will be honest;" "if you promise to *abuse* the marriage obligations," *e. g.*, by onanism (these conditions are not against the substance of marriage or its *tria bona*); "I marry you until I find a richer girl;" "as long as you remain faithful;" "on condition that I (or you or both of us) have a *right* to abuse marriage, *i. e.*, that I do not assume the obligation of the *bonum prolis;*" "on condition that I promise now to observe chastity in such a way as not to give you the radical marital rights," all these conditions are against the substance of marriage.[28]

Of the above mentioned kinds of conditions, the condition properly so called, is that whose happening is contingent in the future, for the nature of a true condition is to suspend the effect of the transaction and its resulting obligations and to make that act exist or not according to the existence or not of the condition in reality. This is the Roman law principle of conditions.[29] Hence besides past and

[28] In most of the examples above, future conditions were used to illustrate, but each class could be exemplified also by past or present conditions, except "those against the substance" which division includes only so-called *future* "conditions against the substance."

[29] *Cf. Institutiones* III, *de verborum obligatione,* XV, 6: "Conditiones quae ad praesens, vel praeteritum tempus referuntur, aut statim infirmant obligationem, aut omnino non differunt, veluti, si Titius consul fuit, vel si Maevius vivit, dare spondes? Nam si ea ita non sunt, nihil valet stipulatio; sin autem ita se habent statim valet."

present conditions, also a necessary one lacks the nature of a true condition.[30] The impossible condition too is only one in a wide sense, for it is objectively certain it will not happen and hence the validity and obligation of the act cannot be suspended.

Attention might be called here to what is called a *tacit* condition, that is, they are contained in the act though unexpressed. *Conditio juris* or *conditio tacita* are not true conditions, but only terms for describing the requirements necessarily presupposed by the essential nature of a juristic act, *e. g.*, the death of the testator before the death of the heir, is a *condicio juris*, of the institution's taking effect.[31] "Nam si ea exprimuntur quae actui tacite insunt, verius non conditio intelligitur, sed magis monito quaedam, quae nihil mutat, quippe eadem est vis taciti et expressi." [32] The tacit conditions may be general, *i. e.*, present in every contract, they are imbedded in the very act (*inest in actu*), either from the very nature of the thing (*ex natura rei*), *e. g.*, "I donate the next crop, if there be a next crop" or "I marry you if you consent, if God wills it;" or from the disposition of the law (natural, divine positive, ecclesiastical and legal); *e. g.*, "I marry you unless you are my sister." Others are special, which are present in some act or kind of act in particular, *e. g.*, in willing marriage, if no diriment impediment is present or intervenes, if the transaction remains in the same *status quo*. The special ones may be contained intrinsically, *e. g.*, in the marriage, for no marriage can exist without them, *e. g.*, "I marry you if you are not my sister." [33]

The general conditions do not suspend the contract, because they do not suspend the consent, any more than if they were not expressed. Thus these general conditions work nothing if expressed in the same way as they are understood in every contract; *e. g.*, a legacy left to one if this one be willing. They do operate, if otherwise expressed, *e. g.*, "if the legatee *will have declared* himself to be willing," this condition suspends the legacy, nor is he a legatee before

[30] *Institutes,* III, XV, 6: "quae enim per rerum naturam sunt certa, non morantur obligationem, licet apud nos incerta sint;" *cf.* Schmalzgrueber, lib. IV, tit. V, n. 1.

[31] *Cf.* Sohm-Ledlie, *Institutes of Justinian,* p. 214.

[32] Gasparri, *De Matrimonio* (1932), n. 79.

[33] *Cf.* Sanchez, *De Matr.*, lib. V, disp. II. Schmalzgrueber, lib. IV, tit. 5, n. 1.

this declaration, and if he refuses to do so, he never becomes the legatee. If this condition was expressed in no way at all he would immediately acquire the legacy even though he were ignorant of the transaction.[34]

Intrinsic conditions which are necessary and inherent in marriage and without which the marriage could not exist, do not if expressed make a *conditional* contract, *e. g.*, "I marry you if you are not my sister;" "if you consent." Such are tacitly and intrinsically included in the very contract, and in its very essence, since without these, the contract falls. All teach thus.[35]

Though it is true an intrinsic (*ex natura rei or ex lege*) condition if expressed *per se* effects nothing as a condition, yet whether expressed or not the effect of the act or the consent is suspended till the *conditio juris* is verified and this *ex natura rei*, not *ex natura conditionis*, *e. g.*, in a marriage by means of a procurator, the *mandans* writes to the girl: "I marry you if you consent." [36] The future necessary condition, if seriously placed as such, follows the same principle as the intrinsic condition *inest in contractu*.

They effect nothing as far as the validity of the contract is concerned. But as far as liberty from punishment is concerned, the *expressed condicio juris* is efficacious to free from penalties those who contract in bad faith, *e. g.*, one who knowingly contracts with a blood relative under the condition, "if you are not my blood relative within a forbidden degree," by no means incurs a penalty, for the sinister wicked affection of the parties to marry, which the Church punished especially in the past, is eliminated by the condition.[37] Of course if the condition is *expressed* in a *manner differently* than it inheres in the contract, then it has the effect of a condition, *e. g.*, "I marry you if the court declares you are not my sister." This condition adds a note over and above what is contained in the *condicio juris*, namely the declaration of the court.

The so-called *interpretative* condition is no condition at all, but only a fiction. By it is understood that no actual condition was made

[34] *Cf.* Sanchez, *loc. cit.*, n. 6.

[35] Sanchez, *loc. cit.*, n. 13.

[36] *Cf.* Pichler, *Candidatus Juris Prudentiae Sacrae* (1733), p. 356.

[37] *Cf.* Schmalzgrueber, *loc. cit.*, Sanchez, *De Matrimonio*, lib. V, disp. I, n. 14.

explicitly, but it is considered to have been implicitly understood that the person *would have made* a condition if he knew the circumstances. For instance if the nupturient had known the defects of the woman, he never would have married her, or if he had suspected these defects of the woman, he would have placed an explicit condition to his marital consent. This interpretative conditional consent has no juridical effects simply because it does not exist, in the case, to produce any effects. What would have happened is not the point at issue but what actually did happen, what actually was the quality of his act of willing. It was absolute and not conditional, though it was accompanied by simple ignorance or simple error about the presence of the defects of the woman. "Consensus interpretativus certe non sufficit, et nec consensus nomen meretur, qui *exstitisset* in aliqua hypothesi, sed de facto numquam exstitit." [38] "Nec producit effectus juridicos conditio interpretativa, *i. e.*, conditio quae explicite apposita non fuit sed quae censetur implicite adfuisse, ut si sponsus cognovisset defectus sponsae numquam eam in matrimonium duxisset." [39]

Since marriage by nature and positive Divine Law is indissoluble, a resolutive condition can not be added to marital consent, without destroying the latter and therefore preventing the effect, marriage. A condition is suspensive when the commencement, and resolutive when the termination, of the operation of the act is made to depend on the occurrence of the condition, *e. g.*, "I marry you, if my father consents;" "I marry you until I find a richer girl."

> On the fulfillment of a suspensive condition, the juristic act produces *ipso jure* its normal legal results. . . . And conversely, on the happening of a resolutive condition the normal effects of the act ceases *ipso jure*. . . . If A makes over property by way of a gift to B subject to a suspensive condi-

[38] Gasparri, *De Matrimonio* (1932), n. 781; *cf.* Gougnard, *De Matrimonio*, p. 142.

[39] Gougnard, *De Matrimonio*, n. 30. Of course we speak here not of substantial error or error of quality redounding to substantial error, which invalidates the consent and marriage. But there is no condition present if one contracts in such a disposition, that if he had known this or that, which at the moment of the contract he was ignorant of or in error, he would not have contracted. Thus the consent and the marriage on this head of a so-called interpretative unverified condition would not be invalid.

> tion—subject, for example to B's passing an examination—B (the donee) becomes owner of the property *ipso jure* the moment the condition is fulfilled; till then A (the donor) remains owner. If the condition was meant to be resolutive, *i. e.*, if the intention was that B should be owner, unless he failed in his examination, the ownership would vest in B at once, but on the fulfillment of the resolutive condition (*i. e.*, on B's failure to pass) it would divest again and revert *ipso jure* to the donor. Until, therefore, the condition is fulfilled, the ownership vests, in the former case, in the donor; in the latter case, in the donee; but in either case it is a mere interim ownership, a defeasible ownership (*dominum revocabile*), that is, an ownership which is liable to divest and revert to another person.[40]

Dies is a future event which is *certain* to happen, and on the occurrence of which the operation of the juristic act is either to commence (*dies a quo*) or to terminate (*dies ad quem*). *Dies incertus quando* is the term applied when it is uncertain at what particular time the *dies* will occur, as when the liability of a surety is to cease on the death of the debtor. If there is uncertainty as to whether the *dies* will ever occur at all—as when A promises to give B $100 on the day when he passes his examination—this, though called "*dies incertus an,*" is not properly a *dies* at all, but a condition.[41]

The common law classification of conditions (not applicable in common and English and American laws to *marriage*) consists of three main divisions: conditions precedent (past), the event must have taken place before the rights of the promises arise; conditions concurrent (present), the rights and the happening of the event must take place concurrently or simultaneously; and conditions subsequent (future), the rights are determined by the future happening of the specified event.[42]

[40] Sohm-Ledlie, *Institutes of Justinian*, p. 213.

[41] *Cf.* Sohm, *op. cit.*, p. 215.

[42] Putney, *Conditional Contracts*, Popular Law Library, I, p. 161.

CHAPTER VII

CAN CONDITIONS BE ADDED VALIDLY TO MATRIMONIAL CONSENT?

THE interest one has in a transaction may be of such a nature that he may desire a certain shaping of an event or a circumstance to transpire and be realized simultaneously with the transaction and not before and he may desire the non-realization of the marriage in case the opposite or contrary state of affairs takes place.

It may seem imperative, commendable to him to secure the desired legal issue (the marriage) at the point of time when a future uncertain event is verified, and equally imperative not to desire the marriage if the event be not fulfilled. In other words one may interfere provisionally with the future. It may seem equally imperative to him to will the desired issue (the marriage) if the circumstance *has already* transpired or is simultaneously true in fact at the time of his willing, *e. g.*, "I marry you, if you are now an admiral," and it may seem likewise wise on his part not to desire and will the marriage, if these past or present circumstances are not verified.

Legal procedure has peculiar means to meet this interest and to procure for it the possibility of its satisfaction. This possibility is customarily summed up under the concept of a declaration of will under a condition. It is natural that the concepts of this source have widest scope of development where the will of the legal subject is recognized as an important, a most important factor of legal casuation, and it is just as natural that this means of conditional legal causation has narrower scope if it is within the power of the legal subject to accommodate the juridic situation *at any time* according to circumstances.

Hence it is not public law but private law which makes most use of this concept of conditional decisions and for the same reason within private law, those persons particularly will exercise this means whose sovereign functioning of the will finds limitations in the opposite or contrary rights of others, or who find temporal limitations of their will through death.[1] This is the reason why the private law of property, in so far as it recognizes contractual dispositions *inter vivos causa mortis,* as legal causations of juridic relations, represents the field in which conditional dispositions, will and have attained to the highest perfection in legal technicality. Yet this doctrine is not confined to private law. There is hardly a branch of public law in which such acts are entirely foreign.[2] Private law is freer from the influence of force, or selfish interest of other individuals and could thus more often exemplify the use of this doctrine and, thus developed within the field of private law, it has also served as a model and norm of other juridic branches and departments of law.

To gain a firm basis for the Canon Law doctrine of conditional consent it was necessary to examine briefly the doctrines of Roman Law as was done in the historical part of this work. Roman Law did not succeed in harmonizing its views about the essence of our doctrine. Perhaps for this reason, that Roman dicta were formulated more with regard to individual conditional transactions than under a common accepted definition of the meaning of condition. There was unanimity on one point; these transactions suffered from a peculiar state of being unfinished—unfinished in virtue of an arbitrary private exercise of the will. But in what exactly consists this incompleteness even that was not definitely known as certain. It is probably beyond controversy that the peculiarities of conditional transactions can not be derived from or referred to an incompleteness of the declaration or the consent. It is disputed whether and what sort of will is the cause of the peculiar effects of conditional transactions. It is asserted that the majority teach that, conditional-will exist only in case the condition is verified; if, frustrated or not fulfilled, the will is simply not considered as existent within the realm of law. Not only the result of the act of willing (the legal situation) but the willing itself is conditional in its existence.[3] The condition is a limitation of the will in its very being. If the will posits itself under a condition, it limits its positing by making its positing (or having been posited) dependent upon the verification of a circumstance.

[1] *Cf.* Hussarek, *Die Bedingte Eheschliessung,* p. 83.

[2] Hussarek, *op. cit.,* p. 184.

[3] Hussarek, *op. cit.,* p. 186

To meet the numerous attacks directed against this conception or interpretation, its holders have tried to analyze the conditioned will. This analysis has brought forth various subtle theories and one must consult the authors.[4]

The divergent shaping of conditional marital contract in Canon Law as opposed to the Roman Law theories, may be briefly mentioned. Roman Law took its dicta not from the nature of the condition in itself, but from the nature of the various conditional transactions and their forms. Therefore, it was not freely developed, but hampered by the historical evolution. It was not developed from universal concepts, but from rigid, positive, material needs and circumstances. One acceptation was used for some affairs, while another doctrine prevailed for other legal relations. Nothing was settled *a priori*, but from sober practical considerations of that which according to circumstances was most conducive to party interest.

Canon Law did not blindly follow or apply Roman Law on conditions to marriage, but *a priori* Canon Law stood for the fact that marriage needed its own law on conditional marital consent. This is a great merit. There was a time when Canon Law had no legal procedure for this doctrine. During various periods of its classical development, Canon Law judged contradictorily, conditional marriage consent. The ancient solutions have only historical interest and are not happy. There was a time when the consent was considered as absolute provided the *tria bona* were safeguarded and any condition was irrelevant, was looked upon merely as a desire; irrelevant for the existence of marriage, or as a *modus*. *Error in personam* and conditions were rejected by the old Canon Law theory. The result was always the same: the marriage was absolute, though there might be an obligation of *modus*.

Later developments of canonists and papal legislation could not be friends with the old Canon Law. They learned from Roman Law the difference between different kinds of conditions, and their effects on consent, or at least they felt these differences. The historical part of this work showed the variation of this finding and how is slowly but victoriously won and at what point it became prevalent. Now

[4] Hussarek *op. cit.*, p. 186 sqq. *Cf.*, also, section on Roman Law Doctrine of Conditions.

there is more light on the conclusions to be drawn from this development; some conclusions are mentioned immediately, others in their proper places later on. They first distinguished between lawful and unlawful conditions, for they affected the marriage differently. Concerning unlawful conditions the old interpretation remained in full force, *i. e.*, they were rejected and marriage is immediately valid, if the parties gave true consent. The *turpes* conditions were rejected by old and new canonists and by the law. The matter is entirely different if lawful future conditions are placed. The fundamental principle is that transactions lack immediate creative or causative power to produce marriage or family status.

Some very few recent canonists, and nearly all Scholastic theologians, under the leadership of St. Thomas and some even to this very day, deny that a conditional consent can be placed. All the reasons by St. Thomas, St. Bonaventure, the other theologians and some ancient canonists prove nothing. Generally they miss the very point at issue, confuse *consent* with *absolute marriage,* cling to certain ancient papal decisions and misinterpret them for the most part. Yet some recent books on marriage persistently give credit to certain of these theologians for perfecting the doctrine on conditions. At least the real point at issue, the placing of a future contingent possible honest condition was never admitted by these authors, and even to this day in spite of legislation and innumerable Roman cases on conditional marriages by the Rota and other congregations some still deny this doctrine. They claim it all amounts only to an *engagement,* that consent must of necessity be renewed even though the condition is verified, and other untenable things. Some forever, to sustain their thesis, use the decision of Urban III couched in ambiguous words, saying that consent is not *de praesenti,* even though it is expressed in the present tense.[5] During this overlong dispute the canonists in general propounded the possibility of this doctrine against the denial of the theologians who involving themselves in, among other things, a faulty understanding of the consent theory, were led by a groundless fear for its safety[6]. Santi-Leitner [7] says the theologians under the

[5] C. 5, X, *de conditionibus oppositis*. IV, 5.

[6] *Cf.* Historical section; *cf.* Santi-Leitner, *Praelectiones Juris Canonici* (Ratisbonae, 1905), lib. IV, tit. V, p. 191 s.

[7] *Praelectiones Juris Canonici* (4 ed., 1905), lib. IV, tit. V, p. 192; "*Theologi*

lead of St. Thomas reduced the contract to one of *sponsalia de futuro.*

Many authors, writes Held, hold and try to persuade others to hold that a future contingent possible honest condition cannot by any means be added to the marriage contract, and if added, not matrimony but engagement is contracted.[8] They use their own interpretation of Urban III's ruling of a marriage on condition of obtaining a father's consent, and the reasoning used by Urban.[9]

That renowned canonist, Father Vermeersch, S.J., writes:[10]

> Thus there are some authors who deny that marriage can be contracted under a future condition, contending that in such a case there is question not of marriage but of conditional betrothal contracted under the semblance of marriage. Opposed to this explanation, however, is the fact that, on the fulfillment of the condition under which the matrimonial pact was concluded, the marriage becomes absolute without a new consent, even though the condition should be satisfied without the cognizance or advertence of the parties. Such is by no means the effect of a betrothal subject to a future condition, for the consent by which marriage is merely promised can never become a valid substitute for marriage consent. Shall we say then, that the recision of a conditional marriage through a subsequent marriage with another party is due to the positive law, which being unwilling to accept conditional marriages as valid, approves them only with the limitation that they shall not overcome agreements contrary to them, if these latter are marriages contracted absolutely with another person? Such an explanation is indeed not impossible, but it is inadmissible for the reason that it can claim no vestige of support in the canonical sources, . . . in ecclesiastical tradition, or in the opinions of the authorities on canon law. The suggestion is entirely gratuitous. Consequently we must hold with Sanchez [11] that in every conditional contract the consent is *per se* revocable up to the moment when the condition is fulfilled.

enim duce *S. Thoma,* Dist. 29, q. unica, Art. 3, q. 3, tenent matrimonium conditionatum reduci ad contractum sponsalium de futuro."

[8] S. Thomas, Suppl., qu 47, Art. 5; Gonzales Tellez, *Commentaria Perpetua,* lib. IV, tit. V, cap. 3.

[9] Held, *Jurisprudentia Universalis,* lib. IV, dist. II, cap. IV.

[10] *Homiletic and Pastoral Review,* XXXIV (1933), 187.

[11] *De Matr.,* lib. V, dist. VIII, n. 5.

Some vainly try to argue that the theologians meant, that while the condition was pending, no marriage was possible. But the texts [12] do not substantiate this assertion. The texts plainly insist that no marriage was possible even though the condition was verified. Only by a new consent could marriage exist.

In the preparatory studies to the Code, says Gasparri, the consultors discussed and contemplated to do away with and *invalidate* marriages entered into under any condition, according to the principle of more recent legislations: *actui legitimo conditio apponi non debet.* Father Wernz worded the canon proposed to this effect, and all the consultors, including the President, gave their consent to the canon. But afterwards, this canon was replaced by Canon 1092, and no more mention of this attempt was made in the acts.[13]

It is passing strange that so many stumble and misunderstand the Roman Law on legitimate acts and repeatedly try to bind marriage under this principle, though many in the past (as pointed out *passim*) have shown the fallacy of such application. Reiffenstuel [14] points out that marriage is not an *actus legitimus* in a technical sense. And even if it were, he teaches that all legitimate acts can receive a past or present condition. "Conditionem de praeterito et praesenti omnes actus legitimi recipiunt." He is treating *ex professo* of this particular *regula juris* (n. 50 rule). In explaining the true meaning of the *regula,* Reiffenstuel says, the reason any legitimate acts do not admit a *future* condition is because it would be contrary

[12] *Cf.* Historical section.

[13] Ex actis praeparatoriis ad Codicem constat inter Consultores actum fuisse de *irritando* matrimonio sub *qualibet* conditione inito juxta principium in recentioribus legislationibus receptum: *actui legitimo conditio apponi non debet.* P. Wernz canonem relativum redegit omnesque Consultores, Praeside non excluso, assensum praebuerunt; sed postea canon redactus disparuit et loco ipsius rel. can. 1092 positus fuit, quin hac de re amplius mentio fiat in actis."—Gasparri, *De Matrimonio* (1932), n. 878, nota 2.

[14] *Tractatus de Regulis Juris; Regula* 50, et lib. IV, tit. V; *cf.* Sanchez, *De Matr.* lib. V, dist. I n. 5, *cf.* Esmein, *Le Mariage,* I, p. 192, who quotes Hostiensis; *Summa,* de condit. oppos., p. 361; Sebastianelli, *praelectiones Juris Can.* (1905), p. 132: "Certissimum est . . . matrimonio posse adjici conditiones, nec enim conjugium inter actus numeratur, qui nec diem, nec conditionem recipiunt reg. 30 juris in Sexto, Sanchez I, n. 5." *Cf.* C. Crosata, *Regulae Juris in Quintum Decretalium,* Comi, 1924.

to the substance of the act. "Cum dies et conditio suspensiva substantiae, seu essentiae illorum, quam ex natura, vel speciali dispositione juris habent, immediate sit contraria." Concerning marriage he says (N. 13); "*Neque sacramentæ* [conditionem recipiunt] *excepto matrimonio.*" "Sic insuper sacramenta cuncta (matrimonio exexcepto) quia sunt tales actus legitimi, quorum valor, et effectus adhibita debita materia, forma, et intentione ministri, suspendi in futurum non potest, conditionem de futuro non recipiunt. Dicitur tamen notanter; matrimonio excepto; . . . tamen aliae conditiones (non turpis vel contraria substantiam honestae etiam de futuro contingenti . . . apponi possunt." Reiffenstuel approves Sanchez in pointing out that the *consent* and not marriage receives the condition.

Moreover the question can be asked whether the Church could invalidate all marriages entered conditionally. And in answering it one must distinguish. She *can* forbid under *invalidity* if she sees fit marriages contracted with an *illegal, immoral,* or *impossible* condition, and probably, honest past and present conditions. But it is very difficult to see how she could *directly* invalidate such contracts with a future honest contingent condition and in effect say to a man: You must either take this woman absolutely or not at all, you cannot safeguard your natural and God-given liberty of choice, it is either, or, *aut, aut.* There are occasions when a person may have several grave reasons to suspend his consent, yes even occasions where he is *duty bound* to do so and duty bound at the same time to express his will to be a husband in the present, though the event is future. But the Church could *indirectly* invalidate marriages entered under future honest conditions, *e. g.,* by legislating that for *validity* this condition *must be expressed in words* before the pastor or bishop, or in any other way she decided. "The liberty of consent is so necessary to contract marriage that one who wants to marry can place a condition." [15]

> Par. 51. An consensus sub conditione datus causa efficiens matrimonii sit, a conditionis impletione dependet. Par. 52. Quando conditio versetur circa futurum contingens, vel non contingens, matrimonium suspenditur, usque dum conditio impleatur. Quod si non impletur, consensus dati effectus

[15] Phillips, *Kirchenrecht,* p. 603.

> cessat. Quando consensus alligatur conditioni de praesenti vel de praeterito, matrimonium validum est vel non, prout conditio impleta jam sit, vel von. Par. 55. . . . conditiones, quae in consensus declaratione haud exprimuntur, pro non appositis habendae sunt [in foro externo].[16]

The Church therefore left man the greatest liberty about marriage and did not and probably could not directly prohibit future honest possible conditional marriages. As far as modern Codes are concerned,[17] they are practically helpless to do ought else than to prohibit or remain silent (as in America) about such conditions and everything considered they act quite logically from their juridic viewpoint, since with them marriage is a purely civil contract; but the Church labors under no such difficulties, for she knows full well the action of consent, or lack of consent, or substantially diseased consent on effecting or not, true valid marriage.

The Anglican Reformation of Henry VIII legislated most improperly that all marriages are valid notwithstanding any pre-contracts; but Edward VI revoked this and went back to the former legislation.[18]

All the canonists of great weight, besides the vast majority of others, maintain and prove conclusively the admissibility of our doctrine on conditions. Schmalzgrueber [19] sums up the very impregnable reasons why conditions can be placed to marriage consent, and at the same time refutes the arguments denying this doctrine.

> Neque obstant argumenta sententiae oppositae. Ad. 1, regulae illae intelligi debent de actibus, quibus ex natura rei, vel ex speciali legis dispositione conditio adjici prohibetur, quod v.g. iis praescripta sit certa forma ut sunt

[16] *Instructio Austriaca* (Romae, die quarta Maii, Anni, 1885).

[17] Italian *Codex Civilis*, 95: "La dichiarazione degli sposi di prendersi rispettivamente in marito e moglie *non puo essere sottosposta ne a termine ne a condizione.*"

"Se le parti aggiungessero un termine o una condizione e vi persistessero, l'uffiziale dello stato civile non potra procedere alla celebrazione del matrimonio." (Quoted from Cerato, *Matrimonium*, 4 ed., 1929, p. 149.

[18] Jn. Fulton, *The Laws of Marriage*, p. 128 sq.

[19] Lib. IV, tit. V, n. 15; *cf.* Pallotini, Tomus XII, pars 2, p. 445; pars 4, p. 504; Wolffgang Schmitt, *Institutiones J. C. Universales*, p. 162; Sanchez, *De Matrimonio*, ilb. V, dist. I; Reiffenstuel, lib. IV. titl. V, n. 1.

sacramenta baptismi, poenitentiae, Eucharistiae etc. Non autem de actibus, qui a voluntate nostra dependent, ut sunt plerique contractus, et inter hos etiam sponsalia, ac matrimonia; haec enim nec certam formam a lege divina habent, neque a jure recipere conditionem prohibentur, imo clare permittitur *c. de illis 3. et cap. super eo 5. hoc tit.* ad. 2. Ad matrimonii essentiam requiritur, ut sit consensus de praesenti, qui habetur, etiamsi addatur ei conditio in futurum pendens; erit igitur ante completam conditionem matrimonium, quamvis nondum in suo esse perfectum; quod novum non est, sed commune cum omnibus actibus, et contractibus, cum conditione in futurum pendente initis.

There are two ways of contracting marriage, says Tamburini:[20] absolutely, when one gives absolute consent and wishes in the very moment it is given to pass dominion of his body; and conditionally, when he wishes to pass dominion only when his condition is verified. Berardi [21] says it is vain to dispute about placing conditions to marital consent, for every condition of any contract suspends the obligation to the future with this difference, if against the substance of marriage the condition destroys the consent. Nor was it worthy, he says, of the theologians of the 12th and 13th centuries to pound this question into dust. It will be emphasized later on, that marriage itself does not receive the condition, but the efficient cause of marriage, namely the consent; this exists, and can therefore receive the condition, marriage does not yet exist.

The Council of Trent on the form of celebration of marriage did not either expressly or implicitly do away with conditional marriage consent. The contrary teaching is erroneous and today completely abandoned.[22]

[20] *Explicatio Decalogi,* Lib. VIII, Tract IV, cap. V. p. 142.

[21] *Canones Gratiani* (*Venetius,* 1783), pars. I, cap. XV, pp. 172, 173.

[22] An indirect authoritative acknowledgement is also contained in the instruction of Cardinal Lambruschini to the Primate of Hungary, 30 April, 1841, *Fontes,* n. 497; and Acta Greg. XVI, III, pp. 122, 124. *Cf.* Hussarek, *Die Bedingte Eheschlieussung,* p. 262.

CHAPTER VIII

RENEWAL OF CONSENT IS NOT NECESSARY FOR VALIDITY

A NECESSARY consequence of the truth of the preceding section, showing that a condition can be validly added to marital consent is, that a new act of the will consenting to marry is not necessary for the existence of the marriage after the verification of the condition. During the pendency of the condition the marriage does not yet exist, but when the condition is verified in that moment there is a valid marriage, without any necessity of renewing the consent. Since the theologians of the past, and some today, following St. Thomas, say the entire transaction amounts only to an engagement (seemingly also overlooking the pre- and post-code conditions for a valid engagement), they are forced to maintain that after the verification of the condition, a new consent must be made before there is a marriage. In fact they generally talk of the necessity to renew the *consent,* yet for the moment forgetting their contention that the first consent is only an *engagement* consent, and if that is renewed a thousand fold it can never effect a marriage. Santi and many others are the authority, that the theologians followed the lead of St. Thomas in this point.[1]

Canonists [2] generally adhered to the juridical concept of a conditional contract, and maintained the accepted doctrine, that when the condition is verified, immediately there is a marriage present and no renewal of consent is necessary. Pope Urban in his famous case [3] on which so many theologians pin their doctrine ruled that the youth, before verification was not bound to consummate the marriage and one can read from the contrary sense, he is bound after the fulfill-

[1] Dist. XXIX, qu. unica, Art. 3, qu. 3; *cf.* Franciscus Santi, *Praelectiones Juris Canonici,* ed. 11, lib. III, p. 100, N. Y., 1892.

[2] Wernz-Vidal, *op. cit.,* n. 515; Sanchez, *De Matrimonio,* V, disp. 8, n. 5; Lugo, *Theologia Moralis,* disp. 22, n. 387; Schmalzgrueber, lib. IV, tit. V, n. 36; Reiffenstuel, lib. IV, tit. 5, n. 17; Van de Burgt, *Tractus de Matri.* (1875), p. 77 s; Rosset, *De Sacr. Matr.,* n. 180.

[3] C. 5, X. *"de conditionibus appositis,"* IV, 5.

ment.[4] In practice we must, said the canonists as far back as Fagnanus, follow the decision of the Sacred Congregation of the Council. The case was this. The parties before the pastor and witnesses gave their consent *de praesenti* under a future, honest, possible, contingent condition. It was fulfilled. The question was asked the Council, is marriage *eo ipso* present, or must they renew the consent before the pastor and witnesses?

In a general congregation of cardinals (narrates Fagnanus) [5] only one cardinal, Alciatus (holding the opinion of the canonists) "quod conditione purificata non sit opus alia iteratione contractus matrimonii coram parocho," held that a new consent before the pastor and witnesses was *not* necessary. All others held it was, though not because the opinion of the theologians won over that of the canonists, but because the cardinals thought the marriage was contracted absolutely, thinking that where the transaction was contracted conditionally it was an engagement transaction and not a marital one. Moreover they thought it safer (*tutius pro securitate conscientiae*) to go again before the pastor because of the decree *Tametsi.* However the case went before the pope who approved the opinion of the canonists that it was not an engagement but a marriage, and he seems to agree that the decree *Tametsi* was not pertinent to the case. The pope St. Pius V approved too the contention of the canonists that after verification of the condition, the consent became absolute and nothing else was required.

The same question went before another Congregation and all except one, Plattus, held no new consent before the pastor or witnesses was necessary. Clement VIII hesitated and doubted about this last decision thinking it was contrary to the Tridentine legislation. He said that, though before the decree *Tametsi* marriage without any solemnity was valid and therefore a conditional marital consent passed into a pure and simple contract and thus into a true marriage, when the condition was verified, yet he thought it was otherwise after this decree. For on the one hand it was certain that the decree required the *forma celebrationis matrimonii* for validity; and on the other hand it did not seem that the form used in the

[4] Santi, *Praelectiones Juris Canonici* (4 ed., 1905), p. 191.

[5] *Commentaria* in *Quartum Librum Decretalium* (Romae 1661), lib. IV, tit. V (*De cond. app.*), n. 4.

beginning (*i. e.*, the *conditional declaration* of consent before the pastor) was sufficient. The pope thought if one *receded* from a condition, there was no solemnity in the resolution of the contract and he felt the consent was not sufficient. The pope therefore gave the question to the Council to answer, and the answer was in favor of the contention of the canonists. The Congregation first observed that there was no parity between the case in which one *receded* from the condition and this case in which the condition was verified. In this second case, by its very nature, the first solemnity before the pastor and witnesses seemed virtually to persevere to the time of fulfillment of the condition, and from this it happens that the consent becomes absolute, and the sole defect which existed in the transaction, namely the suspension of the obligation of marriage is taken away by the fulfilled condition. Therefore there must be a marriage present without a new consent, and the first ceremony substantially fulfilled the requirement of the decree *Tametsi.* The pope approved this, but he did not wish this decision to serve in all cases, but all future cases were to be considered separately and individually with their circumstances.

Naturally in the course of time the affair became more clear till now it is certain that both in the case of revoking the condition, as well as in the verification, marriage is effected, provided the canonical form was observed once, if the parties were bound by the form. "Demum verificata conditione post matrimonii celebrationem, valor matrimonii qui erat in suspenso, quia in suspenso erat ipsemet consensus sicuti, adveniente conditione, consensus purus evadit, ita et consequenter matrimonium ipso jure perficitur quin necessaria sit consensus renovatio." [6]

This follows from the very nature of the thing. (Although the Church in certain cases could demand a renewal of consent, under pain of invalidity. But this renewal would be necessary *ex juris specialis dispositione;* not *ex jure naturali.*) This teaching is valid and true, not only for the marriages exempted from the Tridentine, Pianan, and Code forms, but also for marriages subject to these forms. In this hypothesis, the marriage is canonically celebrated, is immediately present as soon as the condition is verified, whether the

[6] Gasparri, *De Matrimonio* (1932), n. 917.

condition was added manifestly before the pastor and witnesses or not. The reason of this is that marriage is considered as *contracted* (*contrahitur*) when the conditional consent is *declared before the pastor* etc.; not when the condition is verified. It is a *fictio juris* that considers it contracted from the moment of celebration, though the marriage is valid only later.

The disposition of law mentioned above is believed present for those who are subject to a *diriment* impediment (not as impediment). The condition, "if the pope (or bishop) dispenses," is governed by this legal disposition. But it must be understood in this way: not as though from the placing of the condition, the consent is irritated and thus given must be renewed (*ex jure naturae*) but in so far as, regularly at least, the dispensation will not be given in a given case unless with the clause concerning this renewal of consent.[7]

> Ad convalidandum matrimonium irritum ob impedimentum dirimens, requiritur ut cesset vel dispensetur impedimentum et consensus renovet saltem pars impedimenti conscia.
>
> Haec renovatio jure *ecclesiastico* requiritur ad validitatem, etiamsi initio utraque pars consensum praestiterit nec postea revocaverit. (Canon 1133).
>
> Renovatio consensus debet esse novus voluntatis actus in matrimonium quod constet ab initio nullum fuisse. (Canon 1134).

However if a diriment impediment is present, but the consent is given with this *condition* thus: "I marry you, if the pope or bishop dispenses me from this impediment," then *no* renewal of consent is necessary, if the dispensation is granted. Canon 1133 speaks of an *invalid* marriage, not of a conditional consent marriage, which cannot be called an *invalid* marriage. Moreover this canon treats of *convalidating* a marriage entered into with a diriment impediment. In the conditional case, there is no question of convalidating the marriage for it was not entered into with a diriment impediment. It was entered into under a *condition* and when the condition is verified *eo ipso* the consent is absolute. Canon 1133 presupposes an *absolute* consent is present, *ab initio*.

Nevertheless some say in this case of the above condition, the

[7] *Cf.* De Smet, *De Sponsalibus et Matrimonio* (ed. 3, 1920), I, n. 154.

consent must be renewed; others deny it. Chelodi,[8] Vlaming,[9] De Smet,[10] Gasparri,[11] teach the consent must be renewed, at least by positive law, or better because of Roman jurisprudence. But Vidal says Cappello rightly doubts concerning this necessity for which no positive argument can be shown and certainly, as pointed out elsewhere in this treatise and immediately above, the invoking of Canon 1133 does not prove the point. In practice, when a dispensation from a diriment impediment is given, the dispensation itself or the rules governing a rescript of this kind require a renewal of consent. But this is only by force of the dispensation or rules governing rescripts, not by force of Canon 1133. For neither that canon nor any other canon *per se* touches this conditional aspect of the case.

If the parties *publicly* add a condition to their consent and later wish to consent absolutely without awaiting verification, they should take care that it be known publicly and certainly that they mutually and expressly or tacitly receded from the condition and now consent purely. A new celebration is not required, for from the beginning *true marital* consent was given whose efficacy was blocked by the condition, which obex is removed by revocation (just as by verification) of the condition and the first consent attains its full efficacy without anything else being needed. Moreover if the ecclesiastical substantial form of celebration was used, it is sufficient (for the external forum to know that the marriage is valid even though the condition were never verified), after the recession, to notify the pastor about it, but the *forma* must not be repeated. For as was said before, marriage is considered as *contracted* when before the witnesses the conditional consent is declared, not when it is verified. Yet by a fiction of the law it is considered contracted from the moment of celebration, and thus Canons 1094 s. concerning the substantial form of the celebration of *marriage*, are complied with.[12]

[8] *Jus Matrimoniale*, n. 126.

[9] *Praelectiones J. Eccl.*, n. 549.

[10] *De Sponsalibus et Matrimonio*, n. 153.

[11] *De Matrimonio* (1903), n. 994.

[12] *Cf.* Wernz-Vidal, *op. cit.*, n. 514; Pichler, *op. cit.*, n. 5, ad. 5; Gasparri, *op. cit.*, n. 991 (1903); Schnitzer, *op. cit.*, p. 316, n. 10; Leitner in *Archiv f. K. K. Rt.*, 76, p. 260 sq.; Cappello, *op. cit.*, n. 639.

CHAPTER IX

PERSEVERANCE OF CONSENT

It would be inane to speak about conditional consent that *suspends* the marriage, and to speak about the *revocation* of the *condition*, or the revocation of the whole transaction, unless the consent persevered. The doctrine of conditional consent, to which a future condition is added, is based on the *fact* that consent can and does endure unless and until it is retracted by a new act of the will; and the same doctrine is reinforced by the *presumption* of law that the *consent* or the *condition* has not been retracted or revoked, unless the contrary be proven. So before discussing the revocation of the condition or of the entire transaction, it will be useful to recall the principles concerning the perserverance of consent, whether absolute or conditioned.[1]

Consent once given, even in a marriage invalid by reason of an impediment is presumed to persevere, until the contrary is proved. If a person is incapable *ex parte subjecti, et ex lege naturali,* of furnishing *marital* consent, then it seems there is no consent in existence to persevere. For instance, if a perfect idiot, or a baby, or a man perpetually and antecedently impotent, were to utter the material words "I marry you," this would not be *marital* consent. This presumption of law is in favor of the existence of the consent once furnished. There was much disputing in rather recent times whether the consent enjoys this presumption when the ecclesiastical form of celebration required for validity, was not observed. The Holy Office on July 2, 1892, instructed the Archbishop of Cologne in these words: "Praesumptionem stare non pro nullitate, imo vero pro validitate utrorumque matrimoniorum (*i. e.,* mixtorum) sive civiliter sive coram ministro acatholico clandestine contractorum, quae ibidem

[1] In the historical part of this thesis, and in the chapter dealing with the question whether conditions can be validly added to consent; and in other places here and there, the perseverance of consent has been not only assumed but also proved. But it is deemed advisable to briefly touch on it here also.

a jure Tridentino eximuntur."[2] The instruction went on to say, that in more difficult cases, the Holy See must be consulted.[3]

Chelodi says no presumption of *law* exists for the above case wherein the form required for validity was not used, but rather a presumption of *fact*, because when there is a conflict between the divine and human law, the Church prefers to believe the parties wish to marry rather than to live in concubinage.[4] Canon 1093 reads: "Etsi matrimonium invalide ratione impedimenti initum fuerit, consensus praestitus praesumitur perseverare, donec de ejus revocatione constiterit."[5] These principles hold good even though the consent furnished was only a *conditional* consent and not absolute. If retraction of the conditional consent has been proved the marriage can be declared null by force of Canon 1081. If it cannot be proved that it was retracted, the marriage is considered valid (presupposing the condition was verified) by force of Canons 1093 and 1092, because furnished consent is presumed to persevere and marriage is convalidated from the moment of the granting of a dispensation, in case it was invalid on account of an impediment; or the verification of the condition in case the consent was furnished under a future licit condition.[6]

[2] This passage is quoted by the Rota in *AAS*, IV (1912), p. 632, it is referred to in another decision in the same volume, p. 388. It was originally given by the Holy Office, 2 December, 1866, and repeated on 6 September, 1876, and 2 July, 1892. It is not found in the *Fontes*. *Cf.* Chelodi, *Jus Matrimoniale*, ed. 3, p. 124.

[3] *Cf.* R. 19 Maii, 1910 (dec. 17); 23 February, 1912 (*AAS* IV, 377); *AAS* IV, 629, Colonien. 27 August, 1910 (dec. 31) and 10 June, 1912.

[4] Chelodi, *op. cit.*, p. 125.

[5] The *revocation* of consent is presumed, some say, if the other party puts off his consent for a long time. De Smet, *De Sponsalibus et Matrimonio*, n. 101.

[6] *Cf.* Cerato, *De Matrimonio*, p. 158.

CHAPTER X

LICEITY OF PLACING CONDITIONS

Some authors claim it is unlawful to place any kind of conditions. Others require *a most urgent* reason. Some others say a *grave* cause is necessary for the liceity, and some more say no grave cause is necessary, that it is simply licit to place honest conditions. This last seems to be correct. These various views and their proponents will now be more fully mentioned.

Sanseverino, and Gasparri among others[1] seem to think it is illicit to place conditions, saying all are to be deterred by the pastor from doing so. The former says that, though it is valid to place conditions, it is illicit to do so, adding it is not licit, even though the pastor and witnesses assist of their own accord. For the general rule is, sacraments should not be given under condition, except for extreme reasons of urgent necessity, *e. g.*, Baptism, Absolution and Extreme Unction. But in this sacrament there is no such necessity to contract conditionally, for it is simply not necessary to anyone to marry, therefore when one wants to contract with a condition, first try to have the condition first fulfilled, and then have him marry absolutely. From the nature of the Sacrament and the contract, the condition exposes them to much perplexity and quarrelling, and difficulties concerning proof of the verification and other things. This is loose reasoning and erroneous and the same words and reasons were used long ago by Clericatus, who ends his discourse with these words: "Let pastors know that throughout fifty years in the episcopal curia of a very large diocese, I have never heard of a marriage contracted under a condition." [2] Placing a condition to one's marital consent is confounded with confecting a sacrament under condition. Moreover it is the consent or the contract and not the Sacramental character of the same that governs and permits conditions for many good reasons, and since the effect of the contract is suspended, it

[1] Sanseverino, *De Ordinis et Matrimonii Sacramentis* (1642), qu. 2, *De Matr.*, p. 209; Gasparri, *De Matr.* (1932), n. 878; De Becker, *De Matr.*, p. 81.

[2] Joannis Clericatus, *Decisiones de Matrimonio*, ed. 2, Venetiis, 1716.

follows that the sacrament is not there to be suspended by the condition. Cardinal Gasparri writes:[3]

> Equidem matrimonium propter reverentiam Sacramenti et plurium incommodorum pericula, contrahi debet pure et simpliciter, nec parochus sinat unquam in expressione consensus aliquid hujusmodi addi. (*i. e.*, conditio, modus, causa, demonstratio).

Many conditions are added secretly, precisely because of the fear of such refusals.

Cerato[4] requires *urgentissima causa et licentia Ordinarii.* Gougnard[5] says the pastor should allow no such conditions, unless there is *urgentissima causa* and he should consult the ordinary if possible, and use proper precautions.

Cappello,[6] Esmein,[7] Noldin,[8] and many others say a *grave cause* is necessary for the liceity. Cappello reasoning from a study of Canons 6, 23, and 1100 claims the permission of the bishop (this is from the old law) is needed and refers to a decisional case of the S. Congr. Council.[9] This decision by no means proves the point, for it does not touch it. In fact the decision declared the marriage null because of the unverified condition; and it says it makes no difference that the pastor thought he could not assist at a conditional marriage.[10]

[3] *Op cit.*, n. 878.

[4] *De Matrimonio,* p. 148.

[5] *Tractatus de Matrimonio,* p. 142.

[6] *De Matr.*, (1923), p. 660.

[7] *Le Mariage,* I, 171-178; II, 216-218.

[8] *Theologia Moralis,* n. 634.3.

[9] *S. C. C. causa Ulyssibon,* 16 March, 1720, and 8 July, 1924—*Fontes,* n. 3201. (*Thesaurus Resolutorum* I, p. 292); *Fontes,* n. 3278 (*Thesaurus Resolutorum,* III, p. 39-44); Cappello, *De Matr.*, n. 626; Wernz, *Jus Matrimoniale,* n. 297; Schmalzgrueber, lib. IV, tit. V, n. 59; Reiffenstuel, lib. IV, tit. V, n. 22.

[10] *E. g.*, Linneborn, *Grundriss des Eherechts* (1919), p. 331. Some cite Canon 1100 to show a grave cause is necessary for liceity. This canon prescribes the use of rites contained in authorized rituals, but no rite for conditional marriage consent is contained in the Roman ritual. This proves nothing. The ritual has no separate rites for mixed religion marriages, nor for those in which a procurator is used, and for other kinds of marriage celebration, *e. g.*, in danger of death, in secrecy etc., yet given the proper circumstances, no priest needs any permission of the bishop for these marriages, as far as the rite of celebration is concerned.

Phillips [11] says erroneously that the Council of Trent decreed that the *condition* must be placed in the very act of celebration or shortly before it to satisfy the *forma celebrationis.* More recently, for greater security, it needs, he says, the bishop's approval and this is not to be denied arbitrarily.

A suspensive condition, says Bayon, is permitted only for a grave cause, and generally speaking the permission of the bishop is needed, for a formula for such a marriage is not in the ritual or practice of the Church.[12] If permission is granted, he continues, the pastor and witnesses should for liceity, not for validly, know of the condition in the act of the celebration or beforehand, so that in the external form its presence can be proved authoritatively. Vidal maintains that conditions are illicitly placed unless there are grave reasons which ordinarily must be approved by the bishop.[13]

Vlaming [14] says it is licit to place conditions even *absque probata causa,* if honest and not against the substance of marriage consent, for the Code demands no cause to place them, as it does in Canon 1091 for use of a procurator or interpreter. Cappello [15] says this opinion cannot be admitted. He maintains that for liceity the condition must be expressed either in the act of celebration before the witnesses or before celebration in a certain way (*modo certo*) so that in the external forum its placing can be proved, and by both parties placed, and not revoked.[16] But it seems this is not required for the *liceity* of *placing* the condition, but for the *proof of its having been placed.* Accidentally, of course, if a condition is placed by one or both in such a way that it is juridically unprovable, then such a placing of the condition can become morally illicit due, *e. g.*, to scandal, or injury to third persons or even the other party, and to any children that may be born. Even for the *probatio* of the placing of the condition it is not necessary that *both* place it, as Cappello

[11] *Kirchenrecht,* p. 605.

[12] Bayon, *De Matrimonio,* p. 315; Wernz-Vidal, *Jus Matrimoniale,* n. 515.

[13] Wernz-Vidal, *Jus Matr.* (1925), n. 515; *Instr.* Card. R., par. 55.

[14] *Praelectiones Juris Canonici,* n. 551.

[15] *De Matrimonio,* n. 626, nota.

[16] *Op. cit.*, n. 647.

insists. The majority of rotal marriage cases are those in which only *one* party placed the condition, *e. g.*, in the two cases referred to in this very discussion.

It may be added here that the pastor and witnesses need not be present at the placing of the condition or at its fulfillment or even know of it, or its fulfillment, for *validity*. In practice it should be recorded in the marriage record for probative reasons. If both parties come to the pastor and want to contract conditionally, what should be the pastor's practice? He may act, himself, or if he wishes in a complicated case confer with the bishop.[17]

A distinction is to be made says Payen [18] in answering the query, whether it is licit for the parties to contract marriage with a past, present, or even future condition, which is at the same time honest and possible and not against the substance of marriage. The distinction must consider whether the condition is added *outside* the act of celebration, or *in the very act* of the celebration of marriage; also whether the condition is placed by one party only while the other party knows of it, or does not know of it.

"Extra actum celebrationis," nothing prohibits, if a grave cause is present, the both partners, or even one, the other knowing it, to place before the ceremony a condition, before witnesses or even without witnesses. This condition may be present or past or future.

But Payen says that to place the condition before the celebration requires three things for liceity. The permission of the bishop, especially if it is a suspensive condition; that its placing can be proved in the external forum; and thirdly that the pastor and the witnesses should be told of the presence of the condition. In the first rotal trial of a case the decision has this paragraph (p. 565).

> Tandem praeteriri nequit, Pitonium in suis *Disceptationibus Ecclesiasticis* . . . contra Pignatelli aliosque, tenere, matrimonium, quod pure et simpliciter coram parocho et testibus celebratur, ab Ecclesia judicari debere tanquam pure et simpliciter contractum."

[17] *Cf.* Schmalzgrueber, lib. IV, tit. V, n. 42 sq.; Sanchez, *De Matr.*, lib. V, disp. 8, n. 23 s; disp. 13, n. 3 sq.; Rosset, *De Sacramento Matrimonii*, 6 vols., (1895-96), n. 184.

[18] *De Matrimonio*, n. 1727.

Pitonius quotes the decree *Tametsi* in substantiation. The judges were Sebastianelli (*ponens*), Many and Heiner. The second rotal trial [19] with Lega and Persiani and Perathoner as judges, reversed the first decision of the Rota, and the third rotal sentence confirmed the second, namely that the marriage was invalid.

The second decision of the Rota also quotes Pitonius against the above assertion. "Sapientissime Pitonius, a Patronis citatus, ait voluntatem jam manifestatam et aliquam conditionem contractui apponentem non praesumi mutatam fuisse sed continuari." (Acta, p. 971). The decision quotes this rule, " 'Et qui ait mutatam fuisse voluntatem docere id debet'." It is to be noted that all this concerns evidence and proof only, not whether it is licit or not to place an honest condition.

That the other party should be warned of the condition, is true, and it is illicit not to acquaint him of it.[20]

With far greater right did a certain girl act, who marrying an irreligious man, placed an expressed condition that he promise her seriously (*ex animo*) not to interfere with the full Catholic rearing of the children and her own religious freedom.[21]

In the two cases referred to, Payen admits "*Non omnes* tamen condiciones ad liceitatem requisitae servatae sunt in hoc duplici exemplo; *neque* petita est licentia Episcopi; *neque* de apposita condicione moniti sunt parochus et testes." Yet the decisions imply that both the man in the one case, and the woman in the other had a right and justification to place the conditions.

"In ipso actu celebrationis matrimonii" the pastor, according to some, cannot permit a condition to be placed.

> Nullibi prohibitum est, et consequenter *per se licet*, matrimonium sub honesta condicione de praesenti, praeterito vel futuro contrahere—attamen, cum Rit. Rom. tanquam formam matrimonii in facie Ecclesiae celebrandi exhibeat consensum absolutum, et plurima incommodo ex

[19] *AAS*, II (1910), 961-972.

[20] *Cf.* a case where the man had a right to place a condition, "monita sponsa" —*AAS*, II (1910), p. 961-972; *AAS*, III (1911), p. 497-513. *Cf.* the first rotal trial: *AAS*, *I* (1909), p. 561-565.

[21] S. R. Rota, *AAS*, XIV (1922), pp. 512-523.

> adjectis condicionibus enasci pronum sit, *parochus permittere nequit* ut coram se contrahatur matrimonium condicionatum, *nisi* ob causam *urgentissimam,* et, quatenus fieri possit, impetrata Ordinarii venia, et condicione per scripturam expressa, ut de ea postea constare possit.[22]

Not even moral theology demands this. The right to do something, and the judicial proof that one did that thing are two different things. What is necessary to satisfy a court of evidence, is not to be transferred to what is necessary to do a thing. All about writing etc. *per se* concern proof only, unless by law *per accidens,* something probative is demanded for the liceity of the act.

In other words says Payen three things are necessary in order that a pastor licitly permit a conditional consent marriage; first, a grave if not a most grave cause or reason;[23] secondly, the permission of the bishop, unless there is danger in delay; thirdly, proper precautions to prove beyond doubt the placing of the condition. All this probably may bind the *pastor.* It is undoubtedly good pastoral theology, but with the distinctions made above, it cannot be proved or shown that there is any law in the Code prohibiting persons from freely placing future honest conditions to their marital consent. Nor for that matter honest past and present conditions also.

In answering the question whether conditions can be licitly placed it seems certain distinctions should be made. First, if it is licit to do so, does that mean absolutely or within certain limitations, *e. g.,* that there must be a *just* cause, or a *grave* cause, or a *most grave* cause? For if the law, *e. g.,* demanded a grave cause to licitly place a condition, one could assert that the placing of conditions is *per se* licit within the limits of the law. Furthermore if it is licit to place conditions, does that mean provided the ordinary's permission is obtained, if possible, or is this last point not necessary? Again distinctions must be made based on the moral quality of the content of the condition. And finally, in what connotation is the word *licit* or liceity used, in a strict canonical meaning or in the wider meaning of moral theology? And yet another distinction should be made, the lack of which seems to be the reason of the confusion of some authors, namely, one must not confound the lawfulness of an act

[22] Genicot-Salsmann, *Theol. Moralis* II, n. 458.

[23] Chelodi, n. 123.

with the requirements of evidential and probational rules demanded by a court to prove whether that act was placed or not, or if placed whether revoked, or fulfilled.

These things being premised, it can be stated that there is no law in the Code forbidding the conditional consent, in fact the Code legislates about the doctrine and nowhere, not even from the pre-Code law, is there found any legislation as legislation requiring the bishop's permission. It was urged as a safe norm but no canonical obligation exists; only in some cases, *moral* obligations, whether towards the other party or on account of reverence to the sacrament, *e. g.*, by placing a foolish condition or an immoral one.

To place any condition secretly by both or one party is *per se* gravely illicit. To place any condition unknown to the other party is *per se* gravely illicit. He acts validly but is gravely culpable of sin, and he must repair any damage; if any, to the other party. He may even in some circumstances be bound in conscience (as the only means of repairing the damage) to give absolute consent.[24] To place a condition, the other party unwilling, is licit in some cases, *e. g.* if a man suspects that the woman labors under a contagious disease; in other cases, it can be gravely illicit, *e. g.* if the man places a condition that the woman seriously promise to always wear black clothes. To place seriously an impossible condition known as an impossible one, is *per se* illicit and gravely culpable. To place any kind of a condition unknown to the pastor (and probably the witnesses) is not illicit, if it was placed before in such a way that it can be proved easily in the external forum. To place a condition *ex joco* is illicit, grave or light according to circumstances. But to place an honest, future, contingent condition, and to place it openly in a way easily proved, is not illicit, requires no permission of pastor or bishop and requires not even a *grave* cause, any honest even light reason, is sufficient.

It is forbidden under pain of grave sin to contract marriage with an immoral condition, or one that is against the substance of marriage.[25] But this is a prohibition of the moral law not Canon Law.

[24] *Cf.* Cappello, *De Matr.*, n. 597 nota.

[25] S. R. Rota, 10 May, 1916, *AAS*, IX (1917), pp. 32-39; *cf.* Payen, *De Matrimonio*, n. 1727.

CHAPTER XI

TIME AND MANNER OF PLACING THE CONDITION

A FUNDAMENTAL principle of law is that in a contract there must be declared union of wills of the parties no matter to what sphere of law this contract belongs. The decision of will of one and the other must be in agreement (meeting of minds). The declaration of will of the parties enters into the world of legal phenomena as a single contractual will. The potency which here operates, begetting, altering, or destroying, is not merely the sum total of two individual wills but a uniform common will or force (a willing common to both). Legal effects ensue not because A wants the same thing as B, but because A and B have fused their bilateral will into one common act of willing. Legal effects ensue only then, when, and if, the two factors begetting this product are congruent with each other.[1]

Hussarek, among others, concludes from the above principle, that as a consequence *both* parties in the case of a conditional contract, must give conditional consent, and if one only contracts conditionally, the other simply, there is no union of wills and therefore no matrimonial consent, for the act of willing of one is categorical, that of the other casual or conditional. That congruence of bilateral will which is required for a contract does not exist and the result is there is neither union of wills, nor a contract, nor any legal effects. He strongly insists on this, and he will eliminate only this case: if the one who consents first absolutely, later accommodates his will to the other, thus both agreeing under the condition. But this assertion is false. True there is not perfect congruence of the wills during the pendency and since this is so no juridical effects flow, but this congruence of wills is had in the very moment of the verification, for at that moment both consent absolutely. This is abundantly proved also from the numerous cases like this that the Roman curia has decided.

[1] *Cf.*, Dr. Max Ritter Hussarek von Heinlein, *Die Bedingte Eheschliessung* (Wien, 1892), p. 260.

Since the enactment of the decree *Tametsi* of the Council of Trent, the giving of marriage consent is (with exceptions) quite a formal affair, and this decree was superseded by the decree *Ne Temere,* and this in turn by the Code. The declaration of a *conditional consent marriage* is also dependent for its validity on the observance of the laws of the Code concerning the substantial form of celebration. The doctrine according to which the Tridentine form of the celebration of marriage, makes a marriage under conditional consent impossible, is and has been completely abandoned. No renewal of consent was necessary after verification of the condition.[2] There is no controversy any more whether the observance of the formality refers only to a part or to the totality of a declaration of will, nor whether the pastor and witnesses must be present at the expression of the condition. Phillips [3] errs when he says the Council of Trent decreed that the condition, if not placed in the very act of declaring the consent, at least be placed a short time before and clearly and distinctly before the pastor and witnesses of the marriage. Nor does the Code in Canon 1094 demand this. It suffices for validity if they be present at the declaration which is externally *absolute,* though prior to the celebration the condition was made, unknown to the pastor and witnesses. Silence about an illicit condition is *a fortiori* immaterial for these are rejected in the external forum. If a simple declaration were given before the witnesses, without any declaration that the consent is conditioned even though it is true that a different thing is declared (*i. e.,* an absolute consent) from that which is willed (*i. e.,* a conditional consent), nevertheless the *substantial form of celebration is had* and on that score the marriage would not be invalid.

The verbal form or wording in all this is immaterial. "Ad effectum inducendae conditionis magis inspicitur substantia dispositionis et mens disponentium, quam cortex verborum." [4] The parties may express their will by means of a principal sentence with a dependent clause containing the condition. Or they may, *e. g.,* first

[2] *Cf.* Hussarek, *op. cit.* p. 262; Phillips *Kirchenrecht,* p. 416.

[3] *Kirohenrecht,* p. 605.

[4] Quoted from a decision of the Rota, 11 August, 1910, *AAS,* II (1910), p. 967.

agree before the pastor and witnesses that they consent under a condition, and then they may pronounce in solemn phrase the consent to marriage alone and separately. As far as the *probative* demands of the courts are concerned, this complicated transaction must naturally be enacted in such wise that one may argue and conclude from the circumstances, the uninterrupted continuance of the conditional consent, and not suspect a departure from the originally declared conditional consent.

A future licit condition suspends the consent and therefore the marriage in virtue of the law of nature, reenforced moreover by the positive law of the Church (Canon 1092, n. 3). It is immaterial whether this condition or any other condition, is placed or added in the very act of the celebration of marriage, or before this time, provided in the latter case it has not been revoked. If it were revoked before the celebration, then the marriage is entered unconditionally. Likewise it is irrelevant speculatively whether the condition is *deducta in pactum* or not; whether placed by one or both parties. If placed by one it makes no difference (*quoad validitatem appositionis*) whether the other party knew of it or not, or whether the other party did not approve of it. Nor does it matter whether it is placed by one or both publicly or only privately or occultly, because in every case, the validity of the marriage depends on mutual consent and this *ex hypothesi* is suspended.[5] Nor is it any more required (if it ever were) that the one positing the circumstances know the juridical effects of such an addition of a condition.[6] A decision handed down by Lega, Persiani, and Perathoner, has this to say:

> Quare sententia appellata advertit: At, quaeso, an nesciens conditionis valorem nec etiam possibilitatem conditionem apponendi ad effectum qui deinde necessario consequitur potest dici quod matrimonium sub conditione contraxerit? Sed,—uti praedicat effatum—nostra existimatio rerum veritatem non mutat: quare actor ductus persuasione quod enuntiata conditio in contractu—si non verbis, re tamen suberat—eadem sinceritate et simplicitate qua conditionis appositae effectum et indolem se ignorasse fassus

[5] *Cf.* Bayon, *De Matr.* p. 315; Wernz-Vidal *Jus Matrimoniale,* n. 514; Cappello, *De Matr.,* 638, 3; De Smet, *De Sponsalibus et Matrimonio,* n. 151.

[6] *Cf.* De Smet., *op. cit.,* n. 151, who refers to *N. R. th.* (1913), p. 222 s.

est, prosequitur: "aujourd'hui je demande à l' Eglise la nullité de mon mariage pour le motif suivant: Je n'ai voulu me marier qu'à la condition qu'on me prouverait que l'ozène n'existait pas chez ma femme. Or la conditio ne s'est pas verifièe si bien qu'à trois semaines de distance le même docteur niait d'abord et affirmait ensuite l'existence de ce mal."[7]

If the condition is placed occultly, in such a way that its placing can not be proved according to the rules of evidence and proof and the jurisprudence of the external forum, the marriage, if canonically celebrated, is presumed and considered as *valid ab initio* in the external forum of the Church, even though the condition was not verified. On the other hand, once proved that the condition was added, its recall must be proved else the condition is presumed to persevere.[8] The same judges of the Rota in the same case insist that the burden of proof that the condition was revoked falls upon him who asserts its revocation. "Sapientissime Pitonius, a Patronis citatus, ait voluntatem jam manifestatam et aliquam conditionem contractui apponentem non praesumi mutatam fuisse sed continuari. Lege enim cautum est, 'quod quis semel voluit aut noluit, illud semper deinceps velle aut nolle intelligitur quamdiu von retractaverit voluntatem.'" Then the decision quotes a similar rule. "'Et qui ait mutatam fuisse voluntatem docere id debet.'"

If the condition is placed by one, the other party being unconscious of it, the party so doing, gravely sins, for its puts the other person in a very grave position. Those contracting marriage conditionally do not sin gravely if in the act of celebration, they are not in the state of grace, provided they are immune from deadly sin at the time of the verification of the condition, for neither the marriage nor the sacrament is present at the time of celebration, but at the time of the fulfillment of the condition. In past and present conditions the time of celebration and the truth of the condition may coincide and grave sin would be committed, if the parties or party were not in the state of grace when they celebrate the marriage.[9]

[7] *AAS*, 11 August, 1910, II (1910), 968.

[8] *Cf.* De Smet., *loc. cit.;* Bayon, *De Matrimonio,* p. 315.

[9] *Cf.* Bayon, *op. cit.*, p. 315.

It cannot be too often emphasized that in the internal forum (that is in God's sight, and according to the law of nature as respects marriage, and the free will conditioned), the condition, if seriously placed, no matter what kind it is, has its effect. Even though the Church in the external forum presumes (for very many good reasons) there is a marriage, in spite of a future *necessary, evil,* or *impossible* condition being placed, yet it by no means presumes that there was no such conditional consent placed by the contractor, it presumes the condition was place *ex joco.* Therefore in conscience and in the internal forum if the contractor did not will to marry unless the condition be verified, and actually it was not verified, or even if it be an impossible condition, never would marriage be present *de facto* and in the sight of God, for without consent purely given there can be no marriage.[10] Canon 1081, par. 1, reads: "Matrimonium facit partium consensus inter personas jure habiles legitime manifestus; qui *nulla humana potestate supplere valet.*" The above mentioned three judges of the Rota who are eminent canonists, in the same marriage case wherein the marital consent was subordinated to a future honest condition, quote D'Annibale to this effect: "Contractus—matrimonium—uti docet D'Annibale 'qua est contractus naturalis regitur tum jure naturae tum jure evangelico, ubique gentium', et in nota 17 explicat [D'Annibale] 'huic autem juri nulli humanae potestati derogare, subrogare, abrogare datum est.' Sed hic contractus [matrimonialis] cum regatur tantummodo jure naturae, si conditio subsit, *quomodoque* expressa eademque deinceps probetur, matrimonium nullum declarandum est." [11] In other words, the rules of jurisprudence (which does not make doctrinal law but only judges according to doctrinal law) are subordinated to the natural law dictating the absolute necessity of human consent to effect marriage, and *if* it is proved a condition was placed and also proved it was unfulfilled then the court must in the external forum *declare* that no marriage exists. The necessity of human consent for marriage has been the constant teaching of the Church, repeated over and

[10] Thus all the Doctors and Hostiensis and Sanchez, *De Matrimonio,* lib. V, disp. IV; *cf.* C. of Trent, sess. XXIV, *de reform. matr.,* chaps. 1 and IX.

[11] *AAS,* II (1910), pp. 971-972.

over again, especially by our present Holy Father as already quoted.[12]

If the one or both placing such conditions as above are not certain but doubtful of the presence or absence of invalidating conditional consent, then the marriage is judged by the presumption of the external forum, that is, valid, and one or both should reject the condition and there will be marriage *de facto.* What the judge resting on a true presumption, judges in the external forum, is to be observed in the internal forum, when the opposite is not certain. Moreover if there be a doubt in both fora, the judgment is in favor of the validity of the marriage.[13] Enriquez says Sanchez teaches that only in doubt in the external forum, one must judge in favor of the marriage, not in doubt, in the internal forum. Sanchez [14] quotes much authority for his view. He allows this exception, if in doubt, and one marries another, then the certain marriage eliminates the uncertain one. Two principles conflict here: better is the position of the possessor (of marriage in this case); and the principle of liberty and freedom of the will in marriage contracts. It is simply a question of jurisprudence, the rules of which may vary from time to time in its criteria and its applications of the same. It is true, in a sense, to say as the author of an article does,[15] "Canon Law in the external forum takes into account such conditions only as are definitely expressed."

Likewise it is irrelevant as far as the validity of placing a condition is concerned, whether it is *deducta in pactum* or not. There are many explanations, some contradictory of others, of the meaning of the phrase "deducta in pactum." The condition passes into the *pactum* (*i. e.*, the marital contract) in such a way that the condition is said to be *deducta in pactum.* The Roman Congregations and the Sacred Rota in their jurisprudence have varied about the meaning of this phrase, but generally one can say they meant by it the *external* expression of the condition attached to the consent at the moment of the *celebration.* If the condition was attached to the

[12] *Cf.* above references to C. of Trent., *cf.* Code on the liberty of marriage.

[13] *Cf.* Sanchez., *loc. cit.; cf.* Canon 1014.

[14] *De Matr.*, lib. I, disp. 18, nn. 5, 6.

[15] *Cath.. Ency.*, vol. IX, 702 c.

very will internally only, as far as the external forum interest, it was not then *deducta in pactum.* And in this latter case, and in other more or less secret or occult expressions of the condition, prior to the celebration, and not in the celebration, the proof of its placing and the proof of its not being meanwhile revoked was generally so difficult, sometimes impossible, that the jurisprudence would only consider cases in which it was *deducta in pactum* in the above sense.[16]

De Smet [17] explains the phrase thus:

> Sensus formulae "in pactum deducta" est quod conditio afficiat ipsum pactum seu contractum matrimonialem; non significat quod conditio debeat apponi ab utraque parte mutuo pacto in conditionis appositionem conveniente: sufficit ad hoc ut contractus sit conditionatus, quod ab una parte apponatur conditio.[18]

One must not confound the *means of proof*, whence it is evident in the external forum that a condition has been placed, with the *effect* (*jure naturae*) on the consent, of a condition that was actually placed (though probably not proven as having been place); nor confound the means of proof with the *very nature* of the *thing placed.* The condition *deducta in pactum* by no means *per se* affects the validity or the invalidity of the marriage, but this manner of placing a condition only can be considered and must be considered as a most suitable means, not the *sole* means, *to prove* the *placing* of a condition. Therefore even without placing the condition in this manner, it is certain and undoubted that the marriage *depends* on the *condition,* and not on the method of its placing even though the condition is merely internal. "Actus agentis ultra illius intentionem non operatur," as another rotal decision said. Of course, as far as the *external* forum is concerned, the validity or invalidity of a conditional consent marriage will depend on whether a condition *was*

[16] *Cf.* section on the *bonum sacramenti,* where the varying practices of the Roman Curia about this phrase and its meanings are discussed as applied especially to conditions against the substance of marriage.

[17] *Op. cit.* n. 151, nota.

[18] *Cf.* Cappello, *De Matrimonio,* n. 599; *cf.* SRR., *Causa Parisien,* 10 May, 1916,—*AAS,* IX (1917), 33.

proved to have been placed and verified or not, and if the condition is not added in such a way that it can be proved, *e. g.*, if it be not *deducta in pactum,* it will be difficult and sometimes *impossible* to *prove* that the condition was ever added to the consent at all. The court needs a proof of its having been placed and the common and more obvious proof is had when the condition is mentioned in the very contract. (The contract is the external expression of the consent given canonically, that is, generally, before the pastor or his delegate and the witnesses.)

One must not confound an internal *intention* excluding marriage, or the right of the conjugal act, or any essential property, with an internal *condition, e. g.*, a person says *only in his mind,* "I marry you, if my father consents;" or "I marry you, only on the condition that I reserve the radical right to my body." These are examples of the two *conditional* consents. If the mind or the act of the will is internally formulated like this: "I will to contract a soluble (*a vinculo*) union;" or "I will to marry this person in this sense that I do not give her the right to my body," then these are not conditional consents but *intentions* against the substance of marriage. In the first example, "if my father consents," there is a full complete act of the will to marry, which healthy act containing all essentials, is suspended. In the last two examples, there are no complete acts of the will *to marry.* (He may think so or wish it thus.) The act is essentially diseased as a *marital voluntarium,* it is juridically and substantially defective; (it is *not psychological* defective as an act of the *will,* willing something different than true marriage). And moreover this concrete act of the will is not willed conditionally or suspended. The example, "I marry you only on condition that I reserve the radical right to my body," is a conditional consent grammatically, but only in that sense. In reality it is nothing else than an *intention* against the substance. There is present *essentially defective marital* consent and on this score of *defective* consent, all marriage cases in which there was so-called condition against the substance are settled. In reality the invalidity is there because the natural law as defined by Canon 1081, pars. 1 and 2, is not complied with. The marriage is not invalid because the *condition* (so-called) was unfulfilled, it would be invalid if (*per impossible*) it were verified. There is *not* present *ex hypothesi,* in the mind a *marital* consent, that is, an act of the will *to marry* that is juridically essentially healthy. There is lacking, "consensus matrimonialis" which is an "actus voluntatis *quo utraque pars tradit et acceptat jus in corpus, perpetuum et exclusivum,* in ordine ad actus per se aptos ad prolis generationem." [19] And since this is lacking (*defectus consensus*) there is possible no marriage whatever. "Matrimonium facit partium *consensus* . . . , qui *nulla humana potestate suppleri valet.*" [20] And the Code applying this truth to anything that excludes any essential of marriage consent, legislates: "At si alterutra vel utraque pars positivo voluntatis actu excludat matrimonium ipsum, aut omne jus ad conjugalem actum, vel essentialem aliquam matrimonii proprietatam, invalide contrahit." [21] All this is manifestly clear from the very notion and nature of marriage and matrimonial consent.[22]

Therefore the *condition* (*i. e.,* every kind of conditions, except the so-called ones "against the substance") can be placed merely *internally,* as a condition (*e. g.,* if you are a virgin) and this must not be confounded with a defective internal consent. Expressed in the innermost will only, it is a condition, and the objective validity of the marriage depends on its verification. The essentially interior (not expressed) defective consent (on account of an intention against the substance etc. of marriage) causes immediately an invalid marriage. A condition as said before may be added by one, or both, even purely internally, though it makes a world of difference in the external forum and the ecclesiastical courts, for they generally dismiss the case and will not consider it because of lack of, or too great difficulty (generally culpably caused by the party or parties that placed it) of proving its existence. If some canonists so define a condition as not to allow a condition to be externally *unexpressed in any way,* they define erroneously, and generally the reason is because they confuse the principles of the two *fora* and fail to realize that decisions of papal courts upholding the validity of the marriage,

[19] Canon 1081, par. 2.

[20] Canon 1081, par. 1.

[21] Canon 1086, par. 2.

[22] *Cf.* S. C. S. Off., 11 December, 1858; 11 March, 1868, 9 December, 1874, 4 February, 1891. *Coll. S. C. de P. Fide,* nn. 1327, 1427, 1746.

do so in as much as the placing of the condition, or its non-revocation are not proven in the external forum precisely for this reason, that it was placed secretly or only in the will. These authors fail to distinguish between the law or doctrine of conditions *a jure naturae* and the Church Law, *i. e.* ,the jurisprudence of the courts, its rules and procedures that govern only the external forum. These rules of evidence, and the conditions on which they will consider a case may and have varied. For instance there was a time when if both parties placed a condition secretly, the courts would not consider the case at all, applying the doctrine of "clean hands" in accusing the marriage, and this is the court's right to so act. And conversely if the condition were *deducta in pactum,* naturally the Rota, for instance, would have something to work on, and it's placing and non-revocation and non-verification being abundantly proved it would declare the marriage invalid. But even in these cases the Rota never uses the phrase "deducta in pactum" in an absolute sense, but only in a *relative* sense, for in an *absolute* sense the phrase can be used of a condition that is *purely internal,* though it must be in the *relative* sense (*deducta in pactum*) that is, externally expressed, before one can insist on its being considered at all by the courts.

The S. R. Rota in a decision of nullity on account of a condition against the substance of marriage, says the following about the placing of a condition.

> Haec autem conditio adjici potest matrimonio duplici modo. Primo quidem modo, quando haec conditio deducitur in pactum, *i. e.,* quando nupturientes hanc conditionem ipsi inserunt contractui, ita ut sit veluti pars pacti conjugalis, et hunc casum respicit cap. ult. *De Conditionibus adpositis in desponatione,* etc., in quo haec habet Gregorius IX: "Si conditiones contra substantiam conjugii inserantur. . . ." Altero modo conditio adjici potest contractui, quin deducatur in pactum; fieri nempe potest ut aliquis nupturiens ita contrahere sibi proponat, ut obligationes matrimonii essentiales, aut etiam unam ex illis expresse et positive rejiciat, quo in casu, etiam absque pacto, matrimonium nullum est. . . .[23]

[23] 10 Maii, 1916,—*AAS,* IX (1917), 33.

From Canon 1086, par. 1, one must prove the lack of internal consent. This is difficult to do, if the intention or condition was not *deducta in pactum,* even though the recent jurisprudence of the S. Rota does not absolutely demand that the intention or the condition be *deducta in pactum,* as did the older jurisprudence of the Congregation of the Council and the Rota itself.[24]

How very difficult it is at times to *prove* the *placing* of a condition that was not clearly and openly added, and how equally difficult to find out in such cases whether the thing placed was a condition or something else, *e. g.*, an intention, a mode, a *causa,* demonstration, or *error juris* can be readily seen in the famous Boni de Castellane-Gould case,[25] in which even the judges temporarily were at a loss, and in one sentence of which concerning the same case, the judges observed:

> Verum, haec dicta sunt de *veritate speculative* circa consensum ejusque valorem objectivum; si autem quaestio fiat de *casu concreto,* praesertim, quo contrahens erroneam opinionem fovet de dissolubilitate conjugii, sive, ex gentilium corruptelis, sive ex doctrina haeretica, sive ex patriae legibus vel moribus haustam, utrum reapse in matrimoniali consensu praestando vinculum solubile simpliciter et absolute intenderit, *res ardua est dubium dirimere,* et regula quaedam juricandi requiritur.[26]

Therefore we can conclude that the judges can scarcely obtain moral certitude that the particular intention of a soluble marriage prevails over the general intention of marrying according to the intention of Christ and the Author of nature, unless the intention was

[24] For older jurisprudence, *cf.* Rota cases: (19 June, 1909), *AAS,* I, 561, 660 (24 July, 1909), 823 (6 December, 1909), for the more recent jurisprudence, *cf.* S. S. R. Rota, (1 March, 1913), *AAS,* V. 312; (8 February, 1915) VII, 292; *cf.* Vlaming, *Praelectiones Juris Matrimonii* n. 534.

[25] "Paulus de Castellane, vero spe motus recuperandae libertatis . . . matrimonium suum cum Anna Gould nullitatis accusavit ex capite defectus consensus ex parte mulieris, quippe quae matrimonium contraxerit *nonnisi cum intentione* certis in adjunctis, illud solvendi" p. 293. A definitive sentence was given "non constare de nullitate matrimonii in casu."

[26] 8 February, 1915, *in causa Neo-Eboracen., nullitatis Matri.,* (Boni de Castellane-Gould). *AAS,* VII, 295.

deducta in pactum or furnished under a condition;[27] or previously mentioned to a sufficient number of trustworthy witnesses, at a not too great distance of time from the actual celebration of the marriage.

From the beginning, says Cappello,[28] the Rota seems to have had the rule of very ancient jurisprudence which demanded that the intention be *in pactum deducta.* He cites some cases,[29] but lately however, the Rota has admitted this is not required.[30]

Some declarations from Rome, which are alleged for the contrary, and which seem not to admit nullity unless the intention or the condition was *deducta in pactum,* are to be understood of the *praesumptio juris* which militates against a limited consent (or conditional consent) when externally the marriage is celebrated absolutely. This presumption is precisely laid down in Canon 1086, par. 1. The contradictory of this presumption must be very clearly proved, and in practice this will not be easy, unless the intention was expressed by an expressed condition. A few authors have strangely asserted that the *deducta in pactum* method is the *only* means of proof. It is only the *ordinary* and *obvious* means. This presumption can be destroyed by all those arguments or proofs which beget moral certitude concerning the point at issue. Though it is known, as observed before, that the Roman courts have varied in what they consider as being sufficient evidence of a proof of fact in this regard.[31]

Cappello and many authors speak of the *intention* being *deducta in pactum.* An intention may be thus put, but authors even when treating of conditions slip into the use of the word intention being thus placed. It is true an intention against the substance of marriage, as well as a condition against the substance of marriage

[27] Chelodi, *Jus Matrimoniale,* n. 116 note.

[28] *De Matrimonio,* n. 599.

[29] R. 19 January, 1909; 8 December, n. 7, 1909; 28 July, 1909; 17 December, n. 6, 1909; 6 December, 1909; 18 December, n. 11, 1909; 17 March, 1910; 12 December, n. 9, 1910.

[30] Explicitedly, *e. g.,* March, 1913—*AAS,* IX (1917), 32; 7 February, 1915—*op. cit.,* VII (1915), 292.

[31] *Cf.* section on conditions against the *bonum sacramenti.* *Cf.* Cappello, *De Matrimonio,* n. 599.

(although this latter in reality is nothing else than an *intention* against the substance, i.e., a positive act of the will excluding something essential), may both be *deducta in pactum.* But is it true as some authors thus assert that the *condition* is *eo ipso* precisely *every intention deducta in pactum?* The reply must be in the negative, for an intention (generally speaking one against the substance of marriage is the important case) although the intention may refer *only* to the *abuse* of an essential obligation. In this latter case it does not vitiate the marital consent. It is often difficult to ascertain the real content of the intention. It is and remains an intention no matter how it is expressed, or no matter if the parties erroneously used words or phrases or sentences that externally and *per se* signify a condition. On the other hand a condition is and remains a condition no matter how expressed in words. Cappello would be more effective in his correct castigation of certain authors if he had insisted on the essential difference between an intention and a condition, which Vlaming and others seem to confuse. Vlaming writes:[32]

> Iterum tamen monemus, conditionem proprie dictam, seu intentionem in pactum deductam, non esse confundendam cum mera intentione, persuasione, opinione, proposito etc. Illa quidem, non item haec, matrimonium invalidat.[33]

An intention is not the same as a persuasion or an opinion. These are acts of the *intellect,* the intention is an act of the *will.* A true intention against the substance of marriage necessarily excludes marital consent. This is true independently of the fact whether the intention was *deducta in pactum* or not, or whether it was grammatically placed as a *condition.*

As remarked before, the condition presupposes an act of willing *marriage,* (not anything that is less than marriage, or merely labelled marriage by the party) the content of which act of willing is essentially complete with all its notes, and this *voluntarium* is made to depend for its marriage producing effect, on the *verification* of a

[32] *Praelectiones Juris Eccl.,* n. 544.

[33] He refers to Holy Office decisions about error concerning the unity and indissolubility of marriage, in *Collect. S. C. de P. Fidei,* n. 1292, 1299, 2106, 2184, 1283, 1302, 1525.

condition voluntarily placed. All this is so *ex hypothesi.* The positive will of the contractor is not to contract marriage if the *condition* be not verified, and he expresses this will with these or similar words. "I marry you, if the condition I place is verified, but if the condition which I place is not verified or fulfilled, notwithstanding my words 'I marry you,' I exclude matrimony, I do not contract." [34] On the contrary the *intention against the substance of marriage eo ipso* means and denotes and connotes that the *de facto* act of willing in the mind is complete as a psychological entity but in reference to its *object, divinely fashioned marriage,* it is essentially diseased, lacks some essential note and as a consequence there is in the mind no *true marital* consent (but what the person thinks or wills as marriage) and precisely because of this essentially defective consent, is the marriage invalid *ab initio,* and it is not invalid because a juridicially healthy consent was suspended to a condition that was not verified.[35]

Thus in the last analysis the so-called conditions against the *tria bona,* do not invalidate the marriage because of an unverified condition (for even if *per impossible* the condition were verified there could be no marriage), but because the mind of the party simply did not will marriage *in se,* but what he calls or thinks or wants to be marriage. There is no rhyme or reason in talking about the suspension of a consent *per se* incapable of causing a marriage, even if the condition were verified.[36]

The object of true marital consent is absolutely beyond the reach of human beings to change, alter or tinker with. One must will this

[34] *Cf.* Chretien, *Praelectiones de Matr.* (Metis 1927), p. 36, *cf.* Gougnard, *De Matr.* p. 143.

[35] *De Matrimonio,* n. 599. This study concerns *conditions,* but in view of what is said above about "conditions against the substance," I feel justified, when warranted, to speak of *intentions.* Besides to know well when a state of mind has conditional content and when not, it is necessary to discuss intentions *qua* intentions.

[36] It *is possible* to place *a condition* "of divorce" if it signifies only the abuse of the *bonum fidei.* It *is not possible* to place a *condition* of divorce *a vinculo* to marital consent because a *condition suspends* or renders objectively *uncertain,* the effect of an act of the will *to marry,* which act of the will is *ex hypothesi* not present. Marital consent by its very nature includes an *indissoluble bond.*

institution with all its *substantialia*, or *not will it at all.* "Contractus —matrimonium—uti docet D'Annibale, 'qua est contractus naturalis regitur tum jure naturae tum jure evangelico, ubique gentium.' Et in nota 17 explicat, 'huic autem juri nulli humanae potestati derogare, subrogare, abrogare datum est.' "[87]

There is a perfect circle of an *unum totum* in which are three essential blessings, besides for the baptized the totality of a Sacrament, all this fashioned by God, and this as it is *per se, is* and *must be* the *object* of the *marital* consent of every human being. The human will cannot substantially change, limit, modify or rebuild this object of marital consent, namely marriage. Thus it is that an intention by which one says in effect, "I do not will this essential element of marriage, but something else that I fashioned according to my notions and desire," thus it is, that the marital consent in this case is non-existent for nothing can exist if it lacks an essential constituent part; for an essential element is defined precisely as that without which a thing can not be or exist, without which it can not have *esse.* Precisely because of this such marriages cannot be convalidated by a *sanatio in radice.* In one word, strictly speaking, it is *impossible* to have a *condition* that is contrary to the substance of marriage, added to a *true* and essentially healthy act of the will *to marry.*

On the other hand, it is *possible,* to have a condition that (*in se*) is contrary to the substance of true marriage, added to an act of the will to contract a union that is *not marital,* that is *not marriage* (though this union may be, erroneously or maliciously, called marriage by the party or parties). But in this latter possibility, it is essentially a misnomer to call the transaction "an act of the will *to marry*" given under a condition *against* the *substance* of *marriage.* The reason is this. The mutual *matrimonial* consent is precisely and identically this "actus voluntatis" of Canon 1081. And this "actus voluntatis" is precisely and identically (possessing all its *substantialia*) the *traditio* and the *acceptatio.* The *traditio, etc., is* the act of the *will delivering and accepting,* and the delivering and accepting of the rights and obligations *is* the act of the will. The act of the marital will *is not* one thing, and the tradition etc. another thing. No, they are one and the same thing. There is only a *logical* distinction be-

[87] S. R. Rota, 11 August, 1910; *AAS,* II (1910), 972.

tween them, not a *real* one. In other words it is impossible psychologically and in reality to have this mutual act of the will and not to have the *traditio eo ipso*. The two are inseparable. In some other contracts there is a priority of time between the act of the will of *e. g.*, selling and the delivery (at least in some Roman law transactions) but this is not true here. The Code in Cannon 1081, par. 2, very accurately says: "Consensus matrimonialis est actus voluntatis (not any act of the will, but) *quo* utraque pars *tradit* (not, will give) et *acceptat* (not, will receive), *jus* in *corpus*, perpetuum et exclusivuum, in ordine ad actus per se aptos ad prolis generationem." This seems to be precisely the reason, why marriages contracted with a diriment impediment (ecclesiastical or natural) are invalid, the act of the wills was *not* such acts of the wills as demanded by Canon 1081, par. 2. And this too explains how when the impediments are removed (not perpetual natural ones) or the condition is verified, then we have the *simultaneous* act of the *will giving and receiving*. The *sanatio in radice*, and the condition have each a part of an essential that is virtually present when the obex preventing the *traditio* is removed, namely the impediment or the verification or revocation of the condition, and at this moment and only then is there a mutual will giving and receiving. Before this moment, there is only the wish, the hope of giving, or the *inefficacious will to give*, but there is not present before this moment a *will actually giving* over marital rights. To assert such a will is present before the removal of the impediment or fulfillment of the condition is to overthrow and undermine the entire doctrine underlying the right and the ability of the Church to institute diriment impediments, as well as to undermine the doctrine on conditional consent. To maintain that the act of the will, of one who is bound by a diriment impediment, *eo ipso tradit et acceptat jus etc.*, is to maintain the absurdity that the marriage is *valid* in spite of the impediment, for the giving and receiving of marital rights necessarily constitutes a true marriage. The very purpose or effect of an ecclesiastical diriment impediment is to make the person *inhabilis to give* and *receive the jus* mentioned in Cannon 1081, par. 2.

Yet in spite of all this, the Decretals and the Code and canonists have ample justification for speaking of "*condition*s against the substance" if for no other reason than it is a consecrated use, and especially because such intentions if expressed at all are usually expressed in word or phrase that is grammatically conditional. But it is not correct to state that the condition is precisely the intention *deducta in pactum,* for the two things are essentially different, one is a circumstance elevated to effect a suspension of an act, the other in *re matrimoniali* is a diseased content of the will (presupposing of course that it is an "intention against the substance of marriage" and not an irrelevant intention, *e. g.,* to have the intention to make the women live a gypsy life, or to wear black clothes); and these two things can not become identical just because of a mode of their external expression.

Again it may be observed that this defective intention or a condition has very slight chance in the external forum of being *proved* as existent unless its external manifestation or expression was quite clear and obvious, and ordinarily the obvious way is *deducere in pactum.* This last phrase does not mean that the intention or the condition must be in writing, for rotal decisions say it can be verified by words orally expressed only; nor does it mean the condition must be known or placed by both parties. Yes, it can be gathered that the intention or the condition need not be necessarily expressed, or be *deducta in pactum,* for the Rota again has taken cases like these.

Cappello rightly finds fault with certain authors who say the intention excluding marriage, or the *jus ad copulam,* or any essential property, should appear in the formula of the marriage contract or placed expressly as a condition, else the marriage is valid. This is false and to be rejected both because an *intention* against the substance *per se* without being raised to a condition, invalidates according to Canon 1086, par. 2, which simply demands a *positive act* of the *will excluding* something *essential;* the above statement is also false in stating that the intention should appear in the formula of the marriage contract. The same canon says the marriage is invalid without this. The statement is false in saying that unless the intention be made a condition or expressed in the formula the marriage is *valid.* This is diametrically opposed to natural and Canon Law (Canon 1086). Those who teach thus confound the *medium probationis* by which a fact, concerning this exclusion of some essential of marriage, is made certain in the judicial forum of the court, with the very nature of the thing itself, (*i.e.*, the nature and effects of an intention or consent), and with the actual existence of the intention.

As observed more than once, the courts of Rome in their jurisprudence may and have simply refused to consider many cases when the intention or the condition was not *deducta in pactum* (defined differently by the courts at different periods in their history) and thus as far as the courts were concerned, they simply stated, the marriages were valid, meaning, it can not be proved that they are invalid because the proofs are declared insufficient. This is good jurisprudence, but some canonists err in confusing the *stylus curiae Romanae* with the essential doctrine governing intentions against the substance of marriage, and conditions. For after all it is not the courts' place *ex professo to define doctrine* but to render judgements based on doctrine, and good jurisprudence built on doctrine.

In a word this difficult phrase (*deducta in pactum*) simply means in an absolute sense that the condition is a condition, that is, suspends the very marital effect of consent. *Relatively*, as a *probationis medium*, its limits and evidential value have varied according to the way the courts define it, *e. g.*, at one time both parties must agree; at another time one party alone can place a condition as *deducta in pactum* in the sense of the external forum.[38]

Against a simulated consent, *i.e.*, when one uses words expressing consent but has no internal will to contract the marriage, there is the *presumptio juris* of Canon 1086. The Roman law had a like presumption: "Nemo existimandus est dixisse, quod non mente agitaverit." [39]

To overcome this presumption that the words uttered externally reveal the inner intention it is not sufficient to affirm such a contrary simulation, it must be proved. If three things concur this proof is had: The confession of the one who simulated, especially if sworn to immediately after the contract; a manifest reason for the simulation;

[38] *Cf.* De Smet, *De Spons. et Matr.*, 151, n. 1; Cappello, *op. cit.*, n. 599; who cite Rota decisions interpreting the phrase in various meanings, *e. g.*, in a stricter sense; *cf. causa Parisien,* 10 May, 1916, *AAS*, IX, 32.

[39] Fr. 7, par. a, D. 33, 10.

and circumstances before, during, and after the transaction which show the affair was a simulated one.[40]

As observed by Chelodi and Cappello, these principles are applied over and over again in cases before the new Rota. In the beginning it applied the more ancient jurisprudence. Both these authors cite rotal cases illustrating both jurisprudences.

We may conclude this part with the words of Wernz-Vidal: [41]

> Nihil autem refert quoad effectum juridicum, utrum conditio apposita fuerit in actu celebrationis an antea nec revocata; utrum in pactum deducta, vel non; utrum ab una tantum parte, an ab utraque; utrum apposita fuerit publice, an occulte ita ut in foro externo probari non possit, utrum ae ab una dumtaxat parte fuit apposita alteri parti fuerit cognita, vel non. At conditionis occulte appositae et in foro externo non probatae in hoc foro nulla habenda est ratio.

[40] *Cf. S. C. C. causa Chien.*, 12 March, 1729; Richter, *Lehrbuch d. Kath-u. evang. KRS* (1842), p. 281, n. 141; *causa Mutien.*, 8 July, 1725; d. Gasparri, II, 917; *causa Granaten.*, 28 September, 1743—Richter, *op. cit.*, p. 232, n. 59; *C. Parisien*, 7 March, 1885; *AAS* 18, 14-31; Rota, 1 July, 1911; *AAS* III (1911), 525; simulation is proved in these cases. But if the confession of the one who simulated is lacking it seems the proof is then not sufficient, *cf.* 12 August, 1912—*AAS* IV (1912), 708.

[41] *Jus Matrimoniale, Romae,* 1925, V, n. 514; *cf.* Cappello, o.c., n. 638.

CHAPTER XII

THE NATURE AND EFFECTS OF CONDITIONAL CONSENT

The general theory of consent furnished under a condition, as shown in the historical section, was given by Pope Gregory IX,[2] but Cardinal Gasparri,[3] says with the exception of necessary and possible honest conditions. It is true the passage of Gregory does not expressly mention possible future honest conditions, but as brought out before, implicitly and necessarily, and as a consequence, the doctrine about future conditions can easily be seen by a process of elimination.

Cardinal Gasparri and others show that before the Code a condition was classified somehow as an impediment and he says one should interpret the responses emanating from Rome before 1918 according to this impedimental viewpoint. The Council of Trent did not introduce any change in this discipline, nor did its legislation about the form of the celebration of marriage directly touch it. The Code recast the former legislation, and gave it a more precise expression.

Conditional marital consent is consent to which is added a condition, that is, a circumstance to which the consent is bound and

[1] Wernz-Vidal, *Jus Matrimoniale*, n. 509 s.; Leitner, *Lehrbuch des Katholischen Eherechts* (1902), p. 127 s; Aichner, *Compendium Jus. Eccl.* (1895), par. 169; Devoti, *Institutionum Canonicarum libri quator, l.c.*, par. 146; Sanchez, *De Matr.*, lib. V, disp. 1; Van de Burgt, *Tractatus de Matr.* (1875) p. 65 s.; Schulte, *Handbuch des Katholischen Eherchts* (1855), par. 21; Gasparri, *De Matr.* (1904), n. 980; (1932), n. 878; Rosset, *De Sacr. Matri*, 6 vols. (1895-96), n. 170 sq.; Schnitzer, *Katholischen Eherecht* (1918), 314 sq.; Freisen, *Geschichte des canonischen Eherechts*, 2 ed., 1895, p. 232 sq.; Moy, *Das Ehercht* (1883), p. 60, 329; Esmein, *Le Mariage* (1891), I, p. 171 sq., II, p. 216 sq.; Vlaming, *Praelectiones Juris Matr.* 1919, n. 541 sq.; Chelodi, *Jus Matrimoniale*, 2 ed., 1919, n. 123 sq.; Cappello, *De Matr.*, n. 625 sq.; De Smet, *op. cit.* (1920), n. 151 sq.; Cerato, *Matrimonium* (1919), n. 88; Berardi, *Jus Eccl.*, tom III, disp. II, cap. 1, etc.

[2] Cap. ult, X "*De Conditionibus appositis*, IV, 5.

[3] *De Matrimonio* (1932), n. 880.

upon the verification of which the consent has its juridical and matrimonial causing effect.[4] The condition must actually be placed (not merely interpretatively).

It might be well to emphasize here that it is not the *marriage,* but the *consent* that receives the condition. If Freisen thinks he is subtle in insisting, to use the words of Vidal, "non existeret *matrimonia conditionata* (quoad vincula) sed *conditionatam matrimoniorum celebrationem,*" he is as Vidal [5] points out, three centuries late for Sanchez [6] and others before and since have plainly enunciated this. Marriage itself does not receive the condition but the matrimonial consent, that is, the consent given to marriage can depend on a condition, by no means the marriage itself. For as long as the condition is in pendency, "matrimonium quoad vinculum, non est." "Matrimonium ipsum conditionem non recipit, bene tamen ejus consensus. Hoc est consensus praestitus ad matrimonium potest ex condicione pendere, *at matrimonium ipsum* minime. Quia quamdiu conditio pendet, *matrimonium* [quoad vinculum] non est." [7] Pichler says: "Matrimonium sub conditione honesta, extrinseca de futuro contingenti . . . *valet quidem* sed ante eventum conditionis *non absolute.*" [8]

This difference of terminology can be reconciled if one distinguishes consent which is true and revocable from consent which is efficacious and irrevocable. For *consensus conditionatus est verus consensus, sed nondum irrevocabilis et efficax,* to produce its principal effect, namely the bond of marriage, before the verification of the event and therefore it does not follow, that *ab initio* it lacks all efficacy, for it produces a true, not a quasi-obligation of awaiting fulfillment.[9] One should not speak of conditional *marriage,* but of condi-

[4] *Cf.* De Smet, *De Sponsalibus et Matrimonio,* n. 151, for the nature of a condition; and Wernz-Vidal, *op. cit.,* n. 510; Schmalzgrueber, lib. IV, tit V, n. 1 sq.; Reiffenstuel, IV, V, n. 2 sq., et lib. III, tit. 26, *de testamento,* n. 656; Rosset, *op. cit.,* n. 170 s; Ballerini-Palmiere, *Opus Theol. Moral.,* VI, n. 265 s.; St. Thomas, *Theol. Moral.,* 4 D., 29 qu., unica; St. Bonaventure, 4 D., 28.

[5] Freisen, *Geschichte des canonischen Eherechts,* 2 ed. (1893), p. 254; *cf.* Vidal, *Jus Matrimoniale,* n. 512.

[6] *De Matrimonio,* lib. V, disp. 1, n. 5.

[7] Sanchez, *loc. cit., cf.* Reiffenstuel, lib. IV, tit. V, 15; Wernz-Vidal, *loc. cit.*

[8] *Candidatus Juris Prudentiae Sacrae* (1733), n. 3.

[9] Thus Wernz-Vidal, *Jus. Matri.* n. 512; *cf.* Gasparri, *De Matri.* (1903), n. 988; Leitner, *Lehrbuch, des Katholisöhen Eherchts* (1902), p. 131.

tional marriage *consent*. For marriage itself does not receive the condition but the consent. Marriage does not yet exist to receive the condition, the consent does. Marriage *per se* is always absolute.[10] It is more correct to say the internal consent, better the *act of willing* receives the condition rather than the *contract*, for in some cases the expression of the words of consent by both parties, which is the *contract* legally speaking, does not have the condition attached.

Tamburini [11] also long ago complained that some authors make no distinction between conditional marriage and conditional consent and he praises Sanchez for being accurate, adding that consent can be conditional, marriage never, and when the consent is conditioned, there is no true marriage yet and when the consent is purified, there is true absolute marriage.

Canon 1092, n. 3, reads: "Conditio semel apposita et non revocata: Si de futuro licita, valorem *matrimonii* suspendit." Just because the canon does not go on to explain the obvious, and state categorically that, if the condition is verified, marriage immediately arises without any new consent, some theologians say this all amounts to an *engagement*. Even Creusen [12] says this suspension can be understood in a twofold way, first as an engagement and not as marriage, for marriage requires a present *traditio*, and he adds if you admit this opinion of the theologians and a few canonists, it is easily understood why marriage, with a third person is valid, if contracted before verification of the condition; and why, if the condition is verified, the consent must be renewed. Of course he does not admit this opinion. The canon expressly states the validity of the *marriage* is suspended, not the validity of an *engagement*. Others say true marital consent is given, but its efficacy is suspended, till the condition is verified and from the nature of the thing, consent does not have to be renewed. If you adhere to this opinion, says Creusen, it is more difficult to understand the validity of marriage with a third person during pendency, and according to him no one clearly explains it (*"quod nemo clare explicat"*). The explanation from the positive will of the legislator to which the parties should accommodate themselves, to wit:

[10] Bayon, *De Matr.*, p. 306.

[11] *Explicatio Decalogi*, lib. VIII, tract. IV, cap. 5.

[12] *Epitome J. Canonici*, Vol. II, n. 381.

the *Dominium rei, i. e.*, the right in the body is not transferred except by absolute immediate consent as such, or such through the verification of the condition, is erroneous. The true answer is that in every *conditional* marriage contract (and in some civil contracts also), the consent is revocable. Creusen says in some contracts and in marriage the consent is so confirmed by the law that it validly cannot be revoked. This is an important confusion. *Absolute* mutual consent cannot be validly revoked, because simultaneously with it there is the *vinculum matrimonii,* by nature perpetual and indissoluble till death. But the question is not about marriage (*quoad vinculum*) but about the efficient cause of marriage, human consent, and this human consent by natural law is made to depend for its marriage producing effect on a future circumstance, and until this circumstance is verified there is no marriage and anytime before verification one can naturally revoke the condition itself, or the consent itself, validly, and sometimes licitly; sometimes sinfully. That is just the very nature and purpose of a condition, and its application to marital consent is in accordance with the full doctrine of liberty and freedom of choice about marriage.[13]

Cardinal Gasparri puts it this way: [14] "In casu appositae suspensivae conditionis matrimonium non est nullum, sed ejus valor in suspenso est (rel. Canon 1092, n. 3), sicuti in suspenso est matrimonialis consensus, illi conditioni alligatus."

It operates somewhat like consent given when diriment impediments of ecclesiastical origin are present, and if consent is to be renewed in some cases, after the removal of the impediment, it is not from the *natural* law but from *positive Church law,* as is clear in *sanatio in radice* cases. The presumption is that the consent perseveres (Canon 1093) and the obex to its efficacy being removed by lifting the impediment, or by the revocation or verification of the condition, the originally given consent, if actually it has not been positively revoked, produces its natural effect, *i. e.,* the marriage bond. The doctrine that the consent can and does persevere, if it has not been actually and positively revoked, is a certain doctrine and used

[13] *Cf.* Sanchez, *De Matr.*, lib. V, disp. VII, n. 5; Gasparri, *De Matr.* (1903), n. 845 (1932), n. 915.

[14] *Op. cit.* (1932), n. 915; *cf.* Cappello, *De Matr.*, n. 640.

by the Church for ages. It is meaningless for the Code of Canon Law to speak of the revocation of the conditional consent or of the condition alone ("conditio semel apposita et non revocata," Canon 1092), unless the original consent can *per se* persevere. Revocation presupposes perseverance.[15]

Many authors evoking Canon 1133 say, if the condition is, "if the pope dispenses," *ex jure positivo,* renewal of consent is necessary.[16] But Canon 1133 has no application to the case of a *condition,* since the marriage was not *attempted,* nor can it be said that something is *irritum,* which does not yet exist, the marriage exists only when the condition is verified and *eo ipso* from the nature of the condition (or dispensation) it is licit too, and if licit it can not be *irritum.*[17]

The proper rôle of a condition is, it is absolutely bound up with the consent as with the principal object of consent (*i. e.,* marriage) and it forms an *unum,* or unity which becomes and is the very substance of the contract and verified or not, the consent falls or not. The fate and fortune of one is the fate and fortune of the latter. The evidence of this strong binding together into one is shown by the use of such particles and phrases as "if," "unless," "provided that," "on condition that," and expressions of similar import and therefore the conditional circumstance is totally different in effect from that circumstance that may have influenced the giving of consent and perhaps gave cause to it, yet is not bound up with it, but the consent is pure and absolute, and such circumstances are chiefly the *modus, causa, et demonstratio.*[18]

Does any kind of true condition placed to marital consent have force and efficacy? Yes, in the internal forum, if seriously placed, the

[15] *Cf.* Vlaming, *Praelectiones Juris Matrimonii,* II, n. 552; *cf.* on the consent persevering: Linneborn, *Grundriss des Eherechts,* 1933; Canons 1092, 1093 V. Scherer, *Handbuch d. K. Rs.* (1866), II, p. 186; Sagmuller, *Kirchenrechts,* II, 3 ed., p. 144; Ronke, *"Die richlichte Bedeuting des Irritums,"* p. 66 f; Freisen, *Geschicte des Canonischen Eherechts,* 2 ed. (1893), p. 233 f; Esmein *Le Mariage,* ed., 2, 1, 191 f.

[16] Chelodi, *op. cit.,* n. 126; De Smet, *op. cit.,* n. 153; Vlaming, *op. cit.,* n. 549.

[17] *Cf.* in this sense Gougnard, *De Matrimonio,* p. 145; Cappello, *De Matrimonio,* n. 640; Wernz-Vidal, *Jus Matrimoniale,* n. 514.

[18] *Cf.* Vlaming, *op. cit.,* II, n. 538; *cf.* Section on the various kinds of conditions, where the mode, etc., are discussed.

marriage before God and according to natural law is present upon the verification, or the marriage is not present if the conditions are unfulfilled. But by no means is this true in the external forum. Speaking of all kinds of conditions (not only true conditions in the strict sense), some partly from the very nature of the case, partly from Canon 1092 (for the external forum only) *destroy themselves* either by nature or by common law (for the external forum only); others *destroy marital consent,* either by nature or Canon Law explaining the law of nature; others neither destroy themselves (*vitiantur*) nor destroy marital consent (*non vitiant*) for they exert the natural force and efficacy of a true condition and suspend the consent or render its efficacy uncertain.

Or to say the same thing in other words, some conditions, once placed and not revoked before verification, are presumed to effect nothing; for they are vitiated or held as not having been seriously placed, *e. g.*, future conditions that are necessary, or impossible or simply immoral and not contrary to the substance of marriage.[19] Others in both fora render the marriage invalid, namely *future* conditions against the substance.[20] Some other conditions in both fora suspend the validity of the marriage, namely future licit conditions.[21] And finally, some others, namely past and present conditions, whether morally good, bad, or indifferent and in both fora, sometimes destroy the effect of the consent immediately (*i. e.*, if the past or present condition is unverified), sometimes the consent is immediately efficacious (*i. e.*, if the condition is verified).

What conditions destroy themselves?

What conditions destroy the consent and thus render the marriage invalid?

What conditions suspend the consent?

What conditions do not suspend the consent nor destroy themselves nor are destroyed, but render the marriage immediately valid or not according to the conditions being actually or having been in the past fulfilled or not? The answer in detailed application to these queries will be found later on in their respective chapters.

[19] Canon 1092, n. 1.

[20] Canon 1092, n. 2.

[21] Canon 1092, n. 3.

CHAPTER XIII

NECESSARY, IMPOSSIBLE, AND IMMORAL CONDITIONS IN GENERAL

THE next few articles will be devoted to discussions of past, present and future, necessary, impossible and immoral conditions. Some of these (*i. e.*, the future conditions) are rejected by the law just as if they were not placed. But it is well to keep in mind that this law is only a *praesumptio juris tantum,* and this presumption cedes to the truth, even in the external forum. If for instance, these kinds of future conditions were placed seriously and the nupturients intended to make their consent depend on the truth of the condition, then the condition obtains its natural native juridical effect, that is, impossible conditions render the consent inefficacious to produce marriage; necessary ones make the marriage valid when the event is verified; and immoral conditions suspend the effect just as honest ones do. This is true in the internal forum if they were seriously placed, yet if a *proof* of such serious intention were not had, the courts would consider them as not having been placed.[1] It will be useful to preface our discussion with some remarks about what is a *fictio juris* (which is often misapplied to our doctrine of presumptions) and to enumerate the *presumptiones juris* in the Code.

The *fictio juris* is based on the will of the legislator. It is used when there is a right to produce some juridical effect conformable to natural equity. It presupposes something, or feigns something, *receives something for the truth, which in reality is not true,* but could have been very well true physically and morally. Alciatus defined it: "Fictio juris est, legis adversus veritatem in re possibili et justa de causa dispositio." [2]

[1] De Smet, *De Sponsalibus et Matrimonio,* n. 152; Vlaming, *De Matrimonio,* n. 543; Chelodi, *Jus Matrimoniale,* n. 124; Wernz-Vidal, *Jus Matrimoniale,* n. 517; *cf.* L. 9 D., *de novatione,* 46, 2; Schmalzgrueber, lib. IV, tit. V, n. 66; Sanchez, *De Matrimonio,* lib. 5, dist. 3, n. 19.

[2] P. Cerato, *Matrimonium,* ed. 4 (1929), p. 231.

"*Logice* fictio est creatio juridica aliquorum effectuum alterius facti (fingitur super falso)." [3] The word is not to be taken in a moral sense, as though the fiction of law is a juridical lie. A *fictio* supposes either, that there *exists* some facts which in reality *hic et nunc does not exist;* or it supposes that some fact *does not exist* which in reality *hic et nunc does exist.*

By force of this supposition the law recognizes positive or negative effects of the fact which it supposes exists or does not exist. It does not refer therefore to simulation in the true and proper meaning, for the effects, at least indirectly, are referred to a fact that is posited or placed, and to which are ascribed, in the case, effects of another fact that is *supposed* to exist.

The *fictio juris* was due to the demands of rigid formularies and legalisms. The Roman pretors often used it in order to avoid what would appear as novelties in the law, or rather in the interpretation of the law. This device is exceedingly useful for a threefold reason. First, to avoid useless circumlocutions by using simple known formulas; secondly, to integrate the primary notion with its correlates and with other facts; and thirdly, to clearly show the derivation and genesis of something. A *fictio juris* is not *epikeia;* nor the *aequitas canonica* mentioned in Canon 20.

Fictiones juris in re matrimoniali are: (1) When a marriage is healed or sanated in its very root (*consensus est radix matrimonii*) the marriage takes its canonical effects from the time of its invalid contracting (Canon 1138); (2) a child legitimatized by a subsequent marriage, is considered as born in wedlock and therefore is put on an equality with legitimate children (Canon 1116); (3) children born of a putative marriage are considered legitimate, just as those born of a true marriage (Canon 1114); (4) a person conceived is considered born as often as it treats of favorable laws, and therefore has juridical capacity for those favorable laws (*e. g.*, Canon 1116); (5) a condition added to marital consent, which condition is future necessary, or impossible, or base, but not against the substance of marriage, is considered as not having been placed (Canon 1092, N. I.); (6) marriage is *contracted* when before the pastor and witnesses a *conditional* consent is declared. Though the

[3] D'Angelo, *Jus Digestorum*, n. 621.

marriage is valid only at the moment of verification, it is, say some authors,[4] by a *fictio juris,* considered as contracted from the moment of its conditional celebration before the pastor. It is not necessary to resort to a fiction of law in this case. The decree *Tametsi* and Canon 1094 are substantially observed by the above mentioned celebration.

A *fictio juris* differs absolutely from a *praesumptio juris,* nor can the two be confounded or identified. These differences are: the fiction of law is assumed *in casu certo et contra veritatem* to obtain some effect in conformity with natural equity. But a presumption of law is used *in casu dubio,* according to what seems probable, for the purpose of investigating the truth. Proof, direct or indirect, to the contrary, is admitted against the presumption, and if obtained the presumption falls. A fiction of law admits no proof to the contrary. A presumption is a species of proof, not so the fiction. A presumption may also be a presumption of man, the legal fiction is only of the *law.* Many presumptions can concur simultaneously, not so fictions of law. A presumption can be extended from person to person, a fiction can not. A presumption treats about factual things, a fiction about things that are factual and juridical (*facti juris*).[5]

A presumption is the same thing as an opinion. "Praesumptio consistit in admittendis ut certis aliquibus factis incertis quin probentur."[6] Its foundation is reasoning or *argumentum verisimilitudinis,* based on that which, in the same circumstances, ordinarily happens. It has especial importance in the matter of judicial proof, though it is by no means confined to judicial processes. By reason of origin, presumptions proceed either from the law (*praesumptio juris*) or from the judge or priest (*praesumptio facti seu hominis*). The *praesumptiones juris* may be "*juris tantum,*" which admit direct proof to the contrary (*praesumptio cedit veritati*);[7] or "*juris et de jure,*" which do not admit *direct* proof to the contrary.[8]

[4] *Cf.* De Smet, *De Sponsalibus et Matrimonio,* n. 154.

[5] *Cf.* Maroto, *Institutiones Juris Canonici,* n. 213.

[6] D'Angelo, *op. cit.,* n. 627.

[7] L. 40, 4 D, 3, 3.

[8] Venerable Ferrini, maintained that the notion of presumption was entirely

Praesumptiones juris in re matrimoniali are: (1) Marriage enjoys the favor of the law, therefore in doubt the validity is upheld (Canon 1014); (2) the *privilegium fidei* enjoys the favor of law over marriage, and everything else in a doubtful case (Canon 1127); (3) marriage having been celebrated, its consummation is presumed, if the couple have lived together (Canon 1015); (4) if the impediment of impotency is doubtful *juris*, or *facti*, marriage is not to be forbidden (Canon 1068); (5) if one at the time of the marriage contract was commonly considered as being baptized, or if his baptism was doubtful, the validity of the marriage must be upheld (Canon 1070); (6) after puberty, ignorance about the nature of marriage, namely that it is a permanent union between one man and one woman for the purpose of procreating offspring, is not presumed (Canon 1082); (7) the internal consent of the will is always presumed to conform to the words and signs used in the celebration (Canon 1086); (8) the consent once given is presumed to continue (Canon 1093); (9) children are presumed legitimate who were born at least six months from the day of the celebration of marriage, or within ten months from the day of the husband's death, or the dissolution of the marital life (Canon 1115).

Finally it may be stated that Canon 1092, in so far as in the external forum, it considers certain conditions as not placed it is similar to a *fictio juris*, but in so far as the canon *presumes* these conditions were placed not seriously but *ex joco*, etc., it is a *presumptio juris*. Canon 1092 by presumption rejects as not having been added seriously all *future* conditions that are necessary, immoral, or impossible. *Past* and *present* conditions that are necessary, immoral, or impossible conditions are *not* rejected. Each kind of the above conditions will now be considered separately, after first making some remarks about an underlying principle of our doctrine, namely the *favor matrimonii*.

The favor shown to marriage is a certain protection the Church throws around marriage on acount of its excellency and dignity and

unknown to the jurisconsults of the classic Roman era; it was evolved by those of the Justinian era, though others deny this. Ferrini, "*Le presunzioni in dir. rom.*" *Rivista italiania di Scienze guiridiche*, Roma, XIX (1893), p. 258; *cf.* D'Angelo, *Jus Digestorum*, n. 630.

most sacred indissolubility, against whatever attacks its juridicity and validity.[9] This canonical favor of marriage cedes to the privilege of faith. Non-consummated Christian marriages are dissolved by solemn religious profession.

Matrimonium gaudet favore juris, quare in dubio standum est pro valore matrimonii, donec contrarium probetur, salvo praescripto Canon 1127.[10] Every marriage, even a pagan one, if it has the *species matrimonii,* enjoys this favor, with the exceptions mentioned.

It is a general principle that when an act has been performed it ought to be considered valid until it is proved to be null. This applies in a special manner to marriage. To pronounce a marriage null without sufficient evidence is to run the risk of "setting asunder what God hath joined together." The burden of proof lies on the one who attacks the marriage.[11]

The fact of the celebration of marriage, as any fact, is not presumed, but must be proved. But marriage once celebrated provided it did not lack the appearance of marriage (*species matrimonii*) enjoys this favor, for "Tolerabilius est enim aliquos contra statuta hominum dimittere copulatos, quam conjunctos legitime contra statuta Domini separare."[12] Even if it be not clear concerning the contracting of marriage, this case often has enjoyed this favor.[13] This last point has been confirmed by the jurisprudence of the Roman Congregations, the Rota and the Signatura Apostolica.[14]

It is disputed whether this favor holds for marriage contracted in fear, some say it is better to pronounce against the marriage,[15]

[9] The Roman law has a like doctrine in its treatise on the manumission of slaves, called *causa libertatis. Cf.* D. 40, I s, and L.1, D. 40, IV.

[10] Canon 1014; *cf.* Canons 1069, 1119, 1127, 586, par. 3.

[11] *Cf.* Vlaming, *Praelectiones Juris Matrimonii,* I, n. 60; Ayrinhac, *Marriage Legislation in the New Code of Canon Law* (New York, 1918), n. 7.

[12] Innocentius III in c. 47, X *de testibus, etc.,* II, 20; St. Alphonsus, *Theologia Moralis,* lib. VI, n. 907; Sanchez, *Jus. Can. U.,* lib. I, disp. 18, n. 5.

[13] *Cf.* S. C. C. to the Apostolic Vicars of Oceanica, 18 December, 1872; S. C. Off. in instruction to the Bishop of Nesqually (Seattle), 1877; *cf.* Gasparri, *De Matrimonio* (1932), n. 18.

[14] Gasparri, *op. cit.,* n. 20.

[15] *e. g.,* Schmalzgrueber, lib. IV, tit. I, n. 401.

but Cardinal Gasparri says the jurisprudence is against this view. It is because of this favor of the law regarding the validity of marriage, that it operates in the form of a presumption of law, to exclude certain conditions (future immoral, impossible, necessary) which are *a priori* rejected as not placed, in the external forum, but this rejection rests only on a *presumptio juris,* that cedes to the truth.

Thus this *favor juris* implies two things: If it is certain marriage was *celebrated,* always it is held valid till nullity is fully proved. This holds good whether the doubt is *dubium juris, sive facti.* Secondly, even if it be not certain concerning the celebration, provided the marriage can show possession *pro se,* the same principle of Canon 1014 holds good, except when using the Pauline Privilege, therefore marriages of infidel converts will be declared null if there is a prudent doubt about their validity.[16] For such doubtful celebrations the general principles of proof of any fact must be applied, *e. g.,* if witnesses were present who can fully prove it though the *conjuges* deny; if no witnesses were present, but both admit the fact of marriage, unless this is harmful to a third party or to the State; if both deny, *habetur pro non contracto;* if one affirms, the other denies, the former must prove it, and if he fails, the marriage is not sustained.[17]

[16] Ben. XIV in Epis. "*Probe te,*" 15 December, 1751, par. 27; S.O. 9 December, 1874; 19 April, 1889; *ASS,* XXXI, 694; S. O. to Bp. Nesqueally (Seattle) 1877, also 30 June, 1910; esp. Chelodi, *Jus Matrimoniale,* n. 6.

[17] *Cf.* Chelodi, *op. cit.,* n. 6, 7, 129.

CHAPTER XIV

NECESSARY CONDITIONS

ONLY in form are those transactions conditional which are made for their existence dependent on a fact which in its very nature or in virtue of a legal principle must happen in the future. Yet the party or parties may mean seriously to await the actual materialization of the condition, and in this case, the marriage consent is suspended in reality, and also for the external forum if this intention was amply proved, otherwise the court or priest judging would presume it was placed not seriously with the intention of suspending the consent. Necessary future conditions, whether known as such or not by the parties, are by a presumption, held not placed. This *presumptio juris* must cede however to the contrary truth, if this be proved. This is true too of negative impossible conditions. If the necessary conditions be placed seriously so as to suspend, it signifies the party did so to give adequate expression to a presupposition to the resolution of his will. If he seriously thinks it is a future event (legally future) and binds his will to do it, and proves it, then his condition is not considered as not being placed, but is considered as lawfully placed, and the result is valid on verification.

A materialistic philosophic viewpoint will abstract from the operations of natural forces as being necessarily operative by necessary potency and will consider them as furnishing merely the impetus to the causation of the effect. The Romans did not accept in this case any pendency in the transaction, and they made a distinction between two groups of cases, really only one group, viz., in which the condition is necessarily verified, and that in which it necessarily cannot be verified, and they established different principles for either group. The reason why the Romans did so is obscure, but this treatment is an historical fact that influenced jurisprudential evolutions.[1]

[1] *Cf.* v. Hussarek, *Die Bedingte Eheschliessung*, n. 207. "Qui sub conditione stipulatur, quae omnimodo exstitura est pure videtur stipulari." L. 9, par, 1 D., *de novat. et deleg.*, XLVI, 2; *cf.*, Historical Section on Roman Law.

"Conditio semel apposita et non revocata: Si sit de futuro necessaria, pro non adjecta habeatur." [2] A necessary condition *de futuro* works on the same principle as an intrinsic condition that inheres in the contract.[3] If therefore the future condition is intrinsic in the nature of the thing or by disposition of law, *regularly* the marriage is valid without delay. This is true also if the condition is extrinsically necessary, *e. g.*, "if the sun rises." The reason being that the condition is already determined in its cause, and considered as already existing and thus the obligation *eo ipso* arises, though in fact the sun has not yet risen. If the condition is seriously placed as a *conditio sina qua non*, it suspends and the presumption that it was not meant to suspend, cedes to the truth. "If the sun rises" is generally more of a demonstrative than a conditional consent, equivalent to: "As it is certain the sun will rise tomorrow, so it is certain I marry you now." Some authors say it is rejected because it is placed *ex joco*. In a word all agree about the rejection by the Church, but authors differ about the reasons why the Church so legislates.

It is a different story if the meaning is this: "I marry you when the sun rises." This is a predetermination of time. It is marital not engagement consent. It can happen that one or both through ignorance or design wish to wait till the verification of this necessary condition. All these things must be gathered from the circumstances and a study of the individual case.[4] If it is believed contingent, it would suspend; for then in the intention the condition was contingent and therefore the effect of a contingent event would take place. Thus the law about necessary conditions is modified by circumstances, *e. g.*, if a delay is meant, as "if my father dies," though it is *necessary* to die, yet the intention may be, as soon as he dies. Then it suspends. In this case "non statim factus sed faciendus contractus."

If the condition refers to the exploration or declaration of the Church or of men, *e. g.*, "if the Church or the pastor shall judge that there is no impediment between us," then there is a suspension. If the necessary event is uncertain to us, *e. g.*, "if the eclipse of the moon takes place on a certain day," it suspends. A condition in itself con-

[2] Canon 1092, n. 1.
[3] Held, *Jurisprudentia Universalis*, lib. IV, disp. II, cap. 4.
[4] Sanchez, *De Matrimonio*, lib. V, disp. II, n. 1 s.

tingent, and which is necessary and will infallibly evenuate, *e.g.*, "if Anti-christ comes," does not suspend. There would be suspension with this condition: "If Antichrist be born next year."[5]

A consent given with a necessary *present* condition, *e. g.*, "if you are breathing," immediately effects a marriage.[6] An impossible condition negatively put charges into a necessary, true, present one, *e. g.*, "if you cannot touch heaven," and whether one says, such a present necessary is rejected as not seriously placed, or that it is added seriously, since the condition is verified, in either case there is a marriage.[7] If the necessary condition refers to the *past*, the marriage is immediately valid, *e. g.*, "I marry you, if you had a mother, if you were born."

[5] Tamburini, *Explicatio Decalogi*, lib. VIII, *de Matr.*, tract. IV, cap. V, par. 4.

[6] Canon 1092, n. 4.

[7] *Cf.* Reiffenstuel, lib. IV, tit. V, n. 46.

CHAPTER XV

IMPOSSIBLE CONDITIONS

A FUTURE impossible condition is rejected by law. A past or present impossible condition is not rejected by law, yet in the latter case, the marriage is invalid because of the impossibility of the condition being verified.[1]

"Conditio *possibilis* est illa circumstantia quae secundum rerum naturalem ordinem aut necessario existit aut contingenter existere potest." "Conditio *impossibilis* est circumstantia, quae secundum naturalem rerum ordinem vires agentis aut absolute aut saltem physice vel moraliter superat." [2]

A condition may be impossible: *ex natura rei,* that is when nature itself is an impediment prohibiting its existence, *e. g.*, "If you capture a half-horse, or a half-man;" or impossible *de facto,* when by law or nature it can be fulfilled, but which on account of the difficulty involved in fulfilling it, it is judged (relatively) impossible, *e. g.*, for a non-swimmer to negotiate the English channel, or "if you give as a dowry a mountain of gold;" or impossible *de jure* when the law prohibits its fulfillment, and therefore it is considered legally impossible. This latter kind may be either against the substance of marriage, *e. g.*, divorce from the bond, or not against the substance of marriage, *e. g.*, "if you kill my enemy."

Many great controversies there were in the past about the decree of Gregory IX rejecting certain conditions, among which were impossible ones. "Si turpes aut impossibiles fuerint debeant propter ejus favorem pro non adjectis haberi." [3] The controversies were many-sided: about the meaning of the phrase, *"pro non adjectis haberi;"* about what kind of impossibles were rejected; and why they were rejected. Innumerable answers were given to these queries, and many rested on the error that this law was not a presumption, but was valid even in the internal

[1] Canon 1092, n. 1 and n. 4.

[2] *Cf.* Wernz-Vidal, *Jus Matrimoniale,* n. 511.

[3] C. 7, X, *de cond. appos.*, IV, 5.

forum and therefore there were marriages *coram Deo* without consent; if the condition were seriously placed. Sanchez [4] enumerates and explains with their arguments six major interpretations of the papal decree and then adds his own, after rejecting and refuting the others. He first clears the ground and supposes and proves certain fundamentals, the first of which is, that if the condition is thought possible, it is not rejected but has its effect in both fora. He uses extrinsic arguments from Roman law about wills and intrinsic ones, *e. g.*, if it is thought as possible and contingent it has the same effect in the mind and conscience as if it were truly possible and contingent; and if it were *de se* possible, it would not be rejected, therefore it is not rejected when the party thinks it is possible. The second fundamental is: the future impossible condition is held not placed, even though there is knowledge of the impossibility. He proves this well, but insists erroneously that both parties must have this knowledge of the law and the impossibility.

The third fundamental is: a future impossible condition is held not placed, when the intention of the parties is doubtful whether they had a mind to consent or to be jocose when they placed the condition. (In dubio pro matrimonio standum est.) All this being so, Sanchez says the proper meaning of the canon is this: all the faithful when receiving the Sacrament are considered to receive it according to the intention of the Church and when they contract and know the condition is impossible and rejected by the Church as not being placed, and the Church presumes they consented absolutely, then the parties seem to wish to give pure consent and according to the intention of the Church and such the Church judges, unless it is otherwise proved. Sanchez says the reason of the law is the favor of marriage, yet he demands the knowledge of the law, for no law he says binds the ignorant.

Sanchez, and nearly all the others, failing to see the true nature of the papal canon, had to rule out many cases as exceptions. Had they realized that it was a law for the external forum *per se*, they could have held that all future impossibles under all circumstances were rejected in the external forum by a presumption of the law, and if proof against the presumption were had, the external forum would not then reject the condition, and before or after proof, or in defect of this proof, as far as the internal forum was concerned, it all depended on the minds

[4] *De Matrimonio*, lib. 5, disp. III.

and intentions or the wills of the party or parties, whether the condition was placed as a *conditio sine qua non* or not.

The great canonists of the past and recent ones also point out some exceptions to this presumption. Before mentioning these so-called *exceptions,* it can be stated that since the law is a *presumptio juris* only, it stands *per se* in the external forum and, if proof against the truth of the presumption is had, all these so-called exceptions are taken care of, by the law itself simply because it is a legal presumption, and moreover to establish the truth of the cases that are so-called exceptions, is nothing else than breaking down the presumption in a given case. De Smet in his third edition held this was a *presumptio juris et de jure,*[5] which was absolutely false, simply because a condition seriously placed enters into the will and the contract and therefore it must *necessarily* be taken into account if its existence is proved. He receded from this opinion in his fourth edition.[6]

These exceptions are: if one or both think the condition is possible, or are ignorant of its impossibility, then in both fora the marriage is invalid,[7] because then it can't be presumed to have been placed *ex joco* but rather to bind the consent. This is true especially in the internal forum, whether one prudently or imprudently thought it possible. But it is true in the external forum only then when this state of mind is proved, before this moment the Church holds for a valid marriage.[8]

The second exception is when the parties were ignorant of this law. To-day it is certain this ignorance *per se* has no such effect. It may help the judge to ascertain the mind of the party or parties. Sanchez said that, morally speaking, it rarely or never happens, even in the external forum that marriage under an impossible condition is judged valid, because the pontifical law should not be judged as being known to the woman. This statement throws much light on the jurisprudence of those days about ignorance of the canons on conditional consent and other regulations. Suffice to say that it is a verity that,

[5] *De Sponsalibus et Matrimonio,* n. 154, note 1.

[6] *Op. cit.,* n. 154.

[7] *Ibid.,* n. 62; Sanchez, *De Matrimonio,* lib. 5, dist. 3, n. 10.

[8] Pallotini, *Coll. S. C. C.,* verb., "matrimonium," nn. 18 and 21, maintains these exceptions and quotes a causa in Eystadien, 9 February, 1732.

as far as the conscience is concerned, the entire transaction depends on the natural will and the presence or not of the impossible condition *qua* condition.

A third exception: If it is evident from various circumstances, *e. g.*, lack of love, social disparity, etc., one can conclude the condition was placed seriously, knowing it was impossible, and meaning in this way to say, "I do not wish in any way to oblige myself," *e. g.*, if a nobleman said to a poor peasant girl, "I marry you if you bring a mountain of gold as a dowry," then there is no consent, nor a marriage. Such circumstances may prove such a will, another set of circumstances may prove a jocose will without any internal condition.

These authors conclude that a future impossible condition is only then held as not added, when it is doubtful whether the will is serious or not, for in doubt marriage is favored. The Church, as said before, has excellent weighty reasons for presuming one way about certain conditions, and another way about others. Not the least of which is, lest marriage perhaps validly contracted be illegitimately dissolved with danger to souls and the way be open to another (illegitimate) marriage. Nor is this favor adverse to the liberty and free consent required for marriage, for it only operates when the absolute consent of the parties can be presumed.

None of these limitations or exceptions seem to be well founded, for the law speaks universally and makes no distinction between impossible conditions that are known as such or unknown. Moreover, ignorance of law does not excuse from a general rule of law, nor is there any reason to recede from this principle. Such an interpretation would in practice make the law illusory and superfluous since it could not be sustained. It is true and easier to believe that he who thinks a thing is possible and honest could bind his consent to this condition, but he that affirms this must prove it. All this is likewise true of the immoral or illegal condition that is not against the substance of marriage. Error or ignorance *per se* is no exception to the presumption.[9]

Past, present, and future conditions that are impossible do not invalidate the contract, but because of the favor enjoyed by marriage

[9] Wernz-Vidal, *Jus Matrimoniale,* n. 513; Bayon, *Tractatus De Matr.* p. 308; Tamburini, *Explicatio Decalogi,* lib. VIII, tract. IV, cap. V, par. 5.

in the law, *future* impossible conditions are treated *per se* as though they were never added to the consent. The contract is absolute. This is true under the former and the present law. The question is asked how can the Church thus legislate, since consent effects marriage and such conditions rather indicate *per se* dissent since they can never be verified, and moreover other contracts are vitiated by such conditions. Besides some say it is difficult to see any favor of marriage here, since it would be more favorable to marriage that it be very voluntary especially because of its indissolubility and its ends. Because of these and other reasons Durandus [10] confessed he could not see how the Church can presume consent and he leaves the question to more learned doctors to judge.

Some older canonists tortured the text of the law in many ways (*mirum in modum*), of which Sanchez [11] gives six absolutely different interpretations and rejects them all. Sanchez says the common explanation of the law is that such a *future* impossible is not seriously placed with the intention of dissenting, or invalidating the act and thus the Church very properly rejects them just as Roman law does in last wills; and this in favor of the testator whose interest it is to have the will valid and fulfilled, and also in favor of the State, for it is of the highest importance to the State that the last will of men be scrupulously carried out, therefore marriage is no less to be favored.[12]

It has been discussed whether this law is a new one or only a declaration of an old natural law. The truer view, say some authorities,[13] is that it is a new law. The reason is because marriage consent under an impossible condition, considering the case precisely would be null, for *per se* the condition shows dissent rather than consent. But it is held as valid, and the condition is no obstacle, not from the natural law, but by positive papal law. The Church does not supply consent, but only presumes absolute consent. The danger to one soul who seriously placed such a condition and was obliged by sentence of

[10] *Commentarium,* III, dist. 39, qu. 4, n. 9.

[11] *De Matrimonio,* lib. 5, d. 3, n. 2 s.

[12] *Cf.* Schmalzgrueber, lib. IV, tit. 5, n. 5.

[13] Sanchez, *op. cit.,* lib. 5, D. 3, n. 19, who quotes many others; *cf.* Schmalzgrueber, lib. IV, tit. V, n. 66; Wiestner, *Institutiones Canonicae,* lib. IV, tit. V, n. 18.

a judge to cohabit is easily removed if he rejects the condition and renders his consent absolute, and he is bound to do this since he can hardly otherwise ward off damage to himself and his putative wife.

The other opinion maintains it is a declaration of the natural law. For the Pope did not legislate that such conditions be considered as not having been placed, but only that they ought to be so considered, which indicates some anterior law, which can be no other than the natural law. Moreover, prescinding from papal law, if marriage under such a condition would be invalid, the Pope could not confer validity on them, for it would be invalid for lack of consent, and this lack the papal power can not supply. Thus it follows that he who thus contracts seriously, but is unable to prove it, lives in continual fornication using marriage.

A distinction might be in order. In so far as the objective validity or not of the marriage is concerned, it is the natural law. In so far as the *de facto* presumption is concerned it is Church law, simply because the presumption can be false in a given case and therefore contrary to the natural law.

What kind of *future* impossible conditions are rejected? There is unanimity and no doubt that all those *ex natura rei* are *per se* rejected. There are different opinions about those *de facto* impossible. Some wish these not to be rejected, because Roman law on wills do not reject them but vitiate the will; and the canon law speaks of impossible ones, but these are not impossible but only difficult.

Others [14] maintain these are to be rejected. Bartholomew a Ledesm [15] distinguishes: they are rejected in foro *externo* but in foro *interno,* they suspend till verification. But Barbosa [16] says if the condition is so difficult that considering the quality of the person upon whom it is enjoined and if it is equally manifest he can in no way fulfill it, even with the help of friends, such a condition is rejected. If, however, the condition is such that the person upon whom it devolves can through friends and good reputation accomplish it, *e.g.,* "if you give $1,000 as dowry," this condition suspends, since it is not so much impossible as difficult, but difficulty does not liberate.

[14] *Cf.* Schmalzgrueber, *loc. cit.*, Schmier, 1754, *De Matr.*, t. II, Tract II.
[15] *De Matr.*, dub. 25, concl. 8.
[16] *Collectanea Doctorum,* n. 71, ad. rubr. li. t., n. 6.

If the condition is possible and easy for a few, but of the highest difficulty for most people, it is then to all intent and purpose equal to an impossibility for most people, *e. g.*, for John, a pauper, to give $1,000. "Quoad internum unice attenditur intentio contrahentium judicandum fit." [17] This seems to be the true solution.[18] One must remember, however, that we speak here only of the external forum, the internal forum is ruled over by the meaning of the will of him who places the condition. Impossible *de jure* conditions will be discussed in the last two chapters.

Vincentius de Justis [19] quotes Basilius Pontius [20] to the effect that if disqualified persons contract between themselves with an impossible condition, the contract is ridiculous, they do not consent to marriage, nor incur excommunication. If the condition is, "if the pope dispenses," some authors strangely say all such are impossible conditions by law, others say certain such conditions are impossible. This particular condition was treated under the caption of future honest conditions.

Are past and present impossible conditions rejected. Before the Code some authors [21] thought the Gregorian decree was restricted only to future impossibles. Others maintained past and present also were rejected.[22] The reason being because the pope rejected impossible conditions *qua* impossible, not because they obliged to something impossible.

Are these past and present conditions rejected by the new law? De Smet,[23] Gasparri,[24] Cappello,[25] Ayrinhac,[26] and nearly all other

[17] Bonacina, *Opera Omnia,* qu. 2, punct. X, Prop., III; *cf.* Held, *Jurisprudentia Universalis,* Lib. IV, dist. II, cap. IV, who is quite original in his views.

[18] *Cf.* Tamburini, *Explicatio Decalogi,* lib. VIII, Tract. IV, cap. V, par. 5.

[19] *Appendix Casum in S.C. Concilii Resolutorum,* Lucae, 1726, 241.159.

[20] *De Matr.,* n. 35.

[21] *Cf.* Schmalzgrueber, lib. IV, tit. V, n. 72.

[22] *Cf.* Sanchez, *op. cit.,* lib. 5, disp. IV, n. 73; Gasparri, *De Matrimonio* (1932), n. 921; Reiffenstuel, lib. IV, tit. V, n. 46; Durandus, *Commentarium,* IV, dist. 27, Weister *Institutiones Canonicae,* lib. IV, tit. V, n. 24 s.

[23] *De Sponsalibus et Matrimonio,* n. 156.

[24] Gasparri, *De Matrimonio* (1932), n. 921.

[25] Cappello, *De Matrimonio,* n. 642.

[26] Ayrinhac, *Marriage Legislation,* n. 223.

authorities rightly say they are not rejected, applying Canon 1092, n. 4:

Si de praeterito vel de praesenti, matrimonium erit validum vel non prout id quod conditioni subest, existit vel non. Therefore the marriage is null in the external forum and null in the internal forum if the condition is seriously placed, otherwise it is valid.[27] This leads to a discussion of immoral (legally impossible) conditions.

[27] It is a general principle of Roman law and modern laws that the essential elements of an obligation must not involve anything that is impossible, illegal or contrary to good morals or public policy. No one can be bound to do what in the nature of things is impossible: "Impossibilium nulla obligatio est," D. 50, 17, 185. An obligation is also null, the primary object of which is to require something to be done forbidden by law. The law cannot enforce that which it at the same time prohibits. Associated with the above objects are also those against the general moral sense of society and inconsistent with public welfare.—W. C. Morey, *Outlines of Roman Law,* p. 246.

CHAPTER XVI

DISHONEST OR BASE CONDITIONS WHICH ARE NOT AGAINST THE SUBSTANCE OF MARRIAGE

FUTURE immoral conditions are rejected, *e. g.*, "I marry you, if you will kill my enemy;" "if you promise to abuse your marital obligations." *Past* and *present* immoral conditions are not rejected, the marriage is valid if the condition is or was verified; invalid, if the condition is not or was not verified; *e. g.*, "I marry you, if you did kill my enemy last year;" "If you are a thief." [1]

First of all it must be remembered that in *foro conscientiae* the effect of these conditions, whether past, present, or future, depends solely on the meaning of the will of the one placing them. But in doubt concerning this state of mind, the presumption of rejection, of such *future* conditions and the decision of the court, must be upheld. Sanchez [2] says that generally such dishonest conditions are added with the intention or will that they be fulfilled, but this seems to run counter to the wisdom and experience of the Church which enacted this presumption. It is certain that a *future conditio turpis* is held not placed and rejected both by the legislation of Gregory IX and Canon 1092, n. 1: "Conditio semel apposita et non revocata: Si sit de futuro . . . turpis, sed non contra matrimonii substantiam, pro non adjecta habeatur." "Turpis conditio est ea quae legibus divinis et humanis adversatur." "Honesta conditio quae conformis iisdem legibus."

The legislation on this point was before the Code the chapters "Quicumque" [3] and "Si Conditiones." [4] Four diverse interpretations of the first decree are mentioned by Fagnanus.[5] The first says the law contemplate *turpis conditio* not against the substance of marriage. This is the common opinion, says Fagnanus, whose commen-

[1] Canon 1092, n. 1 and n. 4.

[2] *De Matrimonio,* lib. V, disp. XV.

[3] C. 1, X, de condit. appos., IV, V.

[4] *Ibid.*

[5] *Commentaria in Quartum Librum Decretalium,* Romae, 1661, n. 36 s.

tary of both decrees is excellent. The chapter "Si conditiones" rejects base and impossible conditions.

Many answers have been given to the query why does the Church thus presume. But the principal reason is because these *future* conditions incite to sin (*quia ad peccandum incitat*). This is proved abundantly by the great canonists who point out the historical background of this legislation and its superlative wisdom.[6]

The old classical canonists like Sanchez, Reiffenstuel and Schmalzgrueber, as well as some moderns like Wernz and Gasparri, most learnedly justify this presumption and refute the various customary objections. Yet it seems most of them [7] exempt from this *presumptive* law and hold these conditions are not rejected: the usual cases of error of the party believing the condition is honest; secondly, when the base condition known as base was seriously placed to bind the consent, and, lastly, ignorance of one or both of this particular law. But, as said before, there is no need of these exceptions; in fact, they are not exceptions, for even in these cases the law holds until the presumption is abolished by the establishment of such proof of the contrary. Before this proof is accepted as such by the court, the condition is held not placed. Thus these are not exceptions, but rather declarations of papal and episcopal jurisprudence after sufficient evidence is had against the presumption. Before this declaration, as far as the external forum is concerned, the state of mind of the nupturients about the condition is doubtful, thus the presumption of law that the condition was not seriously added to suspend the consent exists till that moment.

"Quae appositio conditionis (et ejusdem sensus) cum sit contra ordinariam formam celebrandi matrimonium, legitime est probanda." [8] And the *favor matrimonii* consists in this: "Jus praesumat in favorem causae, quoadusque contrarium non demonstratur." [9]

Sanchez demolishes the objections [10] of those denying the reason

[6] *Cf.* inter alios: Sanchez, *De Matrimonio*, lib. V, disp. XV.

[7] Schmalzgrueber, lib. IV, tit. V; Wernz-Vidal, *op. cit.*, n. 517; Bayon, *op. cit.*, p. 318.

[8] Wernz, *Jus Decretalium*, IV, n. 300, n. 29.

[9] Santi, *Pralectiones Juris Canonici* (1884), p. 104.

[10] *Op. cit.*, lib. V, disp., XV.

he gives for the presumption, and the objection of those who also deny past and present conditions are not rejected. Sanchez, however, in order to escape what seems to him a great difficulty, insists that the law about future immoral conditions must be understood thus provided the parties know the condition is immoral, for he says if they thought it honest, it would not be rejected. And he insists erroneously that both parties know that the law rejects these base conditions. But as pointed out when speaking about impossible conditions, no exceptions to the law need be made, because if the parties prove their ignorance of the nature of the future condition, then the presumption cedes to the truth. Moreover, if ignorance of this law exempted, then the law would be practically meaningless since very few know the law, and no Roman decision based on such a teaching has come under our notice, but the Rota has taken up and decided cases in spite of the ignorance of the parties concerning the law on conditions. De Lugo [11] reprehends this doctrine about ignorance of the law; and, as Cardinal Gasparri[12] acutely remarks, it may very well be this way: if the contractor under such a condition knows that Canon Law will consider the marriage valid and reject the condition, it can be much more presumed that he added the condition *ex joco* and seriously expressed his matrimonial consent.[13]

Roman Law is in accordance with the Church doctrine. "Papinianus pie et bene: de conditione imposita qua facta ledunt pietatem, existimationem, verecundiam nostram, et generaliter, qua contra bonos mores fiunt, ea nec facere nos posse credendum est.[14] "Pacta quoque et stipulationes turpi conditione apposita nullius momenti fiunt, ut juris esse diximus, cum his apponitur conditio impossibilis de facto." [15]

Modern civil law invalidates the contract itself. "Agreements which either directly or indirectly tend to violate the established rules of decency and morality are void, as being against public policy." [16]

[11] *Theologia Moralis*, n. 356.

[12] *De Matrimonio* (1932), n. 887.

[13] *Cf.* Lehmkuhl, *Theologia Moralis*, vol. II, n. 687.

[14] Bonacinae, *Opera Omnia*, I, 356.

[15] Paulus, *de stipulatione*.

[16] Putney, *Law Library*, Vol. III, p. 139.

"No principle is better settled than that no action can be maintained on a contract, the consideration of which is either wicked of itself or prohibited by the law. There is no recovery on that contract."[17] "A contract that on its face requires an illegal act, either of the contractor or a third party, no more imposes a liability to damages for non-performance than it creates an equity to compel the contractor to perform." [18]

Some have said that the condition, "if you give me so much money," is base because of the Sacrament. But nearly all say it is honest and licit *per se,* if there be a just cause. Is it a crime not to promise to marry, but to give marital consent under the condition "if my wife dies"? Probably all will agree it is base because it is an incentive to crime, but if it be psychologically possible to give such a marital consent while one's wife is living, which is not thus possible to do absolutely, but probably it is no contradiction to give it under this condition, then prescinding from the required form of celebration and from diriment impediments, there would result a marriage at the moment of verification as far as the internal forum at least, and in this way one would probably incur no penalty of crime.

Farrugia [19] strangely says if the base condition is seriously placed, because it is thought to be honest, and moreover there is ignorance of the law, then the marriage is null because of lack of consent, because the precise nature of the condition rather signifies dissent than consent. This is not true, in this case even psychologically the consent is suspended, and if the condition is verified, marriage ensues.

If a third party has perpetrated a crime or will do so, the condition is not rejected as base because it does not incite to sin, *e. g.*, "I marry you, if your enemy has unjustly wounded you," or "if your brother killed that man," or "if that man will be murdered by John." [20]

[17] Marshall, *Common Legal Principles,* vol. I, p. 114: Marshall, Armstrong V, Tolen, 11, Wheat, 258.

[18] *Ibid.,* Soge V. Hampe, 235, U. S., 99. There are penalties for marrying with certain agreements and *a fortiori* if these agreements are elevated to a condition attached to the marital consent. *Cf.* Canon 2319.

[19] *De Matrimonio,* 1924, p. 59.

[20] Gasparri, *op. cit.* (1932), n. 889.

Future immoral conditions are rejected because they incite to sin, therefore we can infer as Sanchez points out that base conditions referring to *past* or *present* events are not rejected simply because they do not incite to sin, but suppose a fact. An example: "I marry you if you are an enemy of Peter; or if you killed that man." This verified, there is a true marriage, otherwise not. Therefore these conditions in a sense are not base, *e. g.*, "si es meretrix;" "si fratrem occideris;" for these treat *non de peccato committendo sed de commisso.*[21]

Under the present law it is certain that past and present base conditions are not rejected. Nearly all commentators agree that paragraph four of Canon 1092 applies to these. "Si de praeterito vel de praesenti, matrimonium erit validum vel non, prout id quod conditioni subest, existit vel non."

Reiffenstuel, Pichler, Wiestner, Bonacina, Schmalzgrueber, and nearly all others testify thus concerning the previous law, and Wernz-Vidal, Gasparri, Bayon, Cerato, Cappello and nearly every author testify the same concerning the law of the Code.

But Chelodi writes: "Hactenus conditio de praesenti aut de praeterito impossibilis habebatur pro non adjecta, eodem modo, a multis, etiam turpis. Attento solo puncto primo Canon 1092, etiam jure novo hoc affirmari posset: at considerato simul puncto quarto contrarium videtur deducendum. Practice res est parvi momenti." [22]

It might be remarked here that these base conditions are also designated as impossible conditions by law. Yet the past and present conditions are not rejected. Future ones since they are against honesty are rejected. Thus if the condition were: "if you truly have killed your brother," or "if you have procured abortion," marriage is valid or not according to the truth of the event.[23]

If the condition is "if you lie with me," authors differ.[24] If the *copula* refers to a time before the marriage, it is a future immoral and therefore rejected. If it refers to a time after the marriage, it is

[21] Gougnard, *De Matrimonio*, p. 145.

[22] *Jus Matrimoniale*, n. 127. For the controversy he refers to Van de Burgt, 102, note 2, and Wernz, IV, 300, note 31.

[23] *Cf.* Gasparri, *De Matrimonio* (1932), n. 921 s; Wernz-Vidal, *Jus Matrimoniale*, n. 513; Bayon, *De Matrimonio*, n. 319.

[24] *Cf.* Sanchez, *De Matrimonio*, lib. V, d. XVI, n. 1.

an honest condition *inest in jure* and has no effect at all. If, before the new law, it referred to the two months of grace, for deliberating on entering religion, it was also a condition *inest in jure.* If the condition is: "I marry you if you now promise seriously to allow the *coitus* before marriage," though it seems to be a present condition, its fulfillment is not simultaneous with the placing of the condition, but subsequent to it, thus it incites to sin and is rejected, for it is equivalent to, if you allow the *coitus* (a future condition therefore).

The condition, "if you killed your father," is not rejected. "If you kill him," is rejected because it is future. If the condition is "if you are a virgin," the marriage depends on the truth of the condtion. "If I find you a virgin," is a future condition honest or base. Honest if by licit means, base *si per coitum experimentum est turpissimum. Per se* this condition is not based on an *actus turpis,* but on the honest condition of the virgin; *per accidens* the condition is base if the meaning is ascertain the truth by a manner that is base.[25]

"If you sin with me, I promise either to marry you or give you so much money." In this case there is no receding from a condition, because he had a choice; and the consent is not marital, but engagement consent.

According to Sanchez,[26] in one case only, a past or present condition would invalidate consent and effect no marriage, namely, if it would attach the marriage in the future, *e. g.,* "I marry you, if you have procured medicine of sterility to use afterwards in marriage;" for this is the same thing as to oblige oneself in future to take the poison. Of course, if the meaning is, "you take on the *obligation* to properly bear children, but you must promise to be recreant to this sacred duty, to abuse it," then there is a marriage, for this then is not against the substance of marriage, and the condition being future and dishonest is rejected.

Some taught without rhyme or reason that vain and impertinent conditions are rejected (thus Sotus, etc., whom Sanchez refutes). The phrase, "if the condition is honest or useful, it is valid," does not *per se* exclude useless and impertinent ones, which do not conduce to a real happy married life, but rather please a queer kink

[25] *Cf.* Sanchez, *loc. cit.*

[26] *Op. cit.,* lib. 5, d. 9, nn. 6, 7; Bayon *De Matrimonio,* p. 319.

in the mind of the one placing it, *e. g.*, "if you are a good bridge player, well mannered, low-voiced."

It is plain, as Sanchez and others point out, these conditions are not dishonest even in relation to the sanctity of marriage, and if such circumstances are elevated to conditions *sine qua non* it is evident they bind, and if future, suspend the consent, and marriage is not valid unless the condition is verified. Moreover, every condition not reprobated by the law can be added, as is gathered from the contrary sense of the chapter, *Super eo, de cond, appos,* "ac conditionem ipsam canonica non improbant statuta," and from the contrary sense of Canon 1092. Therefore, vain conditions are not rejected, nor illegal, for nowhere in the law are they reprobated. They do not incite to sin, though there may be some fault in placing them.

CHAPTER XVII

FUTURE HONEST POSSIBLE CONTINGENT CONDITIONS

The fundamental principles of this particular kind of condition resulting from the definite evolution of canonical doctrine and long imbedded in the legislation are on the one hand, the marital consent under a future licit condition lacks immediate causative or creative power of effectuating the marriage [1] (and the consequences from this for diriment impediments arising during the pendency); and, on the other hand, the claim upon the future expectation of the marriage through the fulfillment of the condition. Only in future does it cause family status. When the condition is verified *eo ipso* the marriage is effectuated without any renewal of consent. There is an essential distinction therefore between engagement consent (simple or conditional) and conditional marital consent. If the future condition be such a one (*turpis, necessaria, impossibilis*) that is rejected by the Church, then a diriment impediment arising (before the actual fulfillment) has no invalidating effect on the marriage in the external forum at least, for the marriage by a *presumptio juris* is immediately valid just as if the condition were not placed at all.

The effects of conditional consent are variously explained.[2] Some give to the verified condition a merely declarative consent to a former consent, that is, a declarative, explanatory, affirmative significance concerning a declaration of will already effected. The condition decides here the force of an effectiveness of a fact already achieved in the past, just as in the case of a judgement.

In other cases, say some, results are obtained in this fashion. The condition is a co-efficient, so that the legal effects represent themselves as effects of two things: the will, in the ordinary typical legal way; and the contingent circumstances or fact. The will is the presupposition of the effectiveness of the condition. Relevant questions are

[1] Pallotini says the marriage is suspended by a true proper contingent condition and quotes the causa, Egystetten Matr., die 17 November, 1731—*Coll. S. C. C., verb.,* "Conditio," par. 2.

[2] *Cf.* Hussarek, *Die Bedingte Eheschliessung,* p. 191.

solved by accepting the conditional fact as the exclusively effecting agent of the legal issue, and the declaration of the will has only the significance of a presupposition preceding the operativeness of this *agens.* This acceptation did not enter into canonical jurisprudence and thus its promoters assert the canonists made use of a fiction. The verified condition operates like this, as if it awakens the marriage consent already given, but, simultaneously with its arising, it is sunk into a charmed sleep, and all at once rises to life. This consent (only virtual and moral) awakens to life *actualiter* and causes the family status. This, according to some, is a fiction, for it is a surrogate in order to adopt the victorious theory of consent also to conditional consent to marriage, so as to make the marriage present wholly and entirely through consent.

But further discussion is useful on account of the fundamental principles we have established.

1. Consent under a condition that is future and licit has no immediate marriage effect. Thus Boniface VIII:

Ille vero, qui sponsalia (*i. e.*, marriage, not engagement)[3]

[3] "But a remarkable change of terminology appears (says Joyce in speaking of the formation of marriage until Gratian, 1140) which seems to indicate an important modification. The Christian writers employ the word *desponsatio* to signify marriage, and term the wife *sponsa* until conjugal life actually began. Von Hörman (*Quasiaffinität,* Innsbruck, 1906, vol. II, pp. 1-223), who first called attention to this, points out that the alteration could hardly have taken place unless the Christians had been accustomed to combine the rites of betrothal and marriage, so that the ceremony was no longer a promise of future marriage, but the actual marriage itself. The Church could then give her blessing to the newly-married pair, since they are already man and wife" (thus Joyce, *Christian Marriage,* p. 46.). Boniface VIII reigned 1294-1303, and Joyce is speaking of the development of the theory of marriage before Gratian's time, who lived at 1140. But this fact was long ago pointed out by the older decretalists and later canonists; some of whom give rules for deciding when *sponsalia* is to be taken as engagement, when as marriage. There was a time when the engagement proper was separated, and a later evolution when both ceremonies were combined, after this latter age *sponsalia* meant both ceremonies and when the canonists spoke of whether the *sponsalia* held in this case or could be broken, naturally they meant the marriage. Esmein has been accused for translating *sponsalia* and *sponsa* or rather "desponsata" as "fiancee," and his reviser says he did so because in the French tongue there is no separate words to show the difference. *Cf.* Esmein-Genestal, *Le Mariage* (1929), p. 119.

> cum aliqua muliere sub condicione contraxit, si postmodum ante condicionis eventum cum alia, prioris consanquinea, per verba contraxerit de praesenti, cum secunda remanere debebit, cum ex *sponsalibus condicionalibus ante condicionem extantem sicuti consensum non habentibus et incertis* nulla publicae honestatis justitia oriatur.[4]

In modern expositions [5] of our doctrine on conditions it is strange, says Hussarek, that no regard is had for this highly characteristic passage. Schulte only mentions it treating the impediment of public honesty. Freisen has no mention of it. Yet it is probably the most important law on the whole matter, for only by it is the significance of a condition made clear.

According to this conditional consent, as far as juridical marital effects are concerned (during pendency), is no consent at all. The conditional will is still uncertain and unfinished and need not be considered at all. Strange to say, remarks Hussarek, the following passage of Urban III's decree, "Super eo," has confirmative significance for our own doctrine: [6] " . . . cum hujusmodi consensus *non sit de praesenti habendus,* licet per verba de praesenti evidentius exprimatur, qui in alieno arbitrio, non habito, sed habendo consistit." This passage is regularly explained by distinguishing *sponsalia de praesenti* and *sponsalia de futuro,* and from this passage one finds that marriage consent under a condition of a third party's assent has the significance of a *desponsatio* and thus does essential justice to Urban III. It is not the true explanation because of Gregory IX's interpretation wherein on account of the *copula* matrimony can be enforced. The contradictory of the opposition to this interpretation is, that on account of the condition, the *copula* can be enforced.

The same view is the result if one considers the manner in which Innocent III placed this doctrine of renunciation through *copula* into the legal system: "cum . . . constet, quod post contracta sponsalia carnalis est inter eos copula subsecuta, pro matrimonio est vehementer quiden praesumendum quia videtur condicione apposita recessisse."[7]

[4] C. un., *de sponsalibus et Matrimoniis,* IV, 1, in VI.

[5] Hussarek, *Die Bedingte Eheschiessung,* p. 192.

[6] C. 5, X, *de Sponsalibus et Matrimoniis,* V, 5; *cf.* Hussarek, *op. cit.,* p. 192.

[7] C. 6, X, *de Conditionibus Appositis,* IV, 5.

If conditional marriage consent is the same thing as engagement then the fiction of renunciation by having sexual intercourse has no meaning at all. This supposition would not have been necessary if conditional marriage contracts were considered engagements. One must rather draw the conclusion that the consent becomes actual and efficacious with the materialization of the condition. The proposition that the *copula* is equivalent to the renunciation of the condition has force and meaning independently of engagement. This latter was outlawed where the decree *Tametsi* was in force, and valid where it was not enforced, at least till the Code.

This view explains a series of important consequences: summed up, that the actual present matrimonial status does not exist yet between the parties.

First, express legal sanction is given to the proposition that the impediment of public honesty otherwise arising from engagement did not arise from conditional *sponsalia* before verification (admitted by the canonists before the Code).[8]

Secondly, almost a universal scientific canonical conviction that the impediment of *ligamen* could not arise from conditional marital consent, during pendency. Sufficient proof is found in the passage of the Glossa Ordinaria to Liber X at the word *praesumendum* in cap. 6 h. t.

> Item quid, si contraho cum aliqua sub condicione deinde cum alia pure? Tenet matrimonium. Sed pone, quod postea existat condicio? Videtur quod teneat primum, quia perinde videtur, ac si a principio pure contraxissent . . . sed secus in matrimonio, quia non trahitur retro, *ubi ab inito non fuit.*[9]

In both these laws about impediments, they differ for engagement and marriage consent.

Thirdly, if during pendency an impediment arises, then there is no marriage even after verification. All the remote effects of a conditional marriage consent are extinguished by this impediment, so that the later removal of the impediment would not restitute that relation which would have immediately made marriage on the verifi-

[8] *Cf.* Cappello, *De Matrimonio*, n. 548.

[9] Quoted by Hussarek, *op. cit.*, p. 195.

cation of the condition. If therefore one performed extra-marital intercourse with another, so that affinity arises (*i. e.*, before the Code), then there is no marriage with this one after verification. The same is true of spiritual relationship, adoption, etc. Marriage with a third party during pendency is valid, and there arises *ligamen* against the conditional marital consent.

It is doubtful whether the same is true of marriage obstacles based on lack of consent (not error). If the consent is free from error it will remain so forever. Therefore the question is only about *vis et metus* practised after consent given under a condition, or abduction against one's will, lunacy, etc. No doubt every one of these circumstances justify receding from the conditional consent.[10]

If the impediment or obstacle is still existent at the moment of verification, then the marriage is under the impediment and therefore invalid. Yet these situations do not necessarily invalidate *still pending* agreements, for the will of marriage is still existent, though juridically irrelevant, yet it was psychologically existent and correct and those circumstances elevated to legal significance and viewed from the psychological defectiveness of the will must be considered from that moment in which the psychological defect is present and the moment to which juridical consequences are to be attached to the will. No attention is to be paid to the other intervals of time. Failure to make use of this right of objecting does not create a legal presumption or prejudice against the one or the other of the parties if—but also for so long as the mental disturbance, insanity, fear, etc. prevents him from exercising or claiming this right of objecting.

Even the remote effects of consent under a condition are destroyed by the revocation of the entire transaction by one party.

The following reasons force one to admit a consequence or conclusion which formerly found little recognition and only since the Code is recognized clearly. Canon Law *presumed* the continuance of the consent till verification or till the lack of it is certainly proved. This proposition is one of the foundation stones of the characteristic interpretation of conditional marriage consent during the classical period of Canon Law. If an argument against this presumption is furnished and proved, then every possibility is removed of having a

[10] *Cf.* Hussarek, *op. cit.*, p. 194.

valid marriage through the latter fulfillment of the condition. Therefore on verification, the marriage exists, only on the supposition of the perseverance of the will. Any argument against this presumption (of the law) or the destruction of it is due to the revocation of the consent not the revocation of the condition.

The material justification of the doctrine of revocability of this conditional marital consent consists in this that either party may validly marry a third one, or create an impediment, *e.g.*, through *affinitas illegitima* (before the Code).

The binding force constraining the parties during pendency is therefore less than the obligation created by canonical *engagements.* Hence one must maintain the possibility of destroying this relation by the mere expression of the will of the party or parties. One must not confound the question of valid revocation with the question of its lawfulness.

Let us use the (pre-Code) doctrine governing the unilateral breaking of an engagement as an anology. If it was broken without sufficient cause, it was subject to ecclesiastical punishment, and Church force could be used to bring about its effectuation. It can be revoked by mutual consent, no special form being necessary. The marital conditional consent effects a valid claim upon the future realization of the marriage through fulfillment of the condition or a circumstance equivalent to verification. Till then the parties are bound to await verification and may not do anything counter to the intention of both parties. Yet a contrary action is not impossible to them, only illicit. Therefore, though every direct effort is excluded, certain remote effects arise from the conditional marital consent. This claim is exceedingly uncertain and precarious as we saw above. If there is *res integra,* that is, if the situation continues as it was up to the verification, marriage at once exists by this very fact without renewal of consent. The manner (*quo modo*) of this is explained variously, some theories are good, others having no merit at all. Hussarek, claims the rational explanation is the following:[11] verification creates the marriage, the reason however for this is found in this circumstance that at the time when actually the whole transaction was agreed upon a

[11] *Die Bedingte Eheschliessung,* p. 199.

union of wills was produced which was equivalent to and corresponds to the requirements of marital consent.

Classical canonical jurisprudence has expressed this by the presupposing the continuance of the consent. Later authors speak of the virtual continuance of the consent, but actually we have here, says Hussarek, a fictitious consent. The occasion of establishing this doctrine was the principle that marriage is made only by the *consensus maritalis de praesenti* of the parties; therefore, in cases where this consent could not be found the fiction of consent was created. This interpretation does not interpret anything, it is only an aid to lazy thinking. It is not needed at all. The consent existed therefore in the legal order, there is no reason to admit—in case there is no revocation—any other results than such as would ensue if the parties gave consent in full knowledge of verification.

In ancient and modern times there were and are attempts to explain marital consent given under a condition as engagement consent, but this is abundantly wrong.[12] The obligation from engagements is far more binding, at least before the Code, while, on the contrary, to engagement is lacking every possibility *per se* of becoming marriage, even before the Code. For the Church only presumed in given cases that the condition was revoked and the party or parties then consented absolutely and without this last part of the presumption even in the external forum the Church could not presume a marriage on account of the *copula* freely exercised during pendency. Marriage now and always needs as a *conditio sine qua non* marriage consent and no other consent under the sun can effect a marriage. Engagement consent (simple or given under condition) can not cause a

[12] Schmalzgrueber mentions (lib. IV, tit V, n. 13), many older authors who held this doctrine. Ballerini-Palmieri (*Opus Theologicum Morale,* p. 237, resp. 29, Vol. 6) says, consent with an honest condition *de futuro* is a contract of engagement only and not of marriage, for this consent is not *de praesenti* and therefore for this reason, there is not marriage without new consent, after the condition is verified, as, he says, teach St. Thomas and others. Sanchez says St. Thomas taught thus. Palmieri continues that Laymanns and others think the contrary is probable. (*Cf.* St. Alphonsus, *Theologia Moralis,* lib. VII, n. 894; Gilbert in his voluminous work also denies our doctrine, using the *actus legitimi* argument. (*Corpus Juris Canonici,* a J. B. Gilbert, 3 tomi; *Coloniae Allobrogum,* Tomus III, Tract. de Sacr. tit. XI, sect. XIV, p. 90; also Soto.)

marriage, but in our case (conditional marital consent) there is no need of further marriage consent for it is already had under a condition.

Abstracting from these positive fundamental principles, (namely that on the one hand conditional marriage consent is suspended in its effect and that it lacks immediate causative power to create a marriage,[13] and on the other hand, there is a claim *de jure naturae et divine positivo,* from the conditional consent when the circumstance is verified, to the obligation of the married status) there are differences (essential ones) that arise from the qualities of the act producing legal status. In one case, marriage consent under a condition is the producing act, in the other case, engagement consent, each bringing forth results according to their respective natures. There is an *essential* difference between these two kinds of consent.[14]

The *essential* differences between these two wills are briefly these. Matrimonial consent creates qualities pertinent to family law, makes two people husband and wife, it affects entirely the legal status of the person and the family. Both with their entire personality are subject to the right of the other party, therefore there is a new status. But this is done too by marriage consent under a condition, which is a germ for its future genesis.

[13] "Actus non consideratur ex die quo gestus fuit, sed ex die quo fuit perfectus in qua conditio impleatur."

"Et donec pendet conditio, non potest dici jus parti quaesitum."

"Nothing is due if unverified, nothing is due of those things placed in the *principio* and the preface of the placing and in all its parts and influences." (Augustinius Barbosa, *Libri Duo Votorum, etc.*, Venetiis, 1711, lib. II, votum 71; lib. III, votum 86, n. 4, and votum 86, n. 33.)

[14] For this very reason the arguments of Enneccerus against the possibility of marital consent being given under a condition in Roman Law cannot be considered valid or conclusive. He says such marriages in Roman Law are invalid for nowhere are they punished in Roman Law. *Cf.* Hussarek, *op. cit.*, p. 200. This is a strange argument in itself, but accidentlly it betrays a woeful ignorance of Roman Law on family life. Roman classic law did not directly legislate about marriage, only about the *probatio* of the fact of marriage. The *paterfamilias* was the law on marriage, and marriage in Roman Law never in its classic eras had a separate title or treatment, but the *Lex Civilis* treated of the *patria potestas* to increase or decrease his patrimony and from this angle only does the law consider marriage.

Engagement consent (if canonical) creates claims ***aiming*** at the creation of a new status; its object is the will of another; it aims at some action of this person, but does not create dominion over the person himself. It is merely an argument for a claim (and since the Code a very slight one, or none, as far as juridically being able to force this other to honor the claim, even though he unjustly refuses). This consent does not contain even the germ of a future marriage, at least not if we admit the views held after Canon Law attained to full development, though during this development (and even today, sad to say, after centuries of legislation on the point) there were and are authors who held a doctrine like this false one. The effectuation of marriage through the *copula* is, or was, a doctrine true or false according to one's understanding of it. It was false if one meant it worked absolutely and in all cases, and before God and the consciences of the parties there was *ipso facto* a true marriage. It was a true doctrine, if it meant only a presumption of the revocation of the condition, thus leaving the marriage consent pure and effecting the marriage. Thus it is easy to see how erroneous and careless are some authors of to-day, especially those still holding the engagement theory, who say these two consents (marital and engagement) have the same object when in reality the object of one consent is the marriage status and all it implies, and the object of the other consent is the will of another, some action of another person.[15]

The effects of contracts or consent entered into under a suspensive condition are essentially marked by the very terms of the concept. This future event is not only uncertain as to the time of its occurrence, but uncertain as to the fact of its occurrence, only such an element is called a condition in the strict sense. From their peculiar operations and effects, the special acceptation of Canon Law was formulated. It will be sufficient and useful to review the results obtained and present them in their context.

According to the distinction between licit and illicit conditions those that do not suspend either by their own nature, *i. e.*, past or present, or by disposition of the law, *e. g.*, an immoral condition, we must proceed from the principle that with the one class, as immediate result, there arises a state of uncertainty whether the marriage will or

[15] *Cf.* Hussarek, *op. cit.*, 200; Scheurl, *Zeitschr.*, Bd. 14, S. 281.

will not ensue. While in the case of the other kind, if not always for the parties, then certainly objectively, it is quite clear and certain whether the condition is brought about or not. The product of the consent given *sub turpi conditione* is among baptized a *matrimonium ratum,* just as if the contract was pure, *i. e.,* at least in the external forum and too in the internal forum if there be any doubt about the state of mind.[16] The same thing holds for conditions not properly such, *i. e.,* those that do not constitute an obstacle of consent: the realized past and present conditions, and the conditions that must necessarily be realized, while the past or present unrealized condition destroys the consent. Too, the perplex condition does not permit arising of legally effective consent. So-called conditions against the substance of marriage fall under the category of perplex conditions.

Licit and true real conditions which alone are possible in matrimonial law, have this effect that the consent does not immediately create marriage, that neither the status of married couple, nor any other effect of marriage relationship is created, in particular no *vinculum naturale matrimonii* whatsoever is established. Rather the effectuation of marriage with all its consequences is dependent on the fulfillment of the condition, for that which creates marriage (*consensus*) is dependent on the condition to which it is bound.[17]

Now arise the engrossing questions, what is the situation up to that moment? How does the marriage result at the time of verification? And what is the situation in case of its frustration?

1. During pendency no bond obtains between the parties, only a certain inhibition or binding of their own wills takes place.

Just as little as one may declare the given consent as preliminarily entirely ineffective, inoperative in law for the time being, just so little does it possess during pendency those effects which are to be obtained as their *finis ultimus,* for it can obtain these effects only in connection and union with the future event as yet quite uncertain. The declaration of consent may be considered (rightly understood of course)

[16] We presuppose naturally that no other *obex* or impediment is present, *e. g.,* marriage with a sister (if the Pope dispenses) for this condition is an impossible one *juris divini secundarii.* The consent and the contract is null because of this very impediment, not because of this condition.

[17] *Cf.* Hussarek, *op. cit.,* p. 239; Gasparri, *De Matrimonio* (1932), n. 915.

merely a presupposition for the marriage-creating generative force of the conditional event. For the time being the consent has created no marriage, not even a right to marriage, *i. e.*, not even an engagement (canonical or non-canonical) but merely a hope of marriage. What is the strength and certainty of this hope?

This expectation certainly would be protected energetically if every disturbing, impedient influence were held away from the future evolution of the legal relationship thus established, as far as lies in the province of law. The germ implanted should be allowed to develop into a plant according to circumstances, so that nothing would hinder the strength and certainty of this hope. No disposition of the parties should (ideally speaking) be allowed to interfere. Those in position to prevent the verification should have no legal permission to do so, but also no legal possibility to do so (ideally speaking again). This status now being in a process of development would then be powerful enough to prevent any voluntary interference with its full bloom. This is the ideal.

The effect of the conditional basis of a status according to Roman Law may be mentioned.[18] The civil law of Rome has established norms not only for the conditional placing and basing and proof of objective concrete rights, but it has also given us two interesting cases of real restraint upon one's status, *i. e.*, the whole status is tied down to certain things. The one is *status personae*, and *status rei* is the other. A slave bequeathed to another cannot be manumitted during the pendency of a condition. A piece of property by legacy under a condition cannot be placed outside of commerce through the burial of a corpse thereon, by the heir during the pendency of a condition, the condition being that the land is given on condition that it be used as a burial ground.[19]

Canon Law denies that any basis of a status can be created by conditional marital consent. This law has made essentially different rules about conditions in her marriage legislation. According to Canon Law the parties are not affected in any way by the conditional contract, regarding their personalities, so they can indeed posit actions by

[18] *Cf.* historical section.

[19] *Cf.* Hussarek, *op. cit.*, p. 240; I, II D. *de manum*, 40, 1; I, 34 D. *de rel.*, II, 7.

which the well-founded hope of marriage is completely destroyed, that is juridically, and not *per se* morally. The relationship between them does not preclude the possibility of a legal union with a third party, *i. e.,* it does not create the impediment of *ligamen,* nor did it produce (before the Code) the impediment of public honesty. In one word, it places no obstacle to valid marriage with a third person nor is this relationship charmed and protected against the entrance of a marriage impediment (between the *nupturientes*) during pendency. Finally, either of the parties can rescind the entire relationship through recession or by mutual consent. One may characterize all this in one sentence: conditional marital consent creates no (new) status during pendency, or modification of one's status. As Freisen points out [20] during pendency there is no marriage, no engagement, yet there is more than a mere legal nothing, there is a restraint on the will, not a marriage bond. There is a real restraint on the will, say v. Scheurl [21] and Phillips [22] that permits the principle of validity of a marriage bond with a third person as an exception, and Phillips says this is the prevailing doctrine, (probably true of the German canonists of his era). This relationship it is true does create a certain (moral not legal) restraint on one's will. From it results an obligation (not in law) on both to keep their word and abide by this given word, for as a rul- they may not licitly enter into a legal relation (engagement or marriage) with a third person, or posit any fact impeding the future arising of marriage. Every action which opposes this duty of loyalty (which duty of course may lawfully *i. e.,* morally cease) is opposed to good morals, but not *per se* opposed to good law, as some say. Canon Law does not give any detailed dicta or definitions of these points.

There is similarity between some of these principles and those governing the relationship of engagement. But they are not obvious conclusions from the latter relationship, as Hussarek thinks.[23] We must guard against the identity of these two relations, as this author mentioned above, justly remarks. An *engagement* creates a right

[20] *Geschichte des Canonischen Eherechts* (1893), p. 252.
[21] *Cf.* Hussarek, *op. cit.,* p. 241.
[22] *Kirchenrecht,* p. 408.
[23] *Op. cit.,* p. 241.

(moral right at least since the Code) to marriage, just as an obligation contract creates a *jus ad rem,* and the canonical election also creates a *jus ad rem.* It is an actually present, definite and certain claim. It has a positive and a negative side. The positive side consists herein: the parties are obliged in due time (*suo tempore*) to enter marriage, an obligation for the fulfillment of which, the use of ecclesiastical punishment was (not now since the Code) permitted. In so far it is an analogy to the obligation in a certain sense, claimed upon family law (a claim to a transaction which is neither by nature against family law, nor constitutes the source of legal family claims). Its negative side is an obligation to loyalty in virtue of which both must, apart from general moral obligations, preserve towards the other carnal purity and chastity and avoid every action creating or preparing a legal or factual obstacle of a future marriage contract. The actual existence of this bi-lateral claim has even a certain influence upon the family status of the engaged, in so far as neither could marry (before the Code) a relative of the other because of the impediment of public honesty. Yet there is on the other hand such an essential difference between engagement and marriage, that one may not conceive of the former as a preliminary in the process of marriage, and that a marriage consent is necessary for marriage in spite of the engagement.

It is just this characteristic mark of engagement that is wanting to conditional marriage consent, namely, the right to enter into marriage; after formal engagement there exists (morally *per se,* since the Code, not juridically) a coercion to matrimony. This characteristic is denied to conditional marital consent by the very nature of the case (for the condition is placed precisely to save the liberty in case the condition be not verified, and the will has equally this content; "I expressly do not will to marry you if this condition be frustrated") and it is also denied in law, beginning with the Decretals of Gregory the Ninth, for conditional marriage consent during pendency.[24] There exist however a moral and juridical coercion to consummate the existent marriage after fulfillment of the condition. Just as no right to marriage, so no modification of one's status is caused by conditional marriage consent. No impediments arise *eo ipso* because of this con-

[24] C. 5, X, *de conditionibus appositis,* IV, 5.

sent, and no renewal of consent is necessary for valid marriage, after the verification of the condition.

Marriage is not made by the verification of the condition, but by the consent given under a condition, plus the verification. The consent, not *ex tunc* but *ex nunc*, which consent *ex nunc* exists simultaneously with the verification of the condition which the will freely placed. Before the Code, this relationship during pendency was changed into marriage by the *copula sequens* freely had. Changed thus as far as the external forum, not necessarily for the internal forum unless this *presumptio juris et de jure* actually corresponded with the truth in a given case, namely that the condition was revoked and the consent was given absolutely.[25]

After the condition is verified, the originally conditioned consent is thereby purified. It now creates the marriage (if no diriment impediments intervened, and if the condition was not actually recalled). Of course the continuance of the consent is presumed to persevere till this moment, and rightly presumed. This is not *per se* a fiction of its existence at the moment of verification.[26] It may be a fiction *per accidens* or rather a presumption (if the party or parties actually did recall the consent) and then there is no true marriage although the external forum will hold there is until revocation of the entire consent is proved. In doubtful cases one must favor the non-revoking of consent and therefore hold for a valid marriage on verification of the condition. It is not true nor logical to declare or consider as the law creating element or ingredient, not the continuance of the consent, but only the fulfillment of the condition as the creating fact or ingredient, the only element and factor that brings about marriage in this case. *Per se* and in itself the verification of a condition could never conceivably make a marriage, as is seen if the same circumstances were raised to a condition in contracting a purchase of, say, vegetables or iron and steel. At the moment of fulfillment, the parties are really married. The relation between them is either a *matrimonium legitimum tantum* or *ratum tantum*. A recession from this marriage (except by the *privilegium fidei*, special papal power, or by the solemn vows)

[25] Whether this presumption still holds after the code, cf., chapter on: *Copula* as surrogate of fulfillment.

[26] As Hussarek insists on p. 244.

is excluded. If only now the content of a diriment impediment arises, it cannot nullify the existent marriage. Now arises the impediment of *ligamen salvo privilegio fidei* (Canon 1069) and certain relationships (Canon 1076, 97, 1077). Either one may insist on the consummation of the marriage. In brief, there arises the same marriage and relationship as if they had originally consented absolutely.

No renewal of consent is necessary for validity of the marriage.[27] Such a renewal would only be a testimony that the consent was not revoked. It does not affect the marriage. This declaratory renewal of consent, is not bound to the form of celebration of the decree *Tametsi* or the Code. To enter the fulfillment of the condition into the marriage register, and in the place where the conditional consent was already noted, is a matter of good order in the interest of family relations and, did the frequency of open cases demand, it would be quite fitting to make a corresponding direction by way of diocesan legislation. This notation is probably imposed by the new Code. To make the now existing marriage retroactive or begin from the time of the first declaration of conditional consent *de futuro* is preposterous.

The significance of such retroactivity can only be found in this, that the impediment or obstacle had meanwhile no force and marriage with a third party, during pendency, is null and void, or the death of one during pendency would operate the dissolution of the retroactively accomplished marriage, and also the invalidation of such conditional consent. All this does not happen. The principle of the *glossa* is a faithful expression of the certain doctrine: "Non traditur retro ubi ab initio non fuit."

If the condition is frustrated, the ineffectiveness of the conditional contract is decided, therefore a new consent of the parties corresponding to all the requirements would be necessary for marriage. The carrying out of intercourse after this frustration, has in itself no

[27] *Cf.* Hussarek, *op. cit.*, p. 244; Phillips, *op. cit.*, p. 403, for older literature; Barbosa, *Collectanea*, h. t., n. 7; Fagmanus: "Sanctissimus nempe Pius V probavit sententiam canonistarum, quod purificata condicione per consensum patris matrimonium sit perfectum, nec opus esse alia iteratione contractus coram parocho. . . . . Concilium autem Trident. nihil ad hanc rem facere." *Op. cit.*, *IV, de cond. oppos.*, chap., *super eo*, p. 38, n. 5.

marriage creating force. Since marriage with a third party during pendency is valid *ab inito,* the frustration of the condition has no influence upon its validity. Through the elimination of the materialization of the condition the relationship of fidelity existing during pendency has been cancelled and nothing hinders the parties entering into a new union. The recall of the conditional consent, that is, the revoking of the act of the will, by one or both, has the same effect as the frustration of the condition or the arising of an impediment. The only difference is, or was, sometimes ecclesiastical punishment could be inflicted on account of the violated fidelity.

The future honest possible licit condition suspends the marriage in both *fora.* The conditional contract must not be confounded with an innominate contract (*facio ut facias*). In the former there is undertaken the obligation, once the condition is verified to carry out the conditioned thing (*i. e.,* they are married and are obliged to its obligations) but there is no obligation in this sense to carry out the condition. In the other kind of contract the obligation is undertaken concerning both things "Suscipitur ad utrumque." *E. g.,* "I marry you, if you give me $1,000," if given, the obligation of married life is induced, but there is no obligation on the other party to give the money. If the transaction is a *facio ut facias,* A obliges himself to enter marriage after the payment of the money, and B obliges herself to pay if they are married.[28]

Since the mutual bond of marriage is by its very nature indissoluble, resolutive conditions are against the substance of marriage and cannot validly be placed. We must understand this about such conditions placed by the parties, for those resolutive conditions which are in the consent *ipso jure,* are not against the substance in the sense that explicit or implicit willing of them destroy the consent. *Engagements* can receive resolutive conditions placed by the parties, and also *jure ipso* or by mutual consent they can be dissolved although contracted absolutely.

The invoking of the rule adopted by Canon Law from Roman Law about *actus legitimi,* as an argument against the doctrine of licit future conditions, is often grossly misunderstood and consequently misapplied. This rule concerned acts which from the very nature of

[28] De Smet, *De Sponsalibus et Matrimonio,* I, ed. III, Brugis, par. 126 s.

the case or by special disposition of the law prohibited the placing of a condition for which certain forms or formulas are required, *e. g.*, the formula of Consecration, or Penance, or Baptism, not acts depending on one's own will as are many contracts, among which are engagement and marriage. For these have no certain form from Divine Law nor by law are prohibited from the use of conditions. Marriage in Roman Law was not what is technically known as a legitimate act. As is well known from the history of our doctrine, even before the chapters *"de illis"* and *"super eo"* our doctrine had legislation for its existence.[29]

To repeat, honest and possible conditions can either be intrinsic ones which are tacitly understood or extrinsic, which in order to be added must be placed or expressed *mente vel verbis*. These latter are past, present, or future. Thus far in this chapter the future honest condition was treated, and a few more remarks will now be added concerning this kind, closing the chapter with a brief discussion of past and present honest conditions. Vain and impertinent conditions are not rejected as illegal.

Some older authors, *e. g.*, Tanner and Sporer, used the Ulpian maxim about culpably impeding verification, to deny that in this case, that verification was necessary. This doctrine was and is good law for many branches of commercial and social life but from the nature of the case cannot be applied to the marriage contract simply because of the absolute necessity of true consent. This is one of many sad examples of bodily applying civil principles to certain canonical affairs, which by nature cannot use certain arbitrary positive rulings of the civilists.

If a potestative condition is such that it could be fulfilled repeatedly, without any great trouble, then it is a *conditio promiscua,* and if there is doubt concerning the interpretation of the will, it is proper to accept it as wishing for its repetition even though the condition was verified already before the consent was given.[30] Some dispute

[29] *Cf.* Schmalzgrueber, lib. IV, tit. V, n. 7 s.

[30] Promiscua conditio 1) a quibusdam sumitur loco "mixta", quae pendet partim ab eventu objectivo partim a voluntate; 2) ab aliis vero jure meritoque sumitur ut aliquid *vulgare, commune, usuale*, cui opponitur *non-promiscua* seu quae raro accidit (Scialoia, Ferrini)"—D'Angelo, *Jus Digestorum,* I, n. 726. An example would be, *e. g.*, "I marry you if you dance with me."

whether a potestative condition is one that depends on an arbitrary will, only of one who has some right, *e. g.*, a parent, or of one who has no right.

In the purely potestative condition, *coitus* used to count as recission from the condition. In a *conditio mixta* verification in many cases, according to the will of the parties, is not only aimed at the success of the condition, but the mere activization of the condition.

The Sacrament of Marriage is present, for baptized parties, in the very moment of verification of the condition, even though the nupturients are asleep at that moment.[31] The reason is because, in order to have marriage it is required by the institution of God and our Lord, a consent perfect and absolute, externally expressed, and such consent before verification is not present, but it is present simultaneously with fulfillment of the condition. The sign of the purification of the consent is the external eventuation of the condition. For the same reason it is not necessary for validity that they know the condition is fulfilled. The same is true of the principal who marries through a procurator. The former may be asleep at the time and ignorant.

> A somewhat remarkable example of marriage *sub condicione* is afforded by a constitution of Archbishop Winchelsey issued at a synod held at Winchester in 1308.[32] He decrees that should a man and woman have already been convicted twice for immoral relations, they should in case of a third relapse be compelled to sign a document declaring themselves to be man and wife if any further fall should occur. The contract ran as follows: *Ego ex nunc accipio te in meam si de cetero carnaliter te cognoscam;* and on the woman's part: *Ego accipio te ex nunc in meum si de cetero fuero a te carnaliter cognita.* In this case marriage was employed not as an inducement to sin, but as a deterrent. It does not appear how far this constitution was put into practice.[33]

[31] Pirhing, *Universum Jus Canonicum*, n. 24; Schmalzgrueber, lib. IV, tit. V, n. 33.

[32] See Lynwood, *Provinciale* (Oxford, 1679), Appendix, p. 37.

[33] Quoted from Joyce, Geo. H., *Christian Marriage*, London, N. Y., 1933, p. 70.

Is the condition "if God wills" a general and a non-suspensive one? Some say it is tacitly in the contract. Others think it is a condition if an impediment is present, otherwise not. If it means the good will of God (*voluntas beneplaciti*) by which He rules or permits things, then it is general and understood in all contracts, therefore it does not suspend. If by it is meant the Divine Will *approbans,* as if they would say, if this contract does not displease God, but pleases Him, then it is not general and it suspends, for many things are done against the approving will of God. Therefore there is suspense till it is certain it pleases God, if an impediment is present; otherwise it is a *present* condition, and there is no suspension, and marriage is immediately present or not, even though the parties may not know yet whether their marriage does meet with the approving will of God. In this sense the glossators and doctors understand it when they call it a condition. Some deny this last statement, but in doubt presume it is meant in the last sense, for it is safer for the soul.[34] The phrase, "if it pleases the Church," is a condition and if any impediment is present it suspends the consent, for it is always understood of the Church's will of approbation, and in the Church is not found that double will as in God, therefore it suspends till the Church approves. Intrinsic conditions which are inherent in marriage and without which it cannot exist, do not make a conditional contract, even if expressed, *e. g.*, "if you are not my sister," for they are tacitly included in the very contract and in its very essence, since without these the contract fails. That is if this circumstance is added absolutely just as it is in the contract, but the same condition, if added differently than it inheres in the contract, suspends, *e. g.*, "if the Church approves, that is, after studying the case, if it then approves." In other words the difference is, "if I am qualified, and if the Church finds me qualified." If one knows the other person is his sister and yet places the above condition, he does not incur punishment, for the Church cannot, or rather does not as a rule, punish an effect which does not follow:[35]

No renewal of consent is necessary, if the condition is verified, but some think there is an exception to this principle if persons bound by

[34] Sanchez, *De Matrimonio,* I, V, disp. I, n. 8.

[35] Sanchez, *De Matrimonio,* n. 13; cf. Canons 2388, par. 1, 646, 2356.

diriment impediments contract with the condition, "if the pope or bishop shall have dispensed," for they say the renewal is demanded by positive law. But there is here no true exception since in the case, the party or parties bound by this impediment are *inhabiles* to give consent that is juridically valid, but as far as the natural law is concerned marriage can certainly become valid without any renewal. Moreover it is not certain that the renovation of consent is necessary because of any positive disposition of Canon Law. Some doubt this, others deny it.[86]

This particular condition may be possible or impossible, and some authors class dispensations which the pope is not accustomed (*non solet*) to grant, as an impossible one. This is false, *per se,* and moreover the same dispensation, *e. g.*, from *disparitas cultus,* is not customary (*non solet*) for Italy, and customary (*solet*) for the United States.

Marriages become valid among relatives, affines and other disqualified persons, if the pope dispenses, for the condition is verified. This condition is not *turpis* but *honesta,* for the parties don't intend to marry *nunc sed tunc; i. e.*, when they receive the dispensation thus becoming qualified. Schmalzgrueber, Reiffenstuel, Pirhing and others say this condition is honest and possible for it is often with just cause sought and received. Such dispensations are a part of Church Law and as much law as the canons and impediments from which one is dispensed. The fact of the celebration takes place when they are *inhabiles,* but it refers to a time when they become qualified. Thus too the condition: "if you become converted from infidelity," is honest and the marriage is valid on verification, without a dispensation, and the Catholic party incurs no Church penalty for thus conditionally celebrating without a dispensation.[87] Vincentius de Justis taught in such conditional cases of blood relatives, etc., no excommunication or other penalty was incurred and after the dispensation was granted, a renewal of consent was demanded only by jurisprudence, not *ex natura rei.* If after asking for the dispensation, the superior refuses, the condition is unverified.[88]

[86] *Cf.* Cappello, *De Matrimonio,* n. 640, Reiffenstuel, IV, 5, n. 647.

[87] *Cf.* Bonacina, *Opera Omnia,* III, n. 23.

[88] *Cf. Appendix Casuum S. C. Concilii Resolutorum,* Lucas, 1726, de Justis, 380.127; 93.215.

Reiffenstuel points out without approval that in his time many authors for various reasons and because of their interpretations of Rotal decisions maintained the condition is invalid because it is impossible and therefore rejected, and the marriage is invalid not because of the condition, but because of the impediment, and therefore if a dispensation was obtained, there is no marriage without a new consent. These authors say what the Pope cannot do by law is considered impossible, but Reiffenstuel says they confound conditions *de jure* prohibited (*e. g.*, to eat meat on Friday) and therefore legally impossible, with the actual condition, "if the Pope dispenses," for this condition is not impossible or prohibited, the thing in the condition is, the condition itself is not. If the Pope validly can, irrespective of whether he is accustomed to or not, to give any particular dispensation, the condition is honest and possible and there are many decisions to this effect.[39]

Neither party is bound to procure the dispensation, yet one is bound to await till the other obtains it, if this other wishes to endeavor to procure it, unless otherwise provided in the contract. Sanchez disagrees with the first part of this statement.[40] The reason is because no one obliges himself to seek the dispensation but only to contract absolutely if the dispensation is granted. Sanches wishes both to be held to the expenses *pro rata,* it being a common business of both. But better is the opinion that the one placing the condition is held only, for the other wills only to marry, not to procure it.[41] If the parties place a condition that is rejected by the law [42] and otherwise they are *inhabiles,* they do incur penalties for the contract is absolute in the external forum at least by presumption.[43]

Some authors teach that if the impediment is one which the Pope ordinarily dispenses, but there is no *causa* present to justify the dispensation, then such a condition is not an honest one, and thus rejected and the contract remains null. This reasoning is not cogent, or rather in practice there is always a *causa* present, e. g., the danger of a civil marriage at least; especially, is it not forceful concerning

[39] Reiffenstuel, lib. IV, tit. 1, n. 33.

[40] Sanchez, *De Matrimonio,* lib. 5, tit. 5, n. 36.

[41] *Loc. cit.*, n. 36.

[42] *Eg., turpis, impossibilis.*

[43] Bonacina, *Opera Omnia,* III, n. 15.

the impediments of minor degree, which according to the Code do not need a *causa* for valid dispensation.[44]

To sum up there are two opinions of this condition. The first teaches the consent is absolutely null *ab initio,* for the condition is legally impossible and therefore to be rejected. The other opinion, maintains it is lawful *per se* to add such a condition and therefore it is not licit but immoral *per se* to revoke it, the other unwilling.[45] The reason is because the condition is honest and not against any law. No law forbids one to contract marriage with this condition, but Canon Law does prohibit one to contract absolutely without a dispensation, and if this be granted the marriage is immediately perfected. This opinion is the true one.

A clause in a *fideicommissum* [46] for one party to marry a blood relative is valid, and should be understood, if the Pope dispenses. It is a condition inherent in the law, (*inest in jure*). If there be no blood relative to marry, then the condition is considered fulfilled for a mixed condition in this case is held verified as often as one cannot fulfill by his act in whose person he ought to fulfill.[47]

[44] *Cf.* Bayon, *Tractatus de S. Matrimonio,* Madrid, Vol. I, n. 783; Salmant, tr. IX, c. VII, pars. IV, n. 39.

[45] *Cf.* Ball-Pal., *Theologia Moralis,* n. 96; Gasparri, *De Matrimonio,* n. 104; Wernz-Vidal, *Jus Matrimoniale,* n. 515; Cappello, *De Matrimonio,* n. 640; Sanchez, 5, 5, 13; 5, 8, 10: etc., apud Bayon, *op. cit.*, n. 785.

[46] It was an imperial rescript of the emperor Augustus who was the first to introduce into the administration of justice the principle that, where a testator requested a person who was benefited under his will to make over the benefit he received to a third party—this is the meaning of *fideicommissum*—the request should be legally enforceable. It was an *informal* bequest in trust. Later on *universal fidecommissa* were introduced. The *fideicommissum* was had where the deceased with a view of conferring a benefit on a third party (often legally incompetent to receive by testament) imposed on another, in precatory terms a purely conscientious obligation (hence the name) to make over to the third person the benefit, thus informally conferred on him. Usually it took the form of a letter (*codicilli*) addressed to the *fiduciarius,* the one on whom the obligation was imposed. This only became legally enforcible in the time of Augustus, before that time the execution of the trust depended solely upon the honor of the heir upon whom the trust imposed. *Cf.* Sohme-Ledlie, *Institutes of Roman Law,* Ed. III, par. 115; W. C. Morey, *Outlines of Roman Law,* N. Y., 2 ed., p. 335.

[47] Augustini Barbosae, *Libri Duo Votorum,* etc., lib. 1, Votum VIII, n. 4.

CHAPTER XVIII

PRESENT AND PAST HONEST POSSIBLE CONDITIONS

Phillips [1] says erroneously that according to c. 5, X *De Cond. Appos.* IV, 5, about conditions *de praesenti,* these conditions exceptionally did not produce the effects of a condition, but of a *consent de futuro* and Urban III was probably induced to make this principle because of a Roman Law precept of heritary law according to which no heir could be an heir under the condition of "if Titus wishes," and that it was justifiable to maintain the same thing in marriage and quite sound legislation to do so. The older canonical development of a conditional *desponsatio* did actually handle this condition as an exceptional thing, but for the doctrine we hold this as established: this condition is to be judged as equivalent, equal with any other honest condition and it has no peculiar nature of its own. The lesser obligation or constraint placed on the will of the *nupturientes* as compared with conditional transactions in Roman Law, is due entirely (both for present and future conditions) to the very nature of marriage and the freedom and liberty of the will (*de jure naturae et canonico*) necessarily bound up with this. It is quite another story if the object of the conditional will were buying or selling or giving of material things as money, animals, produce, etc.

If the condition fails, the contract fails.[2] Past and present conditions of *any species* do *not* suspend. Marriage is valid or not according to the truth or not of the condition.[3]

[1] *Kirchenrecht,* p. 376 sq.; Hussarek, *op cit.,* p. 203.

[2] *Cf. Causa Cameracen,* which the diocesan court declared null *ex capite conditionis* of the presence of a disease, while the Rota in its first turn said "non constat de nullitate," the second and third turn confirmed the opinion of the diocesan court, respectively, August 11, 1910, *AAS, II* (1910), 961 s; June 23, 1911, *AAS, III* (1911), 497 s; *Coll. N. R. th.,* 1913, p. 234 s; *cf.* alsso *causa Limburgensis* 2 January, 1913, *AAS,* V, 45 s; a condition of virginity was placed and after three or four months the woman was *gravida.*

[3] De Smet, *De Sponsalibus et Matrimonio,* Tomus 1, ed. III, par. 126 (1920). Canon 1092, Bayon, *Tractatus De Matrimonio,* p. 319.

> *Quaevis* conditio de praesenti vel de praeterito, sive impossibilis, . . . sive turpis, . . . sive honesta . . . revera non suspendit consensum, sed hic habetur, ideoque matrimonium statim valet ab initio, si condito exsistit; non habetur ideoque matrimonium est ab initio nullum, si conditio non exsistit, licet apud nos adhuc incertum sit (rel. Canon 1092, n. 4).[4]

Now will be discussed past and present honest conditions. If the event which in virtue of the declaration of the legal will, is to establish the intended legal relation in cooperation with it—if this event is realized or frustrated simultaneously with the declaration, or if the realization or frustration are already in the past, in that moment then it is simultaneously with the declaration objectively certain whether the intended effect is realized or not. Subjective uncertainty of the parties, is quite compatible with this objective certainty. If subjective uncertainty is present then the declaration given in conditional form appears to be due to the mature deliberation and circumspection of one or both of the *nupturientes*. If both know of the fulfillment then the mention of the circumstance may be considered as a hint of the motives that guided the parties in making the transaction, and this declaration may serve as a more definite declaration of the will of the parties, but this is entirely indifferent and practically superfluous as far as the existence and the import of the will is concerned. The legal effects appear in both cases. If the past or present condition is or was already frustrated then the transaction is equivalent to one under an impossible condition seriously placed.

Some care must be used in the evaluation of past or present conditions which are unexplorable for human knowledge, *e. g.*, "I marry you, if John died of heart failure;" "if he died in the state of grace."

[4] Gasparri, *De Matr.* (1932), n. 921. "Itaque duo haec conditionem faciunt, delatio et casus, sive incertus eventus. Conditio praesens vel praeteriens non habet dilationem per se, sed per accidens." Roman law has specific rules for a group of cases in which the characteristic legal effect, pendency is lacking in all of them. The legal transaction is simultaneous and perfected with the act of the will and valid or not according to the circumstances. These are past and present honest possible conditions, and those that are rejected as not placed, by the law, (turpis, necessaria, impossibilis). Canonists of the classic era did not go beyond the sources of Roman law in their investigation concerning these.

If the past or present condition was not fulfilled there is no marriage. If they were fulfilled, there is a marriage. This agrees with Canon 1092, n. 4. No kind of past or present conditions, whether honest or base or illegal or necessary or those so-called past or present against the substance of marriage, none of these suspend, none are rejected.[5]

Strictly speaking, a past or present condition cannot be against the substance of marriage, using this last phrase in the meaning it bears in connection with a future condition and keeping in mind the rôle a true marital consent plays in effecting a marriage. This point will be elucidated more in the chapter on conditions that invalidate the consent.

The verification need not be proved before the pastor and the witnesses of the celebration, for validity of the marriage. Peter Ledesma and Bonacina and others asserted it did. Sanchez denied this.

If the condition is later verified, it effects nothing. For instance, "if you are rich," and he is not, but becomes rich later.[6] The reason is the contract receives its legality and its condition from the will and convention of the parties as *regula contractus* 85 *in Sixto* teaches. "Contractus ex conventione legem accipere dignoscuntur." "Per verbum *legem* regula intelligit forman, naturam, et modum obligationis in contractu. . . ."[7] The knowledge or ignorance of the existence of the condition is irrelevant, since these do not bind the consent. Only in this way could the knowledge be effective, if, *e. g.*, the condition is, "If *I know* your father consents."

"Si legitima es," is an honest condition and possible *de praesenti*. Therefore, if it is true, there is a marriage. We cannot make an impossible condition out of this just because in reality she is illegitimate. If so then all illegitimates are matter of impossible conditions. Even if many children were born of this couple, the marriage is invalid *per se*. The *copula* does not convalidate the consent. For this is *post factum*. It is moreover too late to recede from the condition,

[5] Tamburini, *Explicatio Decalogi*, lib. VIII, *de Matr.*, Tract IV, cap. V, par. 2.

[6] Schmalzgrueber, lib. IV, tit. V, n. 19; Schmier, *Jurisprudentia Canonico-Civilis*, lib. IV, tract. II, chap. II, sect. III.

[7] Reiffenstuel, *De Regulis Juris* (LXXXV), Paris, 1870, p. 179.

for the effect of the consent is not suspended, the consent is either efficacious or not immediately. The *copula* may in a given case signify a completely new consent.[8]

The condition, "if you are a virgin," is *per se* honest. But if the one placing it means that he is to find out by his own personal inspection or in any illicit manner, it is *turpis* and therefore rejected as a *future* turpis, for it invites to sin. It is equivalent then to this, "if I find you a virgin." If the meaning is by licit exploration, *e. g.*, by competent women or experts, then the condition is honest and possible.

A recent case tried in the Rota was a condition with this content, "I marry you if you never lived with another woman." After many decisions against the woman, a special commission of five cardinals declared the marriage was invalid because the condition was unfulfilled.[9]

The *cautiones* demanded by the Church in mixed marriages, in themselves, are not conditions that affect the consent, or suspend it. They do not make the marriage immediately invalid if not seriously given in cases of disparity of worship, that is, on the head that they make a *condition* attached to the consent. They can be made a *conditio sine qua non*. There is a marriage declared null by the Rota on this ground.[10] The *cautiones* as a condition really means this: "If you seriously *promise now* not to ever interfere, etc.," that is, an honest condition. If the one placing the condition means: "if you actually will not ever interfere, etc.", they could not be fulfilled till all the children were born and grew up to manhood in the Catholic faith, etc., that is the same thing as "ad Kalendas graecas amandare," in other words, such a condition will never be fulfilled till the one burdened with the conditions dies; or from another viewpoint, whenever he actually does interfere, even if years later, the condition would be unverified, and in this sense it is a resolutive condition and thus it invalidates *ab initio* the consent.

[8] *Cf.* case in Fagnanus, Commentaria in *quartum Librum Decretalium* (1729), p. 40.

[9] *AAS*, X, 1918, 388, in *Causa Versaliln.*

[10] 11 August, 1922, *AAS*, XIV, 512.

Since it is impossible to enter the mind to find out whether he seriously promises, external criteria must be used, *e. g.*, his conduct before, during, and after the celebration, especially such immediate conduct and other adminicular proofs are indications to probe the mind's seriousness at the time of celebration. But the judges must be careful not to ask the person *leading* questions, yet generally any pertinent questions will be more or less leading ones.

CHAPTER XIX

VERIFICATION AND FRUSTRATION OF THE CONDITION

A CONDITIONAL marital consent is not effective in causing the marriage status to arise unless the conditional circumstance is verified. A conditional marital consent is destroyed or juridically ceases to exist if the realization of the conditional event was not, *de facto* realized if the event was placed in the past; or if the event is not now realized, if the event was placed in the present time; or if the condition no longer can be materialized in the future, if the condition is a future one. For instance, "I marry you, if you were once an admiral;" and he never was an admiral, then the condition is frustrated or unfulfilled, and as a consequence the entire conditional transaction passes from the realm of juridical existence. "I marry you, if you are now an admiral;" and if he is not now an admiral, likewise the whole transaction becomes null and void juridically. "I marry you, if and when you actually will be appointed an admiral;" and if legal or other reasons are or become present, making the appointment impossible, *e. g.*, if the law of the land requires as a qualification, that one must be a native-born citizen, and he is not, or if he becomes insane, or blind, etc., then the entire transaction ceases because the condition placed is now frustrated, it cannot be fulfilled.

To ascertain whether a condition referring to the past was verified or not, presents relatively little difficulty. To ascertain whether a condition referring to the present, *i. e.*, to the time when the conditional consent was furnished, offers much more difficulty.[1] To ascertain whether a future condition was verified or not, presents often most complicated difficulty.

The condition is fulfilled if that state of affairs arises in the future, or has already arisen, or is present, of which it can be said that

[1] *Cf.* for present conditions cases in which the Rota found much trouble in deciding: *AAS,* II (1910), pp. 961-972; which case was discussed by the Rota three different times; *cf.* also, *AAS,* XIV (1922), pp. 512-523—in this marriage case, the woman placed as a condition that her irreligious partner seriously promise not to interfere with her or the future children's religious liberty. This marriage also was discussed several times by the Rota.

it is the realization of that which the party or parties placing the condition intended when the condition was placed. To determine his intention is the business of the interpreter of the contract and the guiding norm for this must be the exploration of the true wills of the parties. "Verba conditionis appositae sumenda esse sensu obvio et juxta intentionem dicentis, ex circumstantiis manifestatam." [2]

If the condition was predicated upon the realization of an event, this event must have been realized or materialized. If based on the non-realization of a fact, then the realization of this fact must have disappeared from the realm of possibility. The knowledge, or ignorance, or error of the parties concerning the fulfillment of a condition are immaterial for the entrance of the legal effects of verification. Of course, these states of mind may motivate the one placing the condition to retract the condition and consent absolutely. But this requires a new act of the will. The point is, these mental states *eo ipso* and automatically do not necessarily elide the condition.

A man, before the ceremony took place, added a condition that the woman be free then from a contagious disease which he suspected was present. Her medical doctor assured him she was perfectly healthy. This report made soon before the celebration gave the man joy and relief. Temporarily, especially at the time of the ceremony, he thought the condition was verified and he did not repeat the condition at the ceremony. In a day or so he was disillusioned. The judges of the first trial in the Rota concluded that his joy and state of mind at the time of the celebration, elided the condition and that he consented absolutely. But two later trials denied this, saying among other profound remarks, the following:

> Posita autem conditione, nostra aestimatio quae falso putet hanc fuisse adimpletam, nihil mutat in re. . .
>
> Sed—uti praedicat effatum—nostra existimatio rerum veritatem non mutat; quare actor ductus persuasione enuntiata conditio in contractu—si non verbis, re tamen suberat —eadem sinceritate et simplicitate qua conditionis appositae effectum et indolem se ignorasse fassus est, prosequitur . . .[3]

[2] "Ad effectum inducendae conditionis magis inspicitur substantia dispositionis et mens disponentium, quam cortex verborum." S. R. Rota, *AAS*, II (1910), 967.

[3] *AAS*, II, (1910), 968.

Difficulties arise from such negative potestative conditions whose verification is certain only with the death of the party who is to omit something in virtue of these conditions. For in such cases (*i. e.*, when the one who is to omit something is one of the nupturients, and only in this restricted sense is the term "potestative" used by some authors) it is certain *ab initio* that the condition is realized at the time when marriage can no longer be contracted, for this time coincides with the death of the one who is to omit something; till then he has the *de facto* power to frustrate the condition by not omitting the condition. Such declarations of will are ailing of an internal disease and are therefore null and void. For instance, "I marry you if you *never actually* interfere with my liberty of religion." (This kind of a condition is not to be confounded with one like this. "I marry you if and when you *seriously promise* not to interfere with my liberty of religion.")

The effect is a little different if the condition were something like this (also called by some a potestative condition, and by others a casual condition: "I marry you if your parents never actually interfere with my freedom of religion." In this case, the condition could be frustrated at any time during the lives of the parents and at least the danger of its frustration could perdure up to the death of the surviving parent. Since this is so, the consent is null and void, moreover it is equivalent to a resolutive condition.

A true surrogate of the fulfillment, in the external forum of the pre-Code law was had in the *copula* during pendency of the condition. Whether or not this continues to be the law to-day, will be treated separately later on.

When the condition is verified, *eo ipso* the marriage is present, for the consent now becomes absolute, provided the situation has remained *in statu quo, e. g.*, no diriment impediment has intervened. The situation does not remain *in statu quo* if one party with absolute consent marries a third person; or if one party becomes permanently insane. Even though the condition is later verified, there is no resulting marriage, if the conditional consent, that is, the whole transaction (the consent and the condition) was meanwhile cancelled or revoked by, *e. g.*, a marriage with a third party, or if a diriment impediment supervenes and continues till the condition is verified.

Likewise if, before verification, one party falls into insanity which is present at the time of verification. Some authorities maintain the consent is absolutely extinct once insanity occurs irrespective of whether the insanity continues till the verification of the condition, or ceases before that time. But it is by no means certain that if the mind becomes sane right before and continues sane during the fulfillment of the condition, that psychologically the once given consent does not then exist, and effect the marriage. It seems improbable that the negative contention could be proved.[4]

If the condition is, "I marry you if my father consents," how long must one wait? The answer is given by the use of good sense, the study of circumstances, and the exploration of the will of the nupturient. Suppose the father consents, then recalls it? Some day the condition is verified, others deny. The answer again is found in the will of the party. If the father first is repugnant, then later on consents, authors again are divided about this. Sanchez denies the condition is fulfilled in this case. But once again theorizing is useless, leaving out the will of the party. If the party meant to stake his all on the condition as soon as his father heard of it and irrespective of his later change of will, then it is to be judged according to the first reply of the father. This condition can have a successive tract, and thus it can be verified if the consent of the parties persevere in that will. Some claim the successive tract idea is valid in this sense, that the father did not have to consent immediately but should be given time to deliberate, not in the sense that he can dissent, then consent. If the father died meanwhile, the condition can be looked upon as an impossible one, especially is this true if the condition were, if my father does not refuse, this is verified in the event of his death, before he had a chance to refuse or bless. What if the father has gone away and cannot be reached? Generally the marriage is valid for this condition is regularly placed not to offend his parent and to get his blessing, but in this case the parent can not be offended for he does not know of it. What if the father remains silent? Schmalzgrueber says then the condition is verified, for the parent does not contradict or dissent, which is the meaning of the condition, "if my father consents." This then would be negative, not positive consent, nor does

[4] *Cf.* Wernz-Vidal, *Jus Matrimoniale,* n. 126; Chelodi, *Jus Matrimoniale,* n 126, who it seems favors the exstinction of consent in these circumstances.

the regula juris 44 in Sixto present an obstacle to this conclusion. "Is, qui tacet, non fatetur, sed nec utique negare videtur," for in the case we presume negative consent according to regula juris 43, "Qui tacet consentire videtur." This last rule is particularly applicable to parental approval for marriage.[5] Therefore rule 43 is validly applied to the case proposed; and rule 44 is not pertinent to it.

Some authors, *e. g.*, Peter Ledesma [6] taught as certain, that the marriage is not valid till the condition was verified before the pastor and witnesses, because of the requirements of the decree *Tametsi.* Many canonists have shown the fallacy of this doctrine now abandoned by all, quoting among other arguments the famous case given by Fagnanus, already previously discussed.[7]

If a man contracts conditionally with two women, which one is valid? The learned differ. Some wish the first transaction to prevail according to the regula juris "qui prior," 54 in Sexto: "Qui prior est tempore potior est jure." The true meaning of this *regula* is that in the case of both persons everything else is equal (caeteris paribus, soli excepto tempore) except the time element. Others say the second prevails, having destroyed the first.[8] But due to the natural causative power of marital consent when not obstructed, it is better to distinguish as follows without any regard to the above rule which does not apply to the case. If both conditions are fulfilled at the same time, neither marriage is valid on account of uncertainty, to say the least; otherwise that one prevails whose condition is first fulfilled. The reason is that if during pendency, one simply contracts with a third party, without doubt this last is valid, and in the above case, when the condition is verified, the consent is simple and absolute. It is assumed that it is psychologically possible to have two such conditional consents at the same time. In a given case, the second transaction may intimate a revocation of the first.

The condition is frustrated as soon as and when the possibility of the conditioning event being realized is eliminated, *e.g.*, if the con-

[5] *Cf.* Reiffenstuel, *Tractatus de Regulis Juris*, reg. 43.

[6] *Cf.* section, "Can a Condition be Validly Added to Consent."

[7] *Cf.* Pallotini, *Coll. S. C. C.*, verb. "matrimonium," par. XV. Augustinus Barbosa, among others held the antiquated opinion—*cf. Collectanea Doctorum qui in suis operibus Concilii Tridentini Loca Referentes,* Lugduni, 1686, 261.134.

[8] *Cf.* Sanchez, *De Matrimonio,* lib. V, d. 8, n. 13.

dition is that the woman be now free from contagious disease, and she is not free from it. In like manner operates the arising of a matrimonial impediment between the parties (continuing till verification), and also recession from the contract, *e. g.*, "I marry you, if my father consents," but before the father consents (which he does) the man contracts the diriment impediment of public honesty by living in public concubinage with the girl's mother. In this case the verification of the condition does not effect the marriage, due to the presence of the impediment.[9] If the diriment impediment arises, then vanishes, before verification, the transaction is restored *res integra in statu quo.*

The question when the condition is to be considered as *frustrated* is to be interpreted likewise according to the explorations of the wills of the parties. It is a question of this interpretation whether partial fulfillment is sufficient or is not to be considered at all. Usually the latter case is verified.[10] But not necessarily so. The condition may very well have been placed to enforce an act of obedience. If several conditions are placed, it must be ascertained by interpreting the will whether they were intended alternatively or conjunctively and in accordance with this, fulfillment of one or both must be demanded. "Si plures conditiones conjunctive positae, omnibus parendum est. Si plures separatim: In alternativis sufficit alterum adimpleri cui, libet." "In alternativis debitoris est electio, et sufficit alterum adimpleri." [11] "Alternativa et disjunctiva, idem sunt." For instance, "I marry you if you become an admiral or give me a thousand dollars." [12]

If the parties place a potestative condition which is repeatable, in the *knowledge* that it *already* has been *fulfilled once before,* then it may be regularly accepted that repetition of this action corresponds to their intention. In the other case, the condition is held to be verified if the circumstance has already been realized in the past, in spite of the fact that the parties ignorantly expected it only for the future, *e. g.*, *"I marry you, if you swim the channel,"* and if the one

[9] *Cf. Canons* 1042, par. 2, n. 3; and 1078.
[10] *Cf.* L. 23, D. *de cond.* 35, 1.
[11] Reg. 70, R. J., in VI.
[12] Reiffenstuel, *Tractatus de Regulis Juris,* reg. 70.

placing the condition knows that he already swam it several times before, then it seems the party wills that he do it again, but it is presumed otherwise if the former feats were unknown.

A presumption or supposition for or against verification is recognized just as little by Canon Law as by Roman Law.

Likewise the principle of *regula juris* 66 in *Sexto,* of fictitious fulfillment, "Cum non stat per eum, ad quem pertinet, quominus condicio impleatur, haberi debet perinde, ac si impleta fuisset," rests only on the same interpretation of the will.[13] This *regula* can be misused by a too wide interpretation and it should cede to the principle that the intention of the parties deserve closer attention than the wording of the declaration. "Ad effectum inducendae conditionis magis inspicitur substantia dispositionis et mens disponentium, quam cortex verborum." [14] Canon Law, and the sources, do not recognize the principle: "quotiens per eum, cujus interest condicionem non impleri, fiat, quominus impleatur, perinde haberi, ac si impleta fuisset." [15] It may be correct to apply this to the placing of immoral conditions.

Father Vermeersch gives this case and solution, about the frustration of a condition:[16]

> Titius enters a marital contract with Vincentia a Lutheran, under this condition, if you become a Catholic. For several months she deferred her conversion which Titius regarded as certain and more or less imminent. Impatient at delay, he asks what course is open to him to obtain an honorable release from the inflexible Vincentia.
>
> Solution: Two courses are open to him. Either wait until further delay makes palpable the bad will of Vincentia. Under these circumstances Titius deceived by his error, may regard himself as freed from his pact and may licitly contract with another which he could always have done validity at any time. Or he may cite Vincentia before the ecclesiastical judge and ask him to set a day after which Vincentia will be considered to have failed to fulfill the condition, so that Titius is no longer bound to the pact.

[13] Reiffenstuel, *Tractatus de Regulis Juris,* reg. 66; *cf.* Hussarek, *Die Bedingte Eheschliessung,* p. 247.

[14] S. R. Rota—*AAS,* II (1910), p. 967.

[15] L. 161 de R. J., 50, 17.

[16] *Homilectic* and *Pastoral Review,* (N. Y. 1933), p. 186 s.

CHAPTER XX

REVOCATION OF THE CONTRACT OR OF THE CONDITION

CLOSELY allied with the fulfillment or frustration of the *condition,* is the revocation of the same, and the revocation of the entire transaction. Revocation may be twofold. One by which the marriage is made impossible, that is by receding not from the condition but from the entire contract or transaction, from the consent; the other, if the party or parties who places the condition, withdraws it, and consents absolutely. In the first case, a marriage is now impossible; in the latter, the marriage arises at the moment the condition is revoked.

It is licit in the case of a suspensive condition to recede from the entire affair, by mutual consent. Neither can, before verification, *per se* licitly recede, but both are bound to wait till the event is verified or fails, for that is proper to a conditional contract, that one cannot lawfully revoke his consent, if the other is unwilling, because from this hope arises an obligation *in spe* not *in re.*[1]

Revocation of the consent can be made explicitly by expressed or written words, or implicitly by some act showing a contrary will, *e. g.,* a marriage with a third party, or a serious engagement with another. It can be done publicly or secretly, yes, even by a mere internal act of the will, whether at the time of the actual celebration, or before this act of celebration, or after it. If the condition were publicly added, and then the entire transaction secretly abolished, if the condition is verified, the court will hold the marriage is valid in the external forum, till the occult cancelling of the entire transaction is sufficiently proved. If the condition refers to the past or present, there cannot be any revocation of the *entire transaction,* for the marriage is *eo ipso* valid or not according to the truth of the condition or its non-fulfillment.

[1] Sanchez, *op. cit.,* lib. IV, d. 6, n. 8; Bayon, *Tractatus de Matrimonio,* p. 316.

The other kind of revocation is the cancellation of the *condition,* not the *consent,* by which revocation the marriage is perfected. What was said above, concerned that recall that causes the marriage possibility to perish. But the cancelling of the *condition* only, immediately occasions the marriage to arise. This happens if the parties not wishing to await the verification, will to contract absolutely. In this case if the celebration was made according to Canon Law, to have a valid marriage it is not required by natural or canonical law that there be a new canonical celebration, not even for lawfulness. The parties should simply inform the pastor so he can note it in the marriage record.[2] If the condition refers to the past or present, there can be no revocation of the *condition,* for the marriage *eo ipso* is valid if the condition is or was verified; and invalid if not verified.

If both the nupturients placed the condition, and only one recedes from the same, the *status quo* remains the same, provided the other will persevers and marriage will ensue upon verification of the circumstance. If both placed the condition, and one during pendency revokes entirely his *will* or *consent* to *marry,* there would be no valid marriage, even if the condition is verified. Of course the external forum will decide otherwise, if the verification and not the revocation of the condition is proved. The same reason that forbids only one to revoke his consent, also forbids either from impeding the verification, if the other is unwilling. Both should endeavor to have the circumstance come true. By mutual consent, the parties can lawfully recede from the conditional marital consent itself, or from the condition only; for they can renounce their acquired *jus in spe.*

If the condition was revoked before the celebration, the contract is absolute. But if made before, and not repeated in the celebration, one cannot conclude just because the *words* are pure and absolute, that the condition was revoked. Rather it remains *virtualiter in mente* and it is efficacious.[3]

Once it has been proved that a condition has been added, the burden of proof that it has been revoked, falls upon him who asserts it. If, *e. g.*, the other party, or the *defensor vinculi* asserts it was revoked,

[2] *Cf.* Cappello, *De Matrimonio,* n. 639; Bayon, *op. cit.*, p. 314.

[3] Chelodi, *op. cit.*, ed. III, 1921, n. 123; S. R. Rota, 19 June, 1909 (dec. 8); 11 August, 1910 (dec. 30); 23 June, 1911 (*AAS, III,* 497; *AAS, IX,* 388).

they and not the one placing it, must prove it. This was decisively stated by the judges of the Rota.

> Sapientissime Pitonius, a Patronis citatus, ait voluntatem jam manifestatem et aliquam conditionem contractui apponentem non praesumi mutatam fuisse sed continuari. Lege enim cautum est "quod quis semel voluit aut noluit, illud semper deinceps velle aut nolle intelligitur quamdiu non retractaverit voluntatem, et qui ait mutatam fuisse voluntatem docere id debet." [4]

Thus the future marriage *contract* can be dissolved in two ways: either by the revocation of the *consent;* or as often as for any cause whatsoever, whether culpable or inculpable, the *condition* is not fulfilled, and its possibility of being realized vanishes, and thus vanishes the consent and therefore no marriage is possible. On the other hand, the conditional consent becomes absolute and effects marriage also in two ways: either by the *revocation* of the *condition* or the *fulfillment* of the same. All the above is true even though a *condicio juris in re matrimonali* is verified *legally*, but not *actually.* If the condition is a circumstance of the past or present, then revocation of it is not possible, there is no time to recall it, presupposing that the will is conditioned at the moment of the celebration. To effect a marriage in these circumstances a *new absolute act* of the wills is necessary, provided the condition is not or was not verified. Even in the former law the *copula* in these cases (of past and present conditions), had no presumptive revocatory effect and this from the very nature of the case.

[4] S. R. Rota—*AAS,* II (1910), 971.

CHAPTER XXI

INTERCOURSE AS SURROGATE OF FULFILLMENT OF THE CONDITION

A TRUE real surrogate of the fulfillment of the condition was had in the former law,[1] in the freely had *copula* during pendency. This was a *presumptio juris et de jure,* admitting no direct proof to the contrary. Whether by the law of the Code this fact is also a surrogate, will be the purpose of this article to ascertain. This *copula* was usually represented as a *renunciation* of the condition; or as some say, it is more correct to speak of this sexual union as equivalent to the fulfillment of the condition or better still to use a *modus cogitandi* peculiar to the sources, it operates as if a new unconditional consent were given.[2] A closer and clearer examination of the extent and import of this principle will be useful. According to previous Canon Law the *copula* could become a juridic fact *in re matrimoniali* in a twofold way. It could be an act of contracting marriage (by use of the aforesaid presumption) or an act of consummating marriage. The consideration of this last viewpoint is not relevant to this discussion. Juridically it plays an important rôle in Canon Law. Intercourse as an act of consummating the marriage is a fact, not a legal transaction. A series of legal effects are bound up with this sexual unity, these effects are produced by the intercourse pure and simple without regard to the concomitant intention of either or both *concubentes.* This *copula* is in contradistinction to the *copula* as the constitutive act of marriage, insofar as it constituted a *presumptio juris et de jure.* The former is a mere fact, not a legal action. If the marriage were consummated with or even against the will of one, or if this will were legally defective, this would not alter anything in the import of the *copula* as the act of consummating marriage. The legal results would ensue also in this case. This interpretation is the more obvious as sufficient account of the requirements of the freedom of the will is

[1] C. 5, 6, X, *de cond. appos., IV* 5.

[2] *Cf.* Hussarek, *Die Bedingte Eheschliessung,* p. 248.

had when the *consensus de praesenti* is actually given and therefore consummation appears merely as the fulfillment of a legal obligation *sua sponte* entered upon. This principle exhibits the essential distinction between the *consensus* and the *copula* theories.[8]

If the consummation of the marriage appears as having some real causative effect in originating the legal relationship of sacramental marriage, then this consummation is a legal transaction and no one will easily grant that the direction of the will in this act is a matter of indifference. If, however, all that pertains to the legal transaction of the marriage contract is already comprised in the declaration of consent, and if the consummation deserves no further consideration except as a qualification of an already existing relation, then there is no essential reason why the will of the parties might not be considered immaterial in the consummation.

The effectuation of a condition could formerly by the presumption of law, be through intercourse and this latter was presumed to connote a state of mind and qualification of parties that met all the requirements of a legal transaction. The act of intercourse itself could not meet all these requirements, as some assert. Resting on this presumption, Canon Law privileged the intention of having the *copula,* in certain cases, with contractual force to induce marriage. Every extramarital sexual pleasure being ostracized by the law of God, it was obvious to conclude from a fact which may be in its realization either a crime or a licit legal transaction, a sin or a sacrament, all according to the will present at the time, to conclude from all this, in cases of doubt on these points, rather in favor of the sacrament, which the Church desires, blesses, and ratifies rather than to judge it an illegal action subject to ecclesiastical punishment. Hence it is that the *copula* according to this juridic dictum was considered in some cases as the expression of the will of the *concubentes aiming* at marriage. Common to all of these cases is this, that between the parties to be united in wedlock through this medium of a freely had sexual union, there must have obtained before the act, a legally relevant relation, which relation *in se* was not sufficient to create the marriage, but yet aims at marriage. In all these cases the *copula* is always the marriage forming (declarative) act, not at all the consummation act of an already

[8] *Cf.* Hussarek, *op. cit.*, p. 250.

existent marriage. That which it finds present is a non-marriage, and not the *matrimonium ratum.*

These relations between the *concubentes* are: engagement or marital consent given under a future condition. Engagement thus immediately became marriage. The law accepted the intention made probable through the circumstances of the parties as legally existent and every counter argument against this is excluded. The Council of Trent's decree *Tametsi* affected this principle substantially, as far as *engagement* followed by the *copula* was concerned, for it demanded the presence of the pastor and witnesses for the form of celebrating a valid marriage.

If during the pendency of the future *condition* attached to marital consent, the *copula* was had, there resulted (at least up to the Code Law, if not beyond) in virtue of a legal presumption which considered the act as a renunciation of the condition, a marriage. It is not our affair here, to ascertain the proximate presumptions for the verification of all this. The proximate grounds for these two presumptions differ simply because of the nature of engagement consent and marriage consent, on which one or the other presumption works. These were presumptions of such a nature (*juris et de jure*) as to exclude, as a rule, direct counter proofs to the contrary. Only indirect proofs are admitted, *e. g.*, that no engagement or conditional consent ever existed between the parties. Proofs against the presumed intentions obtaining at the moment of the *copula,* etc., are outlawed.

There is no doubt that *coram Deo* and the consciences of the *concubentes,* in order to effect marriage, a certain role must be played by the will of the parties over and above the fact of there being carnal union. This precisely is the rôle that the Church presumed was played by the wills, as far as the external forum is concerned, because of the *favor matrimonii.* Thus the primary requisite is the existence of the capacity of a free decision of will at the moment of the *copula.* If, *e. g.*, one of the engaged had the *copula* in a fit of insanity or perfect intoxication, there would be another angle. Moreover a correct decision of will must have been formed naturally sufficient for the marriage will. Anything causing an internal disease of this will, affecting its substance also limits and affects the force of the *copula* in its juridic effect. If, *e. g.*, an engaged man forces his partner to sin, the natural requirements of the will are compatible with this, the ecclesiastical ones may not be, but in this case the ancient presumption *juris et de jure* excluded invoking any canons on *vis et metus.* Whether there is or is not *affectus maritalis* present at the moment of copulation, is irrelevant, if one means by this love, honor, etc. But if one understands by it our canonical marital consent, then it is relevant.

For the sexual union to bring about marriage it was necessary that first of all the condition be not yet fulfilled or frustrated. It was only for the period of pendency that the decretals ordained the emergency into existence of marriage through the *copula.* This element or favor was quite objective. Knowledge or ignorance of the parties about the fulfillment or frustration, or their error as to the one or the other, are irrelevant.

The past and present unverified condition, does not and could not be convalidated by the *copula,* for the act is null and the *copula* is one of fornication *per se.*[4] Barbosa cites a case [5] where a marriage with the condition, *si legitima es,* was declared invalid because of non-verification in spite of the sexual union.[6]

If the party or parties were certain concerning the non-verification of the past or present condition and had the *copula,* they were presumed to have given a new absolute consent, if they proved their knowledge.[7]

Today, if for no other reason than the necessity, (in most cases) of the substantial form of the celebration of marriage, the juridical *engagement* followed by the *copula* is no longer a *presumptio juris et de jure* of marriage. The positive disposition of law "Consensus Mutuus" of Leo XIII, February 15, 1892 [8] revoked this universally for *engagements,* but did not revoke or touch upon conditional marital

[4] Schmalzgrueber, lib. IV, tit. V, n. 21, who quotes many authors.

[5] S. C. C., 1620, attestante Sellio.

[6] *Cf.* Schmier 1754, *Jurisprudentia Canonico-Civilis,* lib. IV, Tract. II, n. 68. Schulte, *D. Kath. KR.,* par. 21. *S. C. C., in causa Messin,* 1573; *in c. Gerac.* 1587; 8 March, 1595; 15 July, 1593, Reiffenstuel lib. IV., tit. V, n. 14; Schmalzgrueber, lib. IV, tit. V, n. 21, 54.

[7] Held, *Jurisprudentia Universalis,* lib. IV, d. 2, c. 4, p. 286, who really says there is a receding from the condition, but it is objected it is impossible to recede in the case.

[8] *ASS,* XXIV, 441; *Fontes,* n. 613.

consent followed by the sexual act during the pendency of the condition. So the common opinion of canonists held this last named presumption was valid till the Code.[9]

Whether the *copula* henceforth has any special juridical value or force in marriages under a future condition, is doubtful.[10] It ought to be considered at least, as a mere fact which whether it contains a tacit revocation or not of the condition must be learned from the various circumstances. The *copula* in one case at least can manifest consent, if the marriage is invalid on account of an external but not a public reason.[11]

If two baptized non-Catholics were engaged, and not being bound to the substantial form, nor any diriment impediment being present, and if these have the *copula affectu maritali* there exists a marriage. But if they have the mind to fornicate there is no marriage, for then the consent is lacking which is a *sine qua non* for marriage.[12] This presumption about engagement was made law by Alexander III.[13] In this fashion Angelo in Shakespeare's "*Measure for Measure*" is trapped into marriage with Mariana.[14]

In the new law it is certain according to some, that the *copula* (following engagement or conditional marital consent) is no longer a *presumptio juris et de jure,* or even *juris tantum* in the strict sense, for nowhere is it found in the law. But, some say, it is a *presumptio juris lato sensu seu non juridica* today.[15]

Ayrinhac in his first edition [16] said the presumption probably had

[9] Wernz-Vidal, *op. cit.*, n. 516; Chelodi, *op. cit.*, n. 126; Cappello, *op cit.*, n. 640; Bayon, *op. cit.*, p. 317; J. Bucceroni, *Enchiridion Morale,* 4 ed., 1905, Romae, n. 958; Vlaming, *op. cit.*, II, 141.

[10] The Instructio Austriaca 1855, par. 54, reads: "qui ante conditionem impletam matrimonium consumma; eo ipso conditioni nuntium mittit."

[11] Vlaming, *op. cit.*, II, n. 519.

[12] Gougnard, *De Matrimonio,* p. 16, *cf.* Benedict XIV, *Institutiones Ecclesiasticae,* Inst., LXXXVII, n. 73 s.

[13] C. 3, X, *de cond. app., IV,* 5. Gasparri, *op cit.* (1903), n. 990; Wernz, *Jus Matrimoniale,* n. 298.

[14] Joyce, *Christian Marriage,* p. 89.

[15] *Cf.* Cappello, *op. cit.*, n. 640; Wernz-Vidal, *op. cit.*, n. 516 Chelodi, *op. cit.*, n. 126.

[16] *Marriage Legislation,* p. 222.

not been abolished. The second edition [17] denies it exists now. Presumptive marriages are not expressly mentioned in the Code, but this does not exclude that besides that of Canon 1014, many *presumptiones facti* can be had, except in case of Canon 1972.

In a recent Parisian case the marriage is declared null because of the non-verification of a condition, placed by the woman, that the man seriously promise full religious liberty for herself and the children. He time and again promised, but he did not keep it. The court convinced of the non-revocation of the condition, declared for nullity in spite of many sexual acts intervening.[18]

If two using the canonical form of celebration give marriage consent under a future condition, and during pendency have the intercourse *maritali affectu* then there is a marriage without doubt, before God. On the other hand, if they do not recede from the condition and have the mind to fornicate, there is no marriage before God. In both cases the external forum would probably hold for invalidity, until the receding from the condition, or a new consent, is proved.

If two go before the pastor and say nothing of their condition, the marriage is valid for the external forum which presumes the internal mind conforms to the external words. Before God there is no marriage till verification or revocation of the condition. If only one secretly has the condition, the solution is the same.[19]

If the condition is: "If you have intercourse with me," and the condition is verified, then the condition is rejected as *turpis*, and in the external forum the marriage is valid, but not because of the verification. But if the condition was seriously meant, *coram Deo* the marriage is valid *because* of the *copula*.[20]

Fr. Vermeersch has the following interesting case, in the solution of which he says the presumption still exists. Though this runs counter to nearly all other authors.[21]

[17] *Op. cit.*, p. 225.

[18] S. R. Rota, *AAS*, XIV, 1922, 512-523.

[19] Ayrinhac, *loc. cit.*

[20] Santi-Leitner, *Praelectiones Juris Canonici* (1903), p. 194.

[21] *Cf.* S. R. Rota, *AAS*, XIV, 1922, p. 512 s; *cf.* his case in *The Homiletic and Pastoral Review*, November, 1933, Vol. 34, n. 2.

Ambrose a Catholic fell in love with Susana a non-Catholic whom he thought was disposed to embrace the Catholic faith. He regarded her early conversion as certain and wishing to seal their fidelity and love, he contracts marriage with a condition. Therefore while the girl was being instructed in the faith, he filed a document with a notary in which he declared he was unwilling to consent to the approaching marriage unless Susana abjured heresy. No mention of this document was made to the girl or to the parish priest. He applied for a dispensation for mixed religion and contracted an apparently absolute marriage in the eyes of the Church. After its celebration, she declared she no longer desired to become a Catholic. Ambrose meanwhile had intercourse and was much grieved at this news, and now asks whether he can obtain a declaration of nullity of the marriage.

The solution given is: By the intercourse Ambrose obscured and impaired his clear case. In the first place he had no right while the condition was unverified to consummate the conditional marriage, for under the ancient law, *which has not been abrogated,* those who make use of their conjugal rights before the condition is fulfilled are presumed to have renounced the condition, since this is the only honorable explanation of their course of action. Nor was it right to attach secretly to his consent the condition and to dissimilate this at the celebration of the marriage, which his partner and the priest believed to be absolute.

Consequently it is to be feared that in the external forum his plea for annulment will be denied and that he will receive this answer based on reasonable presumption. *"De nullitate matrimonii non constare."* In the *external* forum, however, from the moment when the girl refused conversion, the condition *sine qua non* Ambrose was unwilling to contract marriage, is lacking, involving necessarily the invalidity of the marriage. Wherefore in the *internal* forum he must abstain from all use of the merely apparent marriage, unless having revoked his clandestine condition, he now gives absolute consent to his marriage with Susana. This consent may be occult provided the stipulated condition remains unknown to Susana. If she has learned of this condition, he must manifest his new consent to her, who in turn must testify to the perseverance of her own consent. Since all the necessary solemnities of the celebration of the marriage have already been observed, the consent need not be renewed in the presence of pastor and witnesses.

If after his petition for annulment in the external forum has been denied, Ambrose is unwilling to cohabit with the woman who has deceived him, he may petition the ecclesiastical judge for perpetual separation from bed and board.

It may be remarked that Ambrose's confessor might expose the case to the Sacred Penitentiary and it is probable it may conclude it is not clear concerning the validity of the marriage and authorize Ambrose to marry another, if he wishes, with instructions that the new marriage be inscribed in the secret archives, and to avoid scandal, celebrated elsewhere.

The decree of Leo XIII, "Consensus Mutuus," referred to above, has been interpreted in various ways. For further clarification, it may be useful to study this closer, in order to see whether it sheds light on the subject of this chapter. First it will be well to give the historical background and to clear up some other questions on which rest our specific query whether *conditional consent* followed by the *copula* during pendency is presumed by *law* to effect an absolute marriage.

First of all a very fundamental question is this. Is *marital* consent expressed by words or signs sufficient or not for the essence of the matrimonial contract, or is consummation of marriage, also required? [22]

The common doctrine today and for some centuries previous is that the consummation is not necessary. Some reasons are as follows: The carnal *copula* belongs to the *secondary* perfection of marriage (*operatio*) not to its primary or first perfection which consists in the very *being* (*esse*) of the thing. This assertion then is proved by its proponents in various ways. One argument is based on *authority.* Peter Lombard, St. Thomas and practically all the Scholastics teach the *consensus* theory and bring forth cogent arguments in its favor.

[22] This seems to be the common understanding of the *copula* theory, but to the writer it seems (as pointed out in the historical section of this work) that the difference between Gratian and Lombard was about the point of time when marriage became *sacramental.* In other words, Gratian held there was marriage before the *copula,* but not a *sacramental* marriage.

Both the proponents and the opponents of this theory cite various papal rescripts and pronouncements for their respective view. The opponents seemingly have in their favor some older papal laws or decisions.

Another argument made much of, in favor of the consent theory is, that long before the Roman Law held that theory, and the popes *adopted* this axiom "Nuptias non concubitus, sed consensus facit," which maxim is expressed in Roman Law in various ways.[23]

But it seems capable of being shown historically that this Roman dictum in the earlier Roman Law referred to the *consensus patris familiae,* and not to the consent of the boy or girl. Later on, no doubt, it began to connote the consent of the boy and girl. Furthermore, even some proponents of the consent theory maintain that the Church did *not* borrow or take her consent theory from Roman Law but from Divine Apostolic positive teaching.

> There has been considerable discussion about the sources of the Church's doctrine on this subject. Some have maintained that, having at first no theory of her own, she took over the principle that the sole essential in marriage is the consent of the parties from Roman jurisprudence. Others have held that the apostles handed down to the Church the teaching which prevailed among the Jews. Others again consider that the principles of Canon Law have their source in early German custom. It may safely be said that all these theories are beside the mark. From the first the Church maintained as divinely revealed certain fundamental principles regarding marriage . . . apart from these she was ready to fall in with the systems in use around her, so far as they accorded with reason. But from first to last she held an independent course. There was much in the Roman system which she could accept: and she admitted likewise certain elements drawn from Germanic custom. But she did not hesitate to reject whatever in them she found at variance with Christian principles.[24]

[23] L. 30 s, D. (R. J.) 50, 17; *cf.* also L. 32, par. 13, D. 24, 1; L. 15, D. 35, 1. *Cf.* Nicolaus I, C. 2, D. 27, 9, 2; Alexander I, c. 14, X, *De Sponsalibus,* IV, 1; Innocent III, in cc. 23 and 25 *X*, *De Spons;* IV, 1; Eugene IV in decree "ad Armenos;" *cf.* Institutiones Justiniani, I, 10; *cf.* L. 2, D. XXIII, 2; *cf.* Joyce, *Christian Marriage,* p. 70; *cf.* Gasparri, *De Matrimonio* (1932) I, n. 8, Note 1.

[24] Joyce, *Christian Marriage,* p. 40.

But granting the dictum is correct and refers to the parties marrying, some maintain it is correct but that it does not exclude something else. This contention is put this way. "Copula carnalis affectu maritali habita facit nuptias."[25] It is certain that in some periods of Roman Law, *consent,* as we understand it now in Canon Law, did not and could not effect a marriage in Roman Law, for this it was necessary that the two parties had *maritalis affectus* which in Roman Law was strictly legalistic though based on fact, *e. g.,* in certain periods it was legally inconceivable that a non-citizen could have this *maritalis affectio,* that is why they had no right to *connubium,* yet our canonical consent is possible to slave and free, to every human being. In fact a Roman citizen could have *maritalis affectio* towards his legal wife, in fact *eo ipso* had it, if she too were a *civis,* but at the same time he could lack the consent required by *natural* law (or what our Canon Law demands) and still at the same time this Roman citizen could have this marriage consent (as we know it in canon and natural law) towards his *concubina* or any other woman and she could have the same towards him.

Santi responds to the argument of Freisen mentioned above, as follows:[26] Since marriage is an act transacted between *men* (*homines*), consent in the mind is *per se* not sufficient, it must be manifested, externalized by clear and indubitable signs (*claris et indubiis signis*) especially by words for the word is a natural index or window of the mind, "vox enim naturalis index mentis." But the *copula* is not such a sign, for it can be doubted whether it was had "maritali an fornicario affectu;" and marriage is so important to the individual and society that it cannot be based on something hidden and occult. But to this reasoning it is objected that for centuries, *presumptive* marriages (based on the doctrine that in a given case the *copula* following engagement or conditional marital consent, had with *maritalis affectio,* in a canonical not a Roman Law meaning), *de facto* did become true marriages recognized by the Church, which considered the *copula* with certain other conditions as a *signum consensus maritalis.*

What are these "certain other conditions" leads us unto the question: "Is carnal intercourse considered as a sufficient sign of a con-

[25] "*Cf.* Freisen, *Geschichte des kanonischen Eherechts,* 1882; 2 ed., 1892.

[26] *Praelectiones Juris Canonici,* lib. IV, tit. I, n. 77.

tract of *engagement* or of *marriage,* and if so, when must it be so considered?"

Is carnal intercourse considered as a sufficient sign of the contract of *engagement?* This question was often posited before the present law. Elsewhere we will discuss the question when from the *copula carnalis,* without any relation or reference to *engagement,* there arises an obligation to contract marriage. Here, is considered intercourse in reference to (*in ordine ad*) the contract of engagement. Does it make engagement?

Generally speaking intercourse between two is not *per se* a sufficient sign of engagement (even in the old law), rather the presumption is that it is a *copula libidinis.* But if the woman is honest, and especially a *virgin,* and at the same time the man gave a clear and certain promise of marriage, this *copula carnalis* is properly (*jure meritoque*) considered in the *external* forum as a sign of consent given by the woman, who is not presumed to have given her body to the man except with the intention of entering marriage by which she trusts that her honor will be protected.[27]

These two elements must concur simultaneously in order to consider the transaction as a contract of *engagement,* for the entire thing is a presumption. For neither from love alone nor marks of affection on the part of the man, can it be presumed that he has the intention of taking on the obligation of entering marriage; nor on the part of the woman can it be presumed she contracts engagement, unless the woman is *honesta.* The S. C. Council never considered such affairs as engagements in those places where morality is corrupted. This presumption of law (*praesumptio juris tantum*) was not abolished by Leo XIII's decree "Consensus Mutuus" of the 15 February, 1892; for this neither specially abrogates the presumption, nor can one content that it touches on this point at all.[28] The papal decree abro-

[27] *S. C. C.*, 26 June, 1841; 9 September, 1843 (Apud Richter et Schulte, *Canones et decreta Tridentini, etc.*, Lipsiae 1853), I. 222, n. 14. *Cf. Santi*-Leitner, *Praelectiones Juris Canonici,* Romae, Neo Eboraci, etc. (1905), IV, tit. I, n. 21.

[28] A suspensive honest condition added to engagement consent, is revoked if during the pendency, intercourse is had, "vel nisi conditio ipsa fuerit revocata expresse vel tacite, *e. g.*, copula carnalis, ex c. 6, *X, de conditionilbus appositis in desponsatione vel in aliis contractibus, IV,* 5."—Gasparri, *De Matrimonio,* (1932) I, n. 80.

gated the presumption that a *marriage* arose under these conditions: A *valid* engagement followed by the *copula*. But our question above refers to an *engagement* being presumed present when a serious promise to marry (not a canonical engagement) is given and this promise is followed by the *copula*.

Now two other questions remain to be answered, namely whether the *copula sequens*, had by canonically engaged persons was a *presumed sign* of marriage so that the Church formerly considered the couple married; and the other query is, whether the *copula sequens, pendente conditione*, had by two who contracted a *conditional* consent marriage, is likewise *presumed* as a *sign* of the marriage contract, so that these two are considered by the Church as married.

First the *presumptive* marriage arising from a *valid* engagement followed by the *copula* will be considered. The history and source of this *presumptio juris et de jure*, and the reasons that prompted Leo XIII to abrogate it are clearly brought out in the decree of abrogation which will now be inserted completely. It must be remembered that the *origin* of this presumption antedated the Council of Trent by centuries and was in force till the decree *Tametsi*, and in places where this decree was never promulgated this centuries-old presumption continued till 1892. After this date there was no place in the entire Latin Church where this presumption was legal.

LEO PP. XIII

Ad Perpetuam Rei Memoriam

Consensus mutuus, unde matrimonia justa nascuntur, non verbis dumtaxat, sed aliis quoque signis exterioribus patefieri ac declarari potest. Quamobrem *Alexander* III. (in c. 15.), *Innocentius* III. (in c. 26), et *Gregorius* IX. (in c.30. *De Spons*. IV. 1) decessores Nostri, merito decreverunt ut carnalis copula, si sponsalia de futuro certa ac valida praecessissent, cum in judicio, tum extra judicium, pro vero conjugio haberetur, nisi impedimentum canonicum obstitisset. Et hac juris praesumptione tantum roboris inesse voluerunt, ut firmum ipsa statueret sanciretque jus nec probationem contrariam ullam admitteret. Deinde vero matrimonia clandestina, id est non praesente Parocho et duobus tribusve testibus inita, quum Concilium Tridentinum irrita infectaque esse jussisset, just illud priscum, ut erat necesse, valere desiit ubicumque promulgata vel moribus usuque recepta Tridentina lex. Quibus autem illa locis non viget, in iis semper Apostolicae Sedis judicium fuit, canones, quos indicavimus, ratos atque firmos permansisse. Sed aetatum decursu, ex conscientia et cognitione christianorum sensim effluxere. Plures enim Episcopi ex iis regionibus, in quibus matrimonia clandestina contra fas quidem inita, sed tamen valida judicantur, haud ita pridem rogati quid populus ea de re sentire videretur, plane retulerunt, canonicam de conjugiis praesumptis disciplinam passim exolevisse desuetudine atque oblivione deletam: propterea *vix aut ne vix quidem contingere ut copula inter sponsos affectu maritali nec fornicario habeatur:* eamque non matrimonii legitimi usum, sed fornicationis peccatum communi hominum opinione existimari: imo vix persuaderi populo posse, sponsalia de futuro per conjunctionem carnalem in matrimonium transire.

His igitur rebus et causis, de consilio Venerabilium Fratrum Nostrorum S.R.E. Cardinalium in rebus fidei Inquisitorum generalium, supra memoratos canones et alias quascumque juris canonici ea de re dispositiones, etiam speciali mentione dignas, per hoc Decretum Nostrum *abrogamus* et *abolemus;* et pro abolitis et abrogatis, ac si nunquam prodissent, haberi volumus.

Simul per has literas Nostras decernimus ac mandamus ut deinceps illis in locis in quibus conjugia clandestina pro validis habentur, a quibusvis judicibus ecclesiasticis, in quorum foro causas ejusmodi matrimoniales agitari et judicari contigerit, copula carnalis sponsalibus superveniens non amplius ex juris praesumptione conjugalis contractus censeatur, nec pro legitimo matrimonio agnoscatur seu declaretur. Hujus tamen auctoritate Decreti induci nolumus *necessitatem formae Tridentinae servandae* ad matrimonii validitatem ubi illa forma modo non viget.

Datum Romae apud S. Petrum, d. 15, February, 1892 Pontificatus Nostri anno decimo quarto.

Leo PP. XIII.

This declaration is very clear in meaning. It narrates the source of the presumption. It treats of and abrogates the *praesumptio juris et de jure* that a marriage arises from a valid *engagement* (not a conditional consent) followed by the carnal *copula.* The decree announces the reasons (abuses etc.) that prompted the abrogation.

From the above decree we can draw these conclusions. The perfect carnal *copula* between two canonically engaged persons was according to Decretal legislation an external sign of the marital contract in the *external* forum, 'sive animus *maritalis* aderat sive '*fornicaria*'.[29] It is not thus in the *internal* forum. In this internal court 'solus *verus* consensus constituit matrimonium.' [30] Hence the reason for so many and such terrible conflicts between the consciences of multitudes who had no intention to marry, yet in the eyes of the Church were considered as married and prohibited from marrying other persons. In the course of time the knowledge of this law was practically lost on the people, yet the law of Trent centuries before the decree of Leo XIII had the effect of absolutely removing the very fundamental basis of these presumptive marriages which effect then and for generations thereafter was so contrary to the opinions of the faithful. After the Tridentine law this presumption was not legal nor reasonable (where the decree *Tametsi* was in force). This decree simply had *declarative* force in places subject to the decree *Tametsi*.

The words and the intention of Leo XIII by no means excluded a valid engagement followed by the *copula,* from becoming thereby a true marriage, but only legislated that no longer would it be *presumed* such. It would have to be *proved* that the *copula* was had with *maritalis affectus,* ("ut deinceps . . . copula carnalis sponsalibus superveniens non amplius ex juris praesumptione conjugalis contractus censeatur, nec pro legitimo matrimonio agnoscatur seu declaretur.")

What was the extension of the Tridentine decree and at what time (if ever) it began to be law (or ceased to be law) in any given place is a most intricate question. Yet even to this day there may be marriages whose validity depends on this point.

There was still another kind of presumptive marriage, namely when *conditional marital* consent, during the pendency of a *future* condition was followed by intercourse. The *carnal copula* in this case too was considered as a sign (*signum*) of the marriage contract, and the marriage was a presumptive one. Again in considering this particular question a distinction between those places were the decree *Tametsi* was in force and those where it was not promulgated must be made. The effect of this decree, chapter one of session 24 of the

[29] Santi-Leitner, *Praelectiones Juris Canonici,* lib. IV, tit. IV, n. 38.

[30] *Loc. cit.*

Council of Trent was that *clandestine* marriages cease to be valid, as well as *presumptive* marriages arising from *engagements* (since the substantial form of celebration was not had). Presumptive marriages arising from *conditional marital* consent followed by the *copula* during pendency were made impossible if the *Tametsi* form of celebration had to be used and was not. If this form was used in the celebration of the conditional marriage, or if it was not used in places not subject to the decree *Tametsi* then *presumptive* marriages from *conditional marital* consent followed by the *copula* during pendency continued in existence.

In other words, in places subject to this decree the *copula* following a conditional marriage contract that was *clandestine,* could not effect a marriage, neither in the internal nor the external forum, because the couple were *inhabiles,* "the Holy Synod renders such wholly incapable of thus contracting and declares such contracts invalid and null, as by the present decree it invalidates and annuls them." [31] But if in these places the substantial form was used for the conditional contract of marriage and intercourse followed, the parties were considered to have receded from the requirement that the future condition be verified according to chapters five and six of this title of the Decretals. "Vel carnalis copula subsequatur, dissolvi non debent, sed firmiter observari . . ." [32] "Qui sub honesta conditione sponsalia contrahit, et ante conditionis eventum desponsatam cognoscit, a conditione recedit." [33] This was the teaching of the canonists, but of course the theologians had to hold such a *copula* effected nothing,[34] because conditional consent is nothing esle than *engagement* consent. Although if, as they maintained it was *engagement* consent recognized as such by the law which they quote from the decree of Urban III and others besides, it would seem logical to follow this up and admit that a presumptive marriage exists, resulting from *engagement* consent followed by the *copula.*

[31] ". . . eos sancta synodus ad sic contrahendum omnino inhabiles reddit, et hujusmodi contractus irritos et nullos esse decernit, prout eos praesenti decreto irritos facit et annullat."—Sess. XXIV, *de reform. matr.,*" c. 1.

[32] Urban III, c. 5, X, *de cond. app.* IV, 5.

[33] *C.* 6, X, *de cond, app.* IV, 5.

[34] *Cf.* Santi-Leitner, *op. cit.* lib. IV, tit. V, n. 15.

In places exempt from the law of Trent, *engagements* followed by the *copula* passed *jure Decretalium* into marriage. "Qui juravit aliquam id uxorem accipere, si centum sibi donaverit, centum non datis, recipere non tenetur, nisi postea pure consenerit, vel eam cognoverit." This text is the foundation for presumptive marriages arising out of *engagement* consent followed by the *copula,* for Alexander III's case was "Ego te in uxorem *accipiam.*" [35] But this was abolished by the decree "Consensus Mutuus."

In places exempt from the law of Trent concerning the celebration, the *copula* following a conditional marital consent, was a presumption that the contractors were considered as having receded from the condition and as having entered marriage absolutely, this too *ex jure Decretalium.*[36] This is the doctrine held by canonists, for the Leonine decree speaks not of presumptive conditional consent marriages, but of absolute consent engagements. Some theologians however must apply the decree "Consensus Mutuus" to a conditional marriage because they say these are nothing else than engagements.

As stated earlier in this chapter nearly all canonists teach that presumptive marriages arising from conditional marital consent followed by the *copula* during pendency, are abolished by the law of the Code. Yet it is probable that this ancient law still is in force, for Canon 6 of the Code seems to indicate this. Father Vermeersch, as stated above, maintains this presumption of law has not been abrogated. But whether it has been abrogated or not, the *copula* following a conditional marital consent, if had with marital intent, *per se* effects a marriage, if no other obstacle is present. A *presumptive* marriage was not based in the past or at present on certitude, but on reasonable conjecture gathered from arguments and circumstances which by their nature frequently indicate an intention to marry here and now. Irrespective of whether the *legal* presumption of the intent to marry exists today, the *presumptio facti* may in a given case indicate the presence of absolute marital consent, and then the court would judge accordingly.

But it must be remembered that even in the former law the *copula* in itself did not indicate, nor is, *per se* a *signum consensus*

[35] *C.* 3, X, *de cond. appos.,* IV, 5.

[36] *CC.* 3, 5, 6, X, *de cond. appos.,* IV, 5.

maritalis. Standing alone it signifies nothing one way or the other. The circumstances, especially a legal relation between the parties must be present. This may be seen from the nature of *stuprum.*[87]

"*Stuprum* communiter dicitur '*illicita virginis defloratio.*'" *But to* determine exactly the notion of *stuprum,* the will of the woman must be explored. If a virgin for the sake of lust consents to intercourse, without any violence on the part of the man, or seduction, this is called simply *defloratio.* But if she is oppressed by violence or terrified by threats, or seduced by blanishments and promises, and then is deflowered, this is *stuprum* in the canonical sense. Thus *stuprum* is either simple which is the *defloratio virginis seductae,* and violent when unwillingly she by force or terrified by threats is deflowered.

A girl who is not modest and chaste, but given to improper conversations, and who associates with suspected company, is not presumed *honesta,* nor *seduced,* but rather is she presumed to have consented through lust. All that was said about *stuprum,* can be applied to an honest widow seduced or violated.

These things premised, it can be stated that the man has no obligation of marrying, arising from simple defloration, for "Scienti enim et consentienti non fit injuria neque dolus," as regula 27, R. J., in Sexto reads.

[87] *Cf.* Santi-Leitner, *Praelectiones Juris Canonici,* lib. V, tit. XVI, n. 6; *cf. loc. cit.* in X.

CHAPTER XXII

CONDITIONS THAT INVALIDATE MATRIMONIAL CONSENT

Article I

Conditions Against the Substance of Marriage in General

§1. *Importance of the Subject*

We are living in times when many views concerning marriage are current, which are completely at variance with the natural law. People marry with the intention of preventing the generation of children which is the primary purpose of the union. Some marry on the condition that in certain eventualities the union be dissolved.

Others are already married and attempt a further union. What are these contracts to be called? They are contracts to practical unnatural vice, they are contracts to commit fornication, adultery, or polygamy. They may be considered by the parties themselves to be marriage contracts of a sort; they are doubtless considered by the world at large to bear sufficient resemblance to marriage to entitle them to be called by that name. But the teaching of the Church is, and always has been, adamant. They may be called anything you like but *de facto* they are not Christian marriage. They may have been contracted with all the solemnity of external rites, with Cardinal Gasparri or the Pope to bless the union, but if the primary purpose of the contract or its essential properties are excluded, there is no marriage contract.

In a matter of this kind, the flaw in the consent may not be sufficiently substantial to affect the validity of the contract. Certain cases of defective consent, arising from ignorance or immoral conditions, are on the border-line and need a careful judicial inquiry before it can be said that the marriage contract was not made. It would be idle for anyone who is not a professional theologian or canonist to come to any decision in such matters. It is for this purpose of sifting the evidence in these cases that matrimonial tribunals exist in most dioceses.[1]

[1] *Six Sacraments* (St. Louis, 1929), "Matrimony," E. J. Mahoney, p. 242.

The above paragraphs show the practical importance and the difficulty of the subject now to be discussed.

Marriage is inherently sacred in its nature. Practically all nations and tribes and laws, in the past, have upheld this natural sacredness. The practices and beliefs and sometimes startling abuses of pagan nations amount in the main not to deliberate denials, but to ignorance and error about marriage and its essential properties. Pagans have never attained the dubious eminence and distinction of malicious *ex professo* denial of the sacredness of matrimony. It is left to the post-Christians, "advanced thinkers" of our own era to cathedratically deny the very essentials of true marriage, which through the teaching and efforts of the Catholic Church has been the main cause of Christian civilization and stability of nations and states.

> Our existing civilization unquestionably rests upon marriage, as the Christian religion has shaped it. For a thousand years, while that order of things which we call Christendom endured, the Catholic Church was the great ethical instructor of the progressive societies of the western world. The keynote of her teaching was duty—the whole duty of man, in all the relations of life. And nowhere was the teaching clearer, loftier, and more fruitful, than in her doctrine concerning matrimony. It is not too much to say that she recreated marriage. That must, beyond controversy, be conceded to her, as a special and unique achievement.[2]

> The holiness of Christian matrimony is connected with our most sacred associations and duties; and it cannot be lost sight of in however small degree, without entailing the most serious consequences. The Church has shown in reference to this subject, a spirit of watchfulness and solicitude, which alone would entitle her to the gratitude of man, and cause her to be regarded as the most faithful guardian of public and private morality. Many of the innumerable contests in which she was compelled to engage with the depositaries of the Civil Power, during the Middle Ages, were in defence of the stability and sanctity of the marriage-tie; and at a later period, she preferred to see England torn from her side, rather than yield compliance with the will of a monarch, who sacrified his country's faith to his enbridled passions. In this matter she knew no distinction between the private man and the monarch . . . Even in our own days,

[2] Wm. S. Lilly, *On Right and Wrong* (London, 1890), p. 204.

> her conservative authority has been exerted in the same cause; and the anger of the first Napoleon was incurred by the refusal of Pius VII, of holy memory to declare invalid a marriage contracted between the Ruler's brother and a Protestant lady of the city in which we are now assembled. . .
>
> We recall these facts, because they most strongly express the principle of the Church in regards to matrimony, and must be regarded by every well regulated mind as among the brightest jewels of her crown. We recall them also in order to enforce our solemn admonition to our flocks, to give no ear to the false and degrading theories on the subject of matrimony, which are boldly put forward by the enemies of the Church. According to these theories, marriage is a mere civil contract, which the Civil Power is to regulate, and from which an injured or dissatisfied party may release himself or herself by the remedy of divorce, so as to be able lawfully to contract new engagements. . . . As the guardian of God's holy law, the Church condemns this false theory, from which would follow a successive polygamy, no less opposed to the unity and stability of Christian marriage than that simultaneous polygamy, which to the scandal of Christendom, is found within our borders. No state law can authorize divorce, so as to permit the parties divorced to contract new engagements; and every such new engagement, contracted during the joint lives of the parties so divorced, involves the crime of adultery. We refer with pain to the scandalous multiplication of these unlawful separations, which, more than any other cause, are sapping the foundations of morality and preparing society for an entire dissolution of the basis on which it rests.[3]
>
> We consider the divorce evil an evidence of moral decay and a present danger to the best elements of our American life.[4]

"The civilization of Christendom—the civilization of which we are heirs—was founded on Christian marriage." This thesis is beautifully and cogently proven by Father Joyce.[5]

[3] *The Pastoral Letter of the American Hierarchy of 1866; cf.* Guilday. *The National Pastorals of the American Hierarchy,* Washington, D. C. (1923), n. 210 s.

[4] *The Pastoral Letter of the American Hierarchy of 1919; cf.* Guilday, *o. c.,* p. 315.

[5] *Christian Marriage* (1933), p. V, p. 11 s; *cf.* Baltimore Councils; *cf.* the

Naturalism and the post-Christian ethics contend there is nothing obligatory in the stability and exclusiveness of marriage. It denies every essential natural and Christian doctrine about marriage: it is not sacred, simply a private affair and a mere convention; God is not its author; the bond is not indissoluble; extra-marital relations are not wrong even socially. The devilishness of these preachments (based on an *ex parte* unscientific and biased and pseudo-anthropology and on a pseudo-science of comparative religion) and their ruinous effects not only on religion but society as well, is evident from this one truth that in the social organism the true units are not isolated individuals, but families.

In spite of this, French materialists of the past generation strove for the abolition of marriage on the ground that it is "the tomb of love, and the chief cause of stupidity (*abetissement*) and ugliness (*enlaidissement*) in the human race." [6]

A veteran statesmen, some years ago, in a conversation spoke of marriage as the "stumbling-stone of the age." The reply was: "So much the worse for the age, for an age which falls upon that stone shall be broken." "Within the Catholic Church, marriage is, of course, what it was. But the State is no longer Catholic; is no longer Christian." [7]

§2. *What Kind of an End, Intention or Content of the Will is Necessary in Order That the Act of the Will Be Essentially Perfect and That Marriage Arises Therefrom?*

Sanchez [8] asks what kind of an end, intention, or content of the

Protestant author, Wm. S. Lilly, *On Right and Wrong*, London, 1890. Chapter IX of this excellent work has for its thesis, "Our existing civilization unquestionably rests upon marriage, as the Christian religion has shaped it, its law, indissolubility, grounded upon the principle of the spiritual equality of woman and man," p. 203 s. *Cf.* Guilday, *The National Pastorals of the American Hierarchy*, Washington, D. C. (1923)—*P. L.* of 1840, p. 136; 1843; p. 156; 1884, p. 248; 1866, p. 210; 1919, p. 315.

[6] Wm. S. Lilly, *op. cit.*, p. 30.

[7] Wm. S. Lilly, *op. cit.*, p. 207

[8] *Disputationum de Sancto Matrimonii Sacramento, Tres Tomi*, Antverpiae, 1620, lib II, d. XXIX; lib. V, d. IX, X.

act of the will is necessary in order that the act of the will be essentially perfect and therefore that marriage arise. His answer is there is no dispute that an intention *deducta in pactum,* which even implicitly excludes any of the *tria bona,* renders the consent and marriage invalid. But he says the dispute and question is when such an intention is retained in the mind. He says there are three opinions on this.

The first opinion teaches there is no marriage, if the parties so contract as to intend to bring up children (*non educare prolem*), to deny the debt (*debitum*), *etc.* Not, however, if they intend to mix sexually with others, for the first suppositions belong essentially to the *bonum fidei,* the latter only accidentally. Three proofs are enumerated. The proponents quote St. Augustine,[9] "those who contract with the intention not to have children, or to kill them, are not married, *non habent connubium.* Another proof: Consent is necessary for marriage, that is at least implicit consent to those things which are of its essence, but the *bona* are essential to marriage at least *in suis principiis,* (teste St. Thomas, 4, D. 31, q. 1, a. 3), therefore to exclude consent in these by a contrary intention invalidates the consent. A third reason is this: Such an intention, although not expressed in words, invalidates, for if the same intention were expressed as a condition it would destroy the consent, being against the *bona.*

After mentioning the proponents of this opinion Sanchez [10] gives the second opinion: An intention against the substance of marriage and its *bona,* retained in the mind, does not invalidate consent and therefore marriage arises, *e. g.,* if one intends to marry only *ad tempus.* The reasoning runs thus: In order to have a marriage the internal consent expressed by external signs are necessary and neither consent *sine signis,* nor *signa sine consensu,* operate anything, therefore every condition expressed by no signs operates nothing.

Sanchez himself holds the third opinion: The one marrying ought to intend, at least implicitly, the *bonum sacramenti,* which intention

[9] Lib. I, *de nupt. et concupiscentia,* c. 15 and 32, q. 2, *P. L.* 44, 420.

[10] Lib. II, d. XXIX.

is present, when he does not have a contrary intention. It is not necessary that one intends implicitly the other two *bona,* wherefore if he has in his heart and mind something against the *bonum sacramenti, e. g.,* intends marriage *ad tempus,* there is no true marriage. If, however, he has an intention against the other two *bona,* retained only in his heart, "nec in pactum deductam," marriage is valid, *e. g.,* if he intends to avoid offspring or having them does not intend *educare prolem,* or to deny the *debitum,* or to commit adultery. His proof of the first part is that it is of the very nature of marriage that the bond is perpetual, and he that intends a bond that is temporary, soluble, intends something against the essence of marriage. His opinion follows logically from the way he defines the essence of marriage as the *vinculum.* His proof that an intention against the other two treasures of marriage effects no invalidity, is simply the statement that these intentions take away nothing pertaining to the substance of the contract, for the party is obliged by the force of the contract not to do anything against these *bona,* in spite of his intention.

Sanchez here, and many others, fall into a begging of the question, for the point in dispute is simply this: Can or do such intentions invalidate the consent, so that he is not obliged by the contract simply because these intentions may prevent a contract arising? He evidently could not see, that it is possible, and a fact for that matter, that if one can have a so-called condition against the substance simply because it is *deducta in pactum,* it and the jurisprudence of the Church presupposes that if the *external* pact invalidates it is simply because of the internal pact of the intention or will.

This is abundantly evident from the very nature of the case, that is, from the necessary nature of a consent directed to effecting a marriage. In other words, using the word condition in the meaning of the phrase "conditions against the substance" there can and must be conditions in the mind, always when seriously expressed by words, and oftentimes when they are not expressed externally at all, *conditio in mente tantum.* Here it is essential also to again recall that these so-called conditions against the substance, are nothing else *in re* than a certain actual human consent labelled marital consent (which all this denotes and connotes) but which in reality *ex supposito* labors under an essential defect in so far as it is true marriage consent, and since nothing can subsist without its substance and essence, this true consent does not actually exist. It is a complete act of the will, a *voluntarium,* but not an act of the will of marrying because of its essential defect.

Per se this study does not deal with *intentions* of marriage, whether against or in conformity with the substance of marriage but with *conditions,* which *ex hypothesi,* by definition, presuppose not only a complete concrete act of willing, a perfect act, but a perfect act, perfect in so far as it aims at marriage as God made marriage with all its essentials, and this complete internally and essentially healthy content of marital consent, is made dependent for producing its effect (*i. e.,* marriage) on the truth of a freely chosen circumstance. But *de facto* conditions against the substance, would be a true phrase if both suppositions were verified: a complete essentially perfect content of the marital consent, and a condition which *per se* equals no complete essentially perfect content of marital consent. It is therefore evident such so-called conditions really denote one human act of the will, not two, and the content of this act of consent is not marital, but what is called marital erroneously or designedly.

Concerning the other two treasures of marriage, it is certain that if the vitiated consent excludes them in a certain way, there is no marriage, whereas in another sense these treasures *quoad* execution may be excluded and there is a marriage. Sanchez failed to see that the essence of marriage which he calls the *vinculum* necessarily even if implicitly includes the other two *bona* in the sense to be now mentioned. But first, as far as the *bonum sacramenti* is concerned, this may be remarked. A man knowing full well that matrimony is indissoluble, can will to be the true husband of a woman, can will to be married to her and no one else and to obligated thus for life and yet have the concomitant depraved intention or purpose of leaving her later and ostensibly marrying another. On the other hand if the intention he has means this: "I do not will to be obligated as a husband for life," he is not married, but if the intention means anything less than that, he is married. The difficulty seems to be helped along by the meaning of the word *intention.* If it be used in the sense that he wills not to give the *jus perpetuum* or to receive it, of course there is no real consent to marriage. But it must be well remembered that not every one who has the intention to divorce means *necessarily* that he reserves the *jus* to divorce *a vinculo* when he desires it. Often it simply reduces itself, especially because of erroneous beliefs about marriage, to a divorce that considers not the bond at all, but the actual legal separation with immunity from punishment by the State if he cohabits with another.

As far as the other two treasures are concerned, the distinction is valid between the *jus* and the *abusus,* the being bound as a married person, and the execution of the essential obligations voluntarily taken. Sanchez says if one wishes absolutely to contract he is obliged thereby not to do anything against the *bona* which is very true, but this is equally true, that if in his mind by an intention, or a condition even only in mind, he does not will to be obliged to *any* one of the *bona* he thereby excludes consent to such an obligation and his actual consent is not marital consent, but something else. For instance, one may will to be bound to tell the truth through taking an oath, but he may at the same time have no intention of actually telling the truth, or living up to his obligation, yet the oath was taken and is valid, and on the other hand, he may internally not will to take the oath, though going through the formalities.

As remarked above, Sanchez in his definition of marriage says it consists neither in internal consent, nor in the external contract, for these are the efficient causes of marriage, which pass away, marriage does not. Nor is the quiddity of marriage the *traditio mutua* of the bodies, for this *traditio* likewise passes away, nor does it consist in the mutual obligation and subjection to render the *debitum,* for these cease by entrance into religion and by adultery, yet marriage remains.

Thus it is clear from these partly correct, partly erroneous conceptions that any reasoning based thereon would partake of such notions. And moreover it is not *matrimonium in facto esse,* that regulates the consent, but *matrimonium in fieri* that effects the latter which, in other words, is the consent effecting marriage. And furthermore the solution of questions against the substance can not be found by looking at marriage and the *bona* as the actually present and actually executed *bona,* but by consent viewed as the *causa efficax* of the permanent state. Besides, this *vinculum* on which Sanchez and so many others lay so much stress as though it were something existing in the real order, is nothing else than the *jus perpetuum* looked at from the threefold aspect of *proles, fides, sacramentum.* Sanchez admits *quoad obligationem* all three *bona* are of the essence of marriage but he does not seem to see the reverse of it.

It is true as Sanchez, St. Thomas and nearly all teach that *quoad executionem,* the *bonum sacramenti* is of the essence of marriage, and it is certain the execution or fulfillment of the other two treasures, are not of the essence of marriage, but it is equally true that it is of the essence of marital consent to *assume the obligation to fulfill* these two *bona,* and it is true therefore in this sense that an intention not to assume these, or rather an intention excluding either of these, invalidates the consent.

The mutual consent of the parties is the human cause of marriage. This consent embraces all the essentials of marriage as God made it. All other things in marriage, *e. g.,* actual intercourse, children begotten, and such like, do not constitute elements of the essentials of consent. "Reliqua omnia sunt media, consectoria, non principalia nec rem conficiunt." [11] "Consensus est radix matrimonii."[12] The Council of Florence teaches that the efficient cause of marriage is mutual consent externally expressed *de praesenti.* The Council of Trent taught the same.[13] The act of the will to marry must exist actually or virtually, not interpretively.[14]

It is the act of the *will* externalized that constitutes the contract. Acts of the intellect, dispositions of the mind, opinions, errors of judgment, are considered only insofar as they affect the act of the will. If any of these intellectual states cause the will to positively not give and receive this right to acts which of their nature tend to generation, which right must be given and accepted as perpetual and exclusive, then the will does not will marriage *in se* and as God made it, but wills something else under the name of marriage. Of the irri-

[11] Franciscus Florens, *Opera Juridica,* II, p. 102.

[12] Vicentius de Justis, *Casuum S. C. C. Resolutor;* Lucae, 1726, 2, 306 in appendix.

[13] *Cf.* Ayrinhac-Lydon, *Marriage Legislation* (1932), p. 191. *Canones et Decreta C. Tridentini,* Sess. XIXIV, *Decret. de Ref. Matr.,* c. 1.

[14] Chelodi, *Jus Matrimoniale,* ch. V.

tating, destroying defects of consent, some affect the intellect: lack of use of reason, insanity, certain kinds of ignorance; others affect the will: simulation, fear contrary to reason, and certain kinds of error. Strictly speaking, a condition attached to the consent is not a defect of the will or its contents. The condition presupposes a full healthy will with all its essentials, and this willing is made to depend for its marriage causing effect, on the verification of the event of the condition.

The marriage can exist without the actual *copula,* but it cannot be validly contracted unless the parties mutually give the *jus ad usum,* at least *implicite.* It is certain that the actual consummation does not pertain to the substance of marriage,[15] but the consent and right to this act does, at least implicitly and virtually. In other words, one must consent to be obligated to the other seeking the debt and one must consent to receive the right to seek the debt himself. Schmalzgrueber says it is certain that the mutual consent and the mutual giving and receiving of this juridical right and its obligations, do not belong to marriage as a permanent union but only to the *vinculum* or bond alone. It is also certain doctrine that this mutual consent belongs to marriage as a *contract* for without this no marital contract can exist.[16]

All the essentials of this consent are had at least implicity by the use of such sentences as, "I take you for my lawful wife;" "I now marry you;" "I do, etc." Indefinite words as, "I wish, I desire, I beseech," are not sufficient for validity.[17]

It may be remarked here that the words used in the celebration, *e.g.,* "I take you for my wife," must not be taken materially, else insane people and little children and joksters would be married, but the words must be taken formally in so far as they impart and signify sufficient and valid consent for the mutual tradition. Thus the decree of the Council of Trent "Tametsi" and the present legislation effect

[15] Schmalzgrueber, *Jus Ecclesiasticum Universum,* lib. IV, tit. I, n. 263.

[16] *Cf.* Schmalzgrueber, lib. IV, tit. I, n. 261, 262, where solid reasons and arguments are drawn from Sacred Scripture to prove this essential character of the marital consent.

[17] *"Cupio, desidero, rogo te"*—Franciscus Florens, *Opera Juridica,* II, 102.

that words uttered not before the pastor and witnesses do not import and contain sufficient consent for marriage.[18]

This consent is also the efficient cause of the sacrament, not the efficient *first* cause which is divine and operates in the parties to salvation, but the second cause or instrumental cause.[19]

Farrugia [20] among many others insist that consent is the efficient cause of marriage, is so far as marriage consists in the consent by which is given the *jus ad copulam* and not directly *jus in copulam seu in usum,* for the use of marriage is not of the essence of marriage. Therefore St. Ambrose referring to the marriage of the Blessed Virgin and St. Joseph says, "Cum enim initiatur conjugium, tunc conjugii nomen adscisitur: non enim defloratio virginitatis facit conjugium, sed pactio conjugalis." [21] Similarly St. Augustine in his treatise *De Nuptiis et Concupiscentia says:* "It would be intolerable to say that the bond of marriage is dissolved, because husband and wife agree to abstain altogether from the use of carnal concupiscence." [22] In the beginning of the seventh century, St. Isidore of Seville, when defining a series of terms relating to marriage in his *Etymologiae,* speaks as follows on the term *conjux:* "The name of 'married persons' is most correctly given to people in view of the initial plighting of their troth, even though consummation has not taken place." [23] Again St. Augustine writes: "Matrimonium non facit coitus, sed voluntas." [24]

The Roman jurists, nearly all say, had laid it down as a principle that the essential element in marriage was the consent of the parties.[25] This doctrine passed into a *regula juris.*[26]

[18] *Cf.* Sanchez, *De Matrimonio,* lib. III, d. IV.

[19] Cerato, *De Matrimonio,* p. 138.

[20] *De Matrimonio et Causis Matrimonalibus* (Taurini-Romae, 1924), p. 23.

[21] *De institutione Virg.,* cap. 6, n. 41—*P. L.,* 16, 316.

[22] Lib. 1, c. 11—*P. L.,* 44, 420.

[23] Lib. IX, c. 7, "Conjuges verius appellantur a prima desponationis fide, quamvis adhuc inter eos ignoretur conjugalis concubitus."—(*P. L.,* 82, 365) taken from Joyce, *Christian Marriage,* p. 44.

[24] Lib. V, *contra Julian,* cap. 16—*P. G.* 58, 80 (c. 1, C. XXVII, q. 2); *Opus imperfectum in Matthaeum.*

[25] L. 30, D. I, 17. "Nuptias non concubitus sed consensus facit." *Cf.* L. 9, Cod. V, 4; Nov. XXII, 3.

[26] L. 30, D. I, 17.

The Church, some say, makes her own the principle of Roman Law: "Sufficiat ad matrimonium solus consensus illorum, de quorum quarumque conjunctionibus agitur." [27] But there were two opinions from the ninth century on about the relation between consent and the *copula*.[28]

Consent makes the marriage, but in Roman Law for long ages that dictum meant the consent of the *paterfamilias,* and the natural consent of a boy and girl meant nothing if this ruler said nay, and if he wanted them married, it was marriage even without their natural consent. The *affectio maritalis* of Roman Law sources is not the same as our canonical consent of the parties. Our canonical consent was possible between a *civis Romanus* and an *ancilla* (*non civis*), yet it could not effect a marriage between them. *Affectio maritalis* was possible only between two Roman citizens of different sexes. It was impossible by law for a *civis* to have this towards a non-citizen. Thus if the canonists took this axiom from Roman Law, they never realized that originally the Romans meant the consent of third parties. The Church drew this principle concerning the consent of the parties from Christ and the Apostles, not from Roman Law.

On the qualities (not the elements) of this consent it is not necessary to delay. It is sufficient to recall these few things. It must be marital, which is implicitly contained in the will of entering a permanent union of marriage; it must be born in the will, that is it must be internal (Canon 1086, par. 2); if merely external the marriage is null and void.[29] Love or *animi inclinatio amorosa* is not required for validity of consent. Thaner errs saying: *consensus juridicus* is not sufficient as in other contracts, but a consent proceeding from love, etc.[30] It must be deliberate and free, that is with sufficient reflection and mature judgment and free; it must be mutual, existing at the same time morally. It must be given by persons qualified to marry, not subject to diriment impediments of natural, divine or human laws.

[27] C. 2, C. 27, q. 2 (Nicholas I, 866).

[28] *Cf. Jus Matrimoniale,* ed. 3 chap. V, p. 117; Joyce, *Christian Marriage,* p. 53 s; *cf.* historical part of this work.

[29] *S. S. C.,* March 7, 1885—*ASS,* XVIII, 14; S. R. Rota, *causa Massilien.,* July 1, 1911—*AAS,* III (1911), 525-531.

[30] De Smet, *De Sponsalibus et Matrimonio* (1927), n. 99 s.

Personal or proper, externally expressed, legimately manifested and, in one sense, absolutely given. Being mutual it is necessary for validity that it be externally manifested. This presupposes mutual presence of the parties (*per se* or *per alios*) and the observance of formalities required by natural, divine, or human law for the validity of the marriage. *Ex jure naturali* no specific formality is required, the mutual exchange of consent without witnesses, etc., is sufficient, and *ex jure positivo,* no special formality was required, before the Council of Trent. This Council demanded such a formality for validity by issuing the decree *Tametsi.*[31] Then followed the decree "Ne Temere" and the legislation of the Code on the substantial form of the celebration of marriage.

For the validity of the marriage contract it is not necessary that the actual consent of both parties be given simultaneously that is one immediately after the other. No distance of time between the consent of one and the other is an obstacle provided the consent given first remains at least *virtualiter,* and probably even *habitualiter.*[32]

Farrugia rebutts the tenet that there is no difference between the *jus* and *usus juris,* remarking that if this be so, then it follows that, after all the ceremonies have been carried out, and there is some delay before the *usus juris,* the parties would not be truly married meanwhile, which is repugnant.[33]

Though the marital consent is twofold: the giving and the receiving of the marriage right, it is evident that there is no necessity to elicit two acts formally and distinctly, but it is sufficient if one *gives* for *eo ipso et virtualiter* he wills to *receive* the *jus in alterum.* This twofold right is, as we saw, perpetual and exclusive. The matrimony *in facto esse* is the *vinculum conjugale* which because of its indissolubility possesses the *bonum Sacramenti* and because of its perpetuity possesses the *bonum fidei.*[34]

[31] Sess. XXIV, *Decretum de Refor. Matrimonii,* c. 1.

[32] Augustinus Barbosa, *Collectanae Doctorum qui in suis Operibus Concilii Tridentini Loca Referentes* (Lugduni, 1686), 251, 29. This principle is used in marriage through a procurator and it solves the question of the meeting of minds when one party only places a condition to the marriage consent.

[33] *De Matrimonio* (1924), n. 33 s.

[34] De Smet, *De Sponsalibus et Matrimonio,* n. 75 s.

Asking what is the essence of marriage, Schmalzgrueber [85] answers it thus: There are six things found in marriage: mutual consent and mutual giving of the bodies for procreational purposes, these two produce a bond the essence of which consists in a right, (*jus*) a mutual obligation to the debt, and from this bond comes a mutual right of seeking the debt. Then follows *usus* and *consummatio.*

Vromant [86] says *traditio et acceptatio juris in corpora in ordine etc.* should be intended directly and *in se,* else there is no contract. But the consent in the properties and obligations of marriage may be given *diverso modo,* not necessarily, *per se* and *directe.* Therefore the consent in the unity and indissolubility, and for baptized in the sacramentality of the marriage, need not be direct *in se* and *explicite,* but an implicit intention is sufficient, which one has who wants to marry truly according to the plan of God, without even thinking or knowing of these properties. There will be occasion when speaking about conditions against the substance to recall these points and to enter further into this consent. But it will be well to consider these same principles now from a negative viewpoint, before actually applying them individually to the three treasures of marriage.

§ 3. *De Vitiis Consensus*

In order to clarify the question about vitiating conditions, it will help to briefly recall the following principles that must be kept in mind later on in these pages. The defects that make marriage consent null are enumerated in the code.[87] Some of the essentials of consent (as also the vices) are *ex parte subjecti:* consent must be *verus, liber, absolutus;* others are *ex parte objecti:* the consent must have as its object the *substance* of marriage and the *tria bona essentialia.* On the part of the *subject* consent is not true by simulation; not free by certain kinds of force and fear; not absolute under certain conditions, honest and possible of the past or present.

On the part of the *object* consent is not valid if marriage itself is excluded by a positive act of the will, or the *jus ad copulam,* or

[85] Lib. IV, tit. I, n. 256.

[86] *Jus Missionariorum;* Tomus V, *De Matr.,* p. 145, Louvain, 1931.

[87] Canons 1082; par. 1; 1083, par. 1, par. 2, nn. 1 and 2; 1086, par. 2; 1087, par. 1; 1092, nn. 2 and 4.

some essential property: unity (*fides*), indissolubility (*sacramentum*). Whether this exclusion is by substantial ignorance, substantial error or *ex industria* is irrelevant. All these beget nullity and actions for declaration of nullity. The phrase *defectus consensus* is used widely and includes any or all of these vices, this phrase is a *genus* and it should be narrowed down in a given case by singling out the particular species of defective consent. *Total* simulation respects the subject of consent, *partial* simulation the *object* of consent, *e. g., jus in corpus,* therefore they are of distinct natures.[38]

Defects *ex parte intellectus seu in cognitione* are: lack of reason, insanity, error, ignorance; *ex parte voluntatis seu intentione aut in libertate* are: simulation, force, and fear. *Vitia consensus* can invalidate the consent and the contract *jure naturae* or *jure positivo.*

Error that is substantial concerning marriage invalidates.[39] Error is the apprehension of a false thing, it is a judgment. Ignorance is a simple lack of knowledge and for a valid marriage it is necessary that the parties are not ignorant of this minimum, that marriage is a permanent society between a man and woman for the purpose of procreating children.[40]

Simple error about the *tria bona, i. e.,* about the unity, indissolubility, and sacramentality (in a wide and narrow sense), by force of which one thinks that marriage is not opposed to polygamy, that complete divorce is licit and marriage of baptized persons is merely a natural contract, does not invalidate. Here is meant *simple* error or mere theroretical error to which nothing is added, neither a condition or a positive intention of the will having as content this error.[41]

If therefore the error (which is in the *intellect*) does not remain exclusively in the intellect but under its influence there is elicited an act of the will excluding any of these essential properties, or if the consent is given with a *condition* excluding any one of these, the con-

[38] *Cf.* F. Roberti in *Appolinaris,* VI (1933), p. 105 s; *Gougnard, De Matrimonio,* n. 31 s; Fourneret, *Le Mariage Chretien,* 5 ed., p. 118.

[39] Canon 104.

[40] Canon 1082.

[41] "Error actum irritum reddit, si versetur circa id quod constituit substantiam actus vel recidat in conditionem *sine qua non; secus actus valet . . .*"—C. 104, *cf.* c. 1084.

sent and marriage are invalid. For then the *will* excludes something essential and the *presumption* ceases that the contractor wished or had the implicit intention to enter marriage as God, through the laws of nature and His Church instituted it. Canon 1086, par. 2, confirms this.[42]

Whether in a given case there was a simple erroneous judgment of the intellect or an efficacious positive prevailing purpose of the will, is a question of fact, in judging which the gravest difficulties occur.[43] The will which is present is not always the will of simply marrying, as some think. What *ignorance* of marriage impedes consent we saw above, therefore if, *e. g.*, the girl thinks that which is called marriage is a society of man and woman *not permanent* but transitory, even though for the purpose of children, this ignorance invalidates the consent. Yet this ignorance must be *proved* for the external forum, for after the age of puberty it is presumed absent.

If the girl does not know the end of marriage is the procreation of children, though she knows it is a permanent society, the consent is null. She does not have to know in what manner precisely children are had. This knowledge too is presumed after puberty, and its absence must be proved, if one wishes a declaration of nullity. The intention *de bono prolis* may be absent, or negatively present, that is not positively excluded. This negative intention is not to be identified with the above substantial ignorance.

If both or one err about the unity, indissolubility or sacramentality of marriage, the marriage is valid even if they think they can have other lovers or partners or seek solution from the bond (Canon 1084). *Ignorance* here means not *in specie* as in moral theology, that is *carentia scientiae debitae* (*ignorantia positiva*) but *in genera*, that is, *carentia verae scientiae* de aliqua re in subjecto capaci, it is *nescientia*, simply negative ignorance. Ignorance pertains to *ideas* and though it is the *mother of error* and hardly ever is there an *actio ex errore* which is not concommitant with ignorance, yet it

[42] *Cf.* S. R. Rota, 27 July, 1917—*AAS*, X, 215 s, *causa Paderbornensis.*

[43] *Cf.* Vlaming, *Praelectiones Juris Matrimonii*, II, p. 150; Wernz-Vidal, *Jus Matrimoniale*, n. 577; Cappello, *De Matrimonio*, n. 583 s.; Gougnard, *De Matrimonio*, p. 159; *cf.* esp. the marriage case three times before the Rota, with contrary decisions, 9 December, 1911, *S. R. R., AAS*, IV, 146; 1 March, 1913, *S. R. R., AAS*, V, p. 312; 9 March, 1915, *S. R. R., AAS*, VII, 292.

differs from error. Error is a *judgment* or a combination of ideas united with a subject and predicate. It is therefore an act of the intellect, *falsum de aliqua re judicium*. The placing of a *condition* is an act of the *will*.

> Qui de aliqua re non *habent veram* scientiam habitualiter, dicitur *ignorare;* qui de aliqua re *judicat* ex *falsa* scientia sive per modum habitus sive per modum actus, dicitur *errare*. Qui de aliqua re habet veram scientiam habitualiter, sed *non actualiter* hanc *scientiam vertit* in eandem rem, dictur laborare *inadvertentia* (completa vel non).[44]
>
> Quidquid impedit causam, de sua natura impedit et effectum; consensus autem est causa matrimonii, ut dictum est, et idea, quod evacuat consensum evacuat matrimonium. Consensus autem voluntatis est actus, qui praesupponit actum intellectus; deficiente autem *primo,* necesse est defectum contingere in *secundo;* et ideo, quando error cognitionem impedit, sequitur etiam in ipso consensu defectus, et per consequens in matrimonio, et sic error de jure naturali habet, quod evacuet matrimonium.[45]

Of course this error must concern the essence of marriage. The difference between simple non-invalidating error about the essence of marriage and its *tria bona,* and substantial invalidating error about the same objects is this: the parties in the first case *think they can* divorce etc.; in the latter case the parties *positively exclude* by an act of the *will* indissolubility of the bond, etc. (*rati se posse, et positive excludere*). Error is called *simple* because it is *not* joined to this positive act of the will excluding the essential property about which there is ignorance and error, this error does not irritate by its nature, though the Church could make this a canonical impediment, but actually for the good of souls she does the contrary.

Consent is sufficient for validity if a person contracts with an *implicit will of obliging* himself, that is, he lacks a contrary will of not obliging himself, namely of excluding marriage itself or all right to the *copula,* or any essential property of marriage. If any of this exclusion is done by means of a condition added to the consent, *a fortiori* the consent is invalid and inoperative, *e.g.*, "I marry you on

[44] *Cf.* Cerato, *De Matrimonio,* p. 131 s.

[45] St. Thomas, *Theol. Moralis, Suppl.,* q. 51, a. 1; *cf.* Cerato, *De Matrimonio,* p. 135.

this condition: that you have the right to prevent every conception;" "if I am *not bound* to render the debt;" "that we have the *right* to seek a divorce *a vinculo;*" "on the condition that I have the *right* to copulate with others," all these render the marriage invalid in both fora.

Often and generally conditions about the *bonum prolis et fidei* are *contra obligationes* which arise from marriage already assumed, against the fulfillment or the carrying out of these obligations, conditions to *abuse* them, rather than conditions against the substance of marriage or the taking on of these obligations. One must always remember that the intention or will to *abuse* one's marital obligations may be elevated into a *condition,* and it is false to conclude that if this intention to *abuse* is put as a *condition* that the marriage is invalid, *e. g.,* "I marry you and give full consent and take on all obligations, but I place this condition that we now promise to *abuse* our obligations to remain faithful, etc." This is gravely wrong but there is a marriage present. Quite a few authors fail to see this essential distinction. The validity as far as being against the substance is concerned is no more affected by this condition, than if it were a *mere purpose* for the object or content of either do not touch the *essentialia.* In doubt whether the will excludes or does not exclude anything essential, whether by a condition or not, the Church generally presumes for the non-exclusion. Of course, the validity of the marriage depends on the verification of the condition, if seriously placed, but in the external forum the condition is rejected as immoral. Among the various defects of consent mentioned above, there is one especially that is more closely connected with our study on conditions, namely, simulation. It may be helpful to recall here the principles governing it, because later on in discussing especially *bonum sacramenti* simulation plays an importane rôle.

Simulation is had when one expresses in proper words marital consent, but *internally* he does not have the mind or will to marry, or to oblige himself, but by a positive act of the will he excludes marriage or some essential property of marriage.[46] Simulation may be

[46] *Cf. S. R. R., causa Oregonopolitana,* 6 July, 1914; *AAS,* VI, 516 s; which quotes the Roman doctrine: "Nemo existimandus est dixisse quod non mente cogitaverit (L. 7, *De suppel. legat.*) licet id ipse affirmet (Ex. I, 5, *De Probat,* C. 5, eod. tit.)."

total or partial. Total, if one excludes marriage itself.[47] In the external forum the internal consent is presumed to conform to the words used in the celebration.[48] This presumption of law cedes to the truth, but the sole confession of the simulator by no means can prove it.[49] "In foro conscientiae, utique, credi potest asserenti se simulate consensisse, quia ibi agitur de bono spirituali poenitentis, et viget principium 'confitenti pro se et contra se credendum est'; in foro autem externo agitur de administranda justitia jus suum petenti, et standum est allegatis et probatis. (Sanchez, disp. 45, n. 2)." [50]

Partial simulation is the exclusion of the right to the *copula,* or some essential property. The external words are *per se* correct, but the person has no will or intention to oblige himself, *i. e.,* he excludes positively in his mind all right to the act, *i. e.,* he excludes the *bonum physicum prolis;* or he excludes unity or *perpetuity, i. e., bonum fidei aut sacramenti,* not theoretically but by a positive act of the will. In these cases there are no marriages resulting,[51] because of essentially defective consent. This exclusion purely internal may be a positive *intention* or by a *condition, e. g.,* in his mind he says, "I marry you, but only on this condition that I give no right to the copula, etc." Thus there may be three kinds of fictitious or simulated consent: (a) one while he pronounces the words has no will to contract; (b) one has *in a sense* the will and intention to contract, but not the will of obliging himself; (c) one has the will to contract and oblige himself, but not of fulfilling the obligations. The first nullifies.[52] The second nullifies.[53] The third is *per se* valid, for obvious reasons, unless *per accidens* this intention or purpose is raised to a *conditio sine qua non* and then the marriage depends (in the internal forum) on its

[47] Canon 1086, par. 2.

[48] Canon 1086, par. 1.

[49] *Cf.* Sipos, *Enchiridon Juris Canonici,* ed. 2, Pecs (1931), par. 131; *cf.* Rota in *causa Oregonapolitana,* 6 July, 1914, *AAS,* VI, 516 s; *AAS,* III, 528 s; *AAS,* IV, 708 s.

[50] *AAS,* VI, p. 517.

[51] Canon 1086, par 2.

[52] *Cf.* S. R. Rota, *AAS,* III, 525; IV, 708; Cappello, *De Matrimonio,* n. 594; Vlaming, *Praelectiones Juris Matrimonii,* II, n. 153; Gougnard, *De Matrimonio,* p. 159; Canon 1086.

[53] *Cf. ibidem.*

verification.[54] The will of taking on the obligation and of violating the obligation are not mutually exclusive.

But in view of what was already said about a *condition* against the substance, though in the form of a condition, it is really an act of the will to marry that is essentially diseased, and there are not two acts of the will, nor (as a condition presupposes) an act of the will to marry which has all the essential content, and this healthy act alone is *suspended* by a *condition.* In the last analysis it is a defective act of the will (*quoad matrimonium*) not defective (*quoad psychologiam*). Simultation, however, connotes *ex industria* a malicious intent,[55] whereas the same effect of invalid consent may not be cupable but due to error passing into judgment and this latter willed innocently or not as a *conditio sine qua non.*[56]

All authors seem to agree about the effect of this simulation and of conditions against the substance (namely nullity of the union) but they say there are two acts of the will, *e. g.*, "Intenditur quidem matrimonium, sed simul non intenditur, quia excluditur essentiale ejus et duo hi actus voluntatis contrarii mutuo se elidunt." [57] This is manifestly erroneous for "Intenditur matrimonium" is not true in reality; it may be true that he intends something which he labels matrimony.

In a concrete case it is often very difficult to judge whether the party had only an erroneous opinion about an essential of marriage, or truly and actually had the positive will of, *e. g.*, contracting a soluble bond. The presumption of law militates against this latter alternative, if the marriage was externally contracted absolutely.[58] One way (but not the sole way as so many authors say) of proving the defective consent would be if the intention were *deducta in pactum* as a condition, *i. e.*, in the sense of an *external* condition.

[54] *Cf.* Cappello, *De Matrimonio*, n. 600; Gougnard, *De Matrimonio*, p. 163.

[55] S. R. Rota, *AAS*, XIX, 1927, p. 219.

[56] *Cf.* on partial simulation, Gasparri, *De Matrimonio* (1904), nn. 919-923; Wernz-Vidal, *Jus Matrimoniale*, n. 461; Chelodi, *Jus Matrimoniale*, n. 116; De Smet, *De Sponsal. et Matrimonio*, n. 533; Sipos, *Enchiridion Juris Canonici*, par. 131.

[57] Sipos, *Enchiridion*, par. 131.

[58] Canon 1086.

The older sententiae and declarations of the Holy See acknowledged nullity of marriage on this head *only* if the intention or condition were externally and provably expressed by being *deducta in pactum.* Even the reorganized Rota followed this rule, but later it admitted the exclusion is possible (and provable) even without any pact or agreement,[59] but this proof is exceedingly difficult to gather.[60]

Sipos [61] has these words:

> Qui positive excludere intendit sacramentum, absolutam autem habet voluntatem contrahendi matrimonii, intentio illa nullum habet effectum, quia matrimonium validum, quod absolute intenditur, eo ipso est sacramentale. Si autem intentio excludendi sacramentum praevaleret voluntati contrahendi matrimonium, nullum esset matrimonium.

The first sentence is erroneous, and in spite of any jurisprudence to the contrary an adult receives no sacrament of marriage, if he *positively* wills not to receive it, and if the contract and the sacrament are *inseparable and the same thing,* he is not married.

It is perfectly evident that the content of the declaration of will, in virtue of which definite legal effects are to be procured, corresponding to the intention of the declarant, may not be in contradiction with this result. The act of the will and its declaration would nullify itself. The legal transaction would enter into opposition with itself, if the contractor makes a condition essentially incompatible with the ultimate purposes aimed at. Such declarations can not be considered juridically as long as the principle is maintained (and it must be maintained as a verity in our doctrine) that a juridic effect must necessarily be brought about by this very decision of the will. In such cases, the declaration of will would not have that content which it pretends to have according to the name it applies to itself. If the condition expressly sanctions nullity of this sort of consent, such consent modified by such conditions are against the substance and essence of marriage. The contradiction may be only internal, or only

[59] *Cf.* Sipos, *op cit.*, par. 131; 1 March, 1913, *AAS,* V, 312; 8 February, 1915, *S. R. R., AAS,* VII, 292; 10 May, 1916, *S.R.R., AAS,* IX, 32.

[60] *S. R. R., AAS,* 6 July, 1914, VI (1914), 520 s—*S. R. R., AAS,* 11 April, 1927, XIX, 217.

[61] *Op. cit.,* n. 131.

external and not internal (in this case it is only apparent contradiction) or internal and external at the same time.

If the decision of the will should be defective, ail of such internal contradictions, but the declaration should be altogether correct and without the internal contradictions being manifested then the case must be judged like one in which the transaction will is declared without actually having an intention or inner act of will, in some cases a mental reservation.

The will with a contradiction tallies with a declaration laboring under a contradiction, *e. g.*, "I marry you, if I marry Helen"; or "I marry, but I do not marry." It is plainly expressed that the parties in spite of the name (marriage) by which they designate their intention in their legal transaction, do intend in reality to obtain or achieve something essentially different from it, *e. g.*, "I marry you on condition that I divorce you *a vinculo* whenever I wish."

It is quite indifferent in what form or mode, or shape this content of the will manifests itself, if only the act of the legal transaction can still be accepted as one. Nothing is present except an external form.

In reality there is really no condition, nor mode, nor modification. For every such modification of a concrete transactional will as opposed to a normal will, presupposes a legally (and in our case, a naturally) valid transaction the effect of which, in the case of a condition is dependent on the verification of the conditioned circumstance. It is simply not sense to speak of conditional declarations if the declarations are invalid. Thus the very title of this chapter is not *ex natura rei* correct, as pointed out previously, but yet there is some justification for its use because externally such fatally diseased wills are often expressed with words denoting a condition and because of this, the law uses this conception. The circumstance, the ingredient which actually operates the invalidity may be contained solely in the mind or expressed in either a principal or a subordinate clause.[62]

The investigation of our question must ascertain what sort of natural and legal content, matrimonial consent must have to be valid, and this was done in the pages immediately preceding. If any essential component is wanting, the consent does not beget marriage. But we must not overlook this fact: there are legal relations that occur so

[62] *Cf.* Hussarek, *Die Bedingte Eheschliessung* (Wien, 1882), pp. 227-238.

often in life that even the laic in law has a general idea of them, even if his concepts literally are not sharply silhouetted, or his thoughts may not be clear at all. That the exchange of fruit for money equals sale and purchase; concession of the use of a thing in exchange for money, is rent or hire; that the appropriation of a thing against the will of the owner, is theft, even the most doltish man in the lowest stratum of society knows these things.

But how surpassingly superior, exalted above these popular lazy conceptions, more sensed and felt and surmised than apprehended or comprehended and actually conceived, is the concept of the jurists on the matter of consent and contract and their relations, and yet for the sake of legal certainty, it is taken for granted that if one declares his will with the employment of such an expression which is just as current with jurists as with laics, that one has fully apprehended this juridic conception.

It cannot very well be even presupposed that even a trained and experienced jurist is fully aware, at the moment when he concludes a transaction, of all the rights and obligations that may arise from the transaction from case to case. But it is quite certain that this is not so, for the layman. At the very best he knows something about the economic aims pursued in affairs and means to attain these ends, yet in spite of this, all the legal rights and duties of the logically developed legal institution are placed upon him too. Mere ignorance about these is not sufficient to render the transaction invalid. For this it is necessary that there be a contradiction against an essential characteristic of the transaction.

This legal (and natural law) principle (*quoad consensum maritalem*) brings it about that we behold the pertinent questions (as witnessed by far too many canonists and theologians) from a false, incorrect, inadequate angle of vision. While as a matter of fact, always the content of the transactional will is in question, the first question that often enters into our field of vision is the liceity or admissability of a special treatment by, *e. g.*, a condition. And he who does not see to the very bottom of this matter will think that alongside the declaration of the will in itself correct, there exists independently an incorrect addition to this act of the will. Nearly all canonists unconsciously, and invalidly pass from the pure logical order into the real order when discussing these so-called vitiating conditions. They [63] and various papal pronouncements speak of the two wills, one general in accord with the institution of marriage by God, the other special containing the vitiating element. In reality there is but one act of the will whose essential notes do not tally adequately with the essential notes belonging to the supposed object of this act of willing, namely, true marriage, whose essence is beyond the reach of human will or desire to alter or touch. On the other hand the *supposed addition* to the will act or the condition is no more than a symptom of the essential incorrectness of the entire act of the will. Therefore canonical jurisprudence speaks of conditions that contradict the essence of marriage, while it would be better to speak of an essentially defective content of the marital consent. Though externally the words may denote a complete act of marital will, to which is added such a condition, *e. g.*, "I marry you only on this condition that it be not for life," yet internally it is psychologically impossible for the contractor to have two internal acts of the will at the same time with contents corresponding to the words used, in other words, it would be to will simultaneously just this: "I marry you, I do not marry you." To give priority of time to either of the supposed two acts of the will only leads us to a *reductio ad absurdum*, keeping in mind the essential causative power of true marital consent, and the lack of such creative power of any other consent though it bears the label of marital consent.[64]

What qualities, what essential notes *true matrimonial* consent must have, the Fathers of the Church have discussed and the result was the formulation of the doctrine of the *tria bona matrimonii: proles, fides, sacramentum* (this last term used not *per se* in a technical dogmatic sense). The procreation of children, the irrefragable fidelity in marriage, the inseparable community of life, all these are to be

[63] *E. g.*, Benedict XIV (as a private canonist), *De Synodo Dioc.*, lib. 13, cap. 22, n. 7.

[64] A man placed a condition, unknown to the woman, against the *bonum prolis*. It was not *deducta in pactum*. The rotal decision has this to say: "Porro haec conditio, quae non est vera et propria conditio, sed potius voluntas contraria substantiae matrimonii, duplici modo intelligi, potest deducta in pactum—*cf. S. R. R. Decisiones*, XI, 1919, p. 146. The decision declared the marriage invalid.

willed by the contracting parties in such a way that their consent is to be true marriage consent answering all natural requirements. As marriage itself receives its consecration and sanctity through those God-given treasures, so must consent correspond and tally with this sanctity and goodness. But because of the principle that it is not necessary to have a clear precise apprehension of all these characteristics of a juridical transaction in one's decision of will, or in one's conceptions, if only a general idea, a mental picture of the same is present, according to all, this is sufficient if only no essential characteristic is *de facto* excluded. And the question in practice shapes itself thus: Whether a concrete marriage consent excluded any of these. If so there is no marital consent and therefore no resulting marrage. On this basis, that is, of anti-essential conditions, the subject of conditions against the substance must be solved. It must be ascertained what Canon Law means by each single treasure of matrimony, *i. e.*, when are they excluded and when not, and under what more definite presuppositions the exclusion of one or more effects the nullity of matrimonial consent, a truly herculean task. The influence of error and ignorance of these *bona,* and the various kinds of such states of mind, especially the action of the will in positively and prevailingly basing or not its willing on these states of mind; or a clear knowledge of these essentials, with deliberate act of the will excluding one or the other, all this is properly not to be treated *ex professo* within the scope of this discussion. It will suffice to endeavor to fix well what the essential content of a marital consent involves, denotes and connotes as an essential minimum without which such consent simply does not exist, and to conclude that, if any of this minimum is lacking, the consequence is to make impossible the arising of marriage. It is *necessary* however in using the conclusions drawn, to study thoroughly *each individual marriage case* in order to explore the facts and rightfully apply these principles of the natural and Canon Law.

The *fides* which upon entering marriage must be present in the intention and therefore willed explicitly or implicitly consists not in the actual future observance of matrimonial fidelity as is clear from the nature of the case, but in the willingness *hic et nunc* to take upon oneself the essential obligation to be obliged all during married life to the fidelity of wedlock. The obligation aims at the future continued actual observance, and this obligation can subsist simultaneously with its non-observance.

Taken in a coarsely sensual acceptation, this *fides* is had, if either party permits himself or herself to be used sexually by the other and shuns carnal intercourse with all others. But a more refined and ideal acceptation or interpretation of this relationship does not content itself with the above sense, but demands a mutual surrender of the parties, a spiritual union into one existence, one being, so that the violation of the fidelity is found even if this harmony of souls, this concord of minds, is destroyed or disturbed. Not only in deed must fidelity be maintained, for as the soul apostatizes from God through work, word, and thought, so also partner becomes a traitor in thought, intention and desire and not merely by criminal action. Now it is true that there is not lacking in moral theology and Canon Law support of this sublime and elevated interpretation of marital fidelity, but the legal juridic order, which demands for its principles sensually, discernible, and papable facts, connects legal consequences only with the coarse sensual violations of this *fides*. Hence in so far as the necessary content of the consent concerns itself with the *bonum fidei*, it considers only such violations. In one word the *bonum fidei* means this: that in the intention of the parties, when giving matrimonial consent, all sexual intercourse with others must be completely and absolutely and forever excluded as a right as long as the marriage exists. Therefore a so-called condition reserving a right to intercourse with a third party, even only once, destroys true marital consent. Thus this fidelity is also absolute in another direction. It does not only know of any exception in favor of a third party, it also does not recognize any exception for any period of time.

The *bonum sacramenti* signifies the indissolubility of the marital relation and bond as long as the life time of the two. This spiritual soul union, this fusion of each other which is the ideal purpose of marriage has no limits either as to its intensity, intimacy, or duration, save that fixed by nature itself. Here it was easier for jurisprudence to describe and define the factual situation in accordance with the ideal. The legal bond is as indissoluble as the ethical bond is supposed to be.

But this unity is to be continued, effected, also beyond the grave.

The witnesses and pledges of this fidelity, for the time coming after the consummation of the earthly pilgrimage of the couple, are the children begotten in their union, the offspring with which God hath blessed the womb of the wife in their devoutly Christian life. In this way their marriage continues even after the parents depart from this existence.

Hence real marriage must be so constituted, that nothing can prevent the blessing and treasure of children, leaving it to God whether He grants or refuses it according to his inscrutable counsels. Hugaccio says at v. *Omne* C. 27 q. 2: "Spes et intencio procreandi prolem et ad cultum et fidem Dei educandi, sive sequitur proles, sive non." The *bonum prolis* consists in the formation, the shaping of the marital union with a view towards the procreation of offspring.

It is towards this three fold marriage treasure, which in reality is simply Christian fidelity to marriage vows in a threefold direction, that the matrimonial consent should be directed. If *fides* is excluded totally in the threefold direction, or only in one or the other direction, there is no marriage consent, even if the declared will or intention arrogates to itself the name of a marriage contract.

It is quite immaterial how this exclusion is expressed, or even if it be unexpressed, but for the external forum of course it must be certain and clearly recognizable. Whether at the time of declaring the consent a special formula is used independently, or whether only one of the parties intends this exclusion, or whether the triple or single fidelity is excluded by words forming a condition, the declared will in these cases is always in contradiction with the essential content of marital consent and therefore legally invalid and incompatible. Gregory IX gives clearest proof of this in furnishing *ex professo* norms just for this case, though it must be observed that his norms and examples can on their face value be interpreted in a way not against the substance of marriage. Two of these examples of Gregory have the form of imperfect conditions, they are not future suspensive, the third has only implicitly the form of a condition for externally it is resolutive or better it is formulated as *dies incertus an et quando.*[65]

[65] C. 7, X, *de cond. appos.*, IV, 5.

Having reiterated the above principles governing marriage consent, now an attempt shall be made to apply these same principles to consent furnished with a so-called condition against the substance or against some essential property of marriage. And in this endeavor it will be necessary to devote some though to several points closely related to *conditions,* namely the effect of a *simple intention* or purpose contrary to matrimonial indissolubility, seeking to find out whether it is equivalent to an actual *condition;* and attention must be directed also to *error juris* concerning especially indissolubility, seeking an answer to the question, is *error juris* also equivalent to a *condition* against the substance or the essential properties of marriage.

CHAPTER XXIII

CONDITIONS AGAINST THE SUBSTANCE OF MARRIAGE IN PARTICULAR

Article I

Conditions Against the Indissolubility of Marriage

§1. *The Nature and Importance of the Question*

It is well known that many marry with the intention or condition of effecting a dissoluble union. Are such unions valid? It is a doctrine of the Church, always taught and defended, that marriage is intrinsically unbreakable. "To that principle [the absolute indissolubility of marriage] the Catholic Church has ever borne unflinching testimony. Divorce in the modern sense (*divortium a vinculo matrimonii*) has no place within her fold." [1] Catholics between themselves rarely contract with a view to divorce *a vinculo,* though the Rota in 1915 annulled such a union.[2] Such a condition is placed sometimes in mixed marriages, though seldom formally expressed.[3]

In non-Catholic marriages such a condition, actual or interpretative, implicit or explicit, is often found, and such marriages sometimes come before the Church Courts for judgment on their validity. The chief reasons why such unions occur are that the indissolubility is little recognized to-day outside the Catholic Church; non-Catholic religions, and laws of States and nations look on marriage as a dissoluble union. Even the Greek and other Eastern Churches, separated from infallibility, officially permit this for adultery, high treason, attempt on life of partner, partial infidelities giving rise to suspicion, intentional abortion, servitude, insanity, leprosy, religious profession, husband's elevation to the episcopate.[4]

[1] This is a tribute of a Protestant philosopher, Wm. S. Lilly. *On Right and Wrong,* p. 206.

[2] *AAS,* 17 April, 1915, p. 442.

[3] Castellane-Gould case, three times before the Rota (condition was alleged), *AAS,* 1912, p. 146; 1913, p. 312; 1914, p. 165; 1915, p. 292.

[4] *Cf.* J. J. Lynch, *Conditional Matrimonial Consent,* Catholic University, Washington, D. C. (1917), p. 3.

In the United States of America and most European countries divorce is legally permissible. It seems the Constitution of the United States gives the Federal Government no power over the subject of divorce. All the States of the Union (except South Carolina) adopted divorce statutes. The causes vary from the single case of adultery (New York and District of Columbia) to as many as nine causes in the State of Washington. The "Omnibus Provision" admits divorces for any cause deemed sufficient by the court. The growth of divorce in the United States chiefly because of these laws is unprecedented, and more than any other modern nation except the pagan nation of Japan.[5]

From this it is evident that the teaching of the true Church on this point is not generally recognized by other religions and the civil power. The result of this fact is that in this country and elsewhere multitudes *do not consider* marriage as an essentially indissoluble union (generally an *error juris* at least). In other words, these thousands are in *error* on this point and under this impression that divorce *a vinculo* is possible and licit, they marry. Some, it can not be doubted, marry with an actual expressed intention or a condition of severing the bond by divorce under certain contingencies voluntarily placed.[6] Since marriages of this kind, be they Catholic, non-Catholic or mixed, are at times brought into the diocesan court, the question of their validity or invalidity is of the greatest practical importance.

In the following pages, we will discuss briefly the property of indissolubility itself, conditions concerning it, and the Canon Law principles governing such conditions, together with their interpretation and application by the ecclesiastical courts, especially in those cases where there is *error juris* on this point.

§2. *The Bonum Sacramenti or the Indissolubility of Marriage*

Those who marry must do so by their own free will as Pius XI recently reiterated, adding that since marriage was instituted not by

[5] *Cf.* Towne, *Social Problems*, chap. XII—"Divorce in the U. S.," *Catholic Encyclopoedia*, Vol. V, p. 67.

[6] "En Amerique presque toutes les jeunes filles, qui se marient, ont cette intention d' user du divorce, si le mariage ne les rend pas heureuses." Statement of an American Protestant in the proceedings of the Castellane-Gould case, *AAS*, 1913, p. 317.

man, but by the Author of nature and man, its essential properties are totally independent of the will of the nupturients. One must will it as it is, or not at all.

The three essentials of marriage (*tria bona*) take their origin not from any human will, but from the Divine Will which fashioned marriage. The *bonum prolis* constitutes marriage's *primary end,* the other two are essential and intrinsic properties of marriage and from another viewpoint also ends of marriage. The exact relation between these three essentials has been the theme of many great minds, as has been mentioned already.[7]

"The *sacramentum* of marriage exists not only among the Latins and Greeks, but also among the faithful and infidels." [8]

The *sacramentum* as already stated differs according to most authors, in an important respect from the other two *bona.* The will to assume the obligation of conjugal fidelity and of procreation, can coexist with the intention or condition to abuse and violate these obligations, for these two intentions are not mutually exclusive, but this intention or condition to violate or abuse cannot bear on the *sacramentum.* In other words this last intention *per se et semper* excludes this *bonum* entirely. The proof of this unique rôle played by the *sacramentum* is left to dogmatic and sacramental theology.[9]

[7] Sanchez, *De Sacr. Matr.,* I, II, disp. 29, n. 5; IV, 9, nn. 2, 3. Wernz, *Jus Matr.,* pars. I, tit. I, n. 52; s; S. Thomas *Theol. Moralis Suppl.,* qu. 49, a. 3.

[8] C. 11, X, *de Transactionibus,* I, 36—Honorius III. "Quo jure matrimonium indissolubile fit, et unde haec indissolubilitas proficicatur?" is the query of the thirteenth dissertation in the second book of Sanchez. He enumerates and explains four answers, the last of which he embraces and which imports two things: "Primum est, aliqualem inseparabilitatem esse de natura matrimonii, et ita competere etiam matrim, rato, de jure divino et naturali: ut optime probant rationes primae sententiae . . . Secundum est, omnimodam indissolubilitatem non competere matrimonio, ex jure naturae, nec ex ratione sacramenti, sed ex significatione, qua Christus eveit illud ad significandam unionem indissolubilem Christi cum Ecclesia per carnem assumptam: et quia haec significatio tantum convenit in matrim. Consummato, ut probavi n. 1 illud solu esse omnino indissolubile." Lib. II, d. XIII, n. 7.

[9] One must not jump to the conclusion that a condition "that we *divorce,*" invalidates. It all depends on what is meant by *divorce* in the minds of the persons, the word has several legitimate and many illegitimate connotations, and it *per se* does not always mean *a vinculo indissolubili.*

This aspect of the marital bond demands the individual life-long society (as a right and obligation) which follows from the consummated sacramental marriage, and from the *matrimonium ratum vel legitimum* as long as this bond is not broken by death or by proper ecclesiastical authority extrinsic to the bond and to the will of the parties.[10] Substantially against this property are conditions restricting (as a right) this society to a certain or uncertain time, *e. g.*, "till I find a richer girl," or, "as long as you please me," or, "till I divorce you *a vinculo.*" [11]

This *bonum* is the bond viewed from its essential characteristic of intrinsic indissolubility, and it is the same as *indissolubilis fides.*

It is certain that this treasure is found in all marriages, even those of infidels. Though some few [12] have thought differently, being confused by the word *sacramentum.*

It might be of historical interest to note the two following unique opinions about the *bonum sacramenti.* Berardi [13] says that the *bona prolis et fidei* ("increase and multiply;" "it is not good for man to be alone") belong to the very origin and institution of marriage, but the *bonum sacramenti* was added (after the fall of Adam) to marriage already instituted, therefore it does not belong to the substance of marriage. Others have said that the *remedium* end, was added after the fall of Adam. Held too [14] has a strange opinion which is,

[10] The gist of the whole matter has been presented in a dozen words by an author who was not only a great artist in romantic fiction, but a profound master of the social sciences. "Nothing more conclusively proves the necessity of indissoluble marriage than the instability of passion."

"Let the perfect ideal of indissoluble marriage be once definitely rejected, and Western civilization will inevitably fall back to that wallowing in the mire from which Christianity rescued it, and in whatever degree you tamper with this ideal, and derogate from its strictness, in that degree do you demoralize woman. Yes and man too . . . The moral tone of society depends upon the chastity of woman. And the chastity of woman depends upon the absolute character of marriage." Wm. S. Lilly, *On Right and Wrong*, p. 220.

[11] *Cf.* Schmalzgrueber, lib. IV, tit. V.

[12] F. Florentis, *Opera Juridica* (Paris, 1679), II, p. 103, who treats at length the *tria bona.*

[13] *Commentaria in Jus Eccl. Universum*, Mediolani (1847), II, *De Matri.*

[14] *Jurisprudentia Universalis*, Fuggerina Boos (1772), 5 vols., IV, *De Matr.*, d. II, cap. I, par. III.

however, identical with the early Romàn viewpoint based on their exalted and pristine conception of *maritalis affectio,* which if it ceased between the two parties, causes marriage *eo ipso* to cease also. But in the early days of Rome *de facto* it was scarcely conceivable that it could cease. It was left to the era of Roman plenty in power and wealth, to run riot in divorce. Held's contention is this. The *vinculum* is not the sole power in the body, but the very habitual union of minds, or consent morally persevering, thus there is no formal marriage (*in facto esse*) abstracting from our first parents, without the consent to persevere.

It seems every author who treats the subject, even though they admit an essential distinction between the obligation and the execution as far as the *bonum prolis et fidei* are concerned, deny it for the *bonum sacramenti,* the gist of their argument seeming to be that if one wills an indissoluble bond, he has such a bond, excluding any intention of divorce. It is true one cannot will and not will at the same time a perpetual bond, or in other words will a perpetual indissoluble bond till death and have the concurrent will to break what he knows is unbreakable as far as his power is concerned. But it is equally true that the same one who wills to be bound by a perpetual indissoluble bond to a particular woman can at the same time have the positive will to leave her and to use civil or heretical church law to obtain a divorce and marry another. But this is against the *bonum fidei* and not against the *bonum sacramenti.* If therefore the *intention* only means this, then the first marriage is valid. If by the phrase "intention against the *bonum sacramenti* is meant, the positive prevailing will to exclude the *obligation* of the *sacramentum,* then of course he is not married.

The Rota in a decision said: "Cum vero *simplex* intentio contrahentis contraria bono Sacramenti seu indissolubilitati matrimonii, diversimode judicanda sit ab intentione contra bonum fidei vel prolis, praestat paulisper immorari in jure hoc in re explicitus declarando." [15]

The decision goes on to say that a *positive* intention to contract a soluble marriage, makes no marriage. Quoting St. Thomas, it affirms the *bonum sacramenti* belongs to the *esse* of marriage, the other two to the *usum* of marriage, not to its *esse.* Yet these other

[15] *AAS,* VI (1914), 516 s; XIX, (1927), 217 s.

two do touch essentially the substance of the marriage *quoad obligationem* and if the *tria bona* are, as is maintained in this thesis, nothing else than three essential aspects of the same bond, which bond is nothing else than a moral *jus*, then the distinction of St. Thomas and others is not valid. The indissolubility rightly viewed pertains also to the *usus* of marriage, from its very necessity of indissolubility. Then the decision continues:

> Deducere aliquam condicionem in pactum matrimoniale nihil aliud significat quam facere talem conditionem partem constitutivam contractus matrimonialis (V. Wernz, *l. c.*, in textu); si autem solubile vinculum positive intenditur, eo ipso, ex sua natura, est pars constitutiva contractus; si, ex altera parte, conditio contra bonum fidei vel prolis etiam positive intenditur, non eo ipso, seu ex sua natura, in contractum ingreditur, quia bonum fidei et prolis consequitur contractum in suo *esse* jam constitutum; ideo, ut talis conditio in contractum ipsum ingrediatur, et consequenter illum irritum reddat, requiritur specialis actus voluntatis, quo non solum positive intenditur conditio contra bonum fidei et prolis, sed etiam ut ita intendatur ut praevaleat intentioni generali contrahendi matrimonium prout ordinarie contrahitur, *i. e.*, prout a Deo institutum est, seu juxta legem Christi seu doctrinam catholicam; praevalet autem huic intentioni generali contrahendi matrimonium prout ordinarie contrahitur, pendet a conditione contra bonum fidei vel prolis. E contra, intention contraria bono fidei vel prolis, contractum matrimonium non irritat, nisi in pactum deducta fuerit.[16]

This line of reasoning about the other two treasures of marriage is only valid, if it all amounts to the *fulfillment* of the obligations, and the decision says this: "Non item intentio contrahendi cum conditione contra bonum fidei vel prolis, quia etiamsi haec conditio positive intendatur non eo ipso est pars constitutiva contractus; intendi enim potest ita ut coexistat cum intentione contrahendi verum matrimonium, videlicet si conditio ista respuat *tantummodo adimplementum* obligationis assumptae."[17] On the other hand if the essential obligation of the *bonum prolis vel fidei* is excluded the marriage is invalid

[16] Causa Oregonopolitana, *AAS*, VI (1914), p. 250.

[17] *Cf.* Ben. XIV, lib. 13, cap. 22, n. 7.

according to Canon 1086, par. 2, which canon is quoted by the Rota in the Marconi-O'Brien case.[18]

The decision goes on to say it cannot be denied that, from pontifical documents and grave authors, a condition to solve a marriage because of adultery or other causes, does not irritate the contract unless it was *"deducta in pactum."* Thus answered the Holy Office on the 2 October, 1680, to the doubt: "An sit validum matrimonium cum intentione foedandi vel solvendi matrimonium? R. Si ista sint deducta in pactum, seu cum ista conditione sint contracta, matrimonia sunt nulla: sin aliter sunt valida." [19]

The Rota decision says of this response that it is clear from the context of documents that it does not mean a distinction between one who contracts, with a positive intention, a soluble marriage, and one who puts this same intention into a condition (*deducta in pactum*), but rather it means the distinction between one who with a concomitant error about indissolubility marries without any positive act of the will to this effect, and on the other hand, one who has the positive intention to contract a soluble marriage.

Thus from this a marriage without error, *e. g.*, a Catholic who knows better yet contracts with the condition *ad tempus* would not come under this response, as far as the second part goes.

" 'Matrimonium facit partium consensus, etc.' ita Canon 1081, par. 1. At non quovis modo assentire conjuges in matrimonium possunt, sed solummodo secundum ejusdem matrimonii naturam." [20]

"Sedulo tamen animadvertendum est, non omnes obligationes quae ex matrimoniali contractu oriuntur, seu melius, non omnia ejus bona ejusdem esse naturae, ita ut in ipsis obligato ab ejus adimplemento secerni queat, seu jus ab ejus usu. In indissolubilitate namque, seu in bono sacramenti, enunciata distinctio locum non habet." [21]

The decision quotes St. Thomas [22] to the effect that marriage is never found without inseparability, but it is found without *proles*

[18] *AAS*, XXIX (1927), p. 219.

[19] *Cf. AAS*, VI, p. 522, also very many similar instructions of the Holy Office.

[20] *Nullitas matri.*, Marconi-O'Brien, 11 April, 1927, *AAS*, XIX (1927), p. 218.

[21] *AAS*, (1927), XXIX, p. 219.

[22] *Sum. Theol. Suppl.* qu. 47, Art. 3.

and *fides,* because the *esse* of a thing does not depend on its use. *Sed fides et proles in suis principiis* do pertain to the *esse matrimonii.*

§3. *Canon Law on Conditions Contrary to the Indissolubility of Marriage*

Canon Law on conditions contrary to the indissolubility of marriage expressly emphasizes and applies the fundamental natural law on this point.[23]

Benedict XIV makes an interesting application of this law to the union of two Calvinists.[24] Modern authors (canonists and moralists) also set forth the law as to the nullifying action of a condition as well as an intention against the *sacramentum* as distinguished from an intention against the other two *bona.*[25]

Such is the law itself about the *bonum sacramenti,* and some of these authors will be referred to on the *interpretation* and *application* of the law. Now one must see how this law about the *bonum sacramenti* is interpreted and applied.

§4. *Interpretation of This Law*

The law about a condition against the *sacramentum* appears quite clear both in itself and in the reasons on which it is based, yet to apply it to a concrete case certain difficulties arise as to its exact *meaning, scope* and *application.*

[23] *Cf.* the celebrated decretal of Gregory IX, *Si Conditiones,* cap. ult. de condit. apposit., Ben. XIV, *De Synodo,* I. 13, c. 22, n. s; Ben. XIV in *novo Bullario Ordinis Praedicatorum,* tom. I, n. 130, "Cum in Sclavoniae . . . sed fornicarie commiscentur;" classical commentaries on the law of the Decretales recognized as such by the Roman Curia, *e. g.,* Sanchez, V. disp. 9, n. 5; disp. 29, n. 11; *cf.* also on this distinction between an intention contrary to the *sacramentum,* and one against the other two *bona,* Gonzales Tellez, *Commentaria Perpetua* in X, lib. IV, tit. V, n. 9; Petrus de Ledesma, *Instr. de Matr.,* pars II, c. 42; Bonacina, *Opera Omnia,* lib. IV, tit. IV, qu. 2, n. 10; Laymann, *Summa,* lib. V, tr. 10, pars 2, cap. 1, n. 3, etc.

[24] *De Syn,* lib. 13, c. 22, nn. 5, 6, 7.

[25] Gasparri, *De Matr.,* III (1904), II, n. 919; Wernz, *Jus Decret. De Matr.,* IV, pars II, n. 302; Lehmkuhl, *Theol. Moral.* II, n. 879; D'Annibale, *Summula theol. moral.* pars II, n. 303; Ojetti, *Syn. Rerum,* V. I, n. 1434; Ballerini, Palmieri, *Opus theol. moral.,* V, VI, 287; Sebastianelli, *Prael. J. C.,* n. 135; and the writers after the Code quoted *passim.*

The chief questions pressing for a solution are these: I. Are we in this matter to regard a simple intention or purpose contrary to marital indissolubility as equivalent to an actual condition? II. Does a condition opposed to this essential property invalidate marriage if not *'deducta in pactum'?* III. Is *error juris,* by reason of which one contracting marriage intends to enter upon what he erroneously considers a dissoluble union—equivalent to the actual condition contrary to and excluding indissolubility? [26]

1. *Is a Simple Intention or Purpose Contrary to Matrimonial Indissolubility Equivalent to an Actual Condition?* The answer to the first question may be made thus: It is an undoubted fact that a *simple intention* contrary to the *bonum prolis vel fidei* is not equivalent to an *actual condition.* To have a null union because of these two *bona* there must be a true condition present as a constitutive part of the consent, whether *deducta in pactum* or not, if by the phrase is meant an external explicit placing of the condition in the contract or ceremony; or by a positive act of the will excluding these two *bona in suis principiis* as Canon 1086, par. 2, states.[27]

Now according to nearly all authors it is different in case of a simple intention against the *bonum sacramenti.* In this case they say, an intention, a purpose, or any act of the will concerning this property is *equivalent* to an *actual* condition. This evidently must be equivalent by necessity to a *positive act* of the will excluding for only this kind the Code outrules, but any intention concerning the abuse of this *sacramentum* is a positive act of the will excluding, according to the distinction held by these proponents.

The reason for this seeming anomaly is found in the fact that this *bonum* admits of no distinction between the assumption of the obligation involved and the fulfillment of the obligation assumed. The assumption is the fulfilment evidently, because it is a bond by nature

[26] The same questions may be posited about the other two essentials of marriage, *bonum prolis* and *bonum fidei* and the same reasoning applies to the solution, keeping in mind what was said about the intention (positive act of the will) excluding the *sacramentum. Cf.* Lynch, *Conditional Marriage Consent,* which confines itself to the *bonum Sacramenti.*

[27] *Cf.* Canon 1092, n. 2; *cf. Theologisch-praktische Quartalschrift,* 1934, p. 381.

unbreakable, but this is not literally a bond as an *ens reale,* but a *jus perpetuum,* which is a *moral* something. The other two *bona* do admit this distinction, yet to the author it seems these other two are only two other aspects of this *jus perpetuum.* This *jus* is *perpetuum* in duration, *exclusivum quoad alios* (fidei), and ordained *ad actus* per se aptos ad prolis generationem (bonum prolis).[28]

It is *certain* that if by a positive act of the will, or by a true condition the *essential* obligations of these two *bona* are not even assumed there is no marriage. It is equally certain that a simple contrary intention against these two *bona* (understood by the Code as simple, because it is not a positive act of the will excluding an essential) caused by *error juris,* etc., does not invalidate as Canon 1084 teaches, for the party has a true will to marry validly and an intention or purpose to abuse the obligations already undertaken. Such a content of the mind is not *exclusive,* they can co-exist, just as one wills to take a valid oath by assuming the obligation entailed to tell the truth, but at the same time has the morally bad purpose of not telling the truth.

But concerning the *bonum sacramenti* no distinction is possible between the assumption of the obligation (of accepting the inviolability of marriage, or no divorce (*ex vinculo*) and the fulfillment of the same (accepting the inviolability of marriage or no divorce), inasmuch as the common opinion says, following the reasoning of, *e.g.,* St. Thomas, that this property belongs to the essence itself of the marriage bond, rather than to the use of marriage.

There is no dispute when the case is posited thus: One wills to contract a true marriage and at the same time intends to exclude the property of indissolubility, then there is no marriage. (But the same statement is exactly true of the other two *bona* being thus excluded.)

There will always be here a discrepancy between the actual (internal) intention or will and the declaration of the intention or will, mental reservation in one case, simulation in the other. Here is discussed for the moment those cases (of real practical importance) in which the party renders *optima fide* (in case of error or ignorance), *mala fide* (in case of knowledge), the declaration of marriage intention, which declaration literally meets all the requirements of Canon

[28] Canon 1081, par. 2.

Law, while the real intent of the will behind all this appears to be entirely against this *sacramentum* and therefore against the substance of marriage. In the evaluation of such a marriage, when submitted to adjudication according to Canon Law, the precedence belongs to the declaration, by presumption, as far as the external forum is concerned, but in the internal forum the *precedence* belongs to the *real* inner intention or act of the will. In this supposition, for the moment is excluded the case of one in simple error about this quality of marriage but who when marrying does not bring it into his will. Excluded too is the case where the opposition to this essential point of Catholic doctrine is expressed in such a way as to reveal that the intention or will of one or both parties is concentrated on this point of diversion, thus altering essentially the entire content of the intention and will to marry by this disease of its essence. To invalidate this legal presumption of the external forum is the business of him who opposes the validity, that is the plaintiff. This presumption springs from a healthy sense of justice desirous of legal certainty. It prevents abuses by malicious cunning for the attainment of shady impure ends.

The difficulty is this, must necessarily and *per se* any kind of an intention, contrary to the *sacramentum,* carry with it the efficacious positive act of the will excluding the *sacramentum?* Even if the answer is yes, we must beware of the manifold meaning and connotation (some false, some true) of the word divorce even when raised to a clearly expressed condition.

It seems false to have recourse here to the theory that there are two acts of the will at the same time, namely one to contract an indissoluble marriage and one to contract a soluble marriage. It seems impossible to have these two acts simultaneously, to will and not will the same thing at the same time, and furthermore *ex hypothesi* (in case of *error juris* being the cause) the intellect and therefore they will know nothing of the indissolubility (*carentia scientiae*) and by error the intellect thinks marriage is soluble, that indissolubility is already not in it by nature, and it is not necessary and foolish to exclude what the intellect falsely thinks is already excluded. All that is in the mind is one act of the will, essentially healthy or not according as the will concentrates on the error and wills marriage as the error thinks it is, or not. In other words it seems that in any case, whether the contractor is in error, doubt, or has true knowledge, there is one act of the will, always psychologically complete, but not always juridically complete as a marital act of willing, then besides there may be in the mind ignorance or error, or in the will a positive intention excluding the *sacramentum,* in the first case, the will is juridically and essentially healthy as a marriage will, in the latter case it is not, though it is a complete act of the will, reaching out to something that is *not marriage* but labelled as marriage.

These writers after fictioning these two opposed acts of the will, end up by stating "evidently these two acts of the will cannot coexist since they are mutually exclusive." Then follows another contradiction "one destroys the other." To do this they must exist simultaneously.

If it be objected that the two acts do not exist at the same time, but that there is a priory in time of one to the other, then all the talk about general intention and special intention falls out, and moreover the prior act works nothing, it is the act of the will that is present when the contract is celebrated according to Canon 1086, and nothing prevents the so-called specific act existing then, it all depends on the one willing.[29]

When it is insisted that any intention contrary to the indissolubility destroys any so-called general intention to will a valid marriage, this insistence seems to overthrow the principle they use about the general intention absorbing the specific one. A passage in a Rotal decision of January 24, 1911, is quoted in support of this point, but this passage speaks of "actus *rejiciendi obligationem,* cum sit magis specificus, certe praevaleat actui magis generali, quia species derogat generi, juxta regulam 34 juris . . ." This is only too true since the act of the will in question is one that actually excludes.

To sum up, it is difficult to see how any kind of intention, aim, purpose, or any act of the will contrary to this propriety must always be held as equivalent (in effect) to an actual condition excluding this property.[30]

Yet the contrary seems to represent the common teaching of

[29] This same thought has been previously touched on here and there at appropriate places.

[30] S. R. Rota, *AAS* (1912), p. 155.

canonists on this point, and this intention may be a virtual one.[31] It is alleged that this equivalence of a simple intention against the perpetuity of marriage, to an actual condition is recognized by the S. R. Rota as proved by its practice. A marriage case in 1913 [32] is mentioned: "ullimodo ergo . . . cui alligetur consensus." But the reasoning in this decision (strange as it was) was overruled by the same Rota in the same marriage case.

In a rotal decision in this pregnant sentence "Verum A. T. optime novit hunc errorem [de indissolubilitate] menti inhaerentem, et non deductum in pactum, matrimonio non officere, ut saepe disertis conceptisque verbis declaravit haec S. C." [33]

2. *Does a Condition Opposed to the Property of Indissolubility Invalidate Marriage if it is not "deducta in pactum"?* The second question is this: Does a condition opposed to the property of indissolubility invalidate marriage if it is not "deducta in pactum"? [34]

It is certain at least speculatively and in the internal forum that such a condition invalidates the consent and the marriage, no matter how that condition is framed or expressed, or whether it is unexpressed externally, known or not to the other party or to others. For a *condition qua condition* when the content is against the substance of a thing, is made a constituent part of the consent. In fact as noted before, strictly it is not a condition in this case, but an act of the will psychologically complete, but incomplete as an act of the will of marrying and inherently possessing an essential disease. The marriage and marital consent are invalid not because of the so-called condition (for a condition makes a full healthy juridical act of the will depend on it) but because of a *defectus consensus.* Canon 1086, par. 2, really governs here, for even a condition externally expressed against the substance simply *indicates* a positive act of the will excluding an essential element. (The marriage would be invalid even if, *per impossibile,* the condition were *verified.*)

But the question is narrowed to this: What *sort* of *proof* of such

[31] Reiffenstuel, lib. IV, tit. 1, n. 346.

[32] Castellane-Gould, *AAS* (1913), p. 329; *cf.* De Angelis, *Prael.,* I, lib. 4, n. 7.

[33] *AAS* (1914), p. 522.

[34] *Cf.* previous chapter on how conditions may be placed.

a condition is required in the *external* forum in order to obtain a declaration of nullity in a Church court? [35]

In the first place, if it be proven that the condition was "deducta in pactum" in this accidental sense of actually being stipulated in the terms of the marriage contract and made a constituent element thereof, then it is evident the union is invalid, for the consent of the contractors must certainly be held to bear on what is expressly stipulated in the contract. Such a marriage would be declared null in the external forum, for Canon 1086, par. 1, reads that the internal consent of the mind is always presumed to conform to the words or signs used in the celebration of marriage.

Is this the only kind of proof sufficient to beget a declaration of nullity? Would it not be sufficient to prove that such a condition *de facto* exists although not externally "deducta in pactum" and even though the terms of the contract implied the intention to contract validly? The answer is affirmative, for Canon 1086, par. 1, is only a presumption that cedes to the truth and besides every condition *qua* condition is *deducta in pactum* (in the substantial sense) and if this fact of its being placed is *proved* in other ways, then the court must render a verdict of nullity. But what is proof and what criteria (some necessarily arbitrary) are used as evidence is left to the prudence and rules of the curial jurisprudence, which, in this very point, has changed more than once.

Many canonists affirmed that the external "deducta in pactum" was necessary to get a decision of invalidity. And they were right as far as jurisprudence was once just that.[36] And quite some few canonists made the tragic error of carrying over this jurisprudence into the internal forum and they taught that, unless the condition was externally *deducta in pactum* in the act of celebration or immediately before, the marriage was valid *coram Deo*. This was a confusion of two distinct things, natural law principles about marital consent was identified with principles of proof of fact of the courts, which latter principles are built ultimately on natural law and partly on arbitrary man-made rules and good experience.

The study of canonists therefore would seem to suggest an affirma-

[35] *Cf.* Instruction of the Holy Office, 19 August, 1857 (Tahiti); *Fontes*, n. 945.

[36] *Cf.* S. C. C., December 2, 1680; *Fontes*, n. 755; *cf.* also *Fontes*, nn. 761, 1005.

tive answer to our original query, but on the other hand, numerous Roman responses appear to give a negative answer. How reconcile this *seeming* contradiction? [37] In conformity with this common teaching is a statement of the Holy Office stating what proofs are regarded sufficient when the conditions was not "deducta in pactum." [38]

Now concerning those responses which seem to contradict the above and to say marriage cannot be declared null on account of a condition opposed to the *sacramentum,* unless that condition is proved to have been "deducta in pactum." The question was asked: "An sit validum matr. cum intentione foedandi vel solvendi matr.?" R. "Si ista sint in pactum, seu cum ista conditione sint contracta, matrimonia sunt nulla, sin aliter sunt valida." [39] The *Instructio Austriaca,* par. 55, reads: "Conditiones, quae in consensus declaratione haud exprimuntur, pro non appositis habendae sunt." [40] There is also the letter of Pius VI to the Archbishop of Prague, 11 July, 1789;[41] and the Holy Office to Japan on February 4, 1891.[42]

A study of the context and circumstances of these responses and instructions reveal they bear only on cases which involve *error juris* about indissolubility, or an intention or condition depending entirely on such error.

> In hujusmodi vero documentis [*i. e.,* the responses demanding that the condition be deducta in pactum, in particular the query and response just quoted here and also in this decision] clarum est ex contextu non agi de distinctione inter contrahentem simpliciter cum positiva intentione matrimonium solubile ex una parte, et ex altera contrahentem cum tali positiva intentione in pactum deducta, sed potius inter illum qui contrahit cum errore concomitanti de indissolubili-

[37] *Cf.* Wernz, *Jus Decretal.,* IV, *De matr.,* n. 302, nota 44; Gasparri, *De Matr.* (1904), n. 1023: Ojetti, *Synop.,* n. 2015 b; Lehmkuhl, *Theol. Moral.,* II, n. 689 s.

[38] To the bishop of Nesqually (Seattle, Wash.)—*AAS,* VII (1915), p. 298.

[39] Collect. S. C. de P. Fidei, Vol. II, p. 83, n. 1427, quoted by Holy Office 9 December, 1874; *AAS,* VII (1915), p. 246; (1914), p. 522; *cf.* Collect. I, n. 1054, *AAS,* VII (1915), p. 297.

[40] Smith, *Marriage Process,* N. Y., 1896, in Appendix; etiam in Aichner, *Compend.,* J. C.

[41] *AAS,* VI, n. 522.

[42] Collectanea, Vol. II, n. 1746, *AAS,* VII, p. 297.

> tate conjugii, menti quidem inhaerenti, quin tamen actu positivo voluntatis conjugium dissolubile intendat, et ex alia parte contrahentem cum positiva intentione matrimonium dissolubile.[43]

Even for such cases the above decisions do not contradict the teaching of canonists that marriage is invalidated by any intention or condition whereby this property is *positively excluded* by the will of the contractor. These responses are not concerned with the speculative question at all (although their wording is quite apodictic, yet it is *presumed* the receiver realizes the courts or Congregations look from the external forum viewpoint). The aim was to give a practical rule to judge concrete cases in the external forum. This rule (since then changed) embodied a *presumptio juris tantum,* to the effect that it is quite difficult, sometimes impossible, to prove satisfactorily to judges the presence of an invalidating condition opposed to the *sacramentum* unless the condition be "deducta in pactum," for it is impossible to enter the mind and explore the will, so only by external signs or actions can it be judged and the best of all *media* is spoken or written words placed as a condition before reliable witnesses. The reason, the basis and the fact, of this presumption of law was already considered, namely that marriage enjoys the special favor of the law, and it is evident, that in the external forum marriage cannot be declared null on account of lack of proof.

Since these decisions concern cases involving *error juris* about this property, they do not cover cases where such error is absent.[44] If therefore it be proved that one knowing of the indissoluble nature of the marriage bond, yet contracts with a condition opposed to it, then the marriage should be declared invalid. Even in this case, unless the condition is "deducta in pactum," it is difficult to prove certainly the placing of the condition and its non-revocation especially when the contract (words used) bear witness to a valid marriage. Only *conclusive* proof can be held sufficient for marriage is a *causa favorabilis.* Proof is more difficult when the condition was placed only by one, and was not agreed to by both. If placed by one and rejected

[43] S. R. Rota, 22 July, 1914, apud *AAS,* VI (1914), p. 522, Smith-O'Kieffe case, Oregon City.

[44] *AAS,* VI (1914), p. 522.

by the other, and the contract is made nevertheless, then the one placing the condition is *presumed* to have withdrawn it, and the marriage is held valid till the contrary has been proved.[45] Some older writers [46] following an opinion of Innocent IV affirm the same is true, if the other party is *silent*. In confirmation of the above main points may be cited the rotal decision wherein a marriage was declared invalid because of a condition contrary to the *sacramentum* though it was not "deducta in pactum," and there was no *error juris*, both parties being Catholic.[47]

> A fortiori ergo, nulla gaudet auctoritate dispensandi ab hoc essentiali Sacramenti qualitate [*i. e., sacramentum*] ideoque omnes declarationes vel instructiones generales ab Ecclesia circa hanc materiam variis temporibus datae, ita prorsus intelligendae sunt, ut qui actu quodam positivo voluntatis in matrimonii celebratione indissolubilitatem excludat, contractum irritum efficiat; sive hic voluntatis actus conditio sit vel propositum, sive in pactum deducatur, sive non, sive sit etiam simplex intentio sive alteri parti manifestata vel non, sive expressa vel tantum in mente retenta. Quoniam vero in foro externo omne factum recte factum praesumitur, donec contrarium probatum sit (et praesertim matrimonium, quod speciali gaudet favore juris), patet quod in foro externo nequeat declarari nullum, propter voluntatem in contrahentibus Sacramenti bono contrariam, nisi haec certa sit et probata. Nec circa bonum Sacramenti recurrit distinctio, quae datur pro ceteris bonis matrimonio essentialibus, scilicet pro bono prolis et pro bono fidelitatis, quorum exclusio nullum reddit matrimonium, si sit *de obligatione non sumenda,* non vero si *sit tantum de non adimplenda.*[48]

There is no conflict here between the doctrine of the Church that it is the internal will that effects a marriage, and the jurisprudence that demanded in the past that this will if conditioned be externally added in the very contract, or the current jurisprudence that accepts any external proofs. It is true that a change of law should be brought

[45] Gasparri, *De Matr.* (1904), II, n. 1003.

[46] *E. g.*, Pirhing, Schmalzgrueber and Fagnanus.

[47] *AAS*, VII (1915), p. 442: Goguel-Gravier case.

[48] *AAS*, VII (1915), p. 452.

about by a *law* and not by explaining away the tenor of old decisions, but this is not the case here as, *e. g.*, one author asserts it is.[49]

3. *Is Error Juris Whereby Marriage is Considered a Dissoluble Union, Equivalent to a Condition Excluding Indissolubility?* The question contemplated by this entire thesis is about *conditions* added to marital consent, and not about *error juris.* But there is a close connection especially in practice between these two subjects, and many cases before the courts often resolve themselves into the question: is there an *error juris* present that was in reality made a condition, though not externally and clearly placed as a condition. Some marriages of persons laboring under this error may come for adjudication before the church courts, and when this happens, testimony is often alleged that the parties made various statements, before marriage about their belief in divorce, or about getting a divorce if the marriage turned out unhappily and other similar remarks. Thus there may be a utility and a justification for discussing this question in the present study.

The indissolubility of the marriage bond is not widely recognized or admitted outside the true Church. The result is perhaps most people outside the Church are under this *error juris.* This is especially true in the United States where three fourths are non-Catholics, and a tremendous proportion of these are not active church members. Nearly all States here have more or less liberal divorce laws.[50]

Error juris is described and defined by Cardinal Gasparri.[51] Error

[49] *Cf.* Hussarek, *Die Bedingte Eheschliessung,* p. 238.

[50] *Cf.* for marriage and divorce statistics in the United States from 1888 to 1931, *The World Almanac and Book of Facts,* New York, 1933, p. 368; *e. g.*, in the year 1888, 28,669 divorces, 5.4 percent of the total marriages; in 1898, 47,849 divorces, 7.4 percent; in 1908, 75,852, 9 percent; in 1919, 141,527 divorces, 12.3 percent; in 1929, 201,468 divorces, 16.3 percent; in 1930, 191,591 divorces; 1931, 183,695 divorces, 17 percent of the total marriages entered that year. Annullments *e. g.*, because of fraud etc. were 4,338 in 1931. "More than 100,000 children are affected by divorces which are granted annually in this country." *Cf.* ibi. p. 235-238 for each State law on divorces and the causes permitting absolute divorce. South Carolina alone does not allow divorce for any cause. Cf. ibi. 1934 ed. p. 246: Cruelty and desertion, conventional legal phrases, the first covering practically any difference of temperament, or tastes, lead in divorce complaints.

[51] *De Matr.*, II (1932), n. 805.

juris circa *ipsum jus* in corpus . . . is had when the contractor thinks, *e. g.*, marriage is a society not for having children, but for mere social purposes, and consents to such. In this case marital consent is absent.[52] After the age of puberty this error is not presumed in the external forum.

Error juris circa *essentialem matrimonii proprietatem* is had, if the contractor either thinks the bond can in some circumstances be broken, or thinks that he can have a second partner at the same time, or finally if he thinks marriage is not a Sacrament. In these cases, it is *certain* that matrimonial consent is present and thus *per se* the marriage is valid even though this error is present, and even though it was the *causa* of marrying, (Canon 1084). "Equidem si contrahens explicito voluntatis actu, *seu vera mentis conditione,* illam proprietatem excluderet, matrimonium irritum esset."[53] But the presumption of law is against this last supposition. Ignorant or perverse Catholics may have such *errores juris.*

It was precisely on the grounds of this error about an essential property that the famous Castellane-Gould marriage was before the Rota three times and finally went to a specially composed body of Cardinals. This type of error is most widespread and therefore the question of its influence on validity of consent is of great practical importance.

At first glance it seems such simple error does invalidate, for does not the will follow the intellect, "nil volitum nisi praecognitum." In our case, it is the impression and judgment (for error is a judgment) that marriage is what Protestantism and Paganism and Civil and common law practices consider it, namely a dissoluble union, and the will reaching out by the intention follows and embraces this false impression of the intellect, and thus naturally purposes to contract a dissoluble union, wherefore it would seem marriage is invalid.

But closer, deeper scrutiny shows this conclusion is not true. First of all the above dictum of psychology is only true if understood properly, and this true application does not in the least militate against an error of judgment being present without destroying the validity of the act of willing. In fact an educated Catholic knowing

[52] Canon 1081, par. 2.

[53] Gasparri, *De Matr.*, II, n. 807.

the true nature of the bond, can will what his intellect tells him is non-existent (a soluble bond). In this case the will does not follow the intellect, but does the contrary.

If this erroneous concept of marriage is set forth *expressly* in the contract, or in connection with the contract, in other words, made a constituent part thereof, the marriage is null. For the will of the contractor certainly bears on what is expressly stipulated in the terms of the contract. If it is definitely stipulated in the contract that only a dissoluble union is intended, then we have the equivalent of a marriage under an expressed condition *deducta in pactum,* against the substance of marriage. There is no room here for the normal *presumptio juris* that the party or parties intended to marry validly and as instituted by the Author of Nature, and thus the union is clearly null. All Roman decisions on this point declare for nullity when the *error juris* in regard to the *bonum sacramenti,* as an intention arising from such error was *deducta in pactum.*

But let us assume, as is most often the case, that this erroneous impression spoken of is not set forth in the contract nor made a constituent element thereof, nor mentioned at all in any way between the parties or to their friends, but on the contrary, the contract by its very form is an apparent manifestation of an intention to contract validly as instituted by God. Then it can be affirmed that the error in question is not sufficient to invalidate marriage.

Let us further assume, as is often the case, that this erroneous impression and conviction about the bond of marriage, is not set forth in the contract, nor made a constituent part of the contract nor of the internal act of the will, and the contract by its very form is an apparent manifestation of a will to contract validly according to the institution of the Author of marriage and nature, but that concomitant with the celebration or before it one or both parties spoke to each other or to friends about this conviction of theirs that marriage is dissoluble, or make statements similar to this, "Let us marry and if we do not get along happily of course we can divorce," this intention or statement arising from and being wholly dependent on such an error, and this intention is actual (or interpretative only) explicit or implicit, then again it can be affirmed, that neither the error in question nor this intention nor these statements about divorce and its availability, are sufficient to invalidate the consent or the marriage.

It is clear, says the usual explanation, that in this case there are two intentions or acts of the will. The general valid one at least implicitly with all its essentials, plus a particular invalid one, entirely sprung from the error by which indissolubility is considered not as an essential of true marriage, and thus the reasoning runs on, since these two are incompatible, they cannot co-exist. One must prevail. In this case the general one prevails.

That is to say, all these marriages of those believing in divorce are valid because the will or intention of contracting a soluble marriage is destroyed by the general intention or will. But it may be pointed out that to destroy, the destroyer first must exist, and the thing destroyed also must exist at the time the destroyer is acting. And besides it seems in some cases (*ex hypothesi*) that this so-called general will to contract an indissoluble union does not exist, if for no other reason than this, that it cannot be willed unless known somehow, but the supposition is these people are totally ignorant of this essential quality of perpetuity that belongs to the bond. In fact they may have a subjective conviction that the bond has the contrary property.

It is not correct to say the two-acts-of-the-will theory agrees with the practice of the Church which never considers the marriage invalid. The practice of the Church is not based on this theory. Theologians have used the theory to try to explain something that the Church holds about these marriages. The theory is only a logical fiction, it does not correspond to the concrete case *in re*, and the mistake is to carry over into the real order what is only an attempted *logical* explanation. But granting that the theory agrees with the practice of the Church, one must make this distinction. It is true it agrees if *simplex error* obtains; but false, if simple error is raised by the will to a positive prevailing act of the will embracing this error.

It will be well now to give the basis in *fact* and in *reason* for this view, which then will be supported and confirmed by showing the teaching of canonists and the decrees and responses of the Roman Curia.

The particular intention to divorce rooted solely in and entirely dependent on the erroneous impression, is derived from non-Catholic doctrine, civil law and popular custom, that marriage is dissoluble by divorce. The person laboring under this error, does not (*per se* and necessarily) by a positive act of his will *definitely* exclude the property of indissolubility; for he erroneously thinks his property has no essential place in marriage, since some non-Catholic religions and State laws do not recognize it. Inasmuch as he thinks this property is not involved or included at all, it would be unreasonable for him to make an attempt to exclude it. Why purpose to exclude what is already excluded? Hence it is only logical to assume that any statements of such a one which appear to express an intention to exclude indissolubility, are rather only the *expression* of the *erroneous opinion* whereby he thinks this property has been excluded by some power extraneous to himself.

As a matter of fact the only way in which this essential property can be excluded (from the act of the marital will) in practice is by a definite act of the contractor's will *actually excluding it* (not from marriage *in se*, but from the sphere of his willing, for marriage *qua* marriage is always intrinsically indissoluble).

For indissolubility is an essential element of marriage, an element placed in it immutably and for the whole human race by the Author of marriage and of nature itself. Consequently it is an element which cannot be excluded by false religions, civil law, custom, or any other power extraneous to the will of the individual. Only in one way can it be excluded. Marriage is a contract and like all contracts is effected by the free will of the contractors. If the contractor of a marriage (so-called) in a concrete case actually excludes by a definite act of his free will the property of indissolubility (excludes it from the sphere of his willing, not from the actual substance of a real marriage) then it is of course excluded from being willed and since to will an essential element of something one at least *implicitly* wills the other essentials, so to exclude positively an essential, one excludes at least *implicitly* all the essentials and therefore the thing (*unum*) itself and the marriage is no marriage but null. In such a case any genuine intention (act of the will going out to a *bonum*) to contract a valid marriage according to God the Author of Nature is absent.

But in our case, no such definite excluding act of the will is posited, nor is it even reasonable (in our case of ignorance, it may be otherwise if one is in doubt or if one knew the truth) that any such act should be elicited.

This similitude may be to the point and useful. A person has a mandate to contract a purchase of potatoes. He wills to act strictly according to the mandate and to buy *potatoes*. But he erroneously thinks potatoes are of the color and property, *e. g.*, of turnips. This is an *error facti*, no doubt. So he points to the turnips and says "I wish to buy these potatoes." It seems evident he wills to buy potatoes and not turnips. So one contemplating marriage has a mandate from God either to will marriage as it is or not at all and if the person is in good faith about his ignorance, he wills conscientiously to act within God's mandate and he does so even though he believes marriage is dissoluble. One in doubt about this property or one knowing the truth about it, may in bad faith overstep the bounds of the mandate by a positive act of the will to choose not marriage but what he calls marriage.

What happens is simply this. The contractor elicits an act of the will, whose content is the intention to marry validly, erroneously thinking the while, that marriage is or has been made dissoluble by reason of the law of the land, or the doctrines of sectarian religions, or the customs and conviction of the people. Inasmuch as these forces are incapable *de facto et de jure* of excluding the element of indissolubility from marriage, it is evident that this property is not *de facto* excluded.

One may object that the contractor, had he but known this property could be excluded by only an act of the will, would have elicited an act definitely excluding it. In other words, he may have had an *interpretative* intention excluding. But as Gasparri and others say, this is only a fiction for intention. It is not an act of the will at all, but is reducible, to and identical with simple error existing merely in the intellect. *Simple* error about this or any other property does not touch the act of the will to marry validly, this act is in the will, the error remains in the intellect. For this intention being the only intention elicited, stands unimpeded by any conflicting act of the will, consequently consent is clearly valid. "In casu simplicis erroris, habetur unicus et sufficiens voluntatis actus."[54] If this simple error was the *causa* of the contract, it is irrelevant for the act is valid, and the cause of the consent is not a condition of that consent.[55]

The doctrine of canonists concerning this error about indissolubility may be noted here.[56] The following author summarizes very well the doctrine of canonists.

Schmalzgrueber[57] asks this question. Are those marriages indissoluble which heretics enter among themselves or with Catholics? That they are not, a very few authors assert, whom he quotes. Their argument runs like this. Because these Protestants do not intend to contract marriage otherwise than they and their sects acknowledge. They however and their whole sects do not acknowledge marriage is a sacrament instituted by Christ, but a mere human contract, civil and soluble, therefore such a marriage, by contracting marriage, they intend and will to enter.

If there were any reason for supposing they will to contract an indissoluble union, it would be because while they wish to marry they always have the general intention of doing so as Christ instituted it, but from this it is not proven, that they contract indissoluble marriage, for the particular judgment prevails over this general intention. Through this error they think only soluble marriage was instituted by God and received into the Church, and by this error they determine to will marriage, as is clear from the practice of Protestant tribunals, to allow second marriages because of adultery.

If by this particular judgment the will is determined, the so-called general will is eliminated. If this particular will does not prevail then that would follow which is against the common sense of all, that there would be no *material* heretics, because this erroneous particular assent arising from false belief would not prevail, but would be corrected by the general assent and orthodox Catholic sense, which they in general give to all revealed truth. If the contrary is not proved, it is presumed marriage is entered into according to the custom of the place where

[54] De Lugo, *De Sacram.*, disp. VII, sect. 8.

[55] Wernz, *De Matrimonio*, n. 304.

[56] *Cf.* among others, Gasparri, *De Matr.* (1904), II, n. 902; Wernz, *Jus Decretalium*, IV, *De Matr.*, n. 228.

[57] *Jus Eccl. Universum*, lib. IV, tit. XIX, nn. 64 to 67.

they live, but heretics commonly intend a soluble marriage, therefore, etc. A consequence of this is, if one of the parties becomes a Catholic, the other remains in the sect, and is permitted by the sect to marry again, and also the convert can marry again since the first is no sacrament but only a human contract and soluble and this is against the substance and treasures of marriage, thus the first union was invalid for lack of marital consent.

Thus argued some Catholic doctors some generations ago, and it is asserted that in our day, especially in the United States, England, France and some other countries too, the strength of these arguments is multiplied, both because of the dogmas or rather lack of dogmas of most sects on this point, the laws of States, and the tremendous use of divorce so that it is no longer looked upon as disgraceful; and the philosophy of refined materialism of the post-Christians.

Voluntas sequitur intellectum, but it is maintained by some that the intellect to-day is quite different from that of say forty years ago. Multitudes actually deny marriage is sacred, perpetual, instituted by God, deny even the divinity of Christ, yes even a God. The intellect does see the companionate marriage idea and the will wills it. Words signify the inner sense of the mind, but the words of many today signify something different than a generation ago for a great number of post-Christians. They liken this reasoning to that used about Anglican Orders: "We know you wanted to ordain priests, but we know too you left out deliberately the Holy Mass idea, it was excluded, therefore there was no sacrament of Orders." [68]

For certain sections or classes of people, it seems the presumption should be for an invalid consent. For other classes a valid consent. But these strata of society do not suffer a sharp definition. There is no doubt but that the Catholic Church still presumes a valid consent generally speaking. But a few thinkers in the Church say that the presumption should be the other way around. But against this is the overwhelming tradition and jurisprudence of the Church for heretics, but especially for pagans in pagan lands, whose abuses and errors about the indissolubility of marriage were much greater, almost second nature in some cases, yet the instructions and responses from Rome never would admit a contrary presumption for places even with

[68] *Cf.* G. H. Betts, *The Beliefs of 700 Ministers,* New York, 1929.

startling customs ingrained for generations, and it was a rare case when the Church would decide a pagan marriage invalid on the score of *bonum sacramenti,* but in practice the difficulty was generally met by the Pauline Privilege or the Privilege of Faith.[59]

It is true that if the presumption for these modern Protestant marriages were for invalidity on the score of the soluble union, it would cause very great amazement, consternation and indignation. But truth is truth, and if the Church legislators were convinced such a presumption more nearly approached the truth, they would not flinch. But if, as asserted by some, the inadequacy of a general presumption *pro* or *contra* for the whole world is easily seen, yet particular presumptions for particular sets of circumstances and beliefs and practices and places would too involve more uncertainty and difficulties than the present presumption that people generally marry according to the nature of marriage and the positive laws of God. Each marriage stands or falls as God sees it, and in practice there is not so much difficulty, for the Church generally has occasion to note the marriages of those of whom one enters her fold. Changing the nature of the presumption would not alter the fact of marriage, or the lack of marriage. A presumption pertains *per se* to the external order and only *per accidens* to the forum of conscience, if, for instance, the person himself is in doubt.

Schmalzgrueber (n. 69 s.) responds to the above opinion with the following reasoning. Either the party or parties contract indeed laboring under this error, but at the same time have the will to contract marriage in such a way as it can be contracted by its divine institution as is *necessary* for the procreation and raising of *legitimate* offspring; or they so enter marriage in such a way that they bind their

[59] The Vicar Apostolic ad Gallas (in Africa) gave what amounted to a study in anthropology in reference to marriage among the Africans, concluding that the slaves had no notion of a true marriage, especially of its perpetuity. His logic seemed convincing, yet the Holy Office (20 June, 1866) takes the same facts and returns in answer a convincing study to the contrary. *Cf. Fontes,* n. 957. A similar penetrating study of pagan abuses and ignorance which the missionaries even in the field did not evaluate properly, but which the Holy Office did, is found in the Instruction to the Vicar Apostolic of Central Oceania, 18 December, 1872, *Fontes,* n. 1024. *Cf.* also a similar masterly penetration given by the Cardinals of the Inquisition. S. C. C. 9 December, 1874, *Fontes,* n. 1036.

will to this error alone and expressly otherwise they do not will to contract than under a condition of a soluble union.

If the first supposition is true, the error is no obstacle to validity. If the second, that condition or positive exclusive intention, annihilates validity and indissolubility. The reason is clear in both cases.[60]

The difficult point is this. With what intention or consent do heretics contract, when they do contract thinking marriage in certain cases is soluble? The answer is, unless the contrary is proven, that it is always presumed they contract with the general intention or will of entering such a marriage as can validly be entered by Christians. Therefore in doubt favor the marriage already celebrated and pronounce for its validity. This rule is received by all and is constant so that the opinion of one eminent doctor for validity, should be preferred to the opinion of many impugning its validity.

From which it follows that the marriage of heretics, if nothing else is lacking, is also a sacrament, for they wish to contract such a marriage as is valid among Christians and in the true Church of Christ and they thus can not otherwise contract it than as a sacrament.

Again it follows, that marriage by heretics, though they think it is soluble in some cases, is indissoluble, for they have when they contract a general active efficacious will of contracting a true marriage, conformable to divine and ecclesiastical tradition and capable for the procreation and education of legitimate children, but such an intention or will virtually includes the indissoluble bond, since this belongs by a true and divine institution and conforms to the Catholic tradition and the substance of marriage or at least flows from it. Therefore . . .

It follows thirdly that the convert can not re-marry on this score. This is clear from the practice of ancient and modern curial practice which never permits converts to re-marry and all this only from a presumption by which these marriages are considered valid, such as would not be if they contracted a temporal union.

The arguments of those who hold the first opinion for invalid marriages, are answered or refuted by these counter ones. Though the heretic when he marries thinks not of confecting a sacrament, yes, even though he expressly does not wish or will to do so, provided his

[60] *Cf.* Suarez, *De Sacr.*, D. 13, sect. 2, par. superest; Lugo, *De Sacram.*, D. 8, n. 131, and others.

consent is not hinged on this intention, then he sufficiently intends to receive the sacrament when he intends to contract a true marriage, for the two, the marriage contract and the sacrament are identical in this case, whence it follows that the intention of receiving the sacrament is already included in the intention of celebrating a true genuine marriage. Probably there is no begging of the question (*petitio principii*) in the above reasoning. If there is it would be in the provision "provided his consent is not hinged on this intention" which others may claim is an impossible assumption in the case. The indissolubility of marriage does not arise from this that marriage is sometimes a sacrament, though Schmalzgrueber and others identify the *bonum sacramenti* with the sacramentality of some marriages, *e. g.,* he says the marriage of infidels is no sacrament, but if both convert, it becomes indissoluble. This is erroneous. It is intrinsically indissoluble just as sacramental marriages are, and extrinsically soluble in some cases, just as *matrimonium ratum* is, though for different causes.

To the argument of the opponents that if there is any reason for judging the marriage is indissoluble, it would be because the general intention prevails over the particular one, but this is not true, it is answered, that this error is an obstacle to indissolubility only then when they bind their consent to it. But they do not always do so, but rather, unless the contrary is proved, there prevails (only by presumption and for the external forum) the general will as is clearly gathered from the doctrine of St. Paul in the first epistle to the Corinthians (VII, v. 12, 13) who counsels the convert spouse that she persevere in the marriage entered in infidelity, if the infidel consents to cohabit with her. But the Apostle could not counsel this unless he thought that the marriages, even of infidels are by divine law insoluble, and that such marriages are contracted in spite of any error about divorce. Moreover Innocent III and all the popes, and the Congregations, especially of the Council and the Faith, thus decided innumerable cases involving this error of divorce.

Besides, what the opponents say about Protestant church courts is not valid, for these do in certain cases grant divorce, not in such a way however that the parties had the intention of entering a soluble marriage, but rather because by error they think these soluble marriages are valid and for certain reasons can be dissolved. But it may be objected that this proves they think a valid marriage is *not indissoluble.*

To the argument, if this erroneous judgment did not prevail, it would follow as a consequence that there would be no material heretics, it is answered: The consequence is denied. There *are* material heretics on this point, when they have inculpably, error on some truth of faith.

The argument that unless the contrary be proved, presume that marriage was entered according to the custom, belief or law of the place, but non-Catholic modern States generally intend a soluble union, the answer is given, that the other presumption is stronger, by which heretics are presumed to wish to contract a true valid marriage, from which they can have legitimate offspring rather than a marriage that is invalid and from which they have nothing but illegitimate or spurious children. This last answer, seems a very cogent reason for the prevailing presumption, though those who positively place as a condition *sine qua non* the right of divorce, also seem to want a marriage whence they can have legitimate children, yet in this case, the marriage is invalid.

If one says, "I marry you on this condition that we get a divorce if etc.," as it stands, the marriage may be valid or not. If it means they contract soluble marriage, the marriage is invalid. If it means, they bind and obligate themselves to an an indissoluble union, but place the condition to divorce one another under certain circumstances then this amounts only to an abuse of the obligation, not of indissolubility but according to even those who hold there is no distinction between the obligation and fulfillment of the *bonum sacramenti,* it is an abuse of the *bonum fidei,* therefore the marriage is valid. Rota decisions already quoted and the popes have said it is an abuse of the fidelity. So one must be careful and not identify every divorce condition as against the substance of marriage or its indissolubility. Besides many may mean a civil divorce which *per se* does not touch the original bond in most laws, but only considers the civil effects, *e. g.*, the new union as legally licit.

Some authors [61] say marriage among Jews is valid even under a

[61] *Cf.* Sanchez, *De Matr.*, lib. 5, disp. 12, n. 2.

condition of divorce according to their rite, for the law of Israel permits this and therefore it is a *condicio juris* and can licitly be *deducta in pactum.* But this law was abrogated by Christ and marriage is restored to its pristine indissolubility, therefore such a condition invalidates. The same must be said of infidels to whom divorce was never permitted. The opinion that Christ's restoration of marriage does not, on this point, bind infidels is not probable.

Moral theologians, too, make clear this same point.[62] The following reasoning about the divorce intention or will is found in the *"Opus Theologicum Morale,"* of Ballerini-Palmieri, Volume VI, page 232. The propositions will be enumerated with little or no comment.

Proposition n. 1: With an expressed pact concerning divorce, marriage is invalid. This is proved from Gregory IX and from reason. Moreover sufficient *external* consent is not expressed, nor *a fortiori* internal consent. There is no external consent in a perpetual bond, rather the opposite.

N. 2: One has in mind only, and marries with the intention that it is proper and licit to divorce, though this is not *deducta in pactum.* There is no marriage. For he only wills a soluble union, therefore if from the confession of both it is clear there was no mind of a true marriage that is sufficient for the court to declare it null, unless the presumption of collusion is present. If this mind is only in one, it is sufficient in the internal forum for him; also for the other party if there be reasons to believe he is telling the truth.[63]

N. 3: If the parties know that in the country where they marry it is legal to divorce, yet at the time of the contract they did not add this limitation that they thus contract with this divorce intent, then if this knowledge about the custom of divorce was had antecedently, that is, if they contracted because they knew it was alright to divorce and would otherwise not have married, then it seems *implicitly* they did not will or wish to obligate themselves perpetually, therefore declare it null.

N. 4: If absolutely ignorant that the bond is perpetual, or if they believed it to be soluble, but did not limit their will or intention at

[62] *Cf.* Lehmkuhl, *Theol. Moralis,* II, n. 688; Benedict XIV, *De Syn. Dioc.,* lib. 13, cap. 22, n. 7.

[63] Sanchez, *De Matr.,* II, 45, nn. 4, 12; Lugo, *De Sacr.,* d. 8, n. 130.

the time of contract to this ignorance or belief, they have a true general will of a true valid marriage, so that this ignorance or error holds itself concomitantly, since without this ignorance or error they would marry anyway. Then the marriage seems valid.[64] This is confirmed for St. Paul tells the *fideles* not to leave their infidel partners, supposing the marriages valid though those Corinthians believed and practiced divorce by Roman Law (1 Cor. VII, 73). Lugo puts it concisely: That error vitiates marriage when from it one limits his intention either by external pact in which he says he contracts in accordance with the law of divorce, or at least interiorly does not will to contract except a soluble union. This is sufficient to invalidate.

Again Lugo says: "When the error is concomitant and one does not contract because he thinks it is soluble, or finally if he has some general will of effecting a valid contract, the marriage is valid. If however this general and efficacious will is lacking and then the second will limits the contract to a soluble marriage, it is invalid. Finally, in doubt, judge in favor of marriage. For everyone is presumed to wish to exercise a valid contract, unless the opposite be proved. This is a common opinion of jurists, which *a fortiori* has place in marriage which is more favorable." Thus Lugo.

For the rules of the external forum to prove whether a condition was expressed or not expressed, and to know the content and sense of the condition one might consult Benedict XIV.[65] These may be briefly stated as follows:

N. 1: If the condition of divorce on account of adultery (belief held by error) is not *expressly* placed, presume a valid marriage because of a general good intention which absorbs the private error.

N. 2: If in the very contract of marriage, this same condition is expressly placed, the error is *not* absorbed but the general will is exstinguished by the error, and marriage is null. A proof is had from the curial practice about Greek marriages. They are denied the faculty to marry another on account of adultery, although these same Greeks contend that for adultery the bond can be broken and they contract with this error.[66]

64 Lugo, *De Sacr.*, d. 8, n. 132.

65 *De Syn.*, lib. 13, cap. 22, n. 7 s; Ballerini, *Theol. Moral.*, p. 233.

66 Ita, S. C. Council, 15 January, 1724; April 13, 1724, where a marriage in

The general doctrine was propounded too by Pius VI, July 11, 1789, to the Archbishop of Prague, against those who say the marriages of non-Catholics are against the firmness of the bond when they intend to marry according to the laws which permit divorce *a vinculo* because of adultery. Pius quotes Benedict XIV and adds:

"If the general intention of marrying according to Christ is believed to prevail over the intention of marrying according to the errors of the sect, for the same reason the intention of marrying according to the law which permits divorce prevails too over the general intention. If not so, no such non-Catholic marriages would be valid, but adultery, but this is far from the practice and doctrine of the Church. For nowhere in the centuries is it heard of that non-Catholic marriages are invalid, because of errors or civil or sectarian laws, nor when converted, were they allowed to marry others. Unless therefore these be true marriages you must say the Church is in a universal error *in se* which is both doctrinal and moral, which no Catholic says."

Nor, says Pius, are there lacking good reasons why marriages according to errors of sects or State laws are not against validity, *modo non deducatur in pactum.* For these people do not think divorce is repugnant to the law of Christ, but according to his teaching and on account of this error they by no means exclude the primary intention of marrying in accord with the divine law confirmed by Christ. But if *deducta* then the condition is against the substance, and the will to marry in Christ is *actually excluded,* because of the repugnance between the law of Christ and the condition of divorce, which actually makes the contract *ineptus.* But the greatest, most powerful reason is that the Church held these marriages valid in ages past (unless as was said the condition was *deducta in pactum*) and it cannot err.

The validity of this teaching is confirmed by many responses and instructions of the Rota and the Roman Congregations, given mostly for places in the world where this error prevails.[67]

Helvetia was held valid, in spite of the formula about divorce in the rite; yet on the other hand there were two or more other answers to the contrary holding the marriages null, one from S. C. Office, one from the S. C. Council, *cf.* Balerini, *Theol. Moralis,* p. 236.

[67] Collect. S. C. P. F., II, n. 1427; *AAS* (1915), p. 296; Pius VI, July 11, 1789, to the Archbishop of Prague, *cf. AAS* (1914), p. 522; for Japan *cf. AAS*

All this agrees with the teaching of Canon 1084 which reads: "*Simplex* error circa matrimonii unitatem vel indissolubilitatem aut sacramentalem dignitatem etsi det causam contractui, non vitiat consensum matrimonialem." The word *simplex* means when the content of the erroneous opinion (*e. g.*, "marriage is soluble") is not positively willed, nor made a *condition sine qua non* of consent.

It is to be noted that *error juris* on this point not only does not invalidate, unless removed to the will and made a constituent element of the consent as a condition or intention *sine qua non* (then of course it is no longer *simplex error juris*) but its presence makes it more difficult to prove the existence of an actual and invalidating condition contrary to the *bonum sacramenti.* For if there is neither error nor ignorance on this point, and the presence of an intention or condition against this *bonum* is proved, then it is evident the party acted in bad faith and knowingly and willingly vitiated the marital consent. On the other hand, he that is in error or ignorance, has no reason to place an expressed condition excluding this property. Hence there is always a strong presumption that *any statement* or purpose on his part to effect a soluble union is rather an expression of his erroneous opinion that marriage is somehow dissoluble, than the manifestation of an explicit act of the will to positively exclude this essential property. From the nature of the case it is extremely difficult to produce proof to overcome entirely this presumption, and it is therefore very difficult to obtain a declaration of nullity on this ground when there is an *error juris* not evidently raised to a provable condition.[68]

4. *Summary and Conclusion.* In the preceding pages, an attempt was made to set forth the sense and scope of the law according to which marriage is invalid if contracted with a condition admitting divorce *a vinculo* and excluding the *bonum sacramenti.* The principles governing cases in which a condition of this sort is alleged to have been made may be summed up briefly, from a practical viewpoint.

[68] *Cf.* Lynch, *Conditional Marriage Consent,* p. 60.

(1915), p. 297, and Collect. P. F. II, n. 1746. These citations typical of many others are sufficient to make certain the principle that *error juris seu theoreticus* about the permanency of marriage, even with a related intention of using divorce, is not sufficient *per se* to invalidate the consent.

To adjudge a marriage invalid in the *internal* forum, it suffices that one of the parties affirm that he contracted marriage with a condition actually and definitely excluding indissolubility. It matters not how the condition was framed, whether as a formal one "*deducta in pactum*" or as a simple intention only in the mind which thus restricted the consent. But mere error on this point is *not* equivalent to such a condition or intention excluding this property.

Although invalidity may be certain in the forum of conscience, it may be *impossible to prove* the invalidity in the external forum. In this court, in view of the privilege and favor enjoyed in law by marriage, there is a presumption of law that a ceremony or contract having the *species matrimonii* is valid, till the contrary is *proved*. The burden of overcoming this presumption rests on the one who attacks the validity.

If it can be proved to the satisfaction of the court that such a condition was *expressly* placed as a part of the contract or a constituent part of the consent, as a condition *sine qua non*, of consent, and also proved it was never revoked, a declaration of nullity can be obtained.

When a condition was not "*deducta in pactum*" in the accidental sense, the presence or absence of such alleged condition may be determined by a consideration of the adjuncts and circumstances of the case, those that preceded, followed and were concomitant with the ceremony.

If both parties offer a sworn confession of the presence of such a condition, and of its non-revocation, and there is no danger or presumption of collusion between them (a very difficult contention) and if to this be added *semi-plena probatio* arising, *e. g.*, from the fact that the law of the land or their religion permitted divorce, then a declaration of nullity may be obtained.[69]

[69] Cardinal Gasparri, *De Matrimonio* (1932), n. 912, insists that we should keep in mind this teaching of Lugo, *De Sacram. in genere*, disp. VIII, n. 130, "Quod si hic animus fuit in utroque conjuge, ex utriusque confessione constabit sufficienter ut matrimonium possit declarari nullum etiam in foro externo, ut docet Sanchez, lib. II, disp. XLV, n. 12, nisi esset collusionis praesumptio. Si autem fuit in solo uno, sufficiet ipsi in foro iterno, imo sufficiet etiam alteri conjugi, si concurrant rationes probabiles ad existimandum ipsum non mentiri, ut docet Sanchez, *l. c.*, n. 4." "Vide etiam Ballerini et Gury *Theol. Moralis*,"

In trying to ascertain whether a condition was added in a marriage celebrated according to civil, pagan, or heretical forms, attention must be given to the words used to express consent and to the formula and ceremonies employed.

Ground for a declaration of nullity is had also even when the condition was placed by one only, the other knowing it or not, provided the presence of the condition and its non-revocation are proved. Silence on the part of the other party or rejection by this party, begets a *presumption* that the condition was revoked.

If the one who is alleged to have contracted with such a condition against indissolubility, was in error at the time about this property, the case is made more complex and difficult of solution. Yet if the *presence* of such a *condition excluding*, is certainly proved and likewise proved it was never revoked, a declaration of nullity may be had. Mere error about this property simply does not essentially affect the consent, unless it takes the form of a condition in the will excluding and generally (for the external forum) externally set forth. Moreover simple error on this point without a true condition is *always presumed* till the contrary is proved. There are excellent reasons already mentioned, for this presumption.

Any chance statements or acts or previous conduct of such a one which *appear* to express an *intention* or *condition* against this essential property being assumed may be merely an expression of the false notion, or opinion whereby marriage was mistakenly thought to be a dissoluble union, and they are not *per se* equivalent or indicative of an act of the will excluding this property.[70]

From this alone that the doctrine of the sect to which one belongs

tom. II, n. 152. If the court will not accept such proof in a given case, the Sacred Penitentary may be asked to do so, even for the external forum. *Cf.* c. 258.

Among the Sioux Indians they marry in order to prove the disposition and qualities of wives, whether they are good and prudent or not. The men have the intention of ridding themselves of unsuitable partners. The Holy Office on May 18, 1892, told the bishop he could accept and believe the convert-Indian's oath that he never intended indissolubility.—*Fontes,* n. 1155.

[70] *Cf.* Instruction C. Office, September, 1877, to Bishop of Seattle, which sets forth what investigation must be made, what sort of evidence must be obtained in cases concerning indissolubility and *error juris*. But a reading of some of the recent Rotal cases is still better for knowing what kind of evidence and proof will or will not satisfy that court.

permits divorce, or the State, or the formula used, no valid conclusion may be drawn as to the will of the parties at the moment of giving consent. On the contrary one must apply the law. *Videte facta!*

In the face of these considerations, and from reading many cases of the Rota, it is only too evident, the difficulty of proving such a condition when error is present and it was not expressly raised to a condition *deducta in pactum.* This difficulty is well illustrated in several cases already mentioned, but particularly in the noted Castellane-Gould case. The party who was alleged to have placed such a condition against indissolubility was in error as to this essential property, but denied that she had placed any actual condition positively excluding it. The case was tried three times before the Rota and then by a higher court, and in the final outcome, the invalidity of the marriage was not admitted.

All that has been said in this section about the *bonum sacramenti* can be validly applied (*mutatis mutandis*) to the other two essential treasures of marriage, except that one must keep in mind the unique invalidating effect of an *intention* against the *sacramentum,* whereas the other two qualities permit the essential distinction between the assumption and the fulfillment of the obligations, so that even an external *condition,* whose content is only *to abuse* these obligations would not invalidate the consent.

The marriage of many to-day who before marriage or in the contract place a clause or have an understanding about possible divorce, are not *per se* to be considered invalid.[71] The sects, in Transylvania and other places, who in the formula of the ritual have a condition of divorce for adultery, *generally* invalidate the marriages, that is, such marriages when brought to our courts, *generally* are declared null, though a few were not, especially if one or both parties were Catholics. The Anglican formula used in the Marconi-O'Brien marriage speaks of fidelity, etc., till death, yet this marriage was declared *null* by the Rota, which said the *formulae* used *per se prove nothing* because the parties use them through necessity. This *only seems* to run counter to the opinion of canonists and the jurisprudence about the sectorian formulas referred to, and to which, among other Popes, Benedict XIV gave much study. But in reality there is no conflict

[71] Gougnard, *De Matrimonio,* p. 159, *cf. L'ami du Clerge* (1924), p. 369 s.

because each marriage was always tried on its own merits. *Videte facta!* was ever the rule. In all doubt whether the *sacramentum* was excluded the *will must be explored.*[72]

Another conclusion is this. It is not necessary directly and *in se* and explicitly to intend or will by one's consent the essential property of indissolubility (or of unity for that matter). It is sufficient to have an *implicit* intention, which is had if one wants to marry as God instituted it, and this can be had even though the party never thinks of it, or even if he is ignorant of the existence of this property.[73]

Again, a man may be convinced that the marriage may be dissolved, and contract with this *conviction,* but he *can* give his consent *absolutely* without making it depend on the possibility of a divorce. Here there is an error, but not a condition.

Another conclusion meriting attention is this: To marry *according to the law of the State,* may mean to contract a *perpetual* union,

[72] *Cf.* Pallotini, *Coll. S. C. C.,* verb. "Divortium," nn. 22, 23, 26, 27, on Lutheran and Calvinist formulas having the divorce clause; also *Fontes,* nn. 883, 894.

The marriage of two Catholics was declared valid who used the Calvinistic form of celebration containing the condition contrary to the perpetuity of marriage. *Cf.* Holy Office, 22 May, 1840; 20 May, 1754. Cardinal Gasparri, *De Matrimonio* (1932), n. 894 s, especially n. 909 s, gives an excellent synopisis of cases wherein heretical formulas were used, and he warns that the various decisions he refers to must be kept before one's eyes in such cases (n. 912). *Cf.* Benedict XIV, *De Synodo,* cap. 22. The substance of the Calvinistic formula (although in accidentals it may differ) consists in this: The Protestant minister says to those about to marry: "Audite S. Evangelium," then he reads to them Matthew, XIX, 9: "Dico autem vobis quia quicumque dimiserit uxorem suam, nisi ob fornicationem etc." Then the parties are warned to restrict their consent thus. Then after the consent is given, they mutually take an oath of fidelity to each other as long as the other party continues faithful.—Quoted from an instruction of the Holy Office to the Vicar Apostolic of Oceania, 6 April, 1843, in *Fontes,* n. 894. This instruction gives minute details about all similar formulas. *Cf. Fontes,* nn. 874, 913.

The Rota in the Oregon case referred to (6 July, 1914, *AAS,* VI, 516 s) profusely and clearly discusses the entire matter about divorce. It makes the distinctions between divorces and divorces according to the various meanings. *Cf.* also Castellanè-Gould case, 8 February, 1915, *AAS* (1915), VII, p. 292.

[73] *Cf.* Vromant, *Jus Missionariorum,* n. 179; Michel, *Le Mariage,* n. 23.

for the laws of most, if not all, States presuppose, and take for granted a perpetual union (in fact it is the professed public policy of most if not all civilized States, *e.g.*, the United States of America, to protect and foster and favor this perpetuity of marriage) and the divorce permit is an exception. On the other hand, to marry according to that *particular specific law* or statute permitting divorce is another thing. Yet it is debatable whether any State *divorce* law even contemplates touching or breaking the marriage *bond.* It is otherwise perhaps in their statutes about violence and substantial fraud concerning marriage. In these cases they intend to *annul* or break or rescind the bond.[74]

The same is true of the marriage laws of heretical sects. One may marry according to the fundamental general law of the sect that considers marriage *per se* is for life. Or one's marriage will may be shaped and intentioned not to the above named law, but solely to the particular law permitting divorce *a vinculo* because of *e.g.* adultery.[75]

A dissolutive condition placed by infidels who intend marriage as they are able, marry validly in spite of this condition born of error.[76] Other practical conclusions about the *bonum sacramenti* may be mentioned.

Strictly speaking no conditions are contrary to the substance of an *actually true marital* content of the act of the will. For one can not have internally this healthy juridical marital will and not have it at the same time, though the external declaration can be without a flaw. In other words, the phrase "a condition against the substance"

[74] "It is forbidden to provide for the possible dissolution of the marriage contract, which the policy of the law is to preserve intact and inviolate . . . Or in other words to allow validity to promises for a future separation would be to allow the parties in effect to make the contract of marriage determinable on conditions fixed beforehand by themselves."—Wm. L. Clarke, *Handbook of the Law of Contracts,* p. 444.—These public policies are still valid and lawyers and jurists find no difficulty in squaring them with easy divorce laws that admit flimsy reasons and evidence.

[75] *Cf.* Cappello, *De Matrimonio,* cap. XII, n. 833 s, about the duties of the parties, Catholic lawyers and judges in reference to modern divorce laws. The doctrine of moralists and the Holy Office have never lost sight of the various usages and meanings of the word divorce in civil phraseology.

[76] *Cf.* Pallotini, *Coll. S. C. C.*, verb. "Divortium," n. 11.

really means *existentially* and in the *real order* an *essentially defective* act of the will *to marry,* not an essentially defective psychological act of the will. In this latter instance it is a complete *voluntarium* or act of willing, but its object or the thing willed is *not* marriage.

Essentially antagonistic to this treasure and quality and therefore equally against the substance of marriage are these conditions *qua* conditions on which the consent depends: I marry you, until I find a richer girl; as long as you remain faithful; as long as you do not commit adultery; as long as you remain pious and good; as long as you please me; as long as you do not quarrel; as long as you do not lose your good name; as long as our life is placid and happy. These are all *resolutive* conditions.

The two *resolutive* conditions from the disposition of the law (solemn religious profession, and papal power as regards ratified marriages only) do not invalidate for they are *condiciones juris.* If the condition concerns itself about the *obligation* of entering the religious state a distinction is to be made. If one intends thereby to give or receive no *jus perpetuum,* it invalidates the union, otherwise it is valid.[77] The use of a *terminus ad quem, e. g.,* "I marry you for seven years," is equivalent to a resolutive condition.

Bonacina [78] says these conditions invalidate: "I marry you, if you always remain at home;" "if you always wear a black dress." These are contrary to the *sacramentum,* since they are resolutive. But if they mean, *e. g.,* "if you seriously *promise here and now* to always stay at home, etc.", then it is not resolutive, but an inane and foolish condition, and the validity of the marriage depends on the serious promise. The same matter, of course, can be placed *per modum modi.* Also invalidating is this resolutive condition, "if you never come to Washington," for this can be negatived up till the moment of death, and therefore it is contradictory. At any moment till death the condition may fail, and strictly speaking marriage can never begin till death, or certainly be invalid at the moment the other one comes to Washington.

This too should be borne in mind. One must not confound and identify *simple* error of the *intellect* of one or both parties, about the

[77] *Cf.* Bayon, *De Matrimonio,* p. 311.

[78] *Opera Omnia,* lib. IV, tit. IV, qu. 2, punctum X, prop. II.

unity or indissolubility of the bond, or its sacramental dignity, with a *positive act* of the *will* of one or both excluding these essentials.

Nor, on the other hand, when a definite external condition is not present, should one immediately conclude that every such case is one of simple error. Undoubtedly many marriages are invalid because of loss of faith plus excessive individualism in religious matters on the part of sophisticates and others. It is not permissible to simply apply a general presumption to a given case and thus settle it. The instruction of the Congregation of the Holy Office to the Bishop of Seattle (24 January, 1877) warns that an *investigation must* be made in *each* marriage case, and this cannot be supplied by any general presumption. All diligence must be used. This was ever the practice of the Roman curia and the burden of instructions which emanated therefrom in this matter.[79]

The instruction of the Holy Office to the Bishop of Seattle, 24 January, 1877,[80] discusses at length the doctrine of indissolubility and vices against it. The instruction marshals in concise array the reasonings of Gregory IX, Benedict XIV and Pius VII, and continues: "Ex nunc relationis principiis, A. Tua facile intelliget admitti nullimode posse ut ex praesumptionibus, quantumvis gravissimis, quis sibi valeat efformare practica quaedam generalia criteria, quorum ope in quocumque dubio de validitate matrimoniorum coram haereticis istis ministellis contractorum, pro eorumdem nullitate et invaliditate sit judicandum: sed juxta mentem et praxim hujus S. Sedis Apostolicae oportere serio et prudenter examinare et perpendere singulos casus occurentes, et nonnisi juxta legitimas deductiones ex tali examine resultantes judicari debere . . ." [81] This instruction is of vital importance on the subject of the marriage of heretics, especially regarding divorce; it tells in detail how to make a complete, sure investigation of the inner will.[82]

[79] *Cf.* Gasparri, *De Matrimonio* (1932), n. 911 s, who goes into detail about this investigation.

[80] *Fontes,* n. 1050.

[81] *Fontes,* n. 1050, 3.

[82] *Cf.* Instruction of Holy Office to the Archbishop of Quebec, June 8, 1836, *Fontes,* n. 874, and that of Holy Office (Mongoliae), 29 November, 1882, *Fontes,* n. 1075. *Cf.* Instruction of Holy Office, 4 February, 1891, concerning the de-

A *pactum per se* has only *demonstrative* and *probative* power, not *substantive* power. It demonstrates a true condition is present, to be placed as a constitutive part of the contract. It proves a *fact*—the existence of the condition. But the validity or not of the marriage depends on the *content* of the pact. This content may embrace, *e. g.*, only the will to *abuse* fidelity, and not be against the substance of, *e. g.*, the *sacramentum*.[83]

scendants of the old Christians in Japan with their pagan errors, etc. Each case must be studies individually, and no general presumptions used to settle them. *Fontes*, n. 1130, *Videte facta!*

[83] *Cf.* Cappello, *De Matrimonio*, n. 633.

CHAPTER XXIV

CONDITIONS THAT INVALIDATE BECAUSE THEY ARE CONTRARY TO THE BONUM PROLIS

ARTICLE I

THE PRIMARY END OF MARRIAGE: ITS MEANING

> Matrimonium in Codice Juris Canonici dicitur contractus (Canon 1012), quem "facit partium consensus inter personas jure habiles legitime manifestatus" (Canon 1081, par. 1); "consensus matrimonialis est actus voluntatis, quo utraque pars tradit et acceptat jus in corpus, perpetuum et exclusivum, in ordine ad actus per se aptos ad prolis generationem" (Canon 1082, par. 2). Matrimonium ergo in "facto esse" consideratum consistit in "vinculo" juridico (Canon 1110), vi cujus "utrique conjugi ab ipso matrimonii initio aequum jus et officium, est quod attinet ad actus proprios conjugalis vitae" (Canon 1111). Proprietates vero essentiales sunt "unitas ac indissolubilitas" (Canon 1013, par. 2), "finis primarius est procreatio atque educatio prolis; secundarius mutuum adjutorium et remedium concupiscentiae" (Canon 1013, par. 1).

THIS description and definition of marriage are formulated by Father Zeiger from the Code and they contain two elements:[1]

> *Elementum juridicum* et *elementum finalitatis*.
>
> Elementum juridicum quo matrimonii essentia reponitur in habitudine juridica inter conjuges, et elementum finalitatis, quo enuniatur conjugium ab ipsa natura, independenter a voluntate nupturientium, ordinatum esse ad certos fines, quorum principalis sit sobolis generatio atque educatio." "Nec videntur, saltem primo aspectu, alia elementa contineri.[2]

[1] Ivo Zeiger, S. J., "Nova Matrimonii Definitio?" *Periodica,* Tomus XX (1931), p. 38.

[2] *Ibid.,* p. 38.

This definition of the Code does not please many moderns and some Catholic authors, the first who boast to amend the nature of marriage;[3] and the Catholics[4] who hold what we hold but want another element. These take their start from the controversy about the genuine concept of the diriment impediment of impotency.

> Matrimonium nec esse nec recte concipi potest sine jure, ex mutuo consensu orto quo conjuges ad fines connubii obtinendos ligantur. Ad essentiam conjugii ergo pertinet elementum juridicum.[5]

Love, only a very imperfect sense, is an essential element. A third element is finality, the ends of marriage. All agree that the procreation of children is the end, or one end, of marriage.

> Sed *qualis* est iste finis? Alii dicunt esse finem tantum operantis, *i. e.,* qui non a natura matrimonio inditus est, sed qui libere a nupturientibus vel permitti vel appeti vel positive excludi possit.
>
> Alii vero concedunt esse finem operis, *i. e.,* a natura necessario praestitutus, sed non finem primarium; consequentia est inter fines matrimonio assignari solitos non haberi hierarchiam quandam, sed omnes independenter ab invicem, in eadem linea positos posse appeti vel excludi. Dummodo ne omnes fines simul positive excludas, poteris jure coniugali uti.
>
> In doctrina autem catholica traditionali, dicunt momentum finis, scl. procreationis, valde exaggerari.[6]

But the Code lays it down that this is the primary end. Now the questions are, how is this to be understood, what is its scope as far as being essential, and are the other ends necessarily subordinate? When does the content of the marital will adequate or embrace this essential end, when does it not? Let us now follow along the reasoning of Zeiger in attempting to answer these queries.

[3] *E. g.,* inter alios: M. Beth, *Neues Eherecht,* 1925; H. V. Keyserling, *Das Ehebuch,* 1926; Lindsey, *Companionate Marriage;* H. Dehmel, *Revolution der Ehe* (Rudolstadt, 1929).

[4] Especially Italians, *e.g.,* Brugi, Miceli, Viglino, Mons. L. C. Medici. *E.g.,* Brugi holds only *in mutuo conjugum adjutori, secumdum Miceli, in complemento personalitatis,* which is further developed by Medici in *Il diritto Ecclesiastico,* XXIX (1928), p. 398 s.

[5] Zeiger, *ibid.,* p. 53.

[6] *Cf.* Zeiger, *ibid.,* p. 54.

The sexual tendency ordinarily tends to the union of the bodies, as to its proximate end. With the help of this instinct men are induced to marry and thus are impelled to have carnal intercourse.

Acting according to this natural instinct (the positive element) and not impeding its natural effects (the negative element) man satisfies that which *in opere conjugii* can be called the human contribution. Thus by the *copula rite posita,* satisfaction and the quieting of the sexual urge is obtained and *activas humana sexualis interim sistit, at natura non sistit.* For the *copula* in its nature is not intended for itself, not as the ultimate end, but as a proximate end, on account of which, as a means to a remote end, which is the *procreatio prolis.* To the human activity (positive and negative) must be added the *opus naturae scl. fecundatio et generatio.* Which remote end can be had *per se* by any complete carnal act in or outside of marriage.

> Ordinate autem et secure atque quantum fieri possit, perfecte neque generatio neque multo minus prolis educatio obtinebitur nisi in matrimonio stabili, perpetuo, monoganico.

From this we infer that marriage was instituted by nature for this purpose, the propagation (in its full sense) of the human race in an ordinary ordered way that is worthily accommodated to the conditions of man. For this most noble end, and most necessary one, the Creator of Nature ordained marriage, or in the words of the school and the Code: "Procreatio et educatio prolis est finis operis primarius matrimonii."

This is an *end.*

> Finis est; non essentia, sed bonum extra rationem essentialem positum, quod ope matrimonii appeti et obtineri potest. Finis operis est, non operantis; independenter enim a libera contrahentium voluntate, ipsa sua natura contractus matrimonialis in hoc tendit, nexu quodam interno et necessario. Iste nexus describi graphice sic potest: Consensus matrimonialis—jus ad actus conjugales—actus carnalis—procreatio et educatio.
>
> Ex quo jam reliquae conclusiones facile et brevi deduci possunt, scl.
>
> 1. Consensus verus conjugalis necessario pro objecto habet

jus ad actus conjugales. Stante ergo consensu non potest non sequi istud jus. Nexus primus ergo est necessarius.

2. Jus vero non importat necessario exercitium juris. Conjuges enim libero consensu continentiam observare possunt. Nexus ergo secundus a libera voluntate viri et feminae dependent. Neque finis procreationis ita essentialis consortio conjugali est, ut necessario obtineri, appeti vel ejus medium *i. e.* commixtio carnalis adhiberi debeat.
3. Actus iste, corporaliter se uniendi ex ordinatione naturae necessario quidem tendit in hoc ut uxor mater fiat; sed hoc obtinetur de facto tantum si impleta est duplex condicio: *a*) Si omnia requisita ex parte naturae adsunt, et *b*) si actus ipse a conjugibus rite est positus. Prima condicio non subest liberae voluntati humanae, nisi negative (non corrumpere naturam). Altera vero subest, et proin in ea finis matrimonii urget eo sensu, quod ob istum finem naturalem conjugibus numquam liceat ponere actum cum positiva exclusione fecundationis. Talis modus esset contra ordinationem naturae, graviter illicitus nec posset ullo alio fine matrimonii (*e. g.*, ob remedium concupiscentiae, etc.) cohonestari.
4. These things having been posited, now we can understand the answer to the question, whether the procreation of children is only the *finis operis primarius,* or also *essentialis et in quo sensu.*

Distinquendum est: si finem essentialem intelligis eum qui necessario obtinendus est ita ut secus ratio et essentia matrimonii deficiat, *nego;*

Si finem intelligis, quem conjuges necessario et essentialiter saltem appetere debent, *nego;*

Tandem si intelligis finem, in quem matrimonium ex interna natura ordinatum est, ita ut quaevis condicio in limine contractus conjugalis contra procreationem prolis apposita, ipsum matrimonium irritet, *concedo.* Et in hoc sensu ipsa finalitas intrat aliquomodo in essentiam matrimonii.[7]

The question may be asked, is the ***possibility of generation*** essentially required for the essence of a true marriage, in such a way that in case of this impossibility, the validity of the marriage is impeded?

[7] Zeiger, *ibid.*, p. 57.

The question redounds to the controversy concerning the genuine concept of impotency. But omitting all other arguments, let us simply recall those things said above about the finality of the sexual tendency. This finality is twofold: one end, by which the *indoles sexualis* tends to human activity (*elementum positivum et negativum*); the other end by which with the help of human activity, the *opus naturae* (*fecundatio, etc.*) is directed. The first finality alone is subject to the power of the parties, the other remains independent of them. The first, therefore essentially as a *jus* affects the very matrimonial consent, the conjugal contract, the other does not. Therefore, one can conclude if the *impossibilitas generandi simul cum impotentia coeundi habetur, matrimonium irritatur; secus non.* Understood in this sense the possibility of generation enters (or rather does not enter or touch) the very substance of marriage.

There is here no contradiction with what was said about conditions invalidating the consent. There is no contradiction because the *conditio* of one having no right to copulate *rite,* invalidates, and to marry a woman *excisa* does not invalidate. There is no contradiction that the first case touches the primary end in its essence and the other case does not, for the difference is this:

> Quod in uno contractu per condicionem pravam contra bona substantialia matrimonii (proles, fides, Sacramentum) appositam ipsum opus humanum et proin consensus vitiatur et tollitur. In altero casu vero opus humanum et proin consensus non attinguntur.

What, if a bad condition is placed that the woman (without necessity) undergo an operation which will render impossible all future generation? If placed to *engagement* consent it is gravely illicit, but the subsequent marriage is valid. If it is placed to the marital consent, Zeiger thinks it is against the *bonum prolis* and destroys the "activitatem humanam in opere conjugii (*i. e.,* sec. elementum negativum 'ne impediatur effectus actus conjugalis' et sic ipsum consensum." The opinion that says it does not invalidate, seems the better one, since it does not interfere with the human activity which begins only when marriage exists. It is of course understood as a future condition on the verification of which, if meant seriously, marriage is effected, and in the external forum (in this view) it is rejected by presumption as a *turpis tantum*.

The *opus naturae* is *per se* independent of, and does not come within the embrace or scope of the marital consent explicity or implicitly. But the condition may be "if you are not *incisa*" and then if it is seriously placed, there would be no marriage if actually she were *incisa*. If the condition were "if you are not sterile" this does not destroy the consent, and if certitude of sterility or fecundity can only be had by actual intercourse or by licit investigation, and if seriously placed, the marriage would depend on the truth of the negative condition. The same condition in practice would generally be ostracized as immoral in the external forum.

> Matrimonium est institutum naturae ea destinatione praeditum ut inserviat ad ordinatam generis humani propagationem . . . Nullo autem modo procreatio prolis est unicus finis, nec necessario obtinendus nec necessario appetendus (dummodo non excludatur) nec amorem conjugalem vel dignitatem personae humanae destruit. Immo eam mirum in modum elevat, sicut perbelle enc. "Casti connubii" exponit, cum enim finis non tantum materialis et pura sit generatio, sed actio maxime spiritualis, quam Codex, Canon 1013, par. 1, nervose proponit "procreatio atque educatio prolis populus Dei et Salvatoris nostri cultui addictus in dies augeatur." [8]

Father Zeiger ends his discussion with these beautiful words:

> Ecclesiae doctrina de matrimonio, aeque remota ab omni exaggeratione et radicalismo, matrimonium in plena sua totalitate complectitur, proponens et defendens et elementum juris et caritatis et finalitatis, inferius et sublime, animale et spirituale, naturam et supernaturalem gratiam, juris rigorem atque caritatis splendorem.

Father Arend [9] sustains these following theses:

> I. Traditio juridica docet matrimonium consistere, ubi solus finis secundarius remedii concupiscentiae obtineri potest.

[8] Zeiger, *ib*. p. 59; *cf*. *AAS*, XXII (1930), 544.

[9] "De genuina ratione impedimenti impotentiae," *Ephemerides Theologicae Lovanienses*, X (1932), 28 s.

> II. Traditio canonica docet in contrahentibus circa prolem sufficere intentionem negativam, scl. non impediendi, sed suscipiendi, si eveniat.

He uses among others, these authorities for the second thesis. St. Augustine;[10] Gratian;[11] St. Thomas;[12] St. Bonaventure;[13] Scotus;[14] St. Antoninus of Florence;[15] and Sanchez.[16] Besides these authorities Father Arend quotes many texts of decretals, and doctors and canonists. His conclusion is:

> Ergo secundum testimonia allata consensus matrimonialis ut sit validus, non debet ferri in generationem ne praesumptive quidem possibilem. Defectus potentiae generandi, etiam cognitus, non impedit matrimonium nec directe nec indirecte ratione vitiati consensus

which of course runs counter to the opinions of many, *e. g.*, Antonelli and Arendt, and the latter has an article "Jus Divinum Arcet a Connubio Ineundo Feminam Recisam" in the above named Review (1932, 432 s.)

Father Arend makes this discerning remark about a faulty definition of marriage:

> Haec definitio nititur confusione finis *extrinseci* (proles) et *intrinseci* (mutua potestas ad copulam) matrimonii. *Hic* utpote principium formaliter constitutivum ingreditur *essentiam* rei, ideoque et *definitionem* ejus; non vero *ille.*

[10] *De bono conjugali,* c. 5, which passage is quoted in the historical section of this work.

[11] C. XXVII, q. 1, c. 41, glossa f.

[12] *Comm. in quattuor Libros Sententiarum,* d. 31, q. 1, a. 3; d. 34, q. 1, a. 2, ad. 3.

[13] *Opera Omnia,* IV, 4 sent., d. 31, q. 3, a. 3; Ad Claras Aquas (1889).

[14] Contrahens non tenetur absolute ad prolem, sed conditionate si eveniat ad gratanter suscipiendam et religiose educandam,"—in 4 sent., d. 31, q. unica, ad 3, Lugduni, 1639, t. IX, 672. Hic textus Scoti inde a Mastrio (in 4 sent., disp. 7, q. 15, n. 411) citatus invenitur: in IV, d. 81, quamvis Scoti in 4 sent. complectatur tantum 50 distinctiones.

[15] *Summa sacrae theologiae, juris pontificii et caesarei,* pars tertia, Venetiis (1571), tit 1, cap. 12, p. 12.

[16] *De Sancto Matr. Sacr.,* II, d. 29, n. 12.

> Secus non habetur definitio *essentialis* sed *causalis*, per notas scl. rei externas.[17]

He too enters into a closer consideration of the *finis*, and since this will illuminate our subject about conditions against the substance, it is helpful to note these distinctions.

Concerning the relations of the ends of marriage among themselves we may note the following, confining ourselves to the *finis operis*, which may be defined as "id ad quod natura opus ordinat." This is twofold: intrinsic and extrinsic.

> *Intrinsecus* est completum esse operis, ejus perfectio in linea suae essentiae. *Extrinsecus* finis est bonum alterius adhibentis opus, bonum, quod alteri independenter a sua intentione per solum usum operis ex intentione naturae affluit, vel bonum, quod opus natura sua natum est parere usu suo. Salvo fine intrinseco salva quoque est *essentia* operis seu ejus "prima perfectio."

Applying these to marriage the result is as follows.

The finis operis *intrinsecus* of marriage is concretely the union of souls of the man and woman founded upon the mutual power of right to use the body for the *copula* (perfectio in linea essentiae). Therefore where this mutual power is given, there is marriage. And to truly contract marriage one must have a body physically fit for the *copula*, the power of which he must give over by the contract to the other.

The finis operis *extrinsecus* of marriage will be "bonum vel bona quae matrimonium natura sua gignit et comparat ineuntibus illud, bona quae ex ipsius essentia affluunt partibus contrahentibus ex matrimonio utentibus secundum ordinem naturae." This end is divided into *finis immediatus et mediatus*. "*Immediatus* (*proximus*) est usus potestatis ad copulam utrinque concessae scl. copula actualis; hic finis merito vocatur et intermediarius, quia in copula ratione sui natura non quiescit. *Mediatus* (*remotus*) a traditione catholica sequente S. Augustinum semper assignabatur triplex: proles, fides, sacramentum." [18]

[17] *Ibid.*, p. 56, note.

[18] *Cf. Ency.*, *Casti Connubii*, *AAS*, December 31, 1930, 543 s.

Now it may be asked what is the relation between these *tria bona* or extrinsic mediate remote ends? Is one of them primary and if so, in what sense is it primary?

> Finem primarium vocamus id quod natura vel Deus per naturam opus instituendo per se, et in ordine ad quod cetera intendit. *Per se, i. e.*, praecise qua instituens hoc opus prae alio, attento elemento *proprio* et *specifico* operis. *In ordine ad quod cetera intendit:* Ergo resultat relatio subordinationis finium secundariorum sub primario. Nota statim: Fines matrimonii *secundarii* sunt *essentiales*, sed non ratione elementi specifici verum ratione elementi generici in essentia.[19]

Some authors do not accept this *subordination*, though not denying the primary end. They say the three ends are co-ordinate and independent of each other, and it seems they are from the viewpoint of marital consent, for it is clear marriage can be entered when there is no hope, in fact, no certitude of children.[20] This is the difficulty. A negative intention or no intention (in one sense) *de prole* is sufficient, for a sterile person can have no more than this negative intention. With this negative intention (to welcome children if they would *per impossible* come) or in other words not to have a positive act of the will excluding children, though using marriage, this is sufficient, says Arend, to have the necessary subordination of ends. Thus the primary end does not amount to much, for this minimum is also required for the other two ends for validity. Arend in answering the objection how can there be subordination to the primary end, in the case of sterile people says the term of subordination is *"ipsa copula, qua secundum rectum ordinem facta, nam copula est materialis inchoatio generationis."*

As in the sacrament of penance the secondary end, the remission of venial sins, is subordinated to the primary end, the remission of mortal sins, though there be no mortal sins to confess.

It is well to recall that the actio *humana* is circumscribed by the proper execution of the *copula*, and the actio *naturae* perfects fecunda-

[19] Arend, *ibid*, p. 58.

[20] *Cf.* Sanchez, *De Matrimonio*, lib. VII, d. 92, n. 25; Zeiger, in *Periodica* (1931), p. 54.

tion. The first alone is subject to the will, and alone is the object of the consent in the marriage contract. The actio *naturae* seems to have place only in the woman; *e. g.*, Vidal [21] writes: "Quae dein (*i. e.*, post copulam) sequuntur, sunt actio naturae, quae unice verificatur in muliere." It is not difficult to admit that the man (*e. g.*, *senex vel phtisiacus*) plays a part in the *actio naturae.* A woman without womb and ovaries and a man with dead seed, affect the *actionem naturae.*[22] Now an endeavor will be made to apply these principles to matrimonial consent, to which is added a condition whose content has reference to the *bonum prolis matrimonii.* First the bonum *physicum* prolis will be discussed, then the bonum *spirituale* prolis, and after this the so-called *honest* conditions against the *bonum physicum, e. g.*, the antecedent vow of celibacy or chastity.

Article II

Conditions Against the Primary End of Marriage

§1. *Bonum Physicum*

Keeping in mind the principles governing valid marital consent and the substantial defects under which actual consent may labor, and recalling the application of these same principles to an intention, or a condition (with or without *error juris*) whose content or object is the *bonum sacramenti,* it will be useful to apply these same rules to the *bonum prolis.*

The *bonus prolis* has reference to the procreation and raising of children. This education, in so far as it is an essential obligation that the marital consent can not positively exclude—includes alimentation and a certain minimum of training in morality. The training and education (in a technical sense) according to the child's status and needs pertain only to the integrity of the *bonum prolis.* Whether it includes for Christian parents a *Christian* education in its essentials, including especially baptism, will be discussed later on. Though the child and his rearing is not of the substance of marriage, yet from

[21] *Jus Matr.*, p. 239.

[22] *Cf.* G. Arend, in *Ephemerides* (1932), 28 s; (1932), 442 s. *Cf.* P. Maroto's study on *Litterae Encyclicae de Matrimonio Christiano,* in *Appolinaris,* IV (1931), 75-96, Gasparri, *De Matrimonio* (1932), n. 503 s.

the consent furnished arises the *obligation* that the sexual act be properly placed, if the other petitions the debt, which act is *ex se* fitted to tend toward the generation of children, and this obligation *excludes* the *right* (not the *fact*) of doing anything illicit to impede the child's generation or raising. Those examples of Gregory IX *e. g.*, "to take poison of sterility," must be understood properly. If they mean one reserves the *right* to take poison, or the right to obligate the other to take it, then the placer of such a condition simply does not give true consent. If they mean, *e. g.*, "you promise to *abuse* your obligation to not interfere with generation by positive means," then there is marriage simply because if the obligation exists, as it does (*ex hypothesi*), marriage exists. One can not abuse an obligation unless the obligation exists.

To reserve the *right* to waste the seed, to procure abortion, or to kill in other ways the born or unborn child, makes it impossible to render valid marriage consent. But to forego this right of positive interference, in other words to will to be obligated to copulate properly (*rite*) and then too, at the same time intend to *abuse* this assumed obligation, in no way affects the consent substantially.[23] Because of the nature and substance of marriage the parties, at least interpretatively, ought to *oblige* themselves not to avoid children by *positive illicit* means.

It is not of the essence of marital consent that *proles et copula* be *expressly* willed or intended, for this consent and its effect can exist with the intention (not the *radical right*) of not consummating the marriage. But marriage can not exist unless by the mutual *traditio et potestas* over the bodies, and since marriage and its bond tends by nature to generate and conserve the species, this *traditio substantially* consists in this, that each one is *dominus* of the other's body and from this intrinsic *dominium* flows the *jus et potestas* of using the body of the other. The consent does not *explicite* consist in or have as its object the *actual carnal copula,* but in the *right* to such *copula.* Carnal intercourse is not of the essence, but its effect and *operatio.*[24]

To the question, "what is the object of the consent, in which it

[23] *Cf.* Schmalzgrueber, lib. IV, tit. V.

[24] *Cf.* Pallotini, *Coll. S. C. C.*, verbum "matrimonium," chap. III, n. 28.

is necessary for the consent to be directed," Sanchez [25] answers that the object is not the actual physical *copula,* but the *jus et potestas* to such a *copula,* in other words the consent is directed implicitly and virtually to the *copula.* The *usus* is not of the essence of marriage, but the right to the *usus* is. Implicit consent in the *copula* is twofold. First *ex parte contractus,* since marriage is ordained for the *copula,* therefore he who explicitly contracts marriage, implicitly consents to intercourse, *ex vi talis contractus.* Secondly, *ex parte contrahentis,* from this viewpoint implicit consent to intercourse is not necessary, for though the party has the intention of not consenting to the *copula,* it is a true marriage. Suarez puts it thus. "In radice et in causa," there is consent to the *copula,* by consenting in marriage which is ordained for this. Therefore *vi contractus,* implicit consent is necessary, but *ex parte contrahentis,* it is not needed.

The formal consent is not directly in the very *copula,* but directly in the power or right of having it. In other words, the consent is only implicitly, remotely, virtually, or *in radice* and *in causa,* in the very *copula,* flowing from the *traditio.* The marital consent can stand with not consenting expressly in the *copula,* not however with the express *exclusion* of the right to the *copula.* The obligations arising from marriage are *ex justitia.* Actual carnal *copula,* mutual actual habitation or actual observance of fidelity are not of the essence of the object of consent.[26]

One can licitly and validly contract for the purpose of a remedy of concupiscence, intending nothing else, provided *proles* is not *positively* excluded.[27]

The unshakable *obligation* of the *tria bona* is one thing, another is their *execution.* The *real* delivery of the thing is not necessary, but the will externally symbolized to deliver, as St. Ambrose de inst. Virg., cap. 6, teaches.[28] If one contracts not intending to be *obliged* to these three treasures, or any one of them he contracts invalidly, for these as oft repeated are *essentialia quoad obligationem,* and such a condition excludes one or all and therefore excludes the essence of

[25] Lib. II, d. XXVIII.

[26] P. Leurenius, S.J., *Forum Ecclesiasticum* (Venetiis, 1729), lib. IV, tit. V.

[27] Ballerini-Palmieri, *Opus Theologicum Morale,* VI, De Matr. resolution, n. XXX.

[28] *Cf.* Pallotini, *ibidem; cf.* Causa Bambergen, March 14, 1856.

marital consent itself.[29] If the words used are doubtful, the common opinion of doctors and tribunals interpret the words of the party or parties in favor of validity of consent, especially if adminicular proofs concur.[30] A vague desire or a simple intention, not a condition, of a woman to defer consummation from fear of maternity does not invalidate.[31]

If both agree to practice onanism or birth control in other ways, after for instance the first, second, or third child, in such a way as to exclude the very marriage *right* to the perfect *copula* the marriage is invalid, and if they explicitly declare thus before witnesses, then juridically and in *foro poli* the marriage is held null. If on the contrary, as is most common and almost always obtains in practice, such a convention does not exclude the *jus,* but is only an agreement (even in the form of a condition to their consent) of a mutual agreement to *abuse* this same right and obligation, then the consent is valid, (if the condition is placed and *verified,* the marriage is also valid).[32] If one says, "I marry you on condition that we avoid children, or commit abortion, etc.," *per se* from these words we can not conclude for validity or invalidity of the marriage. If the meaning is "we take on the essential obligations of the *bonum prolis* but bind ourselves and our consent to the serious promise to abuse these obligations by onanism, abortion, etc.," the marriage is valid, if they seriously promise thus verifying the condition, although in the external forum the condition is rejected as immoral. If the meaning is, "we do *not* take on this essential *obligation,* but reserve the *right* to commit abortion etc." the marriage is invalid. So care must be used and one should not immediately conclude such marriages are invalid because of the words used in the conditional phrase. In other words, the content of the condition may touch an essential (the assumption of the obligation) or a non-essential (the abuse of an obligation

[29] *Cf.* S. C. in Ulyssiponen. Occidentalis, July 8, 1724, referred to by Ben. XIV, lib. 13, cap. 22, n. 10, *De Syn. Dioc.*

[30] *Cf.* Pontius, *De Matr.,* lib. II, cap. 8; Pallotini, *loc. cit.,* nn. 32, 33.

[31] Pallotini, *op. cit., ibidem,* n. 8; cf. Causa Parisien, 28 March, 1857.

[32] Gougnard, *De Matrimonio,* p. 147; vide causam solutam apud S. C. C. apud Analecta Ecclesiastica (1904), p. 294 s.

already assumed). This agrees with Canon 1086 par. 2 and 1092, n. 4.[33]

It seems that some authors *e. g.* Vromant and De Smet do not admit something is against the substance of a thing, when an *essential property* (using the phrase in its strict philosophic sense of something flowing necessarily from the substance of a thing *e. g.* speech from human rationality), is excluded from that substance *de facto* or by one's will. But it seems these authors err for the substance and its properties are an *unum inseparabile.* Moreover the examples given by De Smet may also refer only to the *abuse* of an obligation not to its assumption. In this case they are *turpes conditiones tantum* and follow the rules thereof. Concerning this principle of the essential obligation of the *bonum prolis* and its application several such cases may be consulted.[34]

Canon 1086, par. 2, does not mean one must exclude all three rights of the treasures in marriage, but each or any right; nor does it mean to include the rights pertaining to the *tria bona* not essentially but only integrally, *e. g.*, wicked desires against one's duties, or illicit affection to another, or lack of real love of wife or children.

[33] Canon 1086, par. 2: "At si alterutra vel utraque pars positivo voluntatis actu excludat matrimonium ipsum, aut omne jus ad conjugalem actum, vel essentialem aliquam matrimonii proprietatem, invalide contrahit." *Cf.* Canon 1013 which enumerates the ends of marriage and its essential properties. Canon 1081, par. 2, defines the *jus in corpus.* Canon 1111 reads: "Utrique conjugi ab ipso matrimonii initio aequum jus et officium est quod attinet ad actus proprios conjugalis vitae." Canon 1092, n. 4, legislates: "Si de praeterito vel de praesenti, matrimonium erit validum vel non, prout id quod conditioni subest, existit vel non."

"Contra non esset, salvo meliori judicio, invalidum matrimonium contractum sub conditione occidendi prolem, eam abjiciendi, abortum provocandi, subeundi, pro muliere, ovariotomiam, etc.: hae essent conditiones turpes (et, qua tales, pro non adjectis essent habendae), ac imo repugnantes matrimonio et obligationibus ex eo ortis sed non essent repugnantes matrimonii *substantiae.*" De Smet, *De Sponsalibus et Matrimonio,* n. 155. De Smet adds a note to this passage to the effect that many authors hold that killing, or abandoning or aborting children is repugnant to the substance of marriage, but not a condition of bringing up the children in infidelity or heresy.

[34] S. C. C. apud *Annal. eccl.* (1904), p. 294 s. S. R. Rota, 10 May, 1916, *AAS,* IX, p. 33; case referred to by Benedict XIV, *De Syn. Dioc.,* lib. XXII, n. 10.

The phrase of Canon 1086, par. 2, "omne jus ad conjugalem actum," means that the full perpetual radical right must be given. To exclude this right after, *e. g.*, the first or second child, invalidates the consent. It is false to argue that one must exclude the right for the entire marital life before the consent is vitiated. The right must be perpetual not temporary or partial. The positive act of the will can be an implicit one, when *e. g.* one has an end in mind incompatible with this obligation.[35]

Vromant [36] says this does not pertain to the substance of marriage: "obligatio *educationis* prolis, obligatio prolem non exponendi eamve proprio lacte nutriendi." He refers to certain authors.[37] Vromant thinks with De Smet that the marital contract with a condition of killing the child, throwing it away, committing abortion, suffocating it, etc., is valid, and similar conditions which are against the *bono etiam physico,* are not against the substance, but must be considered *turpes et qua turpes,* held not placed to the contract, provided there remains the right of both *ad copulam per se generationem aptam*. He refers to certain authors.[38] Vromant claims this opinion agrees with Gregory IX "si generationem prolis evites," puta per copulam generationi ineptam. It is sufficient to say, that this runs counter to the traditional teaching of ages and to hang it on a text that can be and has been interpreted in numerous senses, is a very weak procedure. Furthermore it fails to note the meaning of *bonum prolis* in its *essential* aspect as distinguished from the non-essential or integral meaning of *bonum prolis.* Canon 1086, par. 2, speaks of "omne jus." Vidal says all doctors agree that this condition invalidates, for it is against the *bonum prolis.*[39]

Speaking of the *ends* of marriage, the great moralist St. Alphon-

[35] *Cf.*, Appolinaris, I, 1928, p. 355, *cf.*, S. R. R. Decisiones, XI, p. 145 s. *cf.*, Capello, *De Matr.*, n. 598.

[36] *Jus Missionariorum,* n. 175.

[37] Capello, *De Matrimonio,* n. 631, who admits all except the *educatio;* Wernz, *Jus Matr.*, n. 302; Wernz-Vidal, *Jus Matr.*, n. 518, Knecht, *Eherechts,* p. 590 s.

[38] De Smet, *De Sponsalibus et Matrimonio,* n. 155; Vermeersch-Creusen, *Epit. J. C.*, II, n. 381; Ayrinhac, *Jus Pontificum,* IX (1929), p. 33.

[39] *Cf.* Wernz-Vidal, *De Matrimonio,* n. 518; Decree of Eugene IV to Armenians, apud Hardouin, Councils, tom. VIII, n. 440; Ben. XIV, *Syn.* 1, XIII, cap. 22, n. 6; Vatican Schema.

sus [40] reasons thus: there are two *intrinsic essential* ends, the mutual delivery with the obligation of rendering, and the *vinculum indissolubile.* It is certain he says that if one would positively exclude these two ends, the marriage is null. There are two *intrinsic accidental* ends, *procreatio prolis et remedium concupiscentiae.* It is certain, he teaches, that if one excludes these the marriage is valid, and sometimes licit. Of course this is erroneous. These ends cannot be excluded, for they are not accidental but pertain to the substance of marriage. "Nullum matrimonium stare potest sine suis finibus."

A condition repugnant essentially to *one* of the *tria bona* is repugnant at the same time to the other two, for marriage is a *res inseparabilis,* and the *tria bona* are the *vinculum naturale* from a threefold aspect.[41]

He who wills to exclude something of the substance of a thing, does not and can not psychologically or juridically will that thing. For he has in his mind an object totally diverse from that which his external words express; therefore *ex hypothesi,* his juridical consent is absent. If one removes the substance of a thing, the thing itself is removed or destroyed. To know what is of the substance of a thing or of an act one must look and see whether the thing or act can subsist without it.

The *tria bona* are called the *finis operis* of marriage. *Proles* is the *finis genericus* for it refers to the good of the species, the other two are individual and personal. The demands of the primary end most wonderfully takes care of the other two.[42]

The condition "provided you abstain from the use of marriage" (not, *promise* to) is a negative condition that may not be verified till death; therefore it is never valid, and furnishes a perpetual occasion of sin.[43] Generally if convincing proof is had of non-con-

[40] *Theol. Moralis,* lib. VI, tract. VI, *de Matr.,* n. 880.

[41] Pichler, *Candidatus Juris Prudentiae Sacrae* (1733), *De Matr.,* p. 345.

[42] Noldin, *Cursus Theologiae Moralis,* ed. 3, lib. IV, de Sacr., *Veronae,* 1921; Noldin, *Summa Theologicae Moralis, Oeniponte,* 1914, p. 578 s; A. Vermeersch, *Theologiae Moralis Principia,* etc., tom. IV, Romae, 1923, p. 32 s.

[43] *Cf.* defens. Matri. in c. S. C. C., 20 March, 1880, in *ASS,* XIII, p. 454 s; *cf.* for exclusion of the *copula,* "ipsum jus ad copulam," S. C. C. apud Anal. Eccl., 1904, p. 294 s; 10 May, 1916, *AAS,* IX, p. 33; De Smet, *De Sponsalibus et Matrimonio,* n. 155.

summation, and it is doubtful whether the parties had a condition against the substance, one should petition the Holy Father for a dispensation super *rato tantum.*[44]

Practical solutions concerning the *bonum prolis,* that is concerning one of the obligations of the *bonum prolis,* namely the *generation* of offspring may be put thus. It is certain these invalidate the consent. "If you avoid illicitly (*i. e.,* having a *right* to do so, or in other words, not being obliged not to do so properly), the generation of children;" "If I am not bound to render the debitum;" "if you have no right to seek the debitum;" "if I have the *right* to commit onanism."

The following are against the substance if they exclude the *jus perpetuum* to the conjugal act (even for a day or an hour for this right can not be given partially); otherwise they are not against the substance, and this distinction *coram Deo* is valid whether the condition is "deducta in pactum" or not, provable or not: "If you abstain from the use of marriage;" if after the first or second etc. child, we will have no more;" "provided you avoid children till better days."

These conclusions may be made concerning the *bonum prolis conservandae.* The following conditions are certainly against the essence of a marital consent. "I marry you, if you procure abortion as a *right* (not, as an *abuse*);" if you kill your offspring (as a right); or gravely mutilate them (as a right); or render them lame (as a right); or destroy their sight (as a right).[45] The following distinction is in order. If the consent depends on the condition that, *e. g.,* she *seriously promise* the other party to do these things not as a right, or the exclusion of the obligation, but its abuse, and if she does not seriously thus promise them the other party does not will marriage, and if *de facto* she does not seriously promise, then the marriage is invalid *coram Deo* because the *turpis conditio* is not verified. Of course the external forum would reject by presumption this immoral condition.

If the condition has this content: "If you seriously promise to do these things as a *right* (*i. e.,* to exclude the obligation) then

[44] *Cf.* cases referred to in *Rev. des sciences eccl.,* 1905, p. 31; *Canon. Cont.,* 1901, p. 587; 1903, p. 297; *AAS,* X, p. 388; De Smet, *op. cit.,* n. 155.

[45] *Cf.* Bayon, *De Matrimonio,* p. 313; Sanchez, lib. 5, 9, n. 12.

whether she promises or not, the marriage is invalid because of essentially ill consent on the part of the man, at least, for he does not accept his essential rights which are excluded by these conditions, nor does the woman accept her *essential* obligation.

These do not vitiate marital consent: "I marry you provided all or some children are brought up in heresy or paganism," for this is not of the *bonum physicum.* Though the contrary opinion is probable, in Christian marriages, even though Bayon among most others says this opinion is absolutely antiquated. This, it is true, would not follow from the essence and ends of *natural* marriage, but since Christ raised marriage to a Sacrament of the true Church, henceforth then the Sacrament is of the essence of *Christian marriages,* and probably on this score, and in view of the *reasons* of Our Lord in elevating marriage to one of the seven ordinary means of salvation, religious education in the true faith, cannot positively and validly be excluded as a *conditio sine qua non,* of Christian marital consent.

Before the fall of our first parents, the *remedium concupiscentiae* was not an *end* of marriage. Therefore to positively exclude it, before the fall, would not have invalidated consent; to do so after the fall the fall would invalidate; so once, since marriage was not a true sacrament, to exclude it was superfluous, but now to exclude it, invalidates, and probably to exclude positively true religious education, in view of this would also invalidate. At least it is beyond controversy that the *bonum prolis* in its integrity, demands (even of infidel parents) and includes the rearing of children as God wills it. Bayon says this condition of heresy is *per se* immoral, but not irritating, and he says this is the common opinion of doctors and the practice of the Church to-day.[46]

Authors differ about the condition to expose children, to throw them away. Some think (*e. g.*, Bayon) that probably it is not against the substance of the *bonum prolis,* since not all physical care is taken away, since the parents hope others will feed them, especially is it true where orphanages are in the vicinity. In answer it can be said, if they exclude by their condition the obligation to rear and feed

[46] *Cf.* Bayon, *De Matrimonio,* p. 313; Wernz-Vidal, *De Matrimonio,* p. 518, note 32; Capello, *De Matrimonio,* n. 631, Chelodi, *Jus Matrimoniale,* n. 125, Noldin, *Theologia Moralis,* III n. 631.

and clothe the child, even though sure that others will feed them, without any doubt the consent is invalid, for one cannot rid oneself of an essential obligation by such means, otherwise one could exclude the end of *remedium concupiscentiae* because another would satisfy it. Furthermore the arguments from the natural law prohibiting polygamy would fall, for the children in some circumstances may fare better than those of a monogamous union. If the obligation is not excluded, then the condition is not invalidating. In practice if an agreement is pre-nuptial it is commonly only a *modus;* and if it is post-nuptial, as in most cases, it is simply an abuse, of an obligation already assumed.

Ignorance about the substantial object of the matrimonial contract, that ignorance which invalidates, is not had if there is some implicit and confused knowledge that marriage is a permanent union between a man and woman to procreate offspring. There is not required of the parties an explicit knowledge that generation is had by the carnal *copula.*[47] Capello, Vlaming and others deny this last point. "Non enim, jus quod in matrimonio traditur essentialiter consistit in potestate *filios ex conjugio procreandi,* sed in potestate *exigendi usum corporis* seu *copulam* in ordinė ad filiorum procreationem."[48] Against these is the solution of a case in China recently favoring[49] the former viewpoint. This ignorance is not presumed after puberty Canon 1082, par. 2. The age of puberty for this point is governed by Canon 88, par. 2 (under 14 years of age for boys and 12 for girls) not as Farrugia (n. 24) contends by Canon 1067, par. 1, which states a boy must be 16 years completed and a girl 14, for a valid marriage.[50]

Error is a judgement of the intellect, not merely lack of knowledge as is ignorance. It is a false judgment or notion of a thing, considering it other than it is actually. Concerning marriage there may be *error facti, e. g.,* about the physical person, or a quality of the person; or *error juris, e. g.,* about the very substantial object or

[47] Canon 1082, par. 1; De Smet, *De Sponsalibus et Matrimonio,* n. 522 ter.; Gasparri, *De Matrimonio,* n. 791; Wernz-Vidal, *Jus Matrimoniale,* n. 457.

[48] Vlaming, n. 524; *cf.* in same sense, Cappello, n. 582; also Kiselstein, apud *Revue eccl.* de Liege, XVI, 1924, h. 174 s.

[49] Causa V. Chansi Merid., 29 November, 1919, *AAS,* XIII, p. 54 s.

[50] *In Poenalibus,* puberty for both boy and girl may be considered as 14 years complete.

essential properties of marriage. Either kind may be *concomitant,* in so far as it does not influence substantially the marriage consent, *e. g.*, one still might have contracted had he detected the error, though perhaps less promptly; or it may be *antecedent,* it influences substantially the will so that he would not have contracted if he had known.

Error about the very person, whether vincible or not, antecedent or concomitant, invalidates.[51] One cannot maintain that in case of *antecedent* error there is always a *conditioned consent.* One must consider not what *would have* but what *actually did* happen in the will. An interpretative condition is no condition. Nor is it necessary that one think of a condition in the very act of marriage, or know the juridical effect of the condition placed. Any kind of error, that is, no matter what the object is about which one errs, even if it be a vain thing, if made and elevated into *a conditio sine qua non* of the consent would invalidate any effects, for the act is null, the condition being unverifiable.[52] It is a very difficult thing as a rule to prove that such error was made a condition.

Concerning *error juris,* in reference to false essential notions about marriage, there are very peculiar cases, *e. g.*, if one thinks marriage is, *e. g.*, nothing else than a brother and sister relationship and then wills it thus, etc.[53] Error about the essential obligations of the *tria bona,* if elevated to a condition excluding the truth about them, invalidate the consent.[54] Simple error terminates in the intellect; the other kind of error terminates in the will. Antecedent error about the properties of marriages does not *per se* import a positive exclusion by the will of the properties. Fictitious or simulated consent is equivalent to consent positively excluding marriage itself or some property.

Before the Fall of Adam there were two ends, namely the procreation of children and mutual help ("Let us make Adam a helpmate," "It is not good for man to be alone"). After the Fall, the *remedium concupisceniae* became the third intrinsic essential end of

[51] *Cf.* Canon 1083, par. 1; *AAS,* V. 372.

[52] *Cf.* Canon 104; De Smet *op. cit.*, n. 525 s; *cf. S. R. R., AAS,* 30 June, 1910, II, 590, Baltimore case; *cf. S. R. R.*, II, 11 August, 1910, 96; III, 23 June, 1911, 497.

[53] *Cf.* 19 August, 1914, *AAS,* VII, 51 s; cc. 104, 1083, 1084.

[54] *Cf.* (N. Y. case) *AAS,* VII, p. 292; VII, p. 451; X, 216.

marriage. Some say the primary end is *mutuum adjutorium* not the procreation of children. God did not say, they assert, where can I find Adam a *fabrica prolis,* but "let us make Adam a *help-mate*" (Genesis 11, 18 s.) and the Lord said for *him* not for the child. To have any one of these three ends is sufficient for valid marital consent, provided no one in particular is positively excluded.[55]

Cappello [56] says such conditions as, "if you avoid children," or "if you procure abortion," or "if you kill the children," or "if you do not seek the debitum," if simply (*simpliciter*) added, are considered to exclude the "ipsum jus," unless the contrary is proved. This seems to be correct, yet the famous examples of Gregory IX, and these others must be understood in their true meaning, and the law considers them to exclude the right, only if the parties intend to exclude the right. But granting the presumption is as Cappello says, it means little in practice because each individual marriage case like this must, according to the constant instructions and replies of the Roman curia, be considered by the court with all its circumstances in order to explore the inner will behind the expressions used.[56*]

When a limitation of the *copula* is added by way of a condition, the question must be asked, does the limitation refer to the exercise of that right to copulate, or to the right to the exercise of the marriage act. If for instance, the limitation is to once a month, does it mean this is all they intend to use their complete right, or does it mean this is the utmost right the one placing the condition now grants. If the latter is the content of the condition, the marital consent lacks an essential and it is therefore invalid.

The old decretalists and the subsequent ancient canonists, almost invariably (without making distinctions concerning the content of the will act in relation to the essentials of marriage) stated that illicit impeding of children invalidated the marriage. The example of

[55] *Cf.* Bayon, *De Matrimonio,* p. 13; Ballerini-Palmieri, *Theologia Moralis* V, n. 235; Cappello *De Matrimonio,* n. 11; Sporer, *Theologia Moralis,* pars IV, C. 1, sect. III, n. 295.

[56] *De Matrimonio* n. 631. "Obligatio non generandi distinguitur a non executione obligationis; in dubio praesumitur contrahentem habuisse intentionem tantum non exsequendi obligationem; quae tamen praesumptio cedit veritati." —*Appolinaris,* V, 1932, p. 25, *cf. S. R. R. Decisiones,* XI, 145.

[56*] De Smet, *op. cit.,* n. 155.

Gregory IX "si evites prolem," was enough for them, and many modern authors fall into the same fatal error.

The condition "I marry you, if you avoid children" may be meant variously in the mind. If it is meant to suspend, then there is no chance to have it verified, and therefore no marriage. If it means, the other party must now seriously promise to avoid offspring, then a distinction must be made. If it means she has a right to do so, in other words, she promises not to assume the *obligation* of the *bonum prolis*, then there is no marriage possible. If the condition of seriously promising to avoid children means to *abuse* the obligation voluntarily assumed, then the validity of the marriage in the internal forum, depends on the verification of the serious promising. If she does not seriously promise to abuse her duty and obligation the condition is unverified, and there is no marriage consent on the part of the one placing the condition, and therefore no marriage. Of course in the external forum the condition in this last supposition will be rejected as not having been placed seriously, till the contrary is satisfactorily proved to the court. If the condition means to avoid children by licit means, *e. g.*, to use safe periods of time, or by mutual abstention, then it is a licit condition, and the marriage depends on the verification of that promise to thus avoid them. But if the one placing it means this: "I marry you on condition that you *actually* (in the future) avoid children by use of the safe periods, or by a vow, or by mutual abstention, then it ceases to be licit and becomes equivalent to a *resolutive* condition, which kind of a condition is always against the indissolubility of marriage. Because, at any time in the married life, the woman is able to not avoid children and she may have a child, thus the condition is certainly made unverifiable and the marriage would cease. Or if the condition is looked at as a *future suspensive*, then again it cannot be verified till death, and thus there is no marriage meanwhile and no right to marriage acts, which condition too (in this case of avoiding something) is repugnant to a marriage arising.

This same reasoning is valid for all similar expressions used by the parties, *e. g.*, "we marry but we won't have children," or, "we won't have children for the first five years" or, "we will have only one or two children." Though the wording used may not be strictly and grammatically a conditional wording, yet in the intentions of the couple the words may mean to express a condition in the mind, or a positive intention to exclude the assumption of the essential obligation, and on the other hand, the words used may mean to express any of the other significations noted above.

He who contracts a true marriage (thus *ex hypothesi,* giving over and receiving full marital rights) and at the same time has a firm intention or purpose or resolve of avoiding offspring, not only negatively by mutual voluntary non-use, or by denying the *debitum,* but also of avoiding children positively by deprave use, *e. g.,* by onanism, or killing the issue, or by any positive immoral prevention of conception or birth, such a one, in spite of this depraved intention, contracts validly, because the assumption of marital obligations precede their fulfillment and their assumption remains in the essence of marriage, being unaffected by what follows, untouched by what does not become the very object of marital consent. This statement is valid generally and *per se* also for the *bonum fidei,* but the *bonum sacramenti* in one sense admits of no distinction between obligation and fulfillment.[57]

> At caute distinguendum est inter ipsam matrimonialem obligationem et hujus adimplementum. Hoc enim potest contingere, ut contrahens ita sit animo comparatus, ut vere et serio velit contrahere et se obligare, et tamen praevidens matrimonii abusum, v.g. onanismum, pravam habeat voluntatem hoc delictum permittendi, aut etiam committendi, et ita suas obligationes violandi. Hoc in casu matrimonium validum est, quia matrimonii essentia non dependet ab ejus usu. Quam sententiam expressam a D. Thoma . . . Igitur ut in hoc altero casu matrimonium sit nullum requiritur intentio, quae positive et expresse excludat ipsam matrimonialem obligationem, et non tantum hujus implementum. Haec autem intentio dignoscitur praesertim ex adjunctis et circumstantiis, maxima diligentia perpensis, sive antecedentibus, sive concomitantibus, sive subsequentibus matrimonium.[58]

[57] *Cf.* section: "Is a Simple Intention or Purpose contrary to Matrimonial Indissolubility Equivalent to an Actual Condition?"

[58] *S. R. Rota, Causa Parisien,* 10 Maii, 1916, *AAS,* IX (1917), 33 s.

A couple may say before marriage "We will not have any children" and yet these words *per se* do not mean that they do not intend to marry like other people. They may simply wish not to fulfill the obligations. This is most frequently the case with such expressions, and it will often be impossible to have moral certainty that they placed a condition that vitiated the consent. When asked by the judge they often do not understand the distinction between a right and its abuse. They very likely consider themselves married and bound by the laws of wedlock but act contrary to them.

When however one or both are absolutely opposed to a family on principle, simply scoff at the idea of children and use such loose expressions as "no children for us etc." it may very likely be that they exclude the radical right. This principle is affirmed by the Rota in the case of a libertine who scoffed at the thought of children.[59]

Concerning errors of, *e. g.*, infidels about the *bonum prolis,* Vromant writes thus: "Matrimonium erit nullum si alteruter contrahentium hac lege tantum vult contrahere ut sibi liceat adulterare, a conjuge postea recedere, copula abuti contra finem primarium matrimonii, sive haec sint *condicio* sine qua non, sive sint objectum intentionis praevalentis." [60]

The conditional consent, "I marry you if you are fertile," is resolutive and marital consent cannot receive such conditions, except the two that are in the law. Can this particular condition be a non-resolutive one? It cannot be a future suspensive honest. If it is future suspensive then it is a *turpis conditio* which is rejected. It can be a present condition, either honest or immoral and the marriage is immediately valid if the condition is verified though the knowledge is yet future. Though if the means used are immoral, then the external forum will reject its placing unless it is proved to have been seriously placed. If the condition is, "if you beget children," then it is resolutive and invalidates.

[59] *AAS* (1917), IX, p. 35; *cf.* Aryhinac, *Marriage Legislation* (1932), p. 227. Of six cases examined by the Rota in 1929 on the plea of a condition *contra bonum prolis,* five were decided "Non constat;" only one had a clear proof on an invalidating condition. *AAS, XXII* (1930), pp. 177-190. In 1930 there were thirteen cases of a *conditio contra substantiam* decided; only one of these was admitted as proved, the rest rejected. *Cf. AAS, XXIII* (1931), p. 90.

[60] *Jus Missionariorum,* (Louvain, 1931) n. 177.

If the condition is "provided we use marriage only during the safe periods," then if only the right to that extent is given over, it invalidates, but if the abstention is by mutual consent, presupposing full rights *in radice* are transferred to all times, then the condition is not against the substance of marriage, nor is it immoral.[61]

The marriage is invalid if the condition of not using marriage excludes the *right* to the act, and not only the actual exercise of the right. The condition that the man undergo castration by which he becomes impotent and incapable of instituting a true *copula* suitable for generation invalidates.[62]

If the condition has this content, that after the first or second child, the *right* to any further use of the *copula* is excluded, the marriage is invalid.[63] Though in most cases similar conditions generally permit a true marriage, and confine themselves only to the abuse of rights and duties, unless it is otherwise proved.[64]

Thus the conditions: "provided after the second child, we intend to avoid other children;" "provided that till we are better off financially, we exclude all children," invalidate if they intend to exclude the right (*jus*) to the right use of marriage, to *exclude* the *right* even partially for a time; but these conditions do not invalidate, if they are added only secondarily as it were and mean the will or intention of abusing marriage.[65] It is probably not an invalidating condition, the purpose of which is to bring up the children outside the Catholic faith, or other things of this kind, which are not against the *physical* good of the children.[66] Though some authors maintained the contrary for Christian parents and with arguments by no means weak. Canon 2319 excommunicates parents who, through a pact entered into, raise their children outside the Church.

[61] C. J. Ryan, "The Moral Aspects of Periodical Continence," *Ecclesiastical Review*, LXXXIX (1933), 28-39.

[62] De Smet, *loc cit*.

[63] Lemkuhl, *Theologia Moralis*, II, n. 689.

[64] Gasparri, *De Matrimonio* (1932), n. 882.

[65] *Cf*. Cerato, *De Matrimonio*, p. 147; D'Annibale, *Theologia Moralis*, III, 448.

[66] Reiffenstuel, lib. IV, tit. I, n. 371; Gasparri, II (1932), n. 1013 s.

A vague desire and a simple intention to defer for a time the generation of children does not invalidate.[67] To consent on condition not to know the woman is invalid, if the condition excludes the right of either party.[68]

If the condition is internal only and externally the consent is absolute, presumption of law favors the absolute consent having been given according to Canon 1086, par. 1. But there are cases of internal conditions in which nullity was admitted.[69] But if there is convincing proof of non-consummation, a dispensation from *matrimonium ratum tantum* may be obtained from the Holy Father.[70] Otherwise if the doubt still remains, the principle of Canon 1014 is used "in dubio standum est pro valore matrimonii, donec contrarium probetur."

Can the party who put an invalidating condition unknown to the other party be compelled to marry the other party unreservedly if the condition cannot be proved in the external forum? Compulsion would not be *unjustly* brought to bear, else the innocent party would be condemned to a life of celibacy, for no one can licitly enter upon another marriage unless the previous marriage ceremony has been declared null and void or has been dissolved by the Church. However to compel the simulator to marry the girl would hardly make for a happy marriage. Conscientious motives should be brought to bear, but proving of no avail, recourse to judicial compulsion would be in most cases imprudent. The guilty party would in every case be held in conscience to make good all material damage inflicted on the innocent party or the children, if any. The innocent party could not be compelled to accept a revocation of an honest condition, or a new marriage consent in case of a vitiating condition.[71] *Juridically,* there is no action to demand the guilty party to marry the girl. In such difficult cases the innocent party could ask the Sacred Pentitentiary for a declaration of freedom in both fora.

[67] Pallottini, Coll. *S. C. C.*, verb. "matrimonium," n. 8.

[68] Pallottini, *loc. cit.*, n. 9.

[69] *Cf. causam Parisien.*, 17 April, 1915, apud *Can. Cont.* (1915), p. 577; *causam Parisien.*, 26 November, 1921, *AAS,* XIV (1922), 512.

[70] *Cf.* Special Commission of Cardinals, *AAS,* X (1910), 388 s.

[71] Nau, *Manual of the Marriage Laws,* n. 111.

§ 2. *Heresy Condition and Immoral Education*

Whether the marital consent is invalidated by a condition to raise children in heresy, says Pallottini, is greatly disputed. His opinion is, it is invalid *ob favorem religionis fidei.* He refers to a case (Augustana) of November 24, 1742.[72] This distinction is made and defended by Haringer, Weber, Steyart, and Dens, that a condition *deducta in pactum* to bring up children in infidelity or paganism *ipso jure naturali* invalidates, but to raise in heresy or schism or in other crimes, does not invalid consent. All these, according to nearly all writers, are for Catholics simply immoral and are rejected. But if this be so, and they be seriously placed as a *conditio sine qua non,* that is a *serious promise now* to educate them thus, then the validity of the marriage depends on the serious promise, if not made, the union is invalid. Schmier insists the principal end of marriage is not only the generation but the education of children in the true religion.[73]

This opinion of Schmier is not disproved by the common opinion nor by the fact that the Church reprobates such pacts of heresy, but never attacks the marriage. The reason of this may be the Church presumes the general intention in the consent to raise the children as God wills it, and moreover reasons that parents do not exclude positively this good will. It seems all admit, except Boeckhn, that to train the child in any crime or criminal practice, by a condition, does not invalidate. Gougnard[74] says these conditions do not invalidate because these conditions as a rule are not considered as a condition *sine qua non,* but as a pure *modus* added to the contract. This is *per se* not true, moreover if one makes the addition even unknown to the other (the *modus* supposes knowledge by both), then again it would not be a *modus.* He says the parents as *Christians,* not as *parents* are bound to raise the child as a Christian. But in answer to this, one may quote the words of Canon 1113, "Parentes gravissima obligatione tenentur prolis educationen tum religiosam

[72] *Cf.* Wernz-Vidal, *Jus Matrimoniale,* n. 518; esp., Van de Burgt. *Tractatus de Dispensationibus Matrimonialibus,* p. 66 s; Feji, *Dissert. de matr. mixt.* p. 163 s; *Act. theol. Oenip,* IX, p. 170; XIV, p. 535; Lehmkuhl, *op. cit.,* II, n. 689; Gasparri, *op. cit.,* n. 1013.

[73] *De Spons. et Matr.,* III, cap. 5, 571.

[74] *De Matrimonio,* p. 148.

et moralem tum physicam et civilem pro viribus curandi, et etiam temporali eorum bono providendi" True spiritual education belongs at least to the integrity of the *bonum prolis,* which includes not only mere physical well-being, but also moral and spiritual and social well-being.

Such a condition is repugnant to the natural, divine, and ecclesiastical law and gravely sinful under all circumstances, even when the State law, *e. g.,* demands that the boys of a mixed marriage to be brought up in the religion of the father; and the girls in that of the mother. Such a law though unjust and lacking authority before God, nevertheless by its rigor should lessen greatly the number of such marriages in those places. Canon 2319 punishes parents for such agreement, whether conditions or modes.

Even though one may hold that modifications added to the contract to bring up the children in heresy, or without baptism, even if placed as conditions, do not *per se* invalidate the true consent, but being immoral they have no legal force whatever, nevertheless one can not say absolutely, as Scherer and Hussarek [75] do, that the *educatio* of the children has no influence upon marriage or its objectives. *Educare* in the canonical sense of Canon 1013, par. 1, is an essential of the marital consent. "Matrimonii finis primarius est procreatio *atque educatio prolis.*"

Article III

Honest Conditions Against the Bonum Physicum Prolis

Another question often discussed in connection with the papal text and Canon 1092, n. 2, is this: Whether only *turpis* or also *honesta conditio* may be against the substance. In other words, does an honest condition against the substance or only an immoral future against the substance, invalidate. To answer this, other questions must first be settled, namely, if a condition is against the essence of marriage or the *tria bona,* can such a condition be *honesta objectively,* not, subjectively, and can such an honest condition invalidate the consent.

[75] *Cf. S. C. C., in causa Augustana,* 24 November, 1742; *cf.* Hussarek, *Die Bedingte Eheschliessung,* p. 232, note 7.

There are many opinions, though there need be but one, and furthermore it is irrelevant whether it is honest objectively or not, for if the condition excludes marriage itself, or excludes any essential obligation or right, there is *ex natura rei,* no true consent, nor marriage; but if these are not excluded, the marriage is valid if the condition is verified.

Hussarek states well the view of many who claim the marriage is invalid:

> True enough an attitude that contradicts any of the obligations of marriage will regularly oppose Christian morality as such, but it is not necessarily so. It is hard to imagine how the *bonum fidei* can be violated by a *licit* action, but with the other two *bona,* actions may be incompatible which are not only immoral, but may even represent the choice of a higher good than that of married life. There is no doubt that Christian ethics and with them Canon Law attribute to virginal chastity a higher virtue than to matrimonial ethics. The latter is held *good,* the former, *better.* Both goods are however imcompatible with each other. One striving after Christian perfection has only one choice to declare for either one or the other. Hence a marital consent which aims at such an impossible harmonization is invalid because of its inherent contradiction. To declare consent under such a condition is not to declare true marital consent.[76]

If a certain secondary stipulation is antecedently added to the principal marital contract, *salvo vero jure mutuo in corpora,* by which the "conjuges *renutiant tantum licito usui* illius juris," many grave authorities say such antecedent accessory stipulation, though in itself honest, is repugnant to the substance of marriage, as Sanchez,[77] Schmalzgrueber,[78] and others. Pallottini [79] says the common opinion is that an honest condition against the substance invalidates, though he says, others deny this. He lines up quite a few authorities of note

[76] Hussarek, *Die Bedingte Eheschliessung,* p. 233. It may be noted that contradiction and incompatibility are not identical.

[77] *De Matrimonio,* V, d. 10.

[78] Lib. IV, tit. XIX, n. 119.

[79] *Coll. S. C. C., verbum* "matrimonium," n. 10.

for the common opinion of his day. But the contrary opinion which many of the adversaries think is at least probable, and which Benedict XIV [80] said had much probability is held by many others, *e. g.*, Palmieri, Ballerini and Lehmkuhl.[81] Palmieri sees nothing repugnant in a condition of chastity. He reasons very well and answers equally well all the objections against this view.[82]

It will be useful to analyze what the author of the greatest work on marriage, Sanchez, has to say on this subject, and also to consider other great canonists, especially Reiffenstuel and Schmalzgrueber and the commentators on the Code.

Sanchez [83] outlines two main opinions; the first affirms marriage is valid, *e. g.*, on condition to preserve chastity during life. Some reasons are: Gregory IX as is clear from his examples meant only *immoral* conditions; the *actual copula* is not of the essence of marriage, thus the condition not to have the *copula* is not against the essence of marriage, though it is against the *bonum prolis;* the example of Mary and Joseph; if both parties before marriage vowed to enter religion, the marriage is valid, though neither can seek the *debitum* etc.; such a condition seems to be implied in the contract. It suffices to note here that all this really means the condition concerns only the *usus juris,* presupposing the *jus* was given. If the *jus* was given, there is marriage as is seen from fact that intercourse with a third party would be *adultery,* not fornication, there is *ligamen,* etc. Sanchez says this opinion is probable, but his own opinion, namely that the condition does invalidate is much more probable.

The reasons are: When in the very act of the contract a condition is placed that both remain in perpetual chastity, not only is the *copula* taken away, but also the *jus et potestas* to the *copula,* for this obligation efficaciously impedes such *jus et potestas.*

[80] *De Syn.*, XIII, 22.

[81] These favor the validity of marriage. Pichler, *Candidatus Juris Prudentiae Sacrae,* lib. IV, n. 79; Kugler, *De Matrimonio,* n. 519; Lehmkuhl, *Theol. Moralis,* II, n. 690; Ballerini-Palmieri, *Opus Theol. Moralis,* VI, n. 225; Gasparri, *op cit.*, 2 ed., n. 1008; *cf.* Wernz-Vidal, *Jus Matrimoniale,* n. 521; St. Alphonsus, *Theol. Moralis,* lib. VI, tract. VI, *de matr.*, n. 880, Mechlinae, 1882.

[82] *Tractus de Matr. Christiano* (1180), thesis III.

[83] *De Matrimonio,* lib. V, d. X.

Gregory IX did not distinguish between honest or base conditions against the *bonum prolis,* nor does he put the force in the baseness of the condition but in the repugnance to the *bona,* and both good and bad are against the *bona.* He quotes St. Thomas. In vain is the power to copulate, since it is a mortal sin each time.[84] Thus it seems Sanchez takes for granted that the *jus* is excluded *eo ipso* and necessarily by a condition of chastity. He errs here for it all depends on the inner meaning of the will and the meaning of the condition, whether the latter excludes or not the *jus radicale ad copulam.* Thus there are authors who maintain the marriage is valid, others, that it is invalid. But it can not be too often repeated that in a given case a marriage is valid, in another given case it is invalid. Because a vow or a condition of chastity *per se qua* vow or *qua* condition does not in its notes or concepts exclude the *jus radicale.* A true marriage and such a condition are not mutually exclusive and incompatible. The being bound by vow to God to observe perpetual chastity does not make it impossible *per se* to render valid marriage consent. Each case depends on the meaning that the party or parties gives to the vow or condition. If they think erroneously, or not, and if they deliberatey wlll that the vow or condition *they* make excludes the *jus radicale,* no marriage is possible. But an intelligent person knows better, that full marital rights can be given over and the condition or vow can remain intact.

Some authors maintain *eo ipso* (irrespective of the real intent of the parties) the marriage is valid, other authors err likewise in saying it is invalid. While still others see the real point at issue and bring out the distinction made in the above paragraph.

If the *nature* of the firm resolve to keep chastity, or the nature of the vow (both expressed, let us say, in a condition) *in se* and *per se* does not make it possible to give and receive the *jus radicale* of the bodies (which is to be proved by the opponents, else the validity of the marriage is to be upheld by law) then no marriage is possible. But the distinction between the *jus radicale* and the *usus hujus juris* is valid and it is validly applied to the condition of chastity and the

[84] It is also mortal sin under certain circumstances, that arises after marriage, *e. g.*, wife on point of death, yet the power or radical right still persists.

vow of chastity, even by the Rotal decisions, as will be pointed out later on.

Furthermore, it is no casuistical counter-argument to refer to the two months grace of the pre-Code law, to make up one's mind either to consummate marriage or dissolve it eventually by solemn vows. The Church broke the *vinculum,* therefore the Church rightly claims the marital consent was not defective, even with this *condicio juris.* As long as the possibility of sexual intercourse is not excluded by the consent the condition is honest and even licit if the other consents. According to moral theology and Canon Law the *jus radicale* is not essentially a selfish right. If the former *condicio juris* "nisi statum religiosae perfectionis elegero" was not of the nature to invalidate consent because the other party could not *licitly use* the *copula* without the other's consent, how can it now, if it is a voluntary condition of the party? It is a different case, if the condition were "on condition that you must go to religion." But even in this case, a distinction is necessary.

Chelodi [85] maintains that marriage with a pact of perpetual chastity or virginity invalidates the act, saying the general laws do not restrict to base conditions, which is true *ex jure naturali* also, but both laws do restrict to *conditions against the substance,* and these pacts *per se* are not necessarily against the substance. *Per accidens* only, when these conditions violate Canons 1081, par. 2, and 1086, par. 2. These canons and these conditions are not incompatible, accidentally they may be, that is, due to the intent of the party which is over and beyond the real vow or condition of chastity.

Chelodi insists it is no use to distinguish between *jus* and *usus juris,* else the whole affair is a *verbum inane.* But the *jus utendi* is not identical with *exercitium actuale juris utendi,* if it were the newlyweds a moment after the celebration of marriage, would not be married till they had the *copula,* or if the bridegroom dropped dead coming forth from the steps of the church, the girl would not be his widow. If one receives the priesthood with the will of *never exercising* its powers, would this person thereby exclude the sacred Order itself, or the intention of receiving it? The answer is in the negative.

Chelodi admits only the marriage is valid if the purpose of vir-

[85] *Jus Matrimoniale,* n. 125.

ginity is *per modum.* He tries to find support in the Newcastle case of July 27, 1907, wherein there was a written agreement not to consummate. The *defensor vinculi* used the distinction of *jus* and *usus juris,* but the Roman curia dissolved the marriage *super rato ad cautelam.* The real point however is why? The judges were not sure of the minds of the parties whether the agreement excluded the *jus radicale* or not, but they were sure of the non-consummation, so this case proves nothing against our opinion, rather it admits that there is a chance of their being no marriage to dissolve, hence the phrase *ad cautelam.*[86]

In fact, this is the rule, in doubt concerning the nullity of marriage dispense ("si casus ferat") *ad cautelam* super rato tantum.[87]

Wernz-Vidal [88] admit such conditions to keep continency. It is an obligation *per se* taken now in the present, but to be fulfilled in the future, this obligation can be strengthened by a vow. This condition best explains the marriage of Joseph and Mary and other saints, *e. g.*, as the breviary says of St. Pucheria "salva quam Deo voverat, virginitate, conjugem (Marcianum Augustum) sibi delegit."

The actual use of this right *per se* is separable from the *jus* itself, and this actual use can be impeded in many ways, dependently or independently of the wills of the couple. Yes, this impeding can take place as soon as the marriage exists, *e. g.*, if two marry bound by simple vows of chastity. Again, the former law allowed two months to deliberate about entering religion, it was an implicit condition of the right not to use the radical right. This pact is not against any treasure of marriage, not contrary to the *bonum fidei,* for one can not give his body to a third person, nor against the *sacramentum,* because the bond is perpetual, nor against the *bonum prolis,* for one is not obliged to the *copula* except in so far as the other seeks it

[86] *S. C. C., AAS,* XL (1907-1908), 494.

[87] *S. C. C.,* 24 March, 1906, *AAS,* XXXIX, 1906-07, pp. 283-298, this case (p. 298) has a note explaining the use here of the phrase "ad cautelam" saying it was not thus and thus, *e. g.*, an absolute dispensation, but *ad cautelam* refers to the dispensation *super rato,* in so far the "Patres censuerunt in casu adesse grave dubitandi motivum cira nullitatem conjugii propter defectum consensus ex parte mulieris . . ." *Cf.* also the *Instructio S.C.D.S., Pro D. Rato, etc.; AAS,* 7 May, 1923, XV, 389; *cf.* c. 1963, par. 2.

[88] *Jus Matrimoniale,* par. 521.

which right to *actually* use one can renounce. Nor are the parties obliged to the *positive* generation of children, but they are obliged *positively* (presupposing the actual use of the body), not to impede or kill them.

Let us narrow the question accurately. Some things are beyond dispute. No one denies the presence of marriage if both have the purpose or vow already taken of perpetual chastity, in a marriage already contracted.[89] Palmieri [90] says this question probably is well understood by certain writers, but they word it less accurately. This wording is not correct, *e. g.*, "Does a condition contrary to the *tria bona*, if it is honest, invalidate marriage." The point is, is the condition *contrary*, and is it *honest* if it is contrary. It seems evident that no contract can be valid if the requisite substance is wanting, whether the cause whence this defect comes is honest or not. At least civil laws work that way and natural laws too. The word *contrary* also is to be understood, does it mean substantially or only integrally contrary to something?

So let us put the question thus: Does a *condition* to keep chastity (not by both as Vidal desires) [91] but even by one (not necessarily "deducta in pactum" as Vidal again insists), but simply a condition *deducta* or not—does such a condition invalidate because it is essentially contrary to the substance of marriage or the *bonum prolis?* If instead of a condition, it is a secondary stipulation, *i. e.*, a *modus*, there is no dispute, yet a mode and a condition are confounded much by some authors, which Scherer (par. 112) rightly complains of. Some authors as Vidal says give their solution to our problem without making any distinction between the two, thus the difficulty is rather avoided than solved. Even Pichler [92] confuses these, saying the addition is "simul modus et conditio," not averting to the fact that *modus sequitur post contractum jam completum.*

The crux is whether in the *unico contractu matrimoniali*, which consists in the *traditio*, can there be validly placed, *e. g.*, this condition "contraho tecum si te ad continentiam *obligas*." Wernz himself

[89] *Cf.* Ben. XIV, *De syn.*, XIII, c. 22, n. 11.

[90] *Theologia Moralis*, n. 231.

[91] Wernz-Vidal, *Jus Matrimoniale*, n. 521.

[92] *Candidatus Juris Prudentiae Sacrae*, n. 79.

self, says Vidal, saw a contradiction in this supposition, not admitting the distinction between the right and the use of the right. The point is, he that gives the *jus* does not impose the obligation of not using it, but the one that receives this *jus,* accepts it and at the same time imposing on himself the obligation not to use his acquired right in view of his promise, or in view of the similar obligation (*ex promisso vel voto*) taken on by the other party. He that in the marriage contract receives the *jus ad usum* of marriage, impeded by his *own proper consent* as far as the actual exercise of the same right, does not enter a contract that lacks every juridic effect, for mutual consent or dispensation as the case may be can remove this agreement. This reasoning is valid, but only for two who mutually agree. Besides, this one, only taking the promise or vow, known or not to the other, can validly marry too, for in the supposition, both give and receive full radical right. Most, it seems, get tangled up with this question by trying to solve it according to what they hold of the union of Mary and Joseph. But this union need not at all enter the question, for it was *sui generis,* and the real nature of it is only conjecture and probable, but there is no certitude of its nature.

It is said by some that *direct dominion* without *dominium utile* cannot subsist. This is true if by the *dominium utile* is meant the *jus* (*radicale*) *exercendi copulam.* It is false if *dominium utile* means the actual physical exercise of the *copula,* and these writers make it mean this, which is clearly false, else they are proponents of what many think to be the *copula* theory. This assertion is true just because of (not in spite of) the fact that marriage is ordained to the end of the use (*usus*) of marriage, and marriage besides has two other essential ends also. Some writers carelessly use the same terms to express different ideas, *e. g.*, the phrase "jus utendi" signifies for some only the actual use, for others it means the radical right. This latter is correct. It is to be noted too that this phrase "jus exercendi" is used confusedly. The *jus exercendi* is the same as "jus utendi," the same as "dominium radicale," or the "jus ad actus ex se aptos etc." Entirely different is the "*exercitium* juris exercendi," this refers to the actual physical act of intercourse, which the vow or condition *per se* refers to. If the promise is given, the condition is verified, and there is a marriage, otherwise there is no marriage.

Once the substance of the contract has been validly placed, any other addition supervenient or concommitant, whether good, bad or indifferent, whether *de facto* it interferes with the exercise of the rights and duties of marriage, wrongly or rightly so, can not ever invalidate the substance of marriage. These additions can never be against the substance of marriage in the sense of removing what is already there.

The vow of virginity (by one or both) connotes, that the one bound by vow is *bound* by *marriage* to render the *debitum,* and *prohibited* by the *vow* to do so, but in this conflict marriage prevails and even the husband by Church law could dispense from the vow.[93]

Even though the two months grace of law is abrogated, nevertheless the condition, that one be allowed to enter religion before consummation is a licit one, and possible too.

Often this entire question is confused by saying that if the condition is "deducta in pactum" it invalidates, because it means "trado tibi jus quod non recipias." *Per se* a condition does not change its nature or its effects whether it is "deducta in pactum" or not. To assert otherwise is quite false, for the promise of licit abstaining from intercourse may be the content of a condition "deducta in pactum," and if the promise is given, the condition is verified and the marriage is valid. Again, it is false to assert that a condition only then enters into and makes a constituent part of the consent when it is "deducta in pactum," and it is not a part of the consent when not thus placed. A condition *qua talis,* all conditions, no matter how added, by its *very nature* enters into the consent in an essential way, even with a condition not against the substance, marital consent simply is not given if the condition is frustrated. What matters is not the actual manner (*quomodo*) of adding the condition (whether externally or internally, etc.) but the content of the condition, whether it invalidate by its nature or not. Moral qualities of conditions whether good or bad are irrelevant (as far as they concern the substance of marriage) for if in a given case the radical dominion is excluded, so too is the marriage. Absolute and expressed renunciation of the actual use or exercise of a right can happen *post vel ante acceptum jus,* without destroying the contract, for renunciation presupposes one

[93] Gasparri's new idea on Canon 1111 is *ad rem.*

has or will have the *jus radicale.* There is no repugnance in the situation where one receives a right to use and yet does not *exercise* that right to use, whether voluntarily or unwillingly, *e. g.*, in case of the illness of the other party. In other words the marriage is valid if there is not excluded *jus utendi* but *juris (utendi) exercitium.* The same principles govern here about the manner in which the condition is placed, whether "deducta in pactum" etc. as are expressed and applied in the previous section of this chapter when speaking about the *bonum sacramenti.* These principles hold also for conditions concerning the *bonum fidei.*[94]

Thus from the above it is evidently not correct to settle the question on the false principle of the "deductio in pactum." Yet some authors erroneously like to distinguish. First they say what is evident to everyone, if this purpose is added not as a condition but as a *modus* (*per modum modi*) the marriage is valid. But if the purpose and intention is elevated to a *true condition*, another false distinction is made, thus giving two opinions on this point. The first opinion insists that then it is against the substance, and the marriage is invalid, for this condition *eo ipso* takes away the *jus* and the obligation of justice to render the *debitum*, for it begets a contrary obligation in justice not to seek or render. This is based on several fundamental misunderstandings, for the proponents deny it is a valid distinction to say this condition *per se* concerns only the *exercise*, not the *jus radicale* to the *copula*, for the *jus ad copula* is precisely the very use, they insist, and this very use is taken away by the condition, as happens in *res fungibiles* and in servitudes. Let us first note that the one placing the condition of chastity *may mean* internally to exclude the *jus radicale*, but *per se* it is not necessary for one to do so because of this condition. It is not mutually exclusive to, *e. g.*, be a true wife and to be bound by this vow or condition and a marriage with a third is invalid because of the bond of *ligamen.* The truth is the distinction beween the *jus* and *usus juris* is valid and true and traditional

[94] *Cf.* De Smet, *De Sponsalibus et Matrimonio*, n. 156; Wernz-Vidal, *Jus Matrimoniale*, n. 521 s, Cappello, *De Matrimonio*, n. 635 s; Vlaming, *Pralectiones Juris Matrimonii*, n. 546. Some heretics, *e. g.*, Wicleffus, Pelagianus, and the Centuriatores said that vows and conditions like these invalidate the marriage. The Salmanticenses also maintain the same. *Cursus Theologicae Moralis*, tr. IX, *de matr.*, c. VII, dub. III, n. 95.

and there are innumerable cases of the Rota and other Congregations where this distinction is invoked by the learned judges as valid for the *bonum fidei et prolis*. The reference to servitudes is unfortunate, for Roman Law does not bear these writers out. For by Roman [95] and modern laws a servitude or an easement is an incorporeal right distinct from the ownership of the soil, *e. g.*, as to running water or free air. One may have a right of way (*e. g.*, to walk, or to drive animals, etc.) over another's property. Now this right is a right of using (independent *per se* of the owner of the land; he may combine it with his property right or another may have it). This right is not ownership of property. But the possessor of this right may agree (or unilaterally decide) with the owner of the possessor of the property, for certain reasons, *e. g.*, sickness in the latter's house, not to use his right of using the other's property or possession by, *e. g.*, driving a team over it. He thereby does not *per se* nor *per accidens* lose his *jus ad fundum*, or his right of servitude.

The second opinion teaches if the condition over and beyond the natural logical intent and connotation of the words used, means in his mind, to avoid children as a *right* by a *positive* and *illicit* way (some kind of *copula* having been had), then the marriage is invalid. It is not invalid to avoid children by a negative licit way, *e. g.*, by voluntary mutual abstinence, for the essence of the marriage is *mutua traditio et acceptatio* of the bodies for acts *per se apta* for generation, and with this dominion or *right* of use, or *right* to use, there can exist alongside the obligation (on several heads) of not actually using the bodies for this end, since the actual use is separable from direct dominion.[96] For instance, a true husband has the radical right to the *copula*, but other obligations and rights of the wife and even of third parties may, and do prohibit him using the right, *e. g.*, in certain stages of pregnancy, certain advanced illnesses, extreme poverty when the children already born are in dire need, when a third party accidentally would witness the use of this right, etc. It is

[95] *Inst.*, pr. I, *de serv praed.* 2, 3.

[96] The *dominum* of a husband over the body of his wife is not the same kind of dominion which, *e. g.*, a farmer has over his own field or watch. This latter is *dominium reale*. The former is rather like a servitude which is not *realis*.

foolish to say he hereby loses the rights of a husband, and equally foolish to identify the *jus* with the actual use or the *usus juris*. If the two were identical, then when the newlyweds stepped from the alter after the celebration of marriage, they would not yet be man and wife, which is absurd.

If one wishes to follow Cardinal Gasparri's interpretation[97] ". . . suppressa exceptione pro parte quae votum castitatis emiserat," of Canon 1111, all these vows would be irrelevant, even if the content of the condition was the vow content, for though the condition be verified, its substance (the vow) would *eo ipso* remain inoperative from the moment of marriage. In one sense, this opinion that all vows are thus suspended by law at the moment of marriage, does not touch our question, for the post-matrimonial viewpoint is considered, but from another viewpoint it does, for the point at issue is, does this vow invalidate consent precisely because of its post-matrimonial relevance to the non-use of the rights of marriage.

A marriage with a condition by which one was bound to enter religion was decided by the S. C. Council.[98] Some of the conclusions of the Council are these. There can be a true marriage when a vow of virginity preceded, and the union of Mary and Joseph is referred to. Mary knowing by the Holy Ghost that Joseph would never use or seek, She gave over the "*jus ad copulam conjugalem,* quod ad substantiam matrimonii satis fuit, et non consenerit in usum juris illius, quem sibi voto castitatis interdixerat. . ." Another important conclusion is this:

> Et recepta quoque inter Theologos est sententia, matrimonium esse validum, etiamsi contrahatur post conventionem initam abstinendi a quolibet actu conjugali, cum dominium distinguatur ab usu, et verum dominium subsistere valeat cum obligatione seu conditione non utendi re ipsa uti caeteris allegatis. . .
>
> Alii e contra censent validum esse matrimonii contractum sub conditione, quod alter ex conjugibus se obliget ad professionem in Religione emittendam, ex quo conditio haec

[97] But the writer does not agree with Gasparri's opinion, the reasons being those marshalled by Father Lopez. *Cf.* Gasparri, *De Matr.* (1932), n. 429 s., *cf. Periodica,* XXII, 1933, p. 147.

[98] 16 March, 1720, Ulixbonen—*Fontes,* n. 3201.

> non repugnat substantiam matrimonii, quia non repugnat proli: contrahentes etenim non se obligant ad impediendam prolem per media illicita; non fidei, quia contrahentes non se obligant ad communicandum corpus alieno; non indissolubilitati, cum matrimonium adhuc sit indissolubile, uti caeteris allegatis. . .

The above remarks were given, the Council said, to clarify the case and the decision was delayed till July 8, 1724,[99] to hear other witnesses. And the findings were these:

> Cumque pactum emissum ante matrimonium, ingrediendi videlicet Religionem . . . , abstinendi insuper ab usu et consummatione matrimonii *una cum renunciatione cuicumque juri, quod mulieri competere posset super corpore viri,* superaddita expressione . . . multa contra fidem, prolem et Sacramentum, ex hoc infertur ad nullitatem matrimonii. . .

Thus the decision said that from the facts shown, the marriage is null. This decision confirms our thesis of the valid distinction between the *jus* and the *usus juris* and especially does it confirm our insistence that the real inner meaning behind the words used, must be ascertained, for over and above the nature of the vow or condition, the mind may add the exclusion of the *jus radicale.* Videte facta! must ever be the norm to go by. In this case it was said the man had *copula,* but the decision outruled the contention that this *copula* inferred a recession from the vitiating condition. As is evident it could not, since the consent *ab initio* was not marital. Thus decided the Council. And moreover it made no difference said the Council that the condition was not added *in actu celebrationis.* Cardinal Gasparri [100] also refers to this case.

Cardinal Gasparri maintains the validity of this distinction, for the *conjux* loses the *moral* right to the body of the other, but not the *jus juridicum radicale,* in which marriage properly consists. Nor can one object that this right is useless, because he can never use it (morally). This is false, says Gasparri, for it excludes the right of

[99] *Fontes,* n. 3278.

[100] *De Matrimonio,* n. 882.

all others; intercourse with a third party is adultery, not fornication; by mutual consent the restriction can be taken away; one can not use marriage *vi voti;* it would be a sin not against chastity, but against the vow if the husband by force or use of fear obtains the *copula,* it would not be fornication but a sin against his word and a sacrilege. Thus is solved the fundamental argument of the other side.

A condition of seriously promising never to cohabit is not against the substance of marriage, and sometimes marriages of conscience with this tacit or expressed condition is permitted. Though there are some authors who teach the contrary.[101]

A marriage was accused before the court on the head of simulated or fictitious consent.[102] The man, it seems, was a libertine. But the decision while finding no proof of simulated consent, addresses itself to the testimony orally and in writing under oaths of many witnesses to the effect that the man before marriage said he had no intention of cohabiting with the girl, but rather of deserting her. The decision continues (p. 519):

> Docent enim auctores intentionem contrahendi componi posse cum intentione non se obligandi, et juxta plures magnae auctoritatis doctores, invalidum esse matrimonium tali animo contractum. D'Annib. vol. 2, n. 402; Gasparri, vol. 2, n. 919.

Then a quotation is given from Gasparri.

An *intention* contrary to the *bonum fidei vel prolis* (the decision continues) unlike one against the *sacramentum,* does not invalidate marriage "nisi in pactum deducta fuerit." (This phrase is used here in the substantial, not the accidental sense.) "Deducere aliquam conditionem in pactum matrimoniale nihil aliud significat quam facere talem conditionem partem constitutivam contractus matrimonialis." This requires (unlike an intention against the *sacrament*) a special act of the will, by which not only is the intention against the *bonum fidei vel prolis* positively willed, but also that this act of the

[101] *Cf.* Gasparri, *De Matrimonio,* I (1904), n. 7, n. 1013; who favors validity.

[102] S. R. Rota, *causa Oregonopolitana,* 6 July, 1914, *AAS,* VI (1914), pp. 516-524.

will prevails over the general intention of marrying validly. Then the decision explains the valid distinction between the assumption of the essential obligation and its fulfillment, or execution. Sanchez says these intentions (examples of Gregory IX) generally are to be interpreted as referring to the fulfillment only.

> Si vir, itaque, intendit reapse matrimonialem contractum, *i. e.*, vinculum indissolubile, et simul intendit certis in adjunctis uxorem abjicere et alteri mulieri adhaerere, contra bonum fidei seu fidelitatis directe peccat (Sanchez) vinculum intactum manet; si vero dicatur ipsum sibi reservare potestatem in certis adjunctis uxorem abjiciendi et vinculum ipsum violandi, jam non amplius intendit vinculum indissolubile contrahere, seu jus perpetuum et exclusivum tradere—acceptare: hi duo actus voluntatis, nimirum, ex seipsis se mutuo excludunt, quia non solum contrarii sunt, sed contrarii circa idem objectum; per unum scilicet intenditur vinculum indissolubile, per alium idem vinculum indissolubile excluditur.

But (the decision goes on to say) it cannot be denied and pontifical documents and grave authors declare that a condition to break the marriage because of adultery or other causes, does not vitiate the contract "nisi in pactum deducta fuerit." But all these refer to cases where one contracts with concomitant error about the indissolubility of marriage, in one case without any positive act of the will excluding it, and in the other, of a positive act of the will intending only a soluble bond.

Now an intention "deducta in pactum" of breaking the marriage *eo ipso* is positively intended and *eo ipso* it becomes a constitutive part of the contract, not however an intention of contracting with a condition "contra bonum fidei vel prolis, quia etiamsi haec conditio positive intendatur, non eo ipso est pars constitutiva contractus; intendi enim potest ita ut coexistat cum intentione contrahendi verum matrimonium, videlicet si conditio ista respuat tantummodo adimplementum obligationis assumptae." In other words, only if the intention *excludes* the *essential* obligation of the *bonum fidei* or *bonum prolis,* and is put into a condition does it become a constitutive part of the contract. But without it being made into a *condition* it becomes a *constitutive* part of the act of the *will* and it invalidates also in this case.[103]

From the evidence offered the decision draws the conclusion that the man's intention to desert his wife only meant that he did not intend to fulfill his duties, and therefore it is not proved that the marriage is invalid.

Some practical conclusions resulting from our discussion are these: "Licite et (valide) contrahitur in remedium concupiscentiae, nihil aliud intendo, modo proles positive non impediatur." "Valide et licite contrahi potest cum pacto continentiae, sine intentione prolis et remedii concupiscentiae." [104] A condition whose content is to take a vow of perpetual chastity, is not *per se* against the substance of marriage, for of its nature it does not exclude the *jus justitiae ad copulam,* though by the vow the party intends to add the obligation of religion not to seek or render the *debitum.* Many holy couples and saints have done precisely this.[105] Even a so-called honest condition to avoid children invalidates when the *jus radicale* is withheld.[106] The *jus radicale* may also be designated as "nudum domnium." [107] The pact that obliges one of the parties not to demand the *debitum* is not against the *bonum prolis,* which can be generated by *giving.* But if the party has no *radical* right to demand, the consent is invalid.

The pact obliging one or both *not to give* the *debitum* invalidates if the parties excluded or did not receive the *radical* right to *demand,* otherwise the pact is not against the substance.

A condition "provided we observe chastity for one month, or one year, on every Friday, after the first or second child, etc." invalidates if it excludes the *jus radicale* for those periods. If the condition intends only the *exercise* of the radical right (*salvo jure ipso*) then all these cases do not invalidate. The marriage is valid, if the parties agree to the condition. Of course if the conditions [108] mean that "we

[103] *Cf.* Canon 1086, par. 2.

[104] St. Alphonsus, *Theol. Moralis,* lib. VI, tract VI, n. 880.

[105] *Cf.* Bayon, *De Matrimonio,* p. 311; Wernz-Vidal, *Jus Matrimoniale,* n. 521; Cappello, *De Matrimonio,* n. 635; Chelodi, *Jus Matrimoniale,* n. 125.

[106] *Cf. causa rel. Ulyssipon.* July 8, 1724.

[107] Ballerini-Palmieri, *Opus Theol. Moralis,* Vol. VI, *de matr.,* resol. 28.

[108] Vlaming, *Praelectiones Juris Matrimonii,* n. 547; Gasparri, *De Matrimonio,* n. 882.

actually (not only promise to) observe chastity during those periods," and even if the radical right is given, the consent and marriage is invalid for in this case the conditions are resolutive. In spite of denials, this distinction, says Gasparri, is true and valid: "inter exercitium juris et jus exercendi." [100] The conditions which we discuss here in this section, *per se* mean that an obligation (*ex capite alieno*) is contracted *non utendi jure tradito.* In other words, it is sufficient to give the *jus remotum et radicale* to beget children, but it is not necessary for the essence to give the *jus proximum et expeditum.* For instance a minor may truly acquire the *dominium* of marriage, but in certain cases not the *jus expeditum.*

In a marriage case before the S. C. of the Council [110] the man had already a vow of chastity before his marriage, and he placed a condition to live as brother and sister. The girl agreed, but shortly after she petitioned nullity on the head of impotency which she suspected. The "votum theologi" maintained that the marriage because of the vow was doubtfully valid, yes absolutely invalid, quoting Wernz.[111] But the *defensor vinculi* strongly objected saying after outlining the facts and the law: "Ex quo patet decantatam castitatis conditionem in matrimonio observandae haud respicere perpetuam abdicationem usus matrimonii, minusque vero attingere radicale jus utenti matrimonio." The Congregation gave a dispensation *super matrimonio rato tantum in casu.* Of course even pious people may mean by the condition to exclude the radical right, and then there is no marriage, but this exclusion is not to be presumed but proven.

If the condition is unknown or unagreed to by the other party, this *per se* has nothing to do with the validity of the consent, but in such cases the transaction is illicit and gravely so.

In maintaining that even the radical right can be excluded and still there is a marriage, some have said this right and obligation to the *copula* is not of the substance of marriage, since *consent alone*

[100] *Ad rem,* Benedict XIV, *De Syn,* XXIII, 22: "Matrimonii substantiae non repugnat matrimonio *non uti* sed *uti non posse.*" The *jus exercendi* is also called: jus utendi, seu jus radicale vel nudum, seu jus in principiis suis, seu jus remotum.

[110] 24 February, 1894, *causa Varsavien; ASS,* XXVII, pp. 18-32.

[111] *Jus Decretalium,* IV (1890), p. 257.

makes marriage. The reply is: Consent to *what?* If the consent has no need of being directed to certain objects or ends, then two small children, two perpetually insane, two already married, two males even can pronounce the material words and become married. The very reason why some consents are impeded by the law of nature from effecting marriage, is precisely because by that law the consent must be given by persons who can give certain things for specific determined objective essential ends (*tria bona*). Cardinal Gasparri's theory about consent in relation to natural impediments does not draw these conclusions, but his logic seems to lead to such conclusions.[112]

Another conclusion is this. It is true that the actual intercourse can not be demanded nor given if the condition binds both to a vow or to absention. It is true it cannot, *vi voti, vi conditionis;* but it is false, if it is meant they cannot *vi matrimonii.* Also for other moral reasons it cannot be demanded, *e. g.*, on account of insanity, illness, scandal, etc. The content of the condition has *per se* no reference to the substance of marriage, it simply means one or both is bound by his word or by vow to God not to use marriage.

A condition that frees from the obligation *reddendi* or the right *petendi vi matrimonii,* according to all, invalidates. A condition that obligates one not to seek or to give *vi voti* or *vi promissionis* (not *vi matrimonii*) is not contrary to the substance of marriage, for the essentials of the *bona prolis et fidei* are present and safeguarded.

The *jus radicale* and the force of the condition, or the vow, can stand together. By means of the condition the one from whom the *debitum* is sought (*vi matrimonii*) acquires a right (*vi promissionis alterius*) of repelling the petitioner, which right was obtained at the time of the contract. The one vowing by the condition, means you

[112] It is an invalid conclusion that just because the Church *does not grant* a *sanatio in radice* in cases where the impediment was, *e. g.*, a perpetual natural law one, that the Church *can grant* such a *sanatio.* The Holy Office once *ex professo* asserted the Church *could not do so.* Marriage effecting consent is the actual *traditio* of the perpetual, exclusive right in the body for the acts ordained for the generation of offspring (Canon 1081, par. 2). An impotent man cannot have this marriage effecting consent, no matter how vehemently his will works. *Cf.* Gasparri, *De Matrimonio* (1932), n. 813; n. 1215 s.

have the rights of a husband, but you voluntarily promised not to use it. If it was unknown to the husband, on learning it he could validly do away with the force of the vow, always presupposing as a fact, as the Church did, that he is the husband. If he agrees to the condition, he has a radical but not a moral right in view of the mutual agreement.[113] The promise or vow of chastity, the content of the condition, *per se* is to abstain, not to use. It does not exclude the possibility of giving the radical right and therefore true efficacious consent. The one who vows does not give God dominion over her body by the vow, she only promises not to have intercourse *vi voti,* to which both have a right *vi vinculi matrimonialis.*

These conditions are valid ones. "I marry you on condition that I intend never to seek the *debitum;*" "That I render only when asked;" "If you promise to deny me the *debitum* as often as I seek it illicitly." The condition to never cohabit may be valid or destructive, depending on its connotation in the given case. It is valid if the *bonum fidei* and the *bonum prolis* are not excluded. Otherwise it invalidates. The condition to beget children not by right of having the proper *copula,* but only by artificial insemination of the sperm from the putative husband or selected men, invalidates the consent, for the *jus ad actus etc.* is excluded.

If in the various examples of conditions given in this discussion the meaning is not "that you *now promise* etc.", but, "on condition that you *never actually exercise* your right," then the conditions would invalidate the consent. For they would be either future suspensive, which could never be verified till death, because up to this time it is in the power of the other to exercise his right; or the conditions are resolutive, because at any moment in the future if the actual intercourse took place, that fact would resolve the contract, but marriage being indissoluble *ex parte contrahentium,* can not have such conditions added to marital consent.[114]

Finally the following words will be useful for confessors and others:

[113] *Cf.* De Smet, *De Sponsalibus et Matrimonio,* n. 155; *cf.* Rett, "Die Josephsehe"—*Zeitschr. f.k.Theol.* (1909), p. 590 s.

[114] Bonacina, *Opera Omnia,* qu. 2, punct. X, prop. II.

> Novit scilicet A. T. quod si dubium aliquod deprehendatur in alicujus matrimonio circa validitatem, atque ille in bona fide sit, et communi judicio verus conjux existimetur, non possit autem idem moneri absque gravi aliquo periculo, communis doctrina est, silendum esse, illumque in bona fide reliquendum, neque proinde a sacramentis esse removendum.[115]

The so-called marriage of St. Joseph (Josephsehe) is marriage entered into after the example of St. Joseph and Mary, namely with the vow of perpetual and perfect chastity, mutually taken. It may be observed here, however, that it is not certain about the marriage of Joseph and Mary, whether it was a marriage *qua* marriage, or whether there was a condition, or a vow, or a purpose made, etc. In order that these marriages may be entered into, these must be present: (a) the vow must be taken by mutual consent; (b) have the will of contracting a true valid marriage, that is of acquiring and giving all the essential rights, especially the right to intercourse; (c) the promise to forever cede the use of this right acquired through marriage; (d) moral certitude that the danger of violating the vow is excluded. Conditions a, c, and d, are for liceity only.[116]

[115] Holy Office, 9 December, 1874, in Instruction to the bishop of St. Alberta—*Fontes,* n. 1036, p. 348.

[116] *Cf.* Noldin, *Summa theol. moral.,* 1914, p. 586; for a bibliography on "Josephsehen" consult Linneborn, *Grundriss des Eherechts,* 1919, p. 336; Gasparri, *De Matrimonio* (1932), n. 1011; H. Rett, "Die Josephsehe" apud *Ztsch. f. Kath. Theol.,* XXXII (1908), p. 590 s.; Nilles, "De matr. quod vulgo a S. Josepho muncupatur," apud *Act. Theol. Oenip.,* XXV, p. 763 s.; De Smet, *De Sponsalibus et Matrimonio,* n. 155.

CHAPTER XXV

CONDITIONS AGAINST THE BONUM FIDEI

THIS treasure, as far as it is essential to the consent, means the *jus et obligatio* of fidelity, which each party is bound to exhibit towards the other. This means not only the obligation to render the debt, if sought, but also there is no *right* to have intercourse with a third party. Essentially against this *bonum* are conditions by which this *obligation* is excluded, even the radical obligation to place conjugal acts *mutually,* or which impose an obligation or right to prostitute oneself to others whether for gain or not.[1]

Conjugal fidelity in its integrity demands these things of the married. During the life of both there can be no marriage with a third person, nor act of illegitimate affection for a third person; both must render the debt, both must live together in love and friendship.[2]

The intention or the condition against the inseparability of the bond must be clearly distinguished from that against fidelity; thus he who truly intends marriage, *i. e.*, an insoluble bond, and yet, *e. g.*, in certain circumstances intends to reject the woman and adhere to another sins against *fidelity,* but the marriage is valid. Yet it is difficult to see why this can not be called an abuse of the obligation flowing from the *bonum sacramenti.* The word abuse presupposes the existence of this indissoluble bond. But if one reserves to himself the *power* and *right* in certain contingencies of leaving the woman so that he is free from the *bond,* since he does not intend to contract an indissoluble bond, or *jus perpetuum et exclusivum tradere et acceptare,* his consent is essentially ill and invalid for the will of truly marrying is absent. This is essentially against the *bonum sacramenti.*[3] The *bonum fidei* has relations to a secondary end of marriage, but it promotes much the primary end and the remedial end.

[1] *Cf.* Schmalzgrueber, lib. IV, tit. V; *cf. S. C. C.* 2 May and 29 August, 1868, in *AAS,* IV, p. 65 s.; *Instr.* C. R., par. 53; Sanchez, *De Matr.,* lib. V, 12.

[2] Schmalzgrueber, lib. IV, tit. I.

[3] S. R. Rota, 6 July, 1914, *AAS, VI* (1914), 516; Gougnard, *De Matrimonio,* p. 164; Wernz-Vidal, *Jus Matrimoniale,* n. 462.

The *bonum fidei seu fidelitatis* (the blessing of mutual fidelity) belongs to every marriage. This good refers to that secondary end of marriage that is called by the Code (Canon 1013, par. 1) "mutuum adjutorium et remedium concupiscentiae." Specifically it refers more especially to the mutual help, the primary end takes especial care of the remedial end. But all three blessings are different aspects of the one thing, marriage. The three blessings react strongly on each other and invests them with a new excellence. This mutual fidelity of man and wife is not motivated by self-interest, but has in view the spiritual good and the eternal reward of each partner.

God's law of nature and the Church Law do not overlook the realities of human passion and thus the office of marriage is divinely shaped also to this fact.

The blessing of mutual fidelity is based on that essential character of marriage, its unity.

Cappello [4] in speaking of conditions against marital fidelity, says strangely that these conditions are against the substance of marriage "dummodo proprietas essentialis, *i. e.*, unitas vere excludatur, et *non sola obligatio* eam servandi." The exclusion of the *obligation eo ipso* is the exclusion of the *unitas,* and even if the two things are not identical *in re,* numerous decisions of the Roman Curia, some of which were quoted in the section on the *bonum prolis,* insist that if the *obligation* of any of the three *bona* are not assumed the consent is substantially vitiated.

These conditions are certainly invalidating: "I marry you, provided I am allowed to take other wives *qua* wives (and as a right);" "provided it is my right to have relations with other women;" "provided you as a right prostitute your body for lustful gain or no gain;" therefore not only a condition of polygamy and polyandry is essentially contrary to the *bonum fidei,* but also is adultery, as a right reserved, for though it does not exclude the *debitum* with the true wife, it does exclude *exclusivum debitum,* and is therefore invalidating. To *de facto* commit adultery is *per se* not against the essence of this treasure, only its integrity, but it is of the essence that one *obliges* himself by this *fides* not to commit this crime. In a word, the fulfill-

[4] *De Matrimonio,* n. 632.

ment does not pertain to the essence, the obligation of the fidelity does.[5]

The condition to cede the right of intercourse to a third party, invalidates the consent because it is against the essential obligation of the the *bonum fidei.*[6] A condition to concede the radical right to the other, or to reserve it to onself to be an adulterer, invalidates, for it is against the unity and the *bonum fidei* of marriage.[7]

A mere intention against this obligation effects nothing on the consent. Even though the party or parties do not think at all about this obligation, nor expressly oblige themselves to this duty, or even though they know nothing about it, in all these instances the consent is essentially healthy. To vitally affect the marital consent there must be an act of the will or a condition positively excluding the radical right and duty of this treasure.

All the principles and their applications that were noted in regards to the *bonum prolis,* apply equally to the *bonum fidei.* The distinctions between the *jus* and the *usus juris,* and the *abusus juris* are applicable here also. What was said about ignorance, *error juris,* and a simple intention, and a condition "deducta in pactum" as these concerned the *bonum prolis* also apply to this essential of marital consent.

That error *per se* invalidate a marriage, it would be required that at least one party conceive, *e. g.*, that a plurality of wives, or a soluble bond is an essential property of marriage, in such a way that this error nourishes the persuasion that the marital contract otherwise could not exist.[8] It seems it is quite difficult to prove the presence of a condition that is against the substantial obligation of the *bonum fidei.* Certain missionaries and their bishop were quite convinced that the pagans in their district had no conception of a true marriage, and the abuse was ingrained by custom to marry or take a wife for an experiment and on condition that she proved herself capable of

[5] Bayon, *De Matrimonio,* p. 314; Sanchez, *De Matrimonio,* lib. 5, disp. 9, n. 11.

[6] De Smet, *De Sponsalibus et Matrimonio,* n. 155.

[7] *Cf.* Noldin, *Summa Theologiae Moralis* (1914), p. 578; De Smet, *De Sponsalibus et Matrimonio,* n. 155.

[8] Vromant, *Jus Missionariorum,* n. 179; Michel, *Le mariage,* n. 23, pp. 23 s.

household duties and be peaceable, etc. If after a time the man was dissatisfied he put her forth and tried another. There were many other customs about marriage that convinced the missionaries that the marriages were invalid. Much of this error and the resulting practical condition concerned themselves with the *bonum fidei.* Nevertheless the Cardinals of the Inquisition gave the subject deep study and from the facts furnished by the priests in the field they concluded the evidence did not prove substantially defective consent. It was admitted that in a given case the consent may be vitiated, but each case must be studied individually. *Videte facta!* [9]

[9] *Cf.* S. C. S. Off., Instr. (ad Ep. S. Alberti), 9 December, 1874—*Fontes,* n. 1036, pp. 343-354

CHAPTER XXVI

PAST AND PRESENT CONDITIONS AGAINST THE SUBSTANCE OF MARRIAGE

THE difficulty concerning past and present conditions against the substance is twofold: first, in what sense against the substance, against the very assumption of marriage or its essential qualities and obligations, or against the actual carrying out of these assumed obligations (against the substance in this wide, inaccurate, unessential meaning); and the other difficulty is, can a past or present *condition* in either sense *vitiate* the consent, and *can* a past or present condition, be against the substance in the strict and only true meaning of the phrase?

Let it be noted, before giving a categorical answer to these queries, that the discussion concerns a *condition* which is a circumstance on which the marital consent is voluntarily made dependent for its marriage-producing effect. The marital consent, fully healthy and containing no essential illness or defect, is bound up for its effect, to the truth of the condition.

It can be stated immediately that it is, strictly speaking, incorrect to speak of such past or present conditions as "against the substance" in the strict sense, and even in the wide sense.

As usual, in the past, many, and to-day, some, say these past and present conditions (without distinguishing) invalidate marriage. Sanchez, Petrus de Ledesma and others deny this. Some of the arguments are: Gregory IX speaks of *true* conditions, *i. e., de futuro;* one or both parties may intend to commit adultery, become sterile, etc., but this does not touch the essence of marriage *per se,* they only oblige themselves "sic faciendum"; such conditions contain things only against the execution, not the obligations of the three goods of marriage. Other authors even today reject these past and present as not placed. But it is certain they are *not* rejected, and the marriage depends (if they were seriously placed, and since they are conditions) on the truth or not of their being fulfilled *hic et nunc* or in the past.[1]

[1] Sanchez, lib. V; disp. IX, n. 6 s.

Sanchez admits one exception, namely when a condition of this kind would so touch and effect the marriage in the future, *e. g.*, "I marry you if you have gotten or have poison to use in marriage in future to become sterile," for then the obligation amounts to obliging oneself in the future, and therefore the marriage is invalid. Sanchez conclusion is correct, that these additions are not against the substance, but he goes on to give restrictive interpretations of the conclusion. But really what these amount to is that though it is a past or present condition in words, it may have been in the mind a future condition against the substance.[2]

For a condition which does not lead to sin nor impose an *obligation* contrary to the substantial treasures of marriage, is not properly against the substance of the marriage contract, since nothing, in fact, is excluded by the consent from the *substantial object* of *marriage.*

Moreover a past or present immoral condition, which *before* the celebration of marriage is *supposed* as a *fact* already *completed* and *preceding,* does not induce to sin nor *impose* any bond of iniquity. For instance, if the man says "I marry you, if you have taken poison of sterility," or, "if you have had both ovaries removed." But there is an absolute difference between those formulas and this one: "Provided you will take poison of sterility, or will have both ovaries removed."[3]

Past or present conditions of no species are rejected by law whether they be immoral, impossible, necessary, or so-called ones "against the substance." The *only* conditions that vitiate consent are those mentioned in number 2 of Canon 1092. "Conditio semel apposita et non revocata, si de futuro contra matrimonii substantiam, illud reddit invalidum." And the only legislation about past and present conditions is that in number 4 of Canon 1092: "Si de prae-

[2] One author of to-day, maintains erroneously that "present and past conditions are *resolutive,*" because "they make or void the contract as the condition is objectively verified or not." His use of the word "resolutive" is not proper. This word means the transaction is at once effective, and later on, is dissolved. Nau, *Manual on the Marriage Laws* (1933), n. 110.

[3] *Cf.* Sanchez, *De Matrimonio,* lib. IV, disp. IX, n. 6; Schmalzgrueber, lib. IV, tit. XIX, n. 115; Reiffenstuel, lib. IV, tit. I, n. 40; Wernz, *Jus Decretalium,* lib. IV, n. 302. *Cf.* S. C. S. Off., 31 July, 1895—*Fontes,* n. 1174. This response permits a girl who had her ovaries removed, to marry.

terito vel de praesenti, matrimonium erit validum vel non, prout id quod conditioni subest, exsistit vel non."

Every kind of condition provided it is past or present is governed by Canon 1092, n. 4. It is necessary that the condition be truly and properly a past or present one. It would not be truly and properly past or present if it would *substantially affect* the marriage in the future, *e. g.*, "I marry you, if you *have procured* condoms to use in the *future* as a *right* in our marital relations." But outside of this case, past and present conditions "et si specie contra substantiam matrimonii illud non reddit invalidum, si sit impleta. Re seu *proprie* haec condicio non est contra substantiam matrimonii."[4] The prescriptions of Canon 1092, n. 2, are *not to be extended* to true conditions of the past or present which do not touch marriage in the future or are not reducible into an obligatory essential condition *de futuro.*

Some believe from Canon 1092, n. 4, that neither impossible or immoral past or present is rejected by presumption. Cappello says they are, when it is doubtful what the mind of the parties were. Chelodi denies this. The only conditions that vitate the consent are, according to Canon 1092, n. 2, future ones which contradict the substance of marriage.[5] Vlaming says past and present conditions against the substance do not invalidate for Canon 1092, nn. 1 and 2 are about future conditions that are qualified, *e. g.*, necessary, impossible, *turpis*, and *turpis* against the substance, but Canon 1092, n. 4, omits these qualifications entirely. Therefore, he says it seems the old controversy is settled.

Cardinal Gasparri[6] says truly "*quaevis* conditio de praesenti vel de praeterito revera non suspendit consensum; sed hic habetur, ideoque matrimonium statim valet ab initio, si conditio exsistit; non habetur ideoque matrimonium est ab initio nullum, si conditio non exsistit, licet apud nos adhuc incertum sit (rel. Canon 1092, n. 4)." "Si conditio est *turpis* et *verificata* conjugium valet; si non est verificata, non valet, dummodo serio apposita fuerit."[7] Certain com-

[4] *Cf.* Payen, *De Matrimonio,* II, n. 173; Sanchez, *De Matrimonio,* lib. 5, disp. 9, n. 6.

[5] Vlaming, *Praelectiones Juris Canonici,* n. 543.

[6] *De Matrimonio* (1932), n. 921 s.

[7] Cappello, *De Matrimonio,* n. 642.

mentators of the Code[8] say that the principle "de turpi conditione verificata," is valid when the condition is "contra substantiam." This is true, except that as stated above, that condition is not "contra substantiam." Chelodi, of course, say these conditions never invalidate, and he says Aichner[9] is wrong in maintaining they do.

Some conclusions may be stated. Past or present immoral conditions having a reference to the *tria bona* in a wide sense (they cannot *per se* touch these *tria bona* or marriage itself, in the strict sense), do not *induce* to sin, nor impose an immoral obligation, nor invalidate the consent because of being contrary to the substance, etc., of marriage. The marriage may be invalid, but only because the condition is unverified. *E. g.*, "I marry you, if you *had* both ovaries removed, or if they *are* removed." "If you have had relations with so and so, or are *now* his mistress;" "If you now are engaged in prostitution, or were so engaged." Nothing of the substantial object of marriage is excluded by non-future conditions.[10] Such conditions as these invalidate. "If you avoid offspring by wasting the seed;" "if you abort for ten years." If the *actual avoiding* in the future is meant, the condition is resolutive. If the meaning is: If you *promise seriously* to do these things as a *right,* the marriage also is invalid. Strictly speaking in this last case the condition is not a *present* one, though the tense used is present, "promise now," but the promise is subsequent or future to the act of the will of the one placing the condition, and the marriage is invalid, not because of the condition (for she may promise seriously and thus verify the condition, yet the marriage is invalid) but because the external words of the so-called condition really denote an inner will that is essentially defective by lacking an essential. The marriage is invalid and the consent too, not in virtue of Canon 1092, but in virtue of the natural law as defined by Canon 1086, par. 2.[11]

[8] *E. g.*, Chelodi, *Jus Matrimoniale,* n. 127.

[9] *Compendium Juris Eccl.* n. 169, 2.

[10] *Cf.* Lugo, *Theologia Moralis,* n. 361, n. 377; Pichler, *Condidatus Juris Prud.,* nn. 10, 12.

[11] *Cf.* Reiffenstuel, lib. IV, tit. I, n. 40. In the pages following, when I speak of such a condition as "if you promise now" as a present, it is meant as present in expression and tense but with a future connotation or implication, as above.

It is true a *present* condition, strictly must be verified or not simultaneously with the act of the will, *e. g.*, "if you are a virgin," but in the examples used above the condition is "to promise now" which is *to be done,* therefore strictly future. A strict *past* condition does not offer the same difficulty, *e. g.*, "If your father died five years ago." But this condition also: "If you have promised a week ago, or resolved a week ago, to abort for ten years after marriage as a right" even then strictly this condition *per se* does not touch the substance of the marital consent because the marital consent did not yet exist to be vitiated. It is true the promise of a week ago refers to the abuse of marriage, but of a future marriage, but it is equally true that no marital consent *per se* is affected by this promise in the past. The role of a *condition* is to make the now present consent depend for its marriage-producing effect, on the truth of the condition. "If you promised or resolved a week or ten years ago to abuse marriage as a right." If the promise or resolution was made, the past condition was fulfilled and the consent is absolute as soon as made, for the condition really is: "If you promised or resolved ten years ago, etc., then I give absolute consent now to be your husband." In spite of this past resolve, there is no reason whatever to believe that the parties cannot and do not now give marital consent that is essentially healthy. As said above, it is absolutely a different result, if the condition is "If you promise now to abuse, as a right, marriage and its essential obligations."

Suppose the conditions were: "If you have in the past killed your children" or "if you have in the past resolved to kill the children already born of you, as a right," such conditions as is evident, do not affect the marital consent of this marriage.

It is quite *possible* to argue from a condition referring to a situation belonging to the *past,* to an intention of the parties against the substance of marriage in the wide sense of an abuse of the essential obligations, and then the consent is valid, if the condition is verified. (Even if unverified it is equally possible to argue to the present intention of the one placing the condition).

It is also quite possible to argue from a condition referring to a situation belonging to the *past,* to a present intention of the parties against the substance in the strict essential sense, but in this case if the consent is essentially defective, it is not because of the *truth* of the past situation, but because *hic et nunc* the consent (independently of the past event and its fulfillment or not) is essentially vitiated by a positive act of the will that exists now, which act excludes now something essential. The condition, as far as it affects the marital consent, refers only to the truth or not of the past event, not to its content. An intention or a condition must actually enter into the marital consent, as a constituent element to touch the substance.

Past happenings are only facts on whose truth of fact the consent depends for efficacy. The past event *content* is willed in a way, but only *to have happened,* but it (the content) is not willed as a part of the marital consent, and thus the consent is not vitiated, but valid and it is dependent for its efficacy on the truth of the past event, just like an honest past condition.

Even a condition referring to a situation in the past, predicated upon simply destroying marriage or leaving it uninfluenced, leaves the future marriage untouched as far as the contents of the condition are concerned. To say otherwise is to ignore the universal legal principle of which the chapter of Gregory IX, "Si Conditiones," is a corollary, and to this universal principle a quite singular incoherent import is fictioned to it, imagined to it, the scope of which is defined, stencil like, without entering upon the actual crux of the matter. The facts are left out. It is not correct to take such conditions as "I marry you if you now observe chastity;" "if you have preserved virginity," and clothe them with a destructive vitiating effect that arises if the past or present condition exerts an influence upon the future marriage. But here again the truth is veiled and the facts left out.

CHAPTER XXVII

ENGAGEMENTS AND SO-CALLED CONDITIONS AGAINST THE SUBSTANCE

Not only matrimonial consent but also the promise of marriage can be qualified by conditions. Are engagements (*sponsalia de futuro*) invalid under so called conditions against the substance or the *tria bona* of marriage? First of all, they *per se* can not touch the *marriage* or the matrimonial consent from the nature of the case.

Some say, if the condition is so placed, that after the marriage, its fulfillment is against the *tria bona,* then the *engagement* is invalid. If fulfilled before marriage, one must see to what *bonum* it is opposed. If, *e. g.*, it is against inseparability, *e. g.*, "I will marry you, unless before our marriage I find a richer girl," it does not invalidate either the engagement or marriage, for engagements are by nature soluble and they can be contracted with a resolutive condition.

If the engagement condition is against the *bonum fidei, e. g.*, "if you fornicate before marriage," neither the *engagement* is invalid, for it is simply an immoral condition, but being future it suspends; nor is *marriage* invalidated, for the *fides* of marriage arises only after the *jus radicale est traditum.*

If it is against the *bonum prolis, e. g.*, to take medicine of sterility, then marriage and the *sponsalia* are invalid, according to some, for by it the other is obliged to do something against the *bonum prolis,* which *bonum* is promised by marriage, thus it is against the *promised* marriage. But it is better to distinguish, if it means to take steps *before* marriage to become sterile, then both are valid. If it means to promise *now* to take these steps *after* marriage, the engagement is valid if the condition is fulfilled and the marriage is valid, for the condition bound the *engagement* consent, not the *marital* which does not yet exist.

CHAPTER XXVIII

OTHER ADDITIONS TO A CONTRACT

Article I

Modes

Authors treat the *modus* here, because it is similar to a condition. "Modus est adjectio oneris, ad quod post contractum volumus obligare alterum contrahentem." This is regularly indicated by the conjunctive clause, "in order that" (*ut*). A condition can impose an obligation also (*e. g.*, potestative condition) yet this does not suppose a perfect absolute contract, but is a part of the essence of the contract, while the mode is added to a contract already in existence, *e. g.*, "I marry you in order that you will live in my country."

A mode is an accessory and supervenient clause added to an already perfect act, as if persons would agree to contract marriage, and then add that they will not fulfill some of its obligations. A mode *qua* mode *per se* does not become a condition, for the latter suspends the effect of the act till verification; till then no absolute act or obligation arises. With a mode, the act arises immediately with all its effects, even though the mode is not yet fulfilled.

A mode whether possible or impossible, honest or immoral, does not suspend or vitiate the consent or the contract. The immoral and impossible ones are rejected, *e. g.*, "I marry you in order that you help me to kill that person." The possible and honest *modus* begets an obligation of fulfilling that which is the content of the *modus, e. g.*, to live in my country. The modus, is *per se* added to an *already completed act*, thus it has no influence on the validity of the contract,[1] for the consent is not dependent on this (it presupposes a perfect absolute consent) as it depends on a condition.

So-called modes "against the substance of marriage," do not invalidate the union, as is evident.[2] Reiffenstuel refutes Sanchez who

[1] Reiffenstuel, lib. III, tit, XXVI, n. 63.

[2] Sanchez, *De Matrimonio,* lib. V, disp. 19, n. 5; Pirhing, *Universum Jus Canonicum,* lib. III, tit. 9, n. 30.

says the marriage is invalid. It is understood that a *modus* is a *modus,* then there is *ex hypothesi* and *ex natura rei* no effect on the validity of the act. But one must be careful to note that on the one hand, even though the external words or phrases denote a *modus,* yet the person may internally mean it as a condition *sine qua non,* and carelessly or ignorantly *express* it as a *mode,* and on the other hand, what is expressed in the form of a condition may internally be meant as a mode. This is a question of fact, not of law; this observation is true also of the *causa* and *demonstratio,* and if a condition was really meant, then the principles of condition must be used.

Sometimes *in the mind* the addition that externally is expressed as a mode has the nature and force of a condition. To know when it is a mode or a condition one must explore the will of the party and see whether he wished the act to be *eo ipso* valid, or only when the addition is verified. Even an impossible mode does not *per se* affect the validity, *e. g.,* "I marry you in order that you give me a mountain of gold," this mode is rejected. If the mode is impossible by nature, by law, or in fact, then no obligation is induced. If the mode is honest and possible, *e. g.,* "I marry you in order that you live in my home," it obliges in conscience.

If the mode is as they say "against the substance of marriage" or the *tria bona,* what then, *e. g.,* "I marry you in order that you avoid generation;" "in order to find a richer girl." Many authors, *e. g.,* Sanchez, Laymanns, etc., say the union is invalid, for there is no serious will to marry in these cases. Schmalzgrueber says this opinion is probable, but as oft repeated it all depends whether this was the object of the will or not; if so it is an intention or a condition (not a mode) against the substance. Each case must be studied. The latter author says it is the more probable opinion such modes do not invalidate.[3] For from the nature of a mode and *ex hypothesi* the marriage is immediately valid for so it is willed, and anyhow this holds in the external forum which favors marriage. This kind of mode is not a condition *per se,* for consent is given *dependently* on a *condition,* and *independently* of a *mode,* nor is it bound to its existence, therefore there is no obex to the consent. Strictly viewed, it is there-

[3] Schmalzgrueber, lib. III, tit. XXVI, n. 143; Reiffenstuel, lib. III, tit. XXVI, n. 64.

fore incorrect to speak of modes as "against the substance of marriage," all that can be said is this kind of *modus* is contrary to the integrity of marriage obligations in their full bloom.

The mode may be added at the same temporal point of time as the act of marrying takes places, but in respect to the *will* it and its force and meaning, refers to after the marriage obligations are assumed. Bayon[4] says marriage is valid if the immoral mode is placed after the marriage, but invalid if placed before or during the celebration. This is not a valid distinction, because the mode no matter when placed, is by its nature added to an act *perfectly* willed by the parties.

Santi says if the mode is against the substance [which *per se* is impossible] it makes the consent and marriage null, saying the parties are rightly presumed not to wish a true genuine contract of marriage.[5] This, needless to say, is quite erroneous, probably from the example he gives he has in mind the observation made above ("donec inveniam aliam ditiorem"), is not a condition, but a mode, he says.

The modus (so-called against the substance) offers more room for doubt about the intention of the mind. Again *per se* a mode as mode does not affect the existence of the marriage, the latter is presupposed. But though the words used denote a mode, yet the party may mean it internally as a condition. This would cause doubt: "I marry you provided you become sterile," for the conjunction (*ut*) may be a final or a consecutive one. The mode as mode does not suspend but is added to the perfected act, the act is immediately perfected and absolute, and to it the mode is added as an obligation to be carried out in the future, *e. g.*, "I give you this horse (absolute giving) so that you use it thus." A mode does not pertain to the *nature* of the *contract*, but to the *intention* of the *contractor* directed to something else, *e. g.*, "I make this contract to become rich."

The great canonists of the past and present easily annihilate the weak arguments of those saying that the immoral mode has the same nature as a condition against the substance. Much of these lame arguments is based on the ill chosen examples given by Gregory IX; another base of errors is the misapplication of Roman Law principles about *usus* and *usufructus*. But Sanchez did not succeed in

[4] *De Matrimonio*, p. 320.

[5] *Prælectiones Juris Canonici* (1884), p. 111.

freeing himself from this entanglement, and he makes an invalid distinction to settle the difficulties, *i. e.*, if the mode was placed at the time of the contract or after it. This effects nothing. It can be made *ante, in* or *post*, but the fulfillment of the mode is generally in the future, unless it means the other is to seriously promise now to fulfil it in the future.

A mode *qua* mode can not be essentially against the substance, from the very nature of a mode, for it presupposes the substance of the act exists. Yet some authors, *e. g.*, Sanchez, Pirhing, Santi and De Angelis, identifying mode and condition insist the mode invalidates. Vidal agrees with these, for he claims in practice the obligation of the mode added to the marriage contract can be nothing else than a simulated condition *deducta in pactum*. What if it be not *deducta?* Theoretically he admits that a *verus modus* by its nature is added to an already perfected contract. Such reasoning destroys all truth, if a thing is thus in practice, but in the abstract something else, then we have no principles to stand on. Only *accidentally* can a mode or rather a set of words expressing a mode affect marriage itself, and that is when the mind intends an intention or condition against marriage, but ignorantly uses words that express a mode, and the reason why it is an exception is because it is not a mode but a condition, and, strictly speaking, it is no *exception*.

Conditional consent must always be distinguished from consent *cum modo*, which mode enters not into the contract, nor suspends, nor restricts the act of the will or the marital consent itself. This is a condition: "*if* you promise to live in my city;" this is a mode: if one gives absolute consent and demands that the wife promise to live there. The object of the mode and of the condition is the same, "living in my city," but they affect consent differently.[6]

To practice birth control or onanism in marriage can be placed as a *condition* against the *bonum prolis;* or a condition not essentially against this *bonum,* but to *abuse* the obligation; or it can be put as a *mode,* or even a *causa,* or as a *demonstration, e. g.*, "I marry you on condition that I reserve to myself the *right* to practice onanism;" "on condition that I *abuse* by means of onanism the assumed duty and obligation of properly having intercourse;" "I marry you in order

[6] *AAS,* 17 April, 1915.

that you practice onanism;" "I marry you because you are onanistic;" "I marry you who are onanistic." If the *content* of the mode, cause, or demonstration, is elevated into a condition *sine qua non,* then the rules governing conditions prevail. If the condition is really contrary to the substance, it vitiates the consent. If the condition refers only to the abuse of an essential obligation, it is rejected in the external forum as not placed, till proved otherwise. But if it is placed seriously then the marriage depends on its verification.

Article II

Causa and Demonstratio

Marriage consent may have added to it not only a condition but also a cause or demonstration. No kind of *causa* vitiates, or suspends the consent even though error is present, except it is *error personae, e. g.,* "I marry you because you are rich, a virgin, virtuous, because you will avoid children, become sterile, fornicate." The marriage is valid even though she is not rich, a virgin, etc., for the consent is not dependent on this (the *causa* presupposes a perfect absolute consent) as it does depend on a condition. "Causa est ratio ob quam quis contractum conficit." [7] "Demonstratio est affinis *causae* et nihil aliud quam expressio alicujus qualitalis quae supponitur in persona cum qua contrahitur." [8] For instance, "I marry you who are rich." The demonstration *points out,* expresses some *quality* by which the person with whom one contracts is pointed out or determined or known. One may err about the quality, *i. e.,* it may be different than thought, or entirely absent, but this error *per se* does not invalidate the marital consent. The specific difference between the *causa* and the *demonstratio* is that the *causa* expresses the *motive* which moved one to contract, the other indicated a certain intention of the contractor concerning the person or quality, which he has in his mind. Therefore a false cause or demonstration can invalidate marriage under a twofold supposition. If the error of either is *substantial,* that is, if it affects the very person, or if the quality redounds into an error of

[7] Santi, *Praelectiones Juris Canonici,* p. 111.

[8] Santi, *loc. cit.*

person; secondly, if a false cause or demonstration passes into or is made a *conditio sine qua non,* that is, the consent is bound by this error as a condition.[9]

Some say that the *causa* and *demonstratio,* if against the substance of marriage, invalidate. But Sanchez answers that these *per se* never suspend or invalidate no matter what their quality, whether base or against marriage, false or true, *e. g.,* "I marry you because you are sterile; or because you made yourself sterile." [10] The things that vitiate marriage should touch the substance of the contract, but these *ex natura sua* do not do so, they only pertain to the *opinion* of the parties *about things,* or the cause moving them to contract. Error of cause or demonstration do not invalidate marriage unless it be error or person or condition (slavery); which latter is from positive law only. These otherwise are not part of the object of the *contract. Per se,* it was said, for *per accidens,* as just noted, they can touch the substance, *e. g.,* "I marry you because you are freeborn" or "I marry you who are freeborn," or "I marry you because you are the first-born of John." The consent is defective in these cases not because of the falsity of the cause or demonstration but because of the *error personae* involved in the last case, and *error conditionis servilis* in the first two cases. For even though this particular cause or demonstration were not added, the consent would be defective anyhow. The cause or demonstration serve here only to prove the error of person, or servile condition.[11]

One must remember that the same thing (*e. g.,* the same quality, *e. g.,* the piety of the girl), may be made a *cause, demonstration,* or a *condition.* It is difficult sometimes to say what is meant *internally,* judging solely from the expression, *e. g.,* "Contraho tecum quae dabis tantam dotem," can be conditional, or a cause, a demonstration or a *modus,* especially if the cause or demonstration is added with a *future verb,* then the sense is doubtful.

Gasparri [12] says authors propose this case. Cajus marries Bertha,

[9] S. R. Rota, *Causam Limburgen,* 2 January, 1913—*AAS,* V. pp. 45-51.

[10] Sanchez, *De Matrimonio,* lib. V, disp. 9, n. 6.

[11] *Cf.* Sanchez, *De Matrimonio,* lib. 5, disp. 19; Pichler, *Candidatus Juris Prudentiae* (1733), p. 354.

[12] *De Matrimonio* (1903), n. 1023.

no condition being placed, but a short time before he was heard by many to say, he would marry her if she had a dowry of so much, otherwise he would not. After marriage when he found Bertha had nothing, he did not consummate the union. Some answer the marriage is valid.[13] Others deny it.[14] If a true *proper* condition is placed and not revoked nor verified it is evident the union is null. But this is just the point at issue. It can be construed as an error (simple at least) or a *causa* or a condition, hence there is doubt and the union is held valid. Cases of nullity of marriages like this, observes Gasparri, often suffer shipwreck because of lack of requisite proof in the external forum. A *causa* may prompt a person to consent, but once he is determined, he gives the consent absolutely and independently of the cause, *e. g.*, he thinks the girl is honest, he has no doubt of it, and consents absolutely. Or if his disposition is that if the thought occurred to him that she may be dishonest, he would not marrry her, but in reality he does marry her, without making his consent depend on her being honest. We have here only an interpretative intention.[15] No kind of *causa* or demonstration effects the act of the will substantially and *per se,* nor do they suspend the consent.[16] If a *dies certus* or *incertus* is added as a *terminus a quo,* it has the *force* of a *suspensive condition, e. g.,* "I give my consent to be your husband, on the tenth of next February;" or "when my father returns from Europe" (*dies incertus*). If it is added as a *terminus ad quem* it is *equivalent* to a *resolutive condition, e. g.,* "I now marry you for ten years," "or I now marry you until I find a richer girl." The *dies* added as a *terminus ad quem* invalidates the consent.[17]

It will be well to conclude with these quotations.

> *Causa* vel *demonstratio* qualiscumque sive vera sive falsa, honesta vel turpis et substantiae matrimonii contraria vel non contraria von vitiat vel suspendi matrimonium, nisi reducatur ad *errorem* personae at conditionis servilis aut transeat in veram *conditionem.* Nam consensus matri-

[13] Pignatelli, *Const.*, 136; De Angelis, *De confess.*, II, qu. 44.

[14] *E. g.*, the writer of the *Acta S.S.*, I, p. 377.

[15] Ayrinhac, *Marriage Legislation,* 1 ed., p. 217.

[16] Sanchez, *De Matrimonio,* lib. V, disp. 19, n. 2; Reiffenstuel, lib. III, tit. V, n. 61; Schmalzgrueber, lib. III, tit. V, nn. 135-146.

[17] *Cf.* Wernz-Vidal, *Jus Matrimoniale,* n. 519.

monialis non datur *dependenter* a causa vel demonstratione, sed sese habet concomitanter ad illas.[18]

De matrimonio inito sub modo, causa, demonstratione expedita res est, scilicet matrimonium valet, etsi modus . . . sit contra conjugii substantiam: *e. g., Contraho tecum, tu vero generationem prolis evitabis:* nam omnia actum, cui adjiciuntur, illicitum reddunt, sed mimime suspendunt.[19]

[18] Wernz-Vidal, *Jus Matrimoniale,* n. 519.

[19] Gasparri, *De Matrimonio* (1932), II, n. 879.

CHAPTER XXIX

ACCUSATION OF MARRIAGE ON THE GROUND OF CONDITIONS

A PERSON who was culpably responsible for the nullity of the marriage by means of giving consent under a condition is debarred from pleading against the validity in a church court; *e. g.*, the one who placed a condition against the substance of marriage, has no right to petition a review of his marriage. This does not mean that this particular marriage can not be taken up by a court. The other party can do so. If he should present a petition, the court could not accept it and allow him to proceed as plaintiff and any proceedings in which he acted as plaintiff in violation of this rule would be null and void. If one had a right to place an honest condition, then he also has a right to stand in court to ask for a declaration of nullity because of the non-verification of the condition. Many if not most cases tried by the Rota are just this kind of marriages.

It is of importance for those concerned with matrimonial procedure, to distinguish well those who have a right, and those who are prohibited from suing in court, as in the majority of cases brought before ecclesiastical courts the grounds put forward are concerned with consent. The refusal of the right to institute proceedings to the party who is the cause of invalidity is based on the maxim: *"Fraus sua nemini patrocinari debet."* It is a measure to safeguard the sanctity of marriage and to prevent evilly-disposed persons from attempting to render a marriage secretly invalid in the hope of being able later on to have the marriage declared null.

Canon 1971 enumerates those that are qualified or not to accuse a marriage. Canon 1970 legislates that the collegiate tribunal cannot try or decide any marriage case, unless a regular accusation or legitimately made petition has preceded. Canon 1971 says the following persons are capable of attacking a marriage: The married parties in all cases of separation and of nullity, unless they themselves were the cause of the impediment;[1] the prosecutor, in impediments public of

[1] *Cf. AAS,* X (1933), 345.

their very nature. All other persons, even blood-relations, have no right to attack a marriage; they can merely denounce the invalidity of a marriage to the Ordinary or to the *promotor justitiae*.[2] There are some quite difficult points about impediments (including conditions),[3] which are by nature or otherwise occult, and especially about the question when the *promotor justitiae* may act *ex officio* or by request. There have been thorough discussions recently on these points.[4]

Cases of culpable causation of invalidity of marriage occur in conditions against the substance. Instances of *causa honesta et licita* are impotency, ignorance, error, past and present conditions and future honest ones. In practice, the decision whether a party is a *causa culpabilis impedimenti* will rest with the tribunal to which the petition is made for trial and it will be decided by a decree of the tribunal and if unfavorable, recourse may be taken to a higher tribunal within ten days (*tempus utile*).[5]

The Commission that interprets the Code[6] interpreted the word *impediment* in a wide sense to cover *all factors* which may affect the validity of a marriage. Its second reply states that parties debarred from pleading nullity have the right to notify the invalidity of their marriage to the Ordinary or the Promoter of Justice. This is further developed by a reply given concerning Canon 1971.[7] This reply approves the opinion maintained by Noval[8] and Gasparri[9] that rests on the principle that the privation of the right of pleading is a punishment and therefore should be put only on the guilty. "Jus accusandi matrimonium competit conjugibus ex jure naturae ideoque hujus privatio sapit poenam, quae non concipitur sine culpa."[10]

[2] *Cf.* Woywod, *A Practical Commentary on The Code of Canon Law* (1926), II, n. 1876.

[3] 12 March, 1929, *AAS*, XXI, p. 170; 17 February, 1930, *AAS*, XXII, p. 195.

[4] *Cf.* G. Oesterle in *Jus Pontificium*, p. 142, 1932; Roberti, in *Appolinaris*, p. 250, April, 1930; editorial in *Il Monitore Ecclesiastico*, p. 271, September, 1933; *cf.* Noval, *De Processibus*, par. 850; Gasparri, *op. cit.*, n. 292.

[5] *Cf.* Canon 1709.

[6] See above references to the *AAS*.

[7] (*Cf. AAS*, X (1933), p. 345).

[8] *Jus Matrimoniale*, par. 850.

[9] *De Matrimonio*, II, n. 1260.

[10] Gasparri, *op. cit.*, n. 1260.

Protestant critics of the Catholic Church often suggest that she connives at such deliberately invalid marriages.[11] Charges such as these are completely refuted by Canons 1019, 1020, 1027, 1971, which show the care the Church takes to prevent invalid marriages. It is to be remembered that the Marborough-Vanderbilt and the Marconi-O'Brien marriages were celebrated in Protestant churches, and consequently any collusion or negligence in regard to them cannot be charged to the Catholic Church.

The co-authors of an important study entitled "Marriage and the State" [12] have a chapter on marriage exploitation including the "Marriage Market Town" and "Other Forms of Exploitation."[13] They point out that prospective bridegrooms are eminently exploitable and are victims often of sharp practice at the hands of avaricious civil officials and marrying parsons.

> Some cities and towns actually allow such practices (concerning the issuance of licenses, the marriage certificate, and even the wedding ceremony itself) which permit extortions and falsifications, to become habitual.[14]

In the chapter "The Marrying Parson" those who criticize the Catholic Church for simply declaring now and then a *truth,* namely that in a given case there never was a true marriage, should become ashamed of some of their own ministers and remove the blot on certain churches, which is unfair to the vast majority of ministers who are most upright in character.

> Where we have found the same commercial practices among certain ordained ministers that we have found and already described as characteristics of certain civil officiants, there we have felt justified in assuming that these individual clergymen were marrying parsons.[15]

[11] R. H. Charles, *Divorce and the Roman Dogma of Nullity* (England), Fleming, *Church of Rome and Marriage,* who, *inter alia,* distorts the Marconi case.

[12] Mary E. Richmond and Fred. S. Hall, N. Y., 1929.

[13] Pp. 84 to 105.

[14] *Loc. cit.*

[15] *Loc. cit.*

In fact marrying justices sometimes defend their practices saying they are as good as those of some ministers. Only, as stated before, a small minority among ministers of religion can be charged with commercialism and prostituting holy wedlock.

The forms of clerical commercialism are many.

> They include such practices as offering co-operative license clerks a share of the marriage fee; leaving a package of the minister's cards with the clerk to be handed to candidates for matrimony; maintaining a desk in the marriage license office and selling marriage certificates that are designed for framing; maintaining a room or establishing a place of residence very near the court house; putting conspicuous signs outside this residence; employing runners or else personally soliciting patronage from strangers; dividing fees with taxicab drivers who bring candidates to be married; and helping those who apply to be married to evade the marriage laws of their State.[16]
>
> When a bishop, referring to a clergyman in his denomination who has no church and no parishoners, must acknowledge ruefully, "I suppose it is true that he has married more than three thousand couples" . . . when still another—with a charge this time—had to leave town suddenly to escape arrest for performing ceremonies illegally, it seems reasonable to draw again an inference that has often been drawn before; namely, that the churches have a certain responsibility for the existence of the marrying parson.[17]
>
> One California clergyman boasted, that he had performed 247 marriage ceremonies the year before, but only about 15 of these were members of his parish.[18]
>
> One form of evasion consists in misdating the marriage certificate at the request of the marrying pair by entering upon it either an earlier or a later date than the true one.[19]

The non-catholic authors of this Russell Sage Foundation study on marriage, in their section on "Denominational Standards of the Churches" have these words of praise for the Catholic Church.[20]

[16] *Op. cit.* p. 281.
[17] *Op. cit.* p. 281.
[18] *Op. cit.* p. 283.
[19] *Op. cit.* p. 284.
[20] *Op. cit.* p. 244.

> The Roman Catholic Church stands out as the most conspicuous example of a religious organization with definite rules, formulated early, modified from time to time, now explained and enforced throughout all its branches, and interpreted in further detail by an ecclesiastical court.

They note that Canon Law demands diligent investigation by the pastor.

> Cardinal Gasparri thinks it is incumbent upon a parish priest to make such an investigation "even if he should have a moral certainty as to the absence of all impediments in a given case." [21]
>
> The canons of the Protestant Episcopal Church in the United States of America devote less than a page and a half to the subject of the solemnization of marriage.[22]

The Churchman, April 5, 1919, an Episcopalian weekly periodical, arraigns the Church for saying nothing about the wickedness of certain kinds of marriages.[23] In view of these facts sincere critics should have nothing but praise for the law and jurisprudence of the Catholic Church on marriage. The Church by these laws shows her abhorence of such conduct and creates a very effective deterrent against them.[24]

[21] *Op. cit.* p. 246.
[22] *Op. cit.*, p. 247.
[23] *Op. cit.*, p. 247.
[24] *Cf. The Irish Eccl. Review*, M. Browne, November, 1933, Vol. 42, p. 525 s.

APPENDIX

Consent in General as Viewed by Modern Legal Codes [1]

Consent is the very basis of contract as a legal conception. It is only the agreement of two or more persons to do or not to do something that can form a contract, and from the nature of an agreement its most essential constituent is the consent of the parties. Without the meeting of two or more minds, in one and the same intention, there cannot be an agreement. Without consent there may be the shadow but not the substance of a contract. In a general sense, consent is the *quo animo* of the act, to consent is any operation of the will implying positive mental action and consenting is to be willing, as a condition of the mind.[2] This is laid down repeatedly by jurists and judges.

Consent or non-consent is an action of the mind; it consists exclusively of the intention of the mind. Consent has been defined as the concurring of wills. "Voluntas multorum vel plurium ad quos res pertinet." Mere submission is not consent. Every consent involves a submission, but it by no means follows that a submission involves consent. The consent of the will is the only one known to law. There is no such thing as material consent in the case of a rational being, it must be mental consent or nothing.[3]

The term physical consent means the physical expression of consent, because like every other state of mind it can be expressed only physically. But this term is not always used to denote this physical mode of expression of consent but often the absence of those legal qualifications of consent, without which it is generally deemed to have no legal operation or effect, and without which it is sometimes said not to exist at all, at least for the purpose of the law, with reference to which its existence may at the time be in question.[4]

Consent is, in some branches of the law, defined so as to include all those incidents of it, without which it will not have operation in that branch, as if they were its very essentials. To say in any case a consent is no consent at all, tends to throw into the background in these cases, the real question of the

[1] The reader will notice that on the one hand a portion of what follows will not be clear from a canonical viewpoint, and moreover some of the terminology is erroneous and some inexact; and on the other hand, the other portion will be quite cogent and correct. But the text of this chapter is a mosaic of judical pronouncements and legal statutes, and the teaching of legal authorities on the subject. The reason of bringing it in here, is for the purpose of contrast and comparison with our own views on consent, especially, marriage consent.

[2] Whittaker v. State, 50 Wis., 518.

[3] Reg. v. Dee, 15 Cox C. C., 594, per Pallas, C. B., quoted by Huhm Chand, N. A. *Principles of the Law of Consent* (Bombay, 1897), p. 16.

[4] Chand, *op. cit.*, p. 17.

adequacy of every alleged vitiating cause of consent, to divert attention and controversy from the question of any circumstances being or not being sufficient to render consent inoperative in any case. Negative the existence, in any case, of consent, and so far as consent is concerned, there will be no distinction in that case, between the circumstances which are essential constituents of consent and those the observance of which only prevent consent from receiving a certain effect which law assigns only to a consent in a certain branch of law, or with certain qualifications.[5]

There is no consent to an act without knowledge thereof. There are some strange and amusing court cases *ad rem,* in particular concerning a certain surgical operation.[6] But some kind of knowledge of an act though essential to consent is not identical with it. *Volenti non fit injuria, non scienti.* It is not necessary to agree about every circumstance connected with an act. There should be knowledge of the important attributes of the act. This is very true when the attributes are attributes and form part of the act.

The term consent is defined differently in different branches of law and with reference to different matters. Generally this is due to a difference of words and thus there is only an apparent difference. If there be a real difference, it is not due to a different nature of the mental condition or operation which constitutes consent, but to the difference in those aspects of an act which have predominant importance in the several branches of law and in relation to the several matters, respectively. For instance, the law of contracts deals as much with the object to which the act relates as with the act itself. The mode, and the intention and the motive with which the act is done, and the consequences it involves, except as regards the aforesaid object, have, if any, only a secondary importance. Thus this definition of consent is acceptable to legalists. *Pactio duorum pluriumve in idem placitum consensus.* The same thing, in the same sense agreed upon, the thing being the act concerned (*id de quo agitur*).[7] Consent in that branch of law dealing with family relationship will now be briefly noticed.

Marriage consent as viewed by some American States and their supreme courts, may be seen in the statutes of the States and in innumerable judicial decisions of the highest courts. A few States will be picked at random to give some general idea of American legal conceptions about marriage consent.[8]

As to the contract of marriage itself; the law considers it as it considers other civil contracts. It is valid if at the time of its making the parties were willing

[5] This distinction is highly important in those cases where marital consent was given by parties under a diriment impediment of the Church or of nature, and when given with so-called conditions against the substance of true marriage.

[6] Chand, *Principles of the Law of Consent,* p. 20.

[7] *Cf.* Chand, *op. cit.,* "Indian Contract Law," p. 21.

[8] All these are taken from *Marriage Laws and Decisions in the United States,* Geoffrey May, N. Y., 1929; *cf.* Richmond and Hall, *Marriage and the State,* N. Y., 1929.

to contract, were able to contract, and actually did contract in the forms prescribed by law. Marriage in other words is based on the consent of competent parties. Consent alone is the essence of the marriage contract, with consent, no further act such as cohabitation is neccessary.[9]

Kansas: The consent must be to enter the actual marriage status, not some relationship repudiating marital rights.[10]

Michigan: Regardless of ceremony, positive dissent can create no marriage. Consent must be real, deliberate, definite, and irrevocable.[11]

Massachusetts: The validity of a marriage properly contracted is not affected by any collateral agreement of the parties, such as not to live together: the status is fixed when the contract is properly solemnized.[12]

Missouri: Lack of matrimonial consent on part of one party does not prove the invalidity of the marriage where the other party entered the contract in good faith believing that a marriage was being created.[13]

Nebraska: Though consent is necessary to a marriage, a regular ceremony gone through ostensibly in good faith cannot be nullified by a previous agreement of the parties not to consider it binding, for that would allow of a dissolution of marriage by the parties themselves.[14]

New Jersey: Mere words without intent to contract, as in case of a jest, do not create a marriage.[15]

But if the acts and words of a person, followed by matrimonial cohabitation and repute, amount to a statement that the other party is his spouse, no mental reservation or secret intention can deprive such other person of matrimonial rights.[16]

New York: Where the act of marriage was clear a formal ceremony may not be annulled by a mere declaration of either party that they did not intend marriage or by any mental reservation or secret intention,[17] expressed for instance by a silent withholding of assent to the ceremony.[18]

But a marriage ceremony lacking matrimonial consent and gone through as a mere subterfuge to obtain a theatrical engagement without parental consent will be annulled.[19]

[9] May, *op. cit.*, p. 8; *cf.* Blackstone, *Commentaries*, Book 1, Chap. 15, whence the above quotation originates.

[10] State v. Walker, 36 K. 29 (1887).

[11] Roszel v. Roszel, 73 M. 133 (1888).

[12] Franklin v. Franklin, 154 M. 515 (1891).

[13] Imbroden v. St. Louis Union Trust Co., 111 App. 220 (1905), later appeal, 128 App. 555 (1908).

[14] Hill v. State, 61 N. 589 (1901).

[15] McClurg v. Terry, 21 E. 225 (1870); Girvan v. Griffin, 91 E. 141 (1919).

[16] Jackson v. Jackson, 94 E. 233 (1922).

[17] Barker v. Barker, 88 M. 300 (1914).

[18] Everett v. Morrison, 69 Hun. 146 (1893).

[19] Dorgeloh v. Murtha, 92 M. 279 (1915).

North Carolina: Consent of the parties presently to take each other as husband and wife, freely, seriously, and plainly expressed, is necessary to a valid marriage.[20]

Ohio: Mere words without intention corresponding to them will not create a marriage contract.[21]

Pennsylvania: The consent of parties to an alleged marriage is to be determined by what took place at the time of its celebration and is not affected by any secret reservation of one party.[22]

South Carolina: A marriage contract, unless consummated by cohabitation, may be declared void for want of consent of either party or for other cause showing the supposed contract not to have been a contract.[23]

Several States in their statutes do not define marriage. About seven States define it thus: Marriage is a personal relation arising out of a civil contract to which the consent of the parties capable of contracting is necessary.

All the rest of the States have definitions similar or exactly like this: Marriage is a civil contract to which the consent of parties capable of contracting is essential.

Presumptions in Favor of Instruments in American Law

In the interpretation and construction of the contract or intention, a contract is to be so construed as to give effect if possible to every word and phrase. Thus a construction which requires an entire clause to be rejected will not be adopted. When particular words are followed or preceded by a general term the latter is limited in its scope to persons or things of the same general character as those conceived by the particular terms.[24]

When the language of an instrument is susceptible of two constructions, one of which renders it valid, the other invalid, the former will be adopted. For instance, if one comes under the statute of fraud, the other will be adopted. The presumption in favor of the contract's legality is even stronger than the presumption in favor of its validity. Also the presumption is stronger to render it *effective* than *inoperative*.[25]

Can a person show that he meant to do a different thing from that which his actions indicated? A party cannot escape the natural and reasonable interpretation which must be put on what he says and does, by showing that his words were used and his acts done with a different and undisclosed intention.[26]

[20] Statute of Code, No. 2493.

[21] Miller v. Miller, I, O. Dec. (N. P.), 354 (1894).

[22] Barnett v. Kimmell, 35 St. 13 (1859); Torrence's estate, 47 S. C. 509 (1911); affirming 57 P. L. J. 203 (1909).

[23] Statute of Code, n. 5532.

[24] Putney, *Law Library*, Vol. 3, p. 139.

[25] *Ibid.*, p. 139.

[26] Colt, Stoddard v. Ham, 129 Mass. 383.

"The law does not consider secret intentions of a party, the expressed intention must govern in the absence of fraud and mutual mistake." [27]

Concerning the expression of intention, the

> law imputes to a person a state of mind or intention corresponding to the rational meaning, not only of his words, but of his actions as well; and where the conduct of a person towards another, judged by a reasonable standard, manifests an intention to agree in regard to some matter, that agreement is established in law as a fact, whatever may be the real but unexpressed state of his mind on the matter.
>
> If acts are inconsistent as far as his words are concerned, acts in general are accepted as the more reliable guide to the intention and the conduct may in some cases determine the intention, even in opposition to the words.[28]

An agreement to be recognized as such, so as to constitute a contract, must be "an act in the law," that is, have legal effects and therefore the intention must refer to legal relations, so that courts which deal only with legal relations, may take cognizance of it. It must have reference to the assumption of legal rights and duties as opposed to engagements of a social character, or engagements of honor. An agreement resulting in a contract is that form of agreement which directly contemplates and creates an obligation; and the contractual obligation is that form of obligation which springs directly from agreement. Agreements or consent may or may not create obligations and therefore may not result in contracts, *e. g.*, giving gifts. Or agreements may create an obligation only incidentally and remotely and therefore are not contracts. The essence of a contract is in fact the direct purpose of agreement to create an obligation.[29] This is pure Roman law which held that the essence of a contract is to create an obligation enforceable by the State. "Contractus nihil aliud est quam pactum ex quo oritur obligatio." [30]

[27] 129 Mass. 383; Marshall, *Common Legal Principles*, Vol. 1, p. 114.

[28] Wm. L. Clarke, *Handbook of the Law of Contracts*, p. 5.

[29] Clarke, *op. cit.*, p. 5 s.

[30] P. Gudelini, *Novellae*, p. 90.

BIBLIOGRAPHY

Sources

Acta Apostolicae Sedis, Commentarium Officiale, Romae, 1909—

Acta et Decreta Sacrorum Conciliorum Recentiorum (*Collectio Lacensis*), 7 vols., Friburgi Brisgoviae, 1870-90.

Acta Sanctae Sedis, 41 vols., Romae, 1865-1908.

Canones et Decreta Sacrosancti Oecumenici Concilii Tridentini, Romae, 1904, and Neapoli, 1859.

Canones et Decreta Sacrosancti Oecumenici et Generalis Concilii Tridentini, Vindabonae, 1867.

Canones et Decreta Concilii Tridentini accedunt Declarationes ac Resolutiones S. C. C.—Schulte-Richter, Lipsiae, 1853.

Codex Juris Canonici, Pii X, Pontificis Maximi, Jussus Digestus, Benedicti Papae XV, Auctoritate Promulgatus, Romae, 1918.

Codex Theodosianus, Ed. P. Krueger, Th. Mommsen, 3 vols., Berolini, 1905.

Codicis Juris Canonici Fontes, cura Emi. Petri Gasparri editi, 5 vols., Romae, 1925.

Collectanea Sacrae Congregationis de Propaganda Fide, 2 vols., Romae, 1907.

Corpus Juris Canonici, editio Lipsiensis secunda, Richter-Frieberg, Lipsiae, 1922.

Corpus Juris Civilis, Edito Sterotypa, Quinta Decima, Krueger, Mommsen, Berolini, 1928; also edito Stereotypa, Berolini, 1872.

Decreta Concilii Plenarii Baltimorensis Tertii., Baltimorae, 1901.

Denzinger, Henricus, *Enchiridion Symbolorum et Definitionum quae de rebus Fidei et Morum a Conciliis Oecumenicis et Summis Pontificibus Emanarunt.* 9 ed., Wirceburgi, 1900.

Harduin, Jean, *Acta Conciliorum et Epistolae Decretales ac Constitutiones Summorum Pontificum,* 12 vols., Parisiis, 1715.

Jaffe, Phillipus, *Regesta Pontificum Romanorum ab Condita Ecclesia ad Annum post Christum Natum MCXCVIII,* 2 ed., G. Wallenback, Lipsiae, 1881.

Kehr, Paulus Fridolinus, *Regesta Pontificum Romanorum,* 8 vols., Berolini, 1910.

Lancelotti, Paulus, *Corpus Juris Canonici,* 1650.

Mansi, Joannes Dominicus, *Sacrorum Conciliorum Nova et Amplissima Collectio,* 50 vols., Parisiis, 1902.

Migne, P. J., *Patrologia Latina,* Parisiis, 1858-64, 221 vols.

Pallottini, S., *Collectio Omnium Conclusionum et Resolutorum S. C. C.,* tomus XII (1886), tomus XIII (1887), tomus XVII (1893).

Ricobono, Salvator, *Fontes Juris Romani Antejustiniani,* Florentiae, 1909.

Sacrae Romanae Rotae Decisiones seu Sententiae, 8 vols., and appendix, Romae, 1761.

S. Romanae Rotae Decisiones seu Sententiae, vols. I (1909, printed 1912), to vol. XV incl.

Thesaurus Resolutionum Sacrae Congregationis Concilii, 167 vols., Romae, 1718-1908.

AUTHORS

Abbott-Carter, *A Brief on the Modes of Proving the Facts,* Rochester, N. Y., 1922.

Aertnys-Damen, *Theologia Moralis,* 2 vols., Turin, 1928.

Alphonsus, Saint, *Theologia Moralis,* 10 vols., Mechlinae, 1852.

Amos, S., *The History and Principles of the Civil Law of Rome,* London, 1883.

Archiv für Katholisches Kirchenrecht, 1857 to 1934.

Ayrinhac, H. A., *Marriage Legislation in the New Code of Canon Law,* New York, 1918, and ed. 1933.

(Bachofen) Augustine, Charles, O.S.B., *A Commentary on Canon Law,* 8 vols., St. Louis, 1918-1924.

Bardenhewer-Shahan, *Patrology,* St. Louis, Mo., 1908.

Bargilliat, M., *Praelectiones Juris Canonici,* 25 ed., Paris, 1909. 37 ed., Paris, 1923-24.

Bayon, J. G., *Tractatus Canonico—Moralis de Sacramento Matrimonii,* Madrid,

Bonacina, M., *Opera Omnia,* Venetiis, 1705.

Bonaventura, Sanctus, *Opera Omnia,* Ad Claras Aquas (Quaracchi), 1889, Tomus IV.

Benedict XIV, *De Synodo Diocesana,* Romae, 1806.

Bersani, Francesco, *Le Fonti Del Diritto Canonico Prima Della Codificazione,* Romae, 1918.

Bonfante, *Storia del diritto romano,* 2 vols., Milano, 1924.

Bonfante, *Corso di dirrito civile romano,* 2 vols., Romae, 1926-27.

Brancati, D. Laurentius, *Epitome Canonum Omnium,* editio in Germania prima, Coloniae Agrippinae, 1684.

Bucceroni, Januario, S.J., *Institutiones Theologiae Moralis,* editio altera, Romae, 1893.

Buckler, W. H., *The Origin and History of Contract in Roman Law,* London, 1895.

Cappello, Felix M., *Tractatus Canonico-Moralis de Sacramentis,* vol. 3, De *Matrimonio,* 2 ed., Romae, 1927.

Catholic Encyclopedia, The, 17 vols., New York, 1907-1922.

Cavagnis, F., *Institutiones Juris Publici Ecclesiastici,* 3 vols., Romae, 1883.

Cerato, P., *Matrimonium a Codice Juris Canonici integra desumptum,* 4 ed., Patavii, 1927.

Chelodi, Joannes, *Jus Matrimoniale,* 3 ed., Tridenti, 1921.

Chevalier, U., *Repertoire Des Sources Historiques Du Moyen Age,* Topo-Bibliographia, Montbeliard, 1904-1909.

Clericatus, J., *Decisiones De Matrimonio,* Venetiis, 1716.

Cocchi, Guidus, *Commentarium in Codicem Juris Canonici ad-usum Scholarum,* 3 ed., 8 vols., Taurinorum Augustae, 1925-1927.

Corbett, Percy Ellwood, *The Roman Law of Marriage,* Oxford, 1930.

Coronata, M., *Institutiones Juris Canonici,* Turin, 1931.

Cours Alphabetique et Methodique de Droit Canon, M. L'Abbe Andre, Paris, 1844.

D'Angelo, S., *Jus Digestorum,* Tomus I, pars generalis, Romae, 1927.

D'Annibale, Josephus, *Summula Theologiae Moralis,* Romae, 1908.

De Becker, Julius, *De Sponsalibus et Matrimonio Praelectiones Canonicae,* Brussels, 1896.

DeMeester, A., *Juris Canonici et Juris Canonico-Civilis Compendium,* 3 vols., Bruges, 1921-28.

De Smet, A., *Betrothment and Marriage,* 2 ed., 2 vols., Bruges, 1928.

De Smet, A., *Tractatus Theologico-Canonicus de Sponsalibus et Matrimonio,* Bruges, 1927.

Devoti, Joannis, *Institutionum Canonicarum,* 2 vols., Leodii, 1860.

Elbel-Bierbaum, *Theologia Moralis,* 3 vols., Paderbornae, 1894.

Encyclopaedia of Religion and Ethics, Ed. James Hastings, 11 vols., New York, 1908.

Eichmann, Dr. Edward, *Lehrbuch des Kirchenrechts auf Grund des Codex Juris Canonici,* Paderborn, 1923.

Esmein, A., *Le Mariage en Droit Canonique,* 20 ed., Tome Premier, Paris, 1929.

Fagnanus, Prosperus, *Commentaria in quartum Librum Decretalium,* Venetiis, 1729.

Farrugia, P. Nicolaus, O.S.A., *De Matrimonio et Causis Matrimoniis,* Taurini-Romae, 1924.

Ferrara, Orestes, *The Relations Between Public and Private Roman Law During the Republic,* address delivered December 11, 1931, at the Riccobono Seminar of Roman Law, Washington, D. C.

Ferraris, H. Lucii, O. M. Reg. Obs. St. Francisci, *Bibliotheca Canonica, Juridica, Moralis, Theologica nec non Ascetica, Polemica, Rubriscistica, Historia,* 9 vols., Romae, 1885-92.

Ferreres, J., *Compendium Theologiae Moralis,* 2 vols., Barcinone, 1925.

Ferrini, Contardo, *Pandette,* Romae, 1927.

Freisen, Joseph, *Geschichte des Canonischen Eherechts,* Paderborn, 1893.

Fourneret, Pierre, *Le Mariage Chrétien,* 3 ed., Paris, 1921.

Friedlander, G., *Laws and Customs of Israel,* compiled from the codes, etc., London, 1921, and New York City.

Fulton, John, *The Laws of Marriage, Containing the Hebrew, Roman and New Testament Law,* New York, 1883.

Gasparri, Petrus, *Tractatus Canonicus de Matrimonio,* 3 ed., 2 vols., Paris, 1904 (1932), Romae.

Genicot-Salsmans, *Institutiones Theologiae Moralis,* 2 vols., Bruxellis, 1927.

Giraldi, U., *Expositio Juris Pontifici*, Romae, 1769.

Gneist, Rudolphus, *Institutionum et Regularum Juris Romani Syntagma*, Lipsiae, 1858.

Gougnard, A., *Tractatus de Matrimonio*, Mechliniae, 1931.

Grandclaude, E., *Jus Canonicum Juxta Ordinem Decretalium*, Tres Tomi, Parisiis, 1882.

Gudelinus, Petrus, *Liber Sex Commentariorum de Jure Novissimo*, Florentiae, 1839.

Gury-Ballerini, *Compendium Theologiae Moralis*, 2 vols., Romae, 1889.

Heiss, M., *Tractatus Quinque de Matrimonio*, Milwaukee, 1861.

Hinchius, Paul, *System des Katholischen Kirchenrechts*, 2 vols., Berlin, 1869.

Hussarek, Max von, *Die Bedingte Eheschliessung*, Wein, 1892.

Jewish Encyclopedia, The., 12 vols., New York and London, 1906.

Kadushin, J. L., *Jewish Code of Jurisprudence*, 4 ed., 3 vols., New Rochelle, N. Y.

Kenrick, F. P., *Theologia Moralis*, 3 vols., Philadelphia, 1842.

Kendrick, F., *De Contractibus, De Jure et Justitia, et de Matrimonio* (notes).

Knecht, August von: *Handbuch des Katholischen Eherechts*, Freiburg im Breisgau, 1928.

Koeniger, Dr. Albert M. von: *Katholisches Kirchenrecht*, Freiburg im Breisgau, 1926.

Kostler, Rudolf, *Die väterliche Ehebewilligung* (*Kirchenrecheticke Abhandlugun*, Hft., 51), Stuttgart, 1908.

Laboure-Byrnes, *Procedure in the Diocesan Matrimonial Courts of First Instance*, New York, 1928.

Lancelotto, J. P., *Institutiones Juris Canonici*, Venetiis, 1630.

Laurin, Dr. Franciscus, *Introductio in Corpus Juris Canonici*, Freiburg, Brisgoviae et Vindobonae, 1889.

Laymanus, Paulus, *Jus Canonicum*, Dilingae, 1666.

Leage, R. W., *Roman Private Law*, London, 1920.

Lehmkuhl, A., *Theologia Moralis*, 2 vols., Friburg, 1910.

Leitner, Martin, *Lehrbuch des Katholischen Eherechts*, Paderborn, 1920.

Linneborn, Dr. Johannes, *Grundriss des Eherechts*, Paderborn, 1919.

Lijdsman, Bernardo, C.SS.R., *Introductio in Jus Canonicum*, 2 vols., Hilversum in Hollandia, 1924.

Maasen, F., *Geschichte der Quellen und der Literatur des Canonischen Rechts*, Gratz, 1871.

Maine, Sir Henry, *Ancient Law*, London (1861) reprint 1927.

Mansella, Josephus, cura F. Solieri, *De Causis Matrimonialibus*, Romae, 1906.

Manuale Latinitatis Fontium Juris Civilis Romanorum Thesauri Latinitatis Epitome, Henrico Eduaro Dirksen, Berolini, 1837.

Marc-Gestermann, *Institutiones Morales Alphonsianae*, 2 vols., Lugundi, 1927.

Maroto, Phillipus, *Institutiones Juris Canonici ad Norman Novi Codicis,* 2 vols., Romae, 1919-1921.

Marshall, Francis W., *Common Legal Principles,* 2 vols., New York and London, 1929.

Mocchegiani, Peter, O.F.M., *Jurisprudentia Ecclesiastica,* Ad Claras Aquas, 1904.

Morey, William C., *Outlines of Roman Law,* New York and London, 1890.

Mothon, Joseph Pie, O.P., *Institutiones Canoniques,* 3 vols., Paris, 1922.

Noldin-Schmitt, *Summa Theologiae Moralis,* 3 vols., Oeniponte, 1929.

Ojetti, Benedictus, S.J., *In Jus Antepianum et Pianum ex Decreto "Ne Temere" . . . Commentarii.* Romae, 1908.

Pagani, J. B., *Facti Species et Quaestiones de Re Morali,* Romae, 1915.

Payen, G., S.J., *De Matrimonio,* 3 vols., Zi-ka-wei, 1929.

Perrone, Jo., S.J., *De Matrimonio Christiano,* Libri tres, Leodii, 1860.

Perrone, Joannes, S.J., *Praelectiones Theologiae;* 21 ed., Ratisbonae, 1854.

Petrovits, Joseph J. C., *The New Church Law on Matrimony,* Philadelphia, 1921.

Pichler, V., *Candidatus Juris Prudentiae Sacrae,* 1733.

Pirhing, *Universum Jus Canonicum,* 1674.

Prümmer, M., *Manuale Juris Canonici,* Freiburgi, 1927.

Prümmer, M., *Manuale Theologiae Moralis,* 3 vols., Friburgi, 1928.

Reiffenstuel, Anacletus, O.F.M., *Jus Canonicum Universum,* Venetiis, 1735.

Riedler, Franz Jos., *Bedingte Eheschliessung,* Kempten, 1892.

Rittershutius, Cunard, *Expositio Methodica Novellarum,* Florentiae, 1839.

Robertus, Cameracensis, O.M.Cap., *Aurifodina,* Coloniae Agrippinae, 1731.

Roskovany, A., *De Matrimonio in Ecclesia Catholica,* Augsburg, 1837.

Sabetti-Barrett, S.J., *Compendium Theologiae Moralis,* 30 ed., Neo Eboraci, 1924.

Sägmuller, J. B., *Lehrbuch des katholischen Kirchenrechts,* 2 vols., Freiburg, 1914.

Sanchez, Thomas, S.J., *De Sancto Matrimonii Sacramento Disputationum,* Venetiis, 1693.

Santi, Franciscus, *Praelectiones Juris Canonici,* New York, 1886, and latter editions.

Savigny, Federico Carlo di, *Sistema del Diritto Romano Attuale traduzione . . .* di Vittorio Scialoja, volume Terzo.

Savigny, F. C., *System des heutigen romischen Rechts,* 8 vols., Berolini, 1840-49; gallice, Guenoux, Paris, 1855-59.

Schmalzgrueber, Francis, S.J., *Jus Ecclesiasticum Universum,* Ingolstadii, 1728.

Schaff, Philip, *History of the Christian Church,* 3 rev. ed., 7 vols., New York, 1904.

Schaff, Valentine—*"Intention Against the Substance of Marriage"—The Ecclesiastical Review,* January, 1930; *cf.* also his articles; October, 1929; December, 1928; May, 1929.

Schulte, J. F. von, *Die Geschichte der Quellen und Literatur des Canonischen Rechts*, 2 vols., Stuttgart, 1875.

Schulte, J. F. von, *Handbuch des Katholischen Eherechts*, Giessen, 1855.

Schulte, J. F. von, *Die Summa Magistri Rufini zum Decretum Gratiani*, Giessen, 1892.

Schulte, J. F. von, *Die Summa des Paucapalea über das Decretum Gratiani*, Giessen, 1890.

Schulte, J. F. von, *Die Summa des Stephanus Tornacenis über das Decretum Gratiani*, Geissen, 1891.

Schumacher, H., *Das Ehe—Ideal Des Apostels Paulus*, Munchen, 1932.

Scotus, Jn. Duns, *Opera Omnia* (Tomus Decimus nonus) Parisiis, 1894.

Sebastianelli, Guilelmus, *Praelectiones Juris Canonici*, 2 ed., Romae, 1905.

Sehling, Dr. E., *Die Unterscheidung der Verlöbnisse im Kanonischen Recht*, Leipzig, 1887.

Sehling, Dr. Emil, *Zur Lehre von den Willensmängeln im Kanonischen Recht*, Erlangen und Leipzig, 1901.

Sherman, Charles Phineas, *Roman Law in the Modern World*, 2 ed., 3 vols., New York, 1924.

Sipos, Stephanus, *Enchiridion Juris Canonici*, Editio Altera, Pecs, 1931.

Smith, S., *Notes on the Second Plenary Council of Baltimore*, De Matrimonio, chapter XXI, New York, 1874.

Smith, S. B., *The Marriage Process in the United States*, New York, 1896.

Sohm, Rudolph, *Trauung und Verlobung*, Weimer, 1876.

Sohm, Rudolph, *The Institutes*, translated, James Crawford Ledlie, 3 ed., Oxford, 1926.

Stutz, Dr. Ulrich, *Kirchenrechtliche Abhandlugen*, 51 Heft: Die Vaterliche Ehebewilligung, von Dr. Rudolf Kostler, Stuttgart, 1908.

Suarez, Franciscus, S.J., *Opera Omnia*, Parisiis, 1866 (tomus XV).

Tanquerey, Ad., *Synopsis Theologiae Dogmaticae*, 19 ed., 3 vols., Tornaci, 1922.

Tellez, Gonzalez, *Commentaria Perpetua in Singulis Textis quinque Libros Decretalium Gregorii Noni*, Lugduni, 1593.

Thaner, Friedrich, *Die Summa magistri Rolandi nachmals Papstes Alexander III*, Innsbruck, 1874.

Thomas Aquinas—*Summa Theologica*, 6 vols., Romae, 1894 and 1928, Parmae, 1855, Taurini, 1922.

Triebs, Franz von, *Praktisches Handbuch des gelienden Kanonischen Eherechts*, 3 Teile, Breslau, 1925.

Vecchiotti, Sept. M., *Institutiones Canonicae*, 19 ed., Taurini-Romae.

Vermeersch, Arthurus, S.J., *Epitome Juris Canonici*, Mechlinae, 1921.

Vermeersch, A., *Theologia Moralis*, Tractatus VIII, 1923.

Vermeersch-Creusen, *Epitome Juris Canonici*, II, 1925.

Vinnius, Arnaldus, *Institutionum in IV Libros, Imperialium Commentarius*, recensunt Jo. Gottl. Heineccius, J. C. Cui Jacobi Gothofredi, J. C. Historia et Bibliotheca Juris Civilis Romani Praeponitur, accedit ad calicem, Editum Perpetuum Salvii Juliani a Guilelmo Ranchino collectum. Edito novissima, etc., 2 vols., Neopoli, 1772.

Vlaming, Th. M., *Praelectiones Juris Matrimonii*, 2 vols., Bussum in Hollandia, 1919.

Vromant, G., *De Matrimonio*, Louvain, 1931.

Watt, W. A., *The Theory of Contract in its Social Light*, Edinburgh, 1897.

Weber, J., *Die Kanonischen Ehehindernisse*, Freiburg im Breisgau, 1886.

Weister, *Institutiones Canonicae*, Monachii, 1705.

Wernz, Franciscus, S.J., *Jus Decretalium*, 6 vols., Prati, 1911-1915.

Wernz-Vidal, *Jus Matrimoniale*, Romae, 1925.

Windscheid, *Lehrbuch des Pandektenrechts*, Francoforte, 1891.

Woywod, Stanislaus, O.F.M., *The New Canon Law*, New York, 1918.

Woywod, Stanislaus, O.F.M., *A Practical Commentary on the Code of Canon Law*, 2 vols., 3rd revised edition, New York, 1929.

Zollman, C., *American Church Law*, St. Paul, 1933.

UNIVERSITAS CATHOLICA AMERICAE

WASHINGTON, D. C.

FACULTAS JURIS CANONICI

No. 89

1934

ALPHABETICAL INDEX

Accusation of marriage on the ground of conditions added to consent, 350-354.

Bonum Prolis, 241, 242, 284.
- conditions that invalidate, 284 f.,
- meaning of the primary end of marriage, 284-292.
- meaning of the *bonum physicum*, 293-309.
- ignorance and error concerning this end, 302 f.
- heresy condition and immoral education, 310.
- condition to raise children in heresy, dispute about, 310.
- so-called honest condition against the *bonum physicum prolis*, 311.
- vow or condition to preserve virginity, 311 f.
- whether this invalidates is greatly disputed, 312.
- marriage of St. Joseph, 330.

Canon Law—History of condition—see History.

Causa,
- definition of, 80, 346.
- does not suspend the consent, 346.

Condition, Definition of,
- nature of, 81 f.
- species of, 83 f.
- mixed consent, 83.
- future, honest, 84.
- tacit, 85.
- general, 85.
- intrinsic, 86.
- interpretative, 86.
- resolutive, 87.
- can they be added validly to marriage consent, 89 f.
- liceity of placing condition, 105-111.
- some say it is illicit to place condition, 105.
- no grave cause necessary to place honest condition, 107.

Consent,
- renewal of, not necessary for validity, 98.
- perseverance of consent, 103, 104.

Demonstration,
- definition of, 346.
- does not suspend the consent, 346.

Dies, 88, 348.

Engagements and conditions against the substance of marriage, 341.

Favor matrimonii, 141 f.

Ficitio juris,
- definition of, 137.
- *ficitiones in re matrimoniali*, 138.
- *ficitio juris* differs from *praesumptio juris*, 139.

Fides Matrimonii,
- definition of, 238-240.
- conditions against this essential, 331-334.
- error concerning it, 333.

Frustration of the condition—see Verification.

Future honest conditions—see Honest future.

Hebrew Law,
- conditions in, 1-12.
- developed in Jewish Law Books, 10.
- three kinds "if," "from now on, if," "on condition that," 11.
- four essentials for valid condition, 10 f.

History of Canon Law on Conditions, 25-69.
- first emergence of in school of Bologna, 25 f.

Gratian, views of, 25 f.
Paucapalea, 29.
Rolandus, 29.
Stephen of Tournay, 31.
oldest form of doctrine, 31 f.
John Faventinus, 31.
Simon de Bisiano, 33.
Sicard of Cremonia, 33.
first influence of Papal Legislation, 34 f.
Alexander III, 34.
Urban, III, 36.
the completion of the older doctrine, 37 f.
Huguccio, 37.
Transition to the New Doctrine, 39 f.
Bernard of Pavia, 39.
Richard Anglicus, 42.
Tancred, 44, 48.
John Tuetonicus, 46.
the turning point in the doctrine and legislation, 48 f.
Raymond of Pennafort, 50 f.
Gregory IX, 50 f.
Roffredus Epiphanii, 52 .
Goffredus de Trano, 53.
Sinibaldus Fliscus (Pope Innocent IV), 53.
Hostiensis, 54.
Bernardus de Botone, 55.
William Durantis, 57.
Scholastic Antagonism for the doctrine of future honest conditions, 57 f.
St. Thomas Aquinas, 57.
St. Bonaventure, 58.
Petrus de Samspone, 59.
Abbas Antiquus, 59.
The Perfection of the Doctrine, *Liber Sextus,* 60 f.
John Andrea, 62.
Abbas Siculus, 62
Retrospect of Canonical Development, 64 f.
Copula Theory, 67 f.
Honest future possible conditions, 161-182.
suspend consent till verification, 161.
effects of this condition are variously explained, 161.
during the pendency no bond of marriage exists between the parties, 170.
difference during pendency and the status of engagement, 172.
marriage arises at the moment of verification of condition, 178.
renewal of consent not necessary, 179.
the condition "if God wills," 179.
honest past and present condition—see Present and Past Honest.
Indissolubility of marriage, 240, 241, 243, 283.
the importance of the question, 243.
the nature of, 244-250.
conditions against this *bonum,* 250.
meaning, scope and application of the law, 250 f.
is a simple intention against indissolubility equivalent to an actual condition, 251-255.
Interpretation of the law governing this *bonum,* 250.
theory of the two acts of the will, 255.
does a condition opposed to this property invalidate consent if it is not *deducta in pactum,* 255-260.
Is *error juris* equivalent to a condition excluding indissolubility, 260-283.
error juris defined, 260.
propositions of Ballerini—Palmieri about rules for the external forum about divorce conditions, 272, 273.
Immoral conditions that are not against the substance of marriage, 154-160.

future immorals are rejected by law, 154.
past and present are not rejected, 154.
immoral condition also called legally impossible condition, 158.
Impossible conditions, 146-153.
various kinds of, 146.
ignorance of the impossibility, 148.
future impossible condition rejected by law, 146.
past and present impossible, not rejected by law, 152.
Intercourse as surrogate of the fulfillment, 198-214.
copula as a constitutive act of marriage was a *praesumptio juris et de jure*, 198, 211.
qualifications of the state of mind are important, 199.
past and present unverified condition not affected by the *copula*, 201.
has the *copula* henceforth any special juridical value, 202 f.
copula as a sign of engagement, 208.
"consensus mutus" of Leo XIII, 209.
Invalidating conditions,
conditions against substance of marriage in general, 215 f.
importance of the subject, 215-218.
what kind of end, intention or content of the will is necessary that marriage arises therefrom, 218-227.
what vitiates the marriage consent, 228-242.
defects *ex parte subjecti*, 228.
defects *ex parte objecti*, 228.
defects *ex parte intellectus*, 229.
various kinds of error, 229.
simulation, 232.
partial simulation, 233.
consent and the *tria bona*, 238 f.
Marriage,
definitions of, 73-78.
of St. Joseph, 330.
Modern legal codes and consent in general, 355.
marriage consent as viewed by American States and courts, 356.
Modus,
definition of, 80, 342.
added to marital consent, 342.
care must be used to distinguish from condition, 343 f.
does not suspend the consent, 342.
Nature and effects of conditional consent, 131-136.
the consent, not marriage receives the condition, 132.
Necessary conditions, 143-145.
Past and present conditions against the substance of marriage, 335-340.
offer much difficulty, 335.
they do not invalidate the consent, 335.
Praesumptio juris 139.
definition of, 139.
presumptions in marriage law, 140.
Present and past honest, possible condition, 183-187.
are not rejected, 183.
do not suspend, 184.
no kind of honest or past conditions are against the substance of marriage, 185.
present honest and the *cautiones*, 186.
Presumptions in favor of instruments in American Law, 358, 359.
Revocation of the condition, 196.
of the entire transaction, 195.
Roman Law,
conditions in, 13-24.
definitions of, 14.
not used in marriage, 14 f.

the nature of, 17.
improper conditions, 18.
placing of conditions, 21.
effects of conditions, 22 f.
Time and manner of placing condition, 112-130.
One party alone may place, 112.
the condition can be placed before the actual celebration of marriage, 113.
not necessary that condition be *deducta in pactum,* 117.
difference between internal intention and internal condition, 119.
condition can be placed in the mind only, 120.
placing of condition and proof of its placing are two different things, 122, 128.
proof of placing conditional consent, 129.
Verification and frustration of the condition, 188-194.
when is a condition verified, 188.
when is a condition frustrated, 192.
intercourse as surrogate of fulfillment of condition — see Intercourse.

BIOGRAPHICAL NOTE

Bartholomew Thomas Timlin was born in Philadelphia, Pa., on the first of September, 1896. After receiving his elementary education in the public and the parochial schools of that city, he entered St. Joseph's Seraphic Seminary, Callicoon, N. Y., in the fall of 1915, where he completed his classical course in June, 1920. He was received into the Franciscan Novitiate of St. Bonaventure, Paterson, N. J., in August of the same year. After his profession, on August 15, 1921, he attended the prescribed Seminary courses at various study houses of the Province, and was ordained to the Sacred Priesthood on May 29, 1927. He taught philosophy and various subjects in three study-houses of the Holy Name Province; and in September, 1931, his superiors sent him to take up graduate studies in the School of Canon Law of the Catholic University of America. He received the degrees of B.A. in 1924, the M.A. in 1926 from St. Bonaventure College and Seminary, Allegany, N. Y.; J.C.B. in 1931; J.U.B. in 1932; and J.C.L. in 1933 from the Catholic University of America.

CANON LAW STUDIES

1. Freriks, Rev. Celestine A., C.PP.S., J.C.D., Religious Congregations in Their External Relations, 121 pp., 1916.
2. Galliher, Rev. Daniel M., O.P., J.C.D., Canonical Elections, 117 pp., 1917.
3. Borkowski, Rev. Aurelius L., O.F.M., De Confraternitatibus Ecclesiasticis, 136 pp., 1918.
4. Castillo, Rev. Cayo, J.C.D., Disertacion Historico-canonica sobre la Potestad del Cabildo en Sede Vacante o Impedida del Vicario Capitular, 99 pp., 1919 (1918).
5. Kubelbeck, Rev. William J., S.T.B., J.C.D., The Sacred Penitentiaria and Its Relations to Faculties of Ordinaries and Priests, 129 pp., 1918.
6. Petrovits, Rev. Joseph J. C., S.T.D., J.C.D., The New Church Law on Matrimony, X-461 pp., 1919.
7. Hickey, Rev. John J., S.T.B., J.C.D., Irregularities and Simple Impediments in the New Code of Canon Law, 100 pp., 1920.
8. Klekotka, Rev. Peter J., S.T.B., J.C.D., Diocesan Consultors, 179 pp., 1920.
9. Wannenmacher, Rev. Francis, J.C.D., The Evidence in Ecclesiastical Procedure Affecting the Marriage Bond, 1920. (Not Printed.)
10. Golden, Rev. Henry Francis, J.C.D., Parochial Benefices in the New Code, IV-119 pp., 1921. (Printed 1925.)
11. Koudelka, Rev. Charles, J., J.C.D., Pastors, Their Rights and Duties According to the New Code of Canon Law, 211 pp., 1921.
12. Melo, Rev. Antonius, O.F.M., J.C.D., De Exemptione Regularium, X-188 pp., 1921.
13. Schaaf, Rev. Valentine Theodore, O.F.M., S.T.B., J.C.D., The Cloister, X-180 pp., 1921.
14. Burke, Rev. Thomas Joseph, S.T.B., J.C.D., Competence in Ecclesiastical Tribunals, IV-117 pp., 1922.
15. Leech, Rev. George Leo, J.C.D., A Comparative Study of the Constitution "Apostolicae Sedis" and the "Codex Juris Canonici," 179 pp., 1922.
16. Motry, Rev. Hubert Louis, S.T.D., J.C.D., Diocesan Faculties According to the Code of Canon Law, II-167 pp., 1922.
17. Murphy, Rev. George Lawrence, J.C.D., Delinquencies and Penalties in the Administration and the Reception of the Sacraments, IV-121 pp., 1923.
18. O'Reilly, Rev. John Anthony, S.T.B., J.C.D., Ecclesiastical Sepulture in the New Code of Canon Law, II-129 pp., 1923.
19. Michalicka, Rev. Wenceslas Cyrill, O.S.B., J.C.D., Judicial Procedure in Dismissal of Clerical Exempt Religious, 107 pp., 1923.

20. Dargin, Rev. Edward Vincent, S.T.B., J.C.D., Reserved Cases According to the Code of Canon Law, IV-103 pp., 1924.
21. Godfrey, Rev. John A., S.T.B., J.C.D., The Right of Patronage According to the Code of Canon Law, 153 pp., 1924.
22 Hagedorn, Rev. Francis Edward, J.C.D., General Legislation on Indulgences, II-154 pp., 1924.
23. King, Rev. James Ignatius, J.C.D., The Administration of the Sacraments to Dying Non-Catholics, V-141 pp., 1924.
24. Winslow, Rev. Francis Joseph, A.F.M., J.C.D., Vicars and Prefects Apostolic, IV-149 pp., 1924.
25. Correa, Rev. Jose Servelion, S.T.L., J.C.D., La Potestad Legislativa de la Iglesia Católica, IV-127 pp., 1925.
26. Dugan, Rev. Henry Francis, M.A., J.C.D., The Judiciary Department of the Diocesan Curia, 87 pp., 1925.
27. Keller, Rev. Charles Frederick, S.T.B., J.C.D., Mass Stipends, 167 pp., 1925.
28. Paschang, Rev. John Linus, J.C.D., The Sacramentals According to the Code of Canon Law, 129 pp., 1925.
29. Piontek, Rev. Cyrillus, O.F.M., S.T.B., J.C.D., De Indulto Exclaustrationis necnon Saecularizationis, XIII-289 pp., 1925.
30. Kearney, Rev. Richard Joseph, S.T.B., J.C.D., Sponsors at Baptism According to the Code of Canon Law, IV-127 pp., 1925.
31. Bartlett, Rev. Chester Joseph, A.M., LL.B., J.C.D., The Tenure of Parochial Property in the United States of America, V-108 pp., 1926.
32. Kilker, Rev. Adrian Jerome, J.C.D., Extreme Unction, V-425 pp. 1926.
33. McCormick, Rev. Robert Emmett, J.C.D., Confessors of Religious, VIII-266 pp., 1926.
34. Miller, Rev. Newton Thomas, J.C.D., Founded Masses According to the Code of Canon Law, VII-93 pp., 1926.
35. Roelker, Rev. Edward G., S.T.D., J.C.D., Principles of Privilege According to the Code of Canon Law, XI-166 pp., 1926.
36. Bakalarczyk, Rev. Richardus, M.I.C., J.U.D., De Novitiatu, VIII-208 pp., 1927.
37. Pizzuti, Rev. Lawrence, O.F.M., J.U.L., De Parochis Religiosis, 1927. (Not Printed.)
38. Bliley, Rev. Nicholas Martin, O.S.B., J.C.D., Altars According to the Code of Canon Law, XIX-132 pp., 1927.
39. Brown, Brendan Francis, A.B., LL.M., J.U.D., The Canonical Juristic Personality with Special Reference to its Status in the United States of America, V-212 pp., 1927.
40. Cavanaugh, Rev. William Thomas, C.P., J.U.D., The Reservation of the Blessed Sacrament, VIII-101 pp., 1927.
41. Doheny, Rev. William J., C.S.C., A.B., J.U.D., Church Property: Modes of Acquisition, X-118 pp,. 1927

42. FELDHAUS, REV. ALOYSIUS H., C.PP.S., J.C.D., Oratories, IX-141 pp., 1927.
43. KELLY, REV. JAMES PATRICK, A.B., J.C.D., The Jurisdiction of the Simple Confessor, X-208 pp., 1927.
44. NEUBERGER, REV. NICHOLAS J., J.C.D., Canon 6 or the Relation of the Codex Juris Canonici to the Preceding Legislation, V-95 pp., 1927.
45. O'KEEFFE, REV. GERALD MICHAEL, J.C.D., Matrimonial Dispensations, Powers of Bishops, Priests, and Confessors, VIII-232 pp., 1927.
46. QUIGLEY, REV. JOSEPH, A.M., A.B., J.C.D., Condemned Societies, 139 pp., 1927.
47. ZAPLOTNIK, REV. IOANNES LEO, J.C.D., De Vicariis Foraneis, X-142 pp., 1927.
48. DUSKIE, REV. JOHN ALOYSIUS, A.B., J.C.D., The Canonical Status of the Orientals in the United States, VIII-196 pp., 1928.
49. HYLAND, REV. FRANCIS EDWARD, J.C.D., Excommunication, Its Nature, Historical Development and Effects, VIII-181 pp., 1928.
50. REINMANN, REV. GERALD JOSEPH, O.M.C., J.C.D., The Third Order Secular of Saint Francis, 201 pp., 1928.
51. SCHENK, REV. FRANCIS J., J.C.D., The Matrimonial Impediments of Mixed Religion and Disparity of Cult, XVI-318 pp., 1929.
52. COADY, REV. JOHN JOSEPH, S.T.D., J.U.D., A.M., The Appointment of Pastors, VIII-150 pp., 1929.
53. KAY, REV. THOMAS HENRY, J.C.D., Competence in Matrimonial Procedure, VIII-164 pp., 1929.
54. TURNER, REV. SIDNEY JOSEPH, C.P., J.U.D., The Vow of Poverty, XLIX-217 pp., 1929.
55. KEARNEY, REV. RAYMOND A., A.B., S.T.D., J.C.D., The Principles of Delegation, VII-149 pp., 1929.
56. CONRAN, REV. EDWARD JAMES, A.B., J.C.D., The Interdict, V-163 pp., 1930.
57. O'NEIL, REV. WILLIAM H., J.C.D., Papal Rescripts of Favor, VII-218 pp., 1930.
58. BASTNAGEL, REV. CLEMENT VINCENT, J.U.D., The Appointment of Parochial Adjutants and Assistants, XV-257 pp., 1930.
59. FERRY, REV. WILLIAM A., A.B., J.C.D., Stole Fees, X-107 pp., 1930.
60. COSTELLO, REV. JOHN MICHAEL, A.B., J.C.D., Domicile and Quasi-Domicile, VII-201 pp., 1930.
61. KREMER, REV. MICHAEL NICHOLAS, A.B., S.T.B., J.C.D., Church Support in the United States, VI-136 pp., 1930.
62. ANGULO, REV. LUIS, C.M., J.C.D., Legislación de la Iglesia sobre la intención en la applicación de la Santa Misa, VII-104 pp., 1931.
63. FREY, REV. WOLFGANG NORBERT, O.S.B., A.B., J.C.D., The Act of Religious Profession, VIII-174 pp., 1931.
64. ROBERTS, REV. JAMES BRENDAN, A.B., J.C.D., The Banns of Marriage, XIV-140 pp., 1931.

65. Ryder, Rev. Raymond Aloysius, A.B., J.C.D., Simony, IX-151 pp., 1931.
66. Campagna, Rev. Angelo, Ph.D., J.U.D., Il Vicario Generale del Vescovo, VII-205 pp., 1931.
67. Cox, Rev. Joseph Godfrey, A.B., J.C.D., The Administration of Seminaries, VI-124 pp., 1931.
68. Gregory, Rev. Donald J., J.U.D., The Pauline Privilege, XV-165 pp., 1931.
60. Donohue, Rev. John F., J.C.D., The Impediment of Crime, VIII-110 pp., 1931.
70. Dooley, Rev. Eugene A., O.M.I., J.C.D., Church Law on Sacred Relics, IX-143 pp., 1931.
71. Orth, Rev. Clement Raymond, O.M.C., J.C.D., The Approbation of Religious Institutes, 171 pp., 1931.
72. Pernicone, Rev. Joseph M., A.B., J.C.D., The Ecclesiastical Prohibition of Books, XII-267 pp., 1932.
73. Clinton, Rev. Connell, A.B., J.C.D., The Paschal Precept, IX-108 pp., 1932.
74. Donnelly, Rev. Francis B., A.M., S.T.L., J.C.D., The Diocesan Synod, VIII-125 pp., 1932
75. Torrente, Rev. Camilo, C.M.F., J.C.D., Las Processiones Sagradas, V-145 pp., 1932.
76. Murphy, Rev. Edwin J., C.PP.S., J.C.D., Suspension Ex Informata Conscientia, XI-122 pp., 1932.
77. MacKenzie, Rev. Eric F., A.M., S.T.L., J.C.D., The Delict of Heresy in its Commission, Penalization, Absolution, VII-124 pp., 1932.
78. Lyons, Rev. Avitus E., S.T.B., J.C.D., The Collegiate Tribunal of First Instance, XI-147 pp., 1932.
79. Connolly, Rev. Thomas A., J.C.D., Appeals, XI-195 pp., 1932.
80. Sangmeister, Rev. Joseph V., A.B., J.C.D., Force and Fear as Precluding Matrimonial Consent, V-211 pp., 1932.
81. Jaeger, Rev. Leo A., A.B., J.C.D., The Administration of Vacant and Quasi-Vacant Episcopal Sees in the United States, IX-229 pp. 1932.
82. Rimlinger, Rev. Herbert T., J.C.D., Error Invalidating Matrimonial Consent, VII-79 pp., 1932.
83. Barrett, Rev. John D. M., S.S., J.C.D., Comparative Study of the Third Plenary Council and the Code, IX-221 pp., 1932.
84. Carberry, Rev. John J., Ph.D., S.T.D., J.C.L., The Juridical Form of Marriage, 1934.
85. Dolan, Rev. John L., A.B., J.C.L., The Defensor Vinculi, 1934.
86. Hannan, Rev. Jerome D., A.M., S.T.D., LL.B., J.C.L., The Canon Law of Wills, 1934.
87. Lemieux, Rev. Delisle A., A.M., J.C.L., The Sentence in Ecclesiastical Procedure, 1934.
88. O'Rourke, Rev. James J., A.B., J.C.L., Parish Registers, 1934.

89. TIMLIN, REV. BARTHOLOMEW, O.F.M., A.M., J.C.L., Conditional Matrimonial Consent, 1934.
90. WAHL, REV. FRANCIS X., A.B., J.C.L., The Matrimonial Impediments of Consanguinity and Affinity, 1934.
91. WHITE, REV. ROBERT J., A.B., LL.B., S.T.B., J.C.L., Canonical Ante-Nuptial Promises and the Civil Law, 1934.

www.ingramcontent.com/pod-product-compliance
Lightning Source LLC
LaVergne TN
LVHW050300080826
844660LV00012B/662

* 9 7 8 0 8 1 3 2 2 2 7 8 3 *